Metalinguistic
Awareness
and
Beginning
Literacy

CONTRIBUTORS

JEAN F. ANDREWS
Department of Special Education
Eastern Kentucky University

NAVAZ BHAVNAGRI
Center for the Study of Reading
University of Illinois

H. D. DAY
Department of Philosophy and Psychology
Texas Woman's University

KAAREN C. DAY
Department of Elementary, Early Childhood and Reading Education
North Texas State University

JOHN DOWNING
Department of Psychological Foundations in Education
University of Victoria, British Columbia

ANNE HAAS DYSON
Division of Language and Literacy
University of California at Berkeley

LINNEA C. EHRI
Department of Education
University of California at Davis

JEROME C. HARSTE
Reading Education Department
Indiana University

EDMUND H. HENDERSON
School of Education
University of Virginia

ELFRIEDA H. HIEBERT
Department of Curriculum and Instruction
University of Kentucky

DON HOLDAWAY
Lesley College and the Cambridge School District

MARJORIE H. HOLDEN
School of Education
California State University at Dominguez Hills

JERRY L. JOHNS
Reading Clinic
Northern Illinois University

JANA M. MASON
Center for the Study of Reading
University of Illinois

CHRISTINE McCORMICK
Department of Psychology
Eastern Illinois University

LEA M. McGEE
Department of Curriculum and Instruction
Louisiana State University

DEBORAH W. ROWE
Reading Education Department
Indiana University

DONNA M. SCANLON
Child Research and Study Center
State University of New York at Albany

ELIZABETH SULZBY
School of Education
Northwestern University

NANCY E. TAYLOR
Department of Education
The Catholic University of America

SHANE TEMPLETON
Department of Curriculum and Instruction
University of Nevada—Reno

GAIL E. TOMPKINS
College of Education
University of Oklahoma

FRANK R. VELLUTINO
Child Research and Study Center
State University of New York at Albany

LEE S. WILCE
Department of Education
University of California at Davis

DAVID B. YADEN, JR.
Department of Curriculum and Instruction
University of Houston—University Park

Metalinguistic Awareness and Beginning Literacy

Conceptualizing What It Means to Read and Write

Edited by

David B. Yaden, Jr.
UNIVERSITY OF HOUSTON—UNIVERSITY PARK

Shane Templeton
UNIVERSITY OF NEVADA—RENO

WITH A FOREWORD BY
MARJORIE H. HOLDEN

Heinemann
Portsmouth, NH

Heinemann Educational Books, Inc.
70 Court Street, Portsmouth, New Hampshire 03801

LONDON EDINBURGH MELBOURNE AUCKLAND HONG KONG
SINGAPORE KUALA LUMPUR NEW DELHI IBADAN NAIROBI
JOHANNESBURG KINGSTON PORT OF SPAIN

First edition

10 9 8 7 6 5 4 3 2 1

Library of Congress Cataloging in Publication Data
Main entry under title:

Metalinguistic awareness and beginning literacy.

   Bibliography: p.
   Includes indexes.
   1. Language awareness in children.   2. Literacy.
3. Reading (Preschool)   I. Yaden, David B.
II. Templeton, Shane.
P118.M448   1986   401'.9   85-21967

ISBN 0-435-08245-0
Printed in the United States of America.

Designed by Maria Szmauz.

Contents

v

Foreword

I am very pleased to have been asked to write the foreword to this collection. When David Yaden asked me to reminisce on the origin of the term *metalinguistic*, I was reminded of Teachers College as it was in 1967. Those were very exciting days both inside and outside Columbia University. The stream of findings on children's language development was almost as fascinating as the student sit-ins across 120th Street on the Columbia campus.

I have been identified as one of the first to use the term "metalinguistic" in the literature of education and psychology. Indeed, some have suggested that I was the first. However, I cannot claim clear title to the distinction for two reasons. First, David Yaden's (see Yaden and Templeton, this volume) scholarly search for the earliest use of the term reveals that linguists have used it as far back as the 1940s, although to describe aspects of language that are currently associated with sociolinguistics and semantics. Second, others such as Leila Gleitman (Gleitman, Gleitman, and Shipley, 1972) apparently used it at about the same time as I did to describe children's intuitions about, and awareness of, language. My own "discovery" of the term is a little hazy. When I arrived at Teachers College in the late 1960s, my goal was to return to the public schools armed with a Columbia doctorate. I arrived just in time to buy into the new model in psychology—the 1967 streamlined developmental psycholinguist. Somewhere in the transition from classroom teacher to psychologist, the term "metalinguistic" popped into my head as the most appropriate one to describe the behavior I was studying.

The first step in the creative process occurred very early in my graduate school career. The message at TC was very clear. The shades of Thorndike, Lorge, Cattell, and others were palpable. They walked among us. Arthur Gates, although an octogenarian, was still alive, and often at his desk at the Institute of Language Arts. Research was *the* way of life, and it was modeled all around us.

Although I had no clear ideas in mind, I realized I had better get cracking. I also knew that children's language in all forms was my overriding interest. This made Walter MacGinitie the logical person to work with. When I asked him if he would initiate me into the realm of research, Walter's response was to open a drawer, remove a packet of 4 × 6 index cards bound with a rubber band, pass them over, and ask if any of the problems written out on the cards interested me. The first card was the word awareness issue in twenty-five words or so. I never read the rest of the cards. I was immediately and absolutely overwhelmed, because as a first grade teacher I had encountered the problem in several forms without ever thinking about it. Thus was born my research career and my collaboration with Walter MacGinitie.

Retrospectively, it is interesting to see how an empirical, atheoretical investigation, undertaken for practical reasons—we wondered how word awareness affected children's progress at the beginning stages of reading—can lead to increasingly theoretical questions. Having established through our own studies and those of others (at that time it was easy to list all studies of word awareness on a page) that word awareness in young children was lacking or incomplete, the developmental and linguistic implications for this state of affairs began to intrigue me. This progression from the classroom to the ivory tower occurred gradually. The turn to linguistics was inevitable at a time when Tom Bever and Bill Labov opened their classes to TC students, and Chomsky and transformational grammar were on everyone's mind. At the time the arguments between the traditional behaviorists and the Chomskyites were raging. As with many other classroom teachers, behaviorists never convinced me that they held the solutions to all the problems. However, Chomsky, with his vehement stress on the innateness of language, also left questions unanswered. LADs and LASses were interesting metaphors, but transformational grammarians sometimes sounded as if it were only a matter of time before organ transplants would become available for aphasics.

In picking better brains, I came across Chomsky's well-known statement to the effect that in learning a language a child has only to learn the lexical items and the rules for their arrangement in order to become an accomplished speaker. But if a child could do this, he/she would have to have an awareness of the items—at some level. The first study we did on kindergarten children suggested very little awareness of items. As I saw it, as a second-year graduate student, Chomsky had demolished Skinner, but we had at least dented Chomsky.

Intellectually I had reached a watershed. Children's apparent unawareness of the lexical content of their speech was no longer an educational problem to be solved in the name of better teaching of reading. Knowing the rules of grammar for one's native tongue by age five didn't sound nearly as impressive as the ability to arrange the items according to the rules before the items were apparently available qua items.

Neither transformational grammarians nor behaviorists seemed to offer any solution to the problem. However, I felt intellectually closer to Piaget than I did to either Chomsky or Skinner. The notion that children cannot do certain things before a certain age may reflect cultural or familial biases, but I was comfortable both with the idea that biology does set limits, and the idea that there are gray areas where environmental influences can push back these limits to varying degrees.

What Piaget offered was a developmental approach, and a theoretical framework of cognitive functioning into which language possibly might be fitted. It seemed at that time that just as children could perform or respond logically before they could reason logically, they might be able to use language for immediate needs before they could use it or perceive it in situations that were abstract and context-free. The former ability was linguistic. However, after the first study of word awareness, I was more interested in investigating children's intuitions about their language than in their linguistic abilities. It was the need to distinguish between these two abilities—the use of language, and the use of language to analyze and discuss language—that led to the use of the term "metalinguistic." I really cannot say if I first saw the word in linguistic writings. It is certainly true that other meta- terms such as "metamemory" were around, and "metalinguistic" well may have been an unconscious analogical formation, since I was not familiar with the sources David Yaden has uncovered.

The term "metalinguistic ability," as I used it in my dissertation, referred to the awareness of the lexical content of oral language, and to the ability to use language to discuss and analyze language. It seems to me that although Linnea Ehri's (1979) position that children learn much of this as they learn to read is unarguable, this still leaves many interesting questions unanswered. At what age do various metalinguistic abilities appear spontaneously? What interventions hasten their appearance? What are the relationships between metalinguistic abilities and other cognitive activities? What are the practical educational implications of metalinguistic abilities? How early can they be taught? Should they be taught? . . . an inexhaustible list. As a developmentalist and an ex-teacher, I am always curious about which experiences push the age of skill acquisition back into that gray area between bedrock biology and laissez-faire, informal acquisition. Word awareness itself is apparently a much more intractable problem than we ever imagined. The unclarified discrepancies between linguistic definitions of "the word" and printing conventions mar some of the research and muddy some of the theoretical discussion.

Ellen Ryan's and her colleagues' work on bilingualism has provided some interesting ideas and answers to some of these problems, as does the work of those who study differences in performance between normal and handicapped groups. I am particularly fascinated by the work of Cole and Scribner, who have looked at metalinguistic abilities in adults and children in preliterate or quasi-literate societies. If metalinguistic abilities are likely to appear spontaneously at the time children in the Western world are taught to read, biology and external influences may be confounded in many of our studies. Cross-cultural studies are extremely valuable for these and other reasons.

Ehri's work suggests that there may be large individual differences in metalinguistic abilities—perhaps at all ages. If this were true, many studies might need to be reinterpreted, particularly since few of them are experimental or longitudinal. If there are significant individual differences in metalinguistic abilities, then beginning readers who possess a great deal of this ability would find reading facilitated; those who were average in this respect would acquire metalinguistic insights as they learned, and those unfortunates who were below normal in having this capacity would perhaps need special instruction to avoid falling behind their peers. By the same token, the preeminence of literates, bilinguals, and schooled populations in Cole and Scribner's studies may reflect, at least partially, a group with some genetic propensities for language activities.

Certainly knowledge about printing conventions is learned. How learning about printing conventions in alphabetic languages differs from learning about printing conventions in other writing systems may provide interesting insights into how children learn to read and write at the beginning stages, and how different writing systems affect language-processing activities. In any writing system, however, children with some intuition about the nature of language would have a better chance of inferring that the relations between speech and print are ordered and systematic, and of learning the specifics of those regularities.

In support of the individual differences argument, let me add one further thought. Alphabetic writing was invented only once in human history. The individual(s) who conceived and gave birth to this system must indeed have had superior metalinguistic insights. Furthermore, they could not have acquired them from learning to read an alphabetic language!

A developmental interpretation in regard to metalinguistic knowledge, which recognizes individual differences in basic abilities and in rates of development, has practical implications. Bialystok and Ryan (1983) have proposed a model in which knowledge and control gradually emerge and increase. I think much of what I am suggesting could be organized within such a framework.

It is very satisfying to see the central role metalinguistic behaviors have come to occupy in both psychology and education in the last decade. Metalinguistic ability has come to connote awareness of such aspects of language as grammaticality, lexical items, phonemes, and rhetorical devices, as well as the awareness of speech to print regularities. The field has opened out like a funnel, and the implications for increasing knowledge in both applied and theoretical domains have grown just as rapidly. I can recall, when our results on word awareness were still fresh, that there were people who found it amazing that five-year-olds did not know what a word was. I had wanted to do research in a new field where the high-grade ore hadn't all been taken. I am pleased that I was able to recognize gold when I saw it, but I must say truly that I had no idea that there would be an explosion of research which would be booming more than a dozen years later. The techniques for studying metalinguistic ability have become much more refined, and the questions that are being asked are much more sophisticated. For both applied and theoretical reasons, as I read the literature, I believe we are still getting high-grade ore from the mine. I am very pleased to be a part of this volume and a member of this company.

Carson, California   Marjorie H. Holden

Preface

The study of young children's emerging and unique conceptualizations of the processes and elements involved in learning to read and write—herein called *metalinguistic awareness*—is now clearly international in scope. Focused discussions of this phenomenon, variously labeled *metalinguistic awareness, linguistic awareness, language awareness,* or *print awareness,* have begun to appear by interdisciplinary teams of scholars from nearly every continent. Despite the terminological differences, which are not insignificant, the underlying thread which connects them all is the realization that young children as a group embarking on the path to literacy exhibit slowly evolving and widely divergent notions of the tasks expected of them before acquiring a conventional understanding of what it means to read and write. And as will be underscored in this collection, too often it is the case that formal systems of education assume much, but know very little about the actual perceptions and abilities that children already possess before systematic instruction in reading and writing begins. The exact nature of these nascent concepts regarding literacy behaviors and how they are influenced by the structure of orthographies, manual and tactile systems of communication, preschool experience with print, the process of schooling, and differences in children themselves is largely the focus of this book.

The specific aims of the volume are these: (a) Foremost is to discuss metalinguistic awareness within the contexts of *both* beginning reading and writing ability, something which has not been done previously; (b) to highlight important issues in the field, including the causal relationship between spoken language awareness and the influence of print as well as effective instrumentation with which to measure metalinguistic knowledge; (c) to present evidence that children in non-English-speaking countries experience conceptual difficulties in analyzing their own language and script similar to those of American youngsters; and (d) to demonstrate that alternative symbol systems, namely Braille and types of manual language, pose unique and equally challenging problems for visually- and hearing-impaired children learning how to read. In sum, the overall intent of the book is to cast an even wider net around this burgeoning field and to bring more intensely into focus the underlying conceptual foundation needed to successfully master literacy behaviors.

The origin of the present collection was an invitation to David Yaden by a journal editor and publisher to put together a special issue on metalinguistic awareness and reading. Subsequently, initial invitations to submit papers for consideration were extended to Jean Andrews, Marie Clay, Jim and Kaaren Day, John Downing, Linnea Ehri, Elfrieda Hiebert, Don Holdaway, Marjorie Holden, Jerry Johns, Jana Mason, Lea McGee, Elizabeth Sulzby, Nancy Taylor, Shane Templeton, Gail Tompkins, and Frank Vellutino. Each was asked to address a specific issue related to metalinguistic awareness and reading based upon his/her own special expertise and interest in the area. In the ensuing change of direction from journal publication to book, authors were asked to revise and update their papers appropriately for inclusion as book chapters. In addition, invitations to address metalinguistic awareness as evidenced by early writing behaviors were extended to persons knowledgeable in the area and accepted by Anne Dyson, Jerome Harste, and Edmund Henderson. Co-authors Navaz Bhavnagri, Christine McCormick, Deborah Rowe, Donna Scanlon and Lee Wilce were also invited per original authors' request. At this time, Shane Templeton was asked to assume an editorial role as well. An unfortunate occurrence, however, was the voluntary withdrawal of her paper by Professor Clay whose prior international travel commitments came into conflict with the time necessary for the revising of her chapter.

In the editors' view, two conspicuous strengths of the volume are its multidisciplinary aspect reflected in the training and experience of the contributors and the variety of research approaches through which metalinguistic awareness is examined. In addition to wide-ranging reviews and discussions of theory, several data-based investigations representing descriptive, experimental, and longitudinal case study designs are included. An added strength is that for the most part the age of subjects from whom data has been gathered is restricted to preschool and early primary, thereby enhancing the focus of the volume. In a few cases, however, in order to clarify a particular issue or demonstrate the pervasiveness of conceptual problems in older children, data are reported from upper elementary students as well. Readers of this volume, then, can expect the relationship between metalinguistic awareness and growth in literacy to be presented from a multidimensional perspective, without which full understanding of this relationship is made more difficult.

This volume is primarily intended to be of interest to psychologists, linguists, educators, and others studying the developmental nature of children's emerging concepts about the acts of reading and writing. It should serve well as a text for graduate-level courses, doctoral seminars, and other discussions of developing literacy behaviors. The ancillary audience for whom this book is targeted, of course, are teachers, school officials, and educational publishers who largely control the delivery, design, and content of commercial instructional programs in reading and writing, programs which to date do not reflect the current state of knowledge in this field. It is hoped that besides adding to the knowledge base of literacy study, this book may serve as a useful reference for those persons most directly responsible for teaching young children how to read and write.

HOUSTON, TEXAS   DAVID B. YADEN, JR.
RENO, NEVADA   SHANE TEMPLETON

Acknowledgments

While many people were involved in the production of this book, the editors would like to single out a few for special mention. We are particularly grateful to Philippa Stratton, Editor-in-Chief of Heinemann Educational Books, whose foresight, encouragement, and guidance have been indispensable in the book's publication. We would also like to thank William H. Teale for his careful and perceptive reading of an earlier draft and his suggestion to broaden the scope of the volume. To Beth Spencer we owe a special debt of gratitude both for her insightful comments on earlier drafts of several chapters and, even more, for agreeing to take on the laborious task of compiling all of the chapters' references into one list. We would be remiss not to acknowledge as well the assistance and technical expertise given to us by Donna Bouvier in attending to the myriad of details involved in the book's journey from copyedited manuscript to final form.

Finally, we extend our warmest thanks to the contributors themselves, whose extraordinary enthusiasm for this venture has not waned in over two years of negotiations, suggested revisions, and necessary deadlines, any of which might have been reason enough for them to abandon the project altogether. That this volume has come to fruition is a direct result of their professionalism, teamwork, and dedication to their own research endeavors in exploring how it is that young children become literate.

D. Y.
S. T.

Organization of the Volume

The volume is organized into seven thematic sections preceded by an introduction, and a concluding eighth section. The topics proceed from an international overview of metalinguistic awareness and reading research, to theoretical considerations addressing the relationships among metalinguistic awareness and alphabetic orthographies, thence to research addressing the relative contributions of metalinguistic awareness, and spoken and written language to the development of reading ability. Home and school influences on developing literacy and metalinguistic awareness are considered next, then a state-of-the-art review of tests of metalinguistic awareness. The following section addresses children's production of written language and its relationships to metalinguistic awareness, and the thematic sections close with discussion of metalinguistic awareness among visually and auditorially impaired children.

In the introductory chapter, "Metalinguistic Awareness: An Etymology," the editors provide a backdrop for the often cluttered definitional terrain over which theorists and researchers have struggled studying things "metalinguistic." Perhaps not surprisingly, a look at the historical referents of the terms *metalinguistic, metalingual,* and *metalanguage* through this century reveals that current definitions in the literature of education and psychology reflect, in part, older but now-forgotten antecedents indigenous to earlier usages in the fields of philosophy and linguistics. In the editors' view, the present definitional controversy in the field regarding "conscious" versus "unconscious" language behavior as being more genuinely "metalinguistic" can be put into perspective by tracing the term's evolution and obvious malleability within several disciplines. Nevertheless, the diverse array of interpretations of metalinguistic awareness that are considered in Chapter One may perhaps serve to reassure us in our quest for focus and, in the broader context of inquiry, remind us that the study of metalinguistic awareness is a most appropriate point from which to consider the workings of the tacit as well as the conscious mind.

Investigations in metalinguistic awareness have reflected some of the more notable cross-cultural investigations undertaken to date. In Section One, "An International Survey of Reading Research in Metalinguistic Awareness," an encompassing review of contemporary and historical cross-cultural metalinguistic research is presented. In "Cognitive Clarity: A Unifying and Cross-Cultural Theory for Language Awareness Phenomena in Reading," Downing shares the foundations for and modifications of a theory that has attracted considerable interest among the metalinguistic research community. The validity of the theory is tested against results obtained in a number of different cultural, social, and linguistic contexts.

In "Students' Perceptions of Reading: Thirty Years of Inquiry," Johns reviews many of the seminal early studies in this research domain and discusses the somewhat sobering conceptions of reading held by poor readers. Johns also expands on some of his own research, noting in particular some interesting differences in responses between girls and boys regarding the purposes of reading.

Yaden's chapter, "Reading Research in Metalinguistic Awareness: A Classification of Findings According to Focus and Methodology," presents a relatively comprehensive investigation of English-language studies that explore children's understanding of the reading act and of units of spoken and written language. Three rather distinct areas of conceptual development in this research are addressed: (a) nature, purpose, and processes of reading; (b) spoken language units and terms used in reading instruction; (c) print conventions and mapping principles. The review is structured to follow roughly the chronology of research emphases in the field that has come to be called "metalinguistic awareness."

Section Two addresses "Literacy, Metalinguistic Awareness, and the Alphabetic Principle: Theoretical Considerations." Some of the most engaging yet controversial research and thinking in this area has been concerned with the influence of the alphabet as both a cultural invention and a psychological tool. The issue is not merely an academic one: while some theorists have argued for profound changes as a consequence of literacy, some cultural anthropologists and social historians have suggested that literacy does *not* necessarily afford a culture or an individual qualitatively richer psychological and cultural benefits. Henderson's chapter, "Understanding Children's Knowledge of Written Language," surveys a broad range of physiological, historical, and cultural phenomena that have resulted in what he terms the "organic" relationship between speech and print and which underlie children's knowledge of written language.

Regardless of the degree to which consequences of literacy may be wide-ranging, many have argued for at least subtle cultural consequences. In his chapter "The Visual Face of Experience and Language: A Metalinguistic Excursion," Holdaway expresses the strong form of the argument for print being the primary facilitator of metalinguistic awareness. He develops a case for both subtle and profound effects of literacy, the former reflected in the language we use, the latter in the ways in which we encode, organize, and process language and, perhaps more profoundly, thought.

Two issues broached by Henderson and Holdaway—the importance of and instructional emphasis on phonemic segmentation in beginning literacy and the role of print in facilitating this more extensive metalinguistic awareness—are addressed in more empirical depth in Section Three, "Metalinguistic Awareness and Reading Ability: Experimental Investigations of Causal Connections." Two seminal lines of research are represented, each often identified as being at opposite poles from the other. As might be expected, however, such complex issues are rarely either/or, and the research represented in these two chapters enhances the valid points of both. Ehri and Wilce present findings from some very intriguing studies in which they attempted to tease out the relationships between linguistic and orthographic knowledge. In their chapter "The Influence of Spellings on Speech," they trace the developmental effects of exposure to orthographic structure. While acknowledging the possibility of learning phonemic segmentation prior to reading and/or significant exposure to print, they nevertheless succinctly express what may be the *sine qua non* of the "importance of print" school: "since spellings are essentially sound pictures to the tutored eye, they may be worth a thousand spoken explanations."

In their chapter "Linguistic Coding and Metalinguistic Awareness: Their Relationship to Verbal Memory and Code Acquisition in Poor and Normal Readers," Vellutino and Scanlon discuss a line of research that pursues metalinguistic questions beyond the level of young children to a consideration of severely reading-impaired pupils in the upper elementary grades. They note the considerable difficulty that these children have in dealing with language metalinguistically and in using language as a coding medium, and provide insight into possible reasons underlying difficulties in attending to language and lexical features among this reading disabled population.

Whereas the studies by Ehri and Wilce and Vellutino and Scanlon exemplify the content and technique of controlled experimental research, Section Four, "The Influence of Home and School Interventions on the Development of Metalinguistic Awareness," presents and reviews studies that have been conducted in more naturalistic settings. Belying common assumptions about "unstructured" interaction in the home, these studies demonstrate how literate adults, usually unaware, provide a certain informal structure within which conversations about literacy occur.

Hiebert's chapter and the chapter by Mason, McCormick, and Bhavnagri address the home and the preschool setting, while Taylor's chapter synthesizes and reflects on the findings in both contexts. In her chapter "Issues Related to Home Influences on Young Children's Print-Related Development," Hiebert addresses three areas: (a) the influence of individual parent and child differences in experiences with print; (b) informal yet directed experiences with print between parent and child; (c) the nature and appropriateness of home intervention programs.

In "How Are You Going to Help Me Learn? Lesson Negotiations Between a Teacher and Preschool Children," Mason and her coauthors discuss a study conducted in a preschool setting in which a naturalistic experience with print is afforded within a more directed or structured context. They investigate the degree to which reading/writing materials in the home environment, parents' motivation and press for achievement, and parents' interaction with their children contribute to children's readiness to participate in reading lessons. They emphasize the role of *social interactions* in facilitating knowledge about literacy, and within these interactions, the value of children coming to express this thinking to the degree that they are capable.

In her chapter "Developing Beginning Literacy Concepts: Content and Context" Taylor reviews the importance for young children of developing a knowledge base in four general areas: (a) technical aspects of written language; (b) mapping principles that relate speech to print; (c) functions served by written language; (d) schemata that characterize the way written language is organized and expressed. Significantly, she underscores the importance of literacy concepts being experienced across many contexts so that they are less wedded to specific situations. The considerable contribution of the teacher is emphasized; indeed, all three chapters in this section offer some quite specific suggestions for teacher behavior, a concern often distressingly absent in much research in this area.

Section Five, "Tests of Metalinguistic Awareness," comprises the significant chapter by Day and Day. Although the basic ideas underlying metalinguistic awareness are beginning to be incorporated within many informal "readiness" assessments, the domain has been in existence long enough for more deliberate and cohesive analytic and evaluative measures to have been developed. Because of the purported context-specific biases of obtained test results, however, many educators and researchers would bridle at what would be perceived to be yet another intrusion of psychometrics into education. Nevertheless, it is generally acknowledged that testing is an educational fact of life. If the tasks of the test, however, reflect as honestly as possible the phenomenon to be investigated, then results can be used to yield reliable *ongoing* as well as summative information about the nature of students' learning. Day and Day begin their discussion with the first and best known of the newer readiness assessments, Clay's *Concepts About Print* test. They continue their overview by examining the *Test of Early Reading Ability,* the *Written Language Awareness Test,* and the *Linguistic Awareness in Reading Readiness* test. In offering evaluations of each of these tests, Day and Day discuss both the validity of the component metalinguistic-related tasks as well as the practicality of the test administrations. They conclude in effect that rigorous efforts are needed in this area. Educational testing will not fade, and when one considers the alternatives—the common readiness tests according to which significant placement and instructional decisions are made—promising new directions in testing should be applauded and encouraged.

Over the years, the research in the area that has come to be called metalinguistic awareness has, as has other literacy-related research, neglected for the most part the role of *writing*. As noted earlier, writing has in fact been excluded on theoretical grounds from the domain of inquiry. The act of writing, however, perhaps because of the immediacy of its expression and the visible consequences of its application, may be perceived by the young child as "functionally relevant," therefore attributing a positive value to literacy. Dyson, while emphasizing children's "intuitive" rather than overt knowledge of the relationship between spoken and written language, sketches an overview of the symbolic contexts out of which reflective awareness will arise. She pursues two objectives in her chapter "Children's Early Interpretations of Writing: Expanding Research Perspectives": (a) determining whether there is any system to the early writing attempts of children, and (b) intriguingly, highlighting children's understanding of how "meaning is encoded in graphics." Dyson's perspective is necessarily a broad one, addressing much of the recent theory building and research into the more general development of symbolic systems. As children differentiate one or more semiotic or symbolic functions, their conceptions of two-dimensional "graphic" symbolism—pictographic or significatory—are interwoven; the reasons for the gradual differentiation of these symbolic functions reflect the roots of eventual conscious reflection on the nature of the correspondence between the sign, the spoken language, and meaning.

Sulzby's chapter, "Children's Elicitation and Use of Metalinguistic Knowledge About *Word* During Literacy Interactions," focuses on the penultimate linguistic element as its knowledge develops within interaction of a more natural yet structured type. Rather than directly broaching the issue regarding what a "word" is, Sulzby's technique has been to wait until her subjects use the term and then pursue their understanding. Her chapter title suggests the subtle two-way information channel of this exchange, the dynamics of which affect similarly most all of the research in this area: children need information too, even as the researcher is attempting to discern the current state of their knowledge. Of course, the concepts of both researcher and child informant unavoidably change during this exchange so that both participants end with more than they began. Unlike most research directed toward the concept of "word," Sulzby's approach notably has considered the role of writing in the development of this concept.

In their chapter "Metalinguistic Awareness in Writing and Reading: The Young Child as Curricular Informant," Rowe and Harste reexamine the data from the National Institute of Education study by Harste, Burke and Woodward (1981) for instances of metalinguistic behaviors as children generate and comment on writing. Rather than looking at children's knowledge of "word" qua word, for example, they attempt to discuss the "language functions being explored" during instantiations of metalinguistic behavior. Based on their observation of beginning literacy, Rowe and Harste suggest that coming to understand language as an object is a most natural consequence of meaningful experiences with print. In attempting to determine the importance of metalinguistic awareness for literacy, they suggest that successful experiences with literacy do not require particular forms of metalinguistic awareness, that in all language events metalinguistic behavior is a naturally occurring option, and that supportive language learning environments bring about opportunities for explicit awareness of language and language strategies.

Section Seven, "Alternative Symbol Systems: Metalinguistic Awareness in Braille and Manual Language Systems," offers a perspective that, primarily for two reasons, is unique in metalinguistic awareness research. First, there has been very little investigation of visually and auditorially impaired children's awareness of language as an object; second, by investigating these populations insight is afforded into the more general potential for and development of symbolic understanding. When both the usual means of establishing symbol/referent relationships are impaired and a child is presented with only one half of a standard correspondence system, an important research challenge is to probe how "language" as an "object" is realized and its successively more finely differentiated aspects learned.

In their chapter "Visually Impaired and Sighted Children's Emerging Concepts About Written Language," Tompkins and McGee provide a concise overview of the development of Braille as an alternative symbol system and present a comparative study in which they note some striking parallels in the development of metalinguistic concepts between sighted and visually impaired children. Their method involved adapting Clay's *Concepts About Print* test for visually impaired children; this effort alone is a distinguishing feature of this exploratory research.

Andrews and Mason examine briefly the nature of the issue involving competing symbol systems for the hearing impaired and then present their research, suggesting three developmental levels of early print awareness. Although some general developmental parallels with nonimpaired children can be identified, there are some notable differences. These exist primarily at the level of the word and its components, and Andrews and Mason suggest that some quite explicit instruction is necessary in order for hearing impaired children to establish a necessary foundation for analytic strategies.

The volume closes with "Metalinguistic Awareness: A Synthesis and Beyond," in which Templeton discusses both significant issues raised in the volume and some related issues. Despite acknowledging some differences in methodology and interpretations evident in this volume, Templeton suggests that there are stronger commonalities. Not the least of these is most apparently the commitment to understanding, to affording, and to honoring the most facilitative immersion in literacy for our young children. He suggests in addition that, as knowledgeable researchers and educators, we may be more empowered to effect this commitment than we have often believed.

S. T.
D. Y.

Introduction

Chapter 1

Introduction: Metalinguistic Awareness—An Etymology

DAVID B. YADEN, JR.

SHANE TEMPLETON

It is obvious now from even a cursory overview of the literature regarding young children's behaviors toward, and reasonings about, language and literacy tasks that the variety of abilities labeled as "metalinguistic" has taken on protean dimensions. From Holden's earlier use of the term to describe children's conscious awareness of the lexical content of their speech and their ability to use language to talk about language (see Foreword, this volume), the term has been extended to include "intuitions regarding the acceptability, ambiguity, or synonymy of sentences" (Ryan & Ledger, 1984, p. 150); children's knowledge of the structure of stories (McGee, Charlesworth, Cheek & Cheek, 1982); awareness of printed conventions (Moore, 1984); and at the most global level, sensitivity to the distinction of what is *said* as opposed to what is *meant* in both oral and written language, or to put it another way, awareness of the "difference between the linguistic form—at any level, we assume—and its intended meanings and their possible interrelations" (Olson, 1982, p. 159). To be sure, Professor Holden's comment that "the field has opened out like a funnel" (Foreword, p. xii) since her first studies of children's knowledge of "wordness" in the early 1970s can be easily substantiated merely by perusing the references in this book, nearly six hundred of them.

Some researchers, however, have viewed this definitional labyrinth with less than enthusiasm. Valtin (1984a), for instance, has stated that the research area itself has become, in her view at least, virtually "incoherent" (p. 207) due to the spectrum of abilities that can be characterized under the various rubrics of *metalinguistic, language,* or *linquistic* awareness. Even earlier, Marshall and Morton (1978) attempted to distinguish clearly between language production processes and the awareness or monitoring of those processes lest the two be confused and render the terminology related to awareness "totally vacuous" (p. 228).

However, this aforementioned fear may have already come upon us, since attempts to impose some kind of order on the research by way of either classifi-cations of types of awareness (e.g., Clark, 1978; Hutson, 1979; Yaden, this vol-ume) or conceptual models of the emergence of language awareness within lan-guage and cognitive development (e.g., Tunmer & Herriman, 1984a; Valtin, 1984a) have resulted in a clear dichotomy: Either the processes of metalinguistic awareness are "on or off" or they can be represented by degrees of awareness, resulting in what Marshall and Morton (1978) have referred to as an "infinite regress of awareness of awareness of awareness" (p. 229). Thus, consensus of ex-actly what constitutes metalinguistic awareness, or for that matter, any other kind of awareness, still eludes us.

In throwing our own hat into the ring, so to speak, at an attempt to de-scribe the nature of metalinguistic awareness, we will take an approach not tried as yet: tracing the history of the term "metalinguistic" itself. This approach has been chosen (a) for the purely historical interest and the closet philologist in each one of us, and (b) because we suspect that the variation in definitions of the term, since the 1970s in particular, are rooted in earlier uses of it. This in-troduction will not impose yet another fine-grained definition of metalinguistic abilities nor even offer another classification of research in the area, but rather attempt to give a perspective in which present descriptions may be viewed.

Part of the "incoherence" which has been imputed to this body of research can be attributed to the fact that most researchers in the area use the term "metalinguistic" as if its origin were in the 1970s only. While it is true that Holden (1971) and the Gleitmans (1972) were most likely among the first to use the term in the literature of education and psychology as it is applied today, the term itself is indigenous to philosophy as early as the late 1920s and enjoyed a vigorous early attention in linguistics during the 1940s and 1950s as well, cul-minating in a special issue of *ETC*, a journal of semantics, in 1952 devoted to the topic of "metalinguistics," albeit describing something perhaps more familiar today as sociolinguistics.

The material directly following in this introduction provides an excursion of sorts, from the early part of the century to today, examining the term "meta-linguistic" and its various referents for the past fifty years or so. While taking into account several definitions of "metalinguistic" in the past, this discussion does not claim to be comprehensive, largely because of the malleability of the term across several disciplines which include philosophy, psychology, linguistics, English and education, just to name a few. What is hoped, however, is that this historical look, while not providing a definition for "metalinguistic awareness," will at least supply a rationale for several of the ones we already have.

Origin of Metalanguage and Use in Philosophy

In the late 1920s the Polish mathematician-logician Alfred Tarski, in a series of lectures delivered in Polish to the Polish Philosophical Society and the Warsaw Scientific Society, introduced a methodology for analyzing the formal languages of the deductive sciences. These lectures, published under the title *The Concept of Truth in Formalized Languages* (Tarski, 1983), discussed how a formalized language such as is used in logic and mathematics might be analyzed and evaluated in terms of its axioms, syntax, and formulizations (Corcoran, 1983, p. xv). Crucial to this methodology was the distinction between the language being studied, the "object-language" *(Grundsprache)*, and the language in which the investigation was being carried out, the "metalanguage" *(Metasprache)*. While Tarski (1983) went into great depth and technical detail in developing the parameters and nature of a metalanguage, for the purposes of this discussion it suffices to say that metalanguage is simply "language used to talk about an object-language" (Edwards, 1972, p. 68). To put it another way, metalanguage is "a system of propositions about other propositions" (Burchfield, 1976, p. 909). It is interesting to note, in light of current usage in education, that the original referents of both object- and metalanguages were *written* systems rather than spoken. It is perhaps appropriate to point out as well that in their original usage both terms were entirely relative in that a metalanguage could itself be the "object-language" of another describing system of propositions. In this case, the latter set of propositions would be couched in "metametalanguage."

"Metalinguistic," then, was and still is in philosophy the adjective form of "metalanguage" (Burchfield, 1976, p. 909). For example, the statement " 'True' has four letters" makes a metalinguistic statement about the word "true" (Flew, 1979, p. 212). Thus, all of the statements of a metalanguage are "metalinguistic" in that their referent is the linguistic form of another language rather than that language's object- or real-world referents. It is unfortunate that recently Tunmer, Pratt and Herriman (1984b) have proposed that a distinction be made between "metalanguage" and "metalinguistic" awareness, the former referring to such terms as *phoneme* and *word*, and the latter describing the cognizance of these units in speech. This proposed distinction entirely obscures the original derivation and meaning. What has happened since the 1970s is that the term "metalinguistic" has taken on as an additional antecedent some psychological state of mind. We will return to this point later in this discussion, but it is important to note that neither "mental states" nor types of linguistic behavior were included in Tarski's (1983) coining of the term, nor do they have a part in the current usage of the terminology in philosophy today. What vestiges of the original meaning remain in educational usage today will be discussed in another introductory section, entitled "Metalinguistic Terminology." Now, however, we will turn to the carry-over of these terms in the linguistic literature of the late 1940s and 1950s.

Metalinguistics as Science and Language Behavior

There are at least two usages of the term "metalinguistic" and its related form "metalingual" in the literature of linguistics during the mid-century. Roman Jakobson's use of the term "metalingual" to describe an aspect of language development is probably the less well known, but can be seen as the forerunner of its current use in linguistic literature such as is reflected in the writings of Clark

(1978). The more widely known meaning of the term "metalinguistics" during the 1940s and 1950s was as the linguistic science which examined "the relationship of language to the rest of the culture" (Pei & Gaynor, 1954, p. 135). The second of these descriptions will be discussed first.

The Science of Metalinguistics

In the foreword to the special issue of *ETC* on "Metalinguistics," Henry Lee Smith and George Trager (1952) gave an extended definition of the parameters of this budding science:

> The term "metalinguistics" was devised to cover aspects of linguistic science dealing with *the relations of linguistic behavior (language) to other human behavior*. . . . Metalinguistics, however, which may be described as the study of what people talk (or write) about and why, and how they react to it, is concerned with *meaning on all levels* . . . metalinguistics deals also with *the organization of sentences into discourse and the relation of the discourse to the rest of the culture*. (p. 163)

Smith and Trager as well as later linguists, e.g., Postman & Weingartner (1966), give credit to Benjamin Whorf and his work dealing with the relation of language to thought as providing the initial impetus to the development of this new aspect of linguistics. Whorf's view, better known as the Whorf-Sapir hypothesis, in a nutshell was "that the structure of the language one uses 'shapes' not only how one thinks, but what one can think about" (Postman & Weingartner, 1966, p. 198). Whorf himself, however, did not apparently use the term "metalinguistic" to describe his theories; the choice of this term seems to lie with Trager and a group of linguists on the staff of the Foreign Service Institute around 1949.

In the first of several "occasional papers" entitled *Studies in Linguistics*, Trager (1966) categorized the field of linguistics into three basic divisions: (a) Prelinguistics, dealing with the physiological and acoustic properties of language production; (b) Microlinguistics, comprising the central study of language systems, both descriptive and historical; and (c) Metalinguistics, "the full statement of the point-by-point and pattern-by-pattern relations between the language and any of the other cultural systems" (pp. 3–7). Interestingly, Einar Haugen (1951) in a presidential address to the Linguistic Society urged linguists to "reject" Trager's definition of the term in favor of retaining its original philosophic meaning as a descriptor of a special metalanguage comprised of terms such as *phone* and *morph* being generated at the time by American linguists (pp. 231–214). Haugen suggested either "semantics," "ethnolinguistics," or "sociolinguistics" as better suited to describe the relations between language and culture. And it seems over time that the latter term has supplanted "metalinguistics" as the common designation for that particular aspect of language study in linguistics.

Language Behavior as Metalinguistic

In our view, Roman Jakobson was the first to ascribe the related adjective "metalingual" with a function of developing language behavior in the individual, although no conscious mental state was implied in this usage either. Using the philosophic usage as a base, Jakobson, in another presidential address to the Linguistic Society in 1956, described this aspect of language behavior as follows:

We practice metalanguage without realizing the metalingual character of our statements. Far from being confined to the sphere of science, metalingual operations prove to be an integral part of our verbal activities. Whenever the addresser and/or addressee need to check up whether they use the same code, speech is focused upon the CODE and thus performs a METALINGUAL (or glossing function). "I don't follow you—what do you mean?" asks the addressee. . . . And the addresser in anticipation of such recapturing questions inquires: "Do you know what I mean?" Then by replacing the questionable sign with another sign from the same or another linguistic code, the encoder of the message seeks to make it more accessible to the decoder. (p. 86)

Jakobson went on to say that this ability for "metalingual commutation" comprises the very core of language development. He stated that "a constant recourse to metalanguage is indispensable both for a creative assimilation of the mother tongue and for its final mastery" (p. 91). An inability to exchange one sign for another of related meaning was precisely what could be observed in certain language disorders where subjects could not give synonyms for certain words or perform language equations of the form "An adult male goose is a gander" and vice versa. In order to reach to the heart of such problems, Jakobson urged "approaching metalanguage as an innermost linguistic problem" (p. 92).

It is ironic to discover that Marshall and Morton's (1978) attempt to salvage "metalinguistic" awareness from "vacuity" by distinguishing it from merely producing speech is turned on its head in view of Jakobson's earlier definition, which squarely places metalingual operations in the realm of learning to speak. Also the arguments advanced by Tunmer and Herriman (1984a) and Andresen (cited in Valtin, 1984a) for the term referring to a definite reflective awareness of language against the views of Clark (1978) or Mattingly (1984), where conscious awareness plays a lesser role in language development, have little force in that Clark's and Mattingly's views of children's ability to focus on the code are much more consistent with the earlier definition of Jakobson.

It is not, however, that the insistence of Tunmer et al. (1984b) and others for this deliberate, conscious reflection upon language as being the meaning of "metalinguistic" is so much misplaced as it is that the ground swell in cognitive development research has brought a new dimension to the study of the growth of language and literacy in children. It is this research whose immediate roots are visible in Piaget (1924/1974) and Vygotsky (1934/1962) which has forced upon us the uncomfortable notion that children do not qualitively think like adults, nor may they be able to easily or deliberately focus upon either spoken or written language forms as their adult mentors have assumed these past millennia or so. We now turn, somewhat hesitatingly, to try to make some sense of what history has handed us in terms of definitional baggage and what current research demands our attention.

Metalinguistic Awareness in Current Usage

We will not in this section attempt to give a listing of the myriad of definitions of metalinguistic awareness which have been put forward during the last fifteen years or so in the educational and child development literature. We will select only a few as general types and then relate these to past usages as we have described them earlier. Before doing so, however, we would like to point out a couple of the more esoteric definitions of "metalinguistic" phenomena that we have run across in searching its history.

In an article dealing with the characteristics of aphasia, Green (1970) describes a theoretical model of the naming process in patients with language disorders in which the first or "metalinguistic" stage is characterized by the ability to recognize an object and use it correctly but still not be able to verbalize its name. His use of the term *metalinguistic* means literally "without reference to language" (p. 230). Another definition of the term is given by Watkins (1970) in an article entitled "Language of Gods and Language of Men: Remarks on Some Indo-European Metalinguistic Traditions." In this paper, "metalinguistic" is used to differentiate between words having some definite sacred or spiritual connotation and colloquial language. Thus, "metalinguistic" refers to antecedents not common to earth and means literally "above common language."

To say the least, the term "metalinguistic" has proven to be all too "absorbent" in attracting meanings across several disciplines. Thus, in order to clearly distinguish what truly new current work in literacy has added to "metalinguistic's" already long list of courtiers, we are forced to recognize what alternative meanings and nuances came with the word into current educational literature.

Metalinguistic Terminology

The most obvious vestige of the original and current philosophic usage is evident in descriptions of "the language instruction register" (DeStefano, 1972) and "reading instruction register" (Downing, 1976). The various language descriptors, such as *word, sentence, story, paragraph,* or *vowel, consonant, digraph,* are a definite specialized "metalanguage" and statements containing them truly "metalinguistic" in that the referent is the linguistic form of a spoken or written language. In addition, it is appropriate to consider all the statements of phonic generalizations, spelling rules, and definitions of terms as being part of the specialized "metalanguage" of literacy instruction.

As mentioned, Tunmer and Herriman (1984a) add confusion rather than clarity in usage of the term by ignoring the original adjectival status of "metalinguistic" from "metalanguage" by attempting to restrict the meaning of the former to a child's cognizance of these units (i.e., *word, syllable*) in speech only. Given the historical meaning of the terms, "metalanguage" can be couched in both written and spoken form and in reality circumscribes all of language instruction in general. When viewed in this wider context, children's difficulty in recognizing speech elements or the conventions of print may be only a small part of a more pervasive difficulty in dealing with written or spoken language instruction in general, the whole of which must be delivered in metalanguage.

Unconscious Language Behavior as Metalinguistic

Seen also in its original use by Jakobson (1980), Clark's (1978) classification of degrees of awareness, which has been criticized for failing to differentiate conceptually between the stages (Valtin, 1984), cannot be faulted. Clark's (1978) use of the term like others' in this volume (e.g., Dyson; Rowe and Harste) follows Jakobson's use where any recourse to the code itself is considered to be "metalinguistic" by the very fact that the code is either exchanged for another form, manipulated, or monitored in some way. Unless one is willing to deny that Jakobson's former meaning of the term still has validity, then definitions of language awareness which use the word *reflective* to mean any kind of code monitoring (e.g., Clark, 1978, pp. 17–18) or which include notions of *accessibility* to grammatical knowledge without conscious knowledge of it (e.g., Mattingly, 1984) must be considered equally accurate descriptions of "metalinguistic" language behavior.

Language as Object

What is new to the definition of the term in the 1970s is the emphasis not only on being able to focus on the code, but to *know* that one is doing it and to realize the arbitrary nature of language in that the form of language, either written or spoken, is something separate from its meaning. Such views of "metalinguistic awareness" are expressed in the following definitions:

Metalinguistic awareness, the ability to make language forms opaque and attend to them in and for themselves, is a special kind of language performance, one which makes special cognitive demands, and seems to be less easily and less universally acquired than the language performances of speaking and listening (Cazden, 1974a, p. 29).

Thus, one aspect of the development common to *metalinguistic abilities* and concrete operational abilities is an increasing ability to act, think deliberately, and, concomitantly, to place one's self mentally at a distance from a situation and to reflect upon it (Hakes, 1980, p. 38).

Metalinguistic knowledge, or linguistic awareness, involves the ability to focus attention upon the form of language in and of itself, rather than merely as the vehicle by which meaning is conveyed (Ryan, 1980, p. 39).

Metalinguistic ability [is] the ability to reflect upon language as an object of thought rather than simply its vehicle. Children's metalinguistic development reflects their growing awareness of certain properties of language and their ability to make the linguistic forms themselves the object of analysis (Mohanty & Babu, 1984, p. 17).

However precise these definitions may be in circumscribing this new dimension in studying children's growth in language and literacy, they cannot claim exclusively to be defining once and for all what is truly *metalinguistic awareness*, given the definitions of the term which have been in philosophy and linguistics previously. First, there is an overmuch emphasis on spoken language knowledge which is opposite from what *metalanguage* originally referred to in philosophy; second, the exclusion of language behaviors such as the automatic monitoring of speech performance precludes the definition of these latter behaviors as also *metalinguistic* when viewed from Jakobson's former usage.

Summary

Our own position in viewing this plethora of definitions is implied in the title of this book: whatever functional knowledge is required to understand the "strategies and demands of different literacy events" (Rowe & Harste, this volume), whatever "intuitions" are needed to help children begin to realize how language and meaning may be encoded into graphic forms (Dyson, this volume), or whatever explicit conceptualizations of written and spoken language are essential before print becomes meaningful (Ehri; Vellutino & Scanlon, this volume) can all and equally be considered rightfully metalinguistic, since the object of these knowledges, intuitions, and conceptualizations is language itself, in whatever form it may take.

However, in spite of this very global view of metalinguistic abilities, we do not want to detract from or ignore the many interesting and, in our view, crucial questions regarding the exact nature and development of these nascent reasonings about written and spoken language which impinge upon the processes of becoming literate. Professor Holden (see Foreword, this volume) has summarized them well: "At what age do various metalinguistic abilities appear spontaneously?" "What interventions hasten their appearance?" "What are the relationships between metalinguistic abilities and other cognitive activities?" "What are the practical educational implications of metalinguistic abilities?" "How early can they be taught?" "Should they be taught?" And as she further points out, "An inexhaustible list."

To many of these questions this volume should provide considerable insight, particularly since the focus is on supplying direct evidence of the interface of children's developing knowledge of what becoming literate means and their performance in actual tasks of reading and writing. That there is an obvious lacuna in the reading/language arts instructional literature concerning children's conceptual knowledge of literacy behaviors is evidenced by the fact that to the editors' knowledge very few current textbooks (e.g., Aulls, 1982; Cunningham, Moore, Cunningham, and Moore, 1983) give even a passing mention to any of the research in the field, although studies of metalinguistic behaviors have permeated much of the literature for the past fifteen years. Hopefully, this book will begin closing the gap.

Section 1

An International Survey of Reading Research in Metalinguistic Awareness

Chapter 2

Cognitive Clarity: A Unifying and Cross-Cultural Theory for Language Awareness Phenomena in Reading

JOHN DOWNING

A substantial fund of research information on language awareness has grown in the nineteen years since Reid's (1966) pioneering article, "Learning to Think About Reading," was published in Great Britain. Much of this research evidence is reviewed in other chapters in this volume. There is, however, a considerable body of language awareness research that has been conducted in languages other than English and in countries other than the United States. The purpose of this chapter is to review the evidence for metalinguistic awareness across cultures and writing systems. Also, such a review is appropriate for judging the validity of the cognitive clarity theory, because it claims to be a universal explanation of how children learn to read and write in all languages and writing systems. Hence, the focus here is on both language awareness research in different languages and varying types of writing systems.

In order, however, to give the reader an overall theoretical framework within which to interpret the following research, the major tenets of the cognitive clarity theory are briefly reviewed first, as are some general considerations to be made when discussing literacy processes.

Cognitive Clarity and Literacy Processes

A psychological theory of how literacy is learned must be linked with the main body of theory and research in psychology. Most psychologists, when describing reading, label it as "a skill" (e.g., Clay, 1972; Holmes, 1970; Lansdown, 1974; Singer, 1966). Downing and Leong (1982) made a careful analysis of the psychological literature on skill in general, related it to reading behavior in particular, and confirmed that reading does belong in the category of skill.

Any skill, whether it be driving a car, swimming, playing chess, fishing, or reading, has an essential basis in intelligent thinking (Whiting & den Brinker, 1982). The work of practicing a skill to mastery and automaticity cannot begin until the learner comprehends, at least partially, the tasks that he or she is required to undertake in performing the specific skill (Fitts, 1962). The learner must get in mind what has to be done (Bruner, 1971; Cronbach, 1977; Luria, 1976). To understand the tasks involved in acquiring the skill, the learner will need to develop concepts for thinking about it. He or she will also find it useful to know the specialized language for talking and thinking about the skill—the "language instruction register" (DeStefano, 1972).

In learning the skill of reading and the related skill of writing, there are two groups of concepts that people use for thinking about oral and written language and how they are related: (a) *functional concepts*—the various communication purposes of speaking, listening, writing, and reading; and (b) *featural concepts*—the characteristics of spoken language that are represented by written or printed symbols. These functional and featural concepts are put to work by the literacy learner in the "intelligent construction by the child" of these two skills of literacy (Ferreiro & Teberosky, 1979, pp. 344–345).

There is by now a considerable body of research evidence showing that both the language instruction register and its underlying functional and featural concepts are importantly related to success and failure in learning how to read and write (Downing & Valtin, 1984). The precise nature of the causal relationship is still a matter of theoretical debate and research investigation (see Ehri, Vellutino & Scanlon, this volume). The most likely causal connection is an interactional one. The child gains some insight into a linguistic concept and its name. This insight leads to some improvement in understanding the tasks of learning how to perform the reading skill. This improvement, in turn, produces even more insight into that linguistic concept or throws some light on other concepts. Thus, the interactional process leads to cumulative improvement in the learner's comprehension of the language instruction register and the basic functional and featural concepts of language.

The term "metacognitive awareness" refers to all the various new sensitivities that develop in the process of trying to learn to read and write. It includes getting to understand *why* people write, *why* they read, and *how* they write and read in special ways for specific purposes. For example, shopping lists, cookbooks, hymnals, novels, and so forth have different purposes which require different techniques in skilled writing and reading. Metacognitive awareness also includes "metalinguistic awareness," which is the special sensitivity to features of speech and writing and how they are related to each other. For example, the elements of speech sound such as phoneme, word, and sentence have visible counterparts in writing or print.

Downing (1979) proposed the cognitive clarity theory to explain how metacognitive readiness affects children's progress in learning how to read and write. He summarized his theory as follows:

1. Writing or print in any language is a visible code for those aspects of speech that were accessible to the linguistic awareness of the creators of that code or writing system.

2. This linguistic awareness of the creators of a writing system included simultaneous awareness of the communicative function of language and certain features of spoken language that are accessible to the speaker-hearer for logical analysis (cf. Gelb, 1963; Jensen, 1970).
3. The learning-to-read process consists in the rediscovery of (a) the functions and (b) the coding rules of the writing system.
4. Their rediscovery depends on the learner's linguistic awareness of the same features of communication and language as were accessible to the creators of the writing system.
5. Children approach the tasks of reading instruction in a normal state of cognitive confusion about the purposes and technical features of language.
6. Under reasonably good conditions, children work themselves out of the initial state of cognitive confusion into increasing cognitive clarity about the functions and features of language.
7. Although the initial stage of literacy acquisition is the most vital one, cognitive confusion continues to arise and then, in turn, give way to cognitive clarity throughout the later stages of education as new subskills are added to the student's repertory.
8. The cognitive clarity theory applies to all languages and writing systems. The communication aspect is universal, but the technical coding rules differ from one language to another. (Downing, 1979, p. 37)

The term "cognitive confusion" comes from Vernon's (1957) work on reading failure. Her comprehensive and rigorous review of research on the causes of reading disability led her to conclude that "the fundamental and basic characteristic of reading disability appears to be cognitive confusion . . ." (p. 71). Later, Vernon (1971) reaffirmed that "intelligent comprehension" of the task in learning to read is essential (p. 82). Downing (1979) developed the cognitive clarity theory summarized above because

cognitive confusion is the chief symptom of reading disability, according to Vernon. Therefore, if we generalize from her finding, we may postulate that cognitive clarity should be the typical characteristic of the successful reader. He or she will be a pupil who brings clear thinking to the task of reasoning about what to do in learning how to read and write. (p. 10)

Cross-Cultural Research Evidence Related to the Cognitive Clarity Theory

Numerous scientific reports of observations of language awareness phenomena have been published in a variety of languages. Furthermore, in English, French, and Spanish the reports come from several cultures that share the same language. Some of these reports are cited in this section; the list is not meant to be exhaustive.

English

Studies of language awareness have been made in several English-speaking countries. Reid's (1966) investigation in *Scotland* covered both functional concepts and featural concepts in young beginners. She found that they all began at age five with "a general lack of any specific expectancies of what reading was going to be like, of what the activity consisted in, of the purpose and use of it" (p. 58). Also, they had "a great poverty of linguistic equipment to deal with the new experiences, calling letters "numbers" and words "names" (p. 58).

Downing (1970) replicated Reid's study in *England* and obtained remarkably similar results. He also conducted experiments on the children's comprehension of the terms "word" and "sound" in the language instruction register. Downing (1970) reported that both terms were "very poorly understood by five-year-old beginners" (p. 111). In a longitudinal study, Downing (1971–72) traced the same children's cognitive development in these respects during their first school year. He found that the children differed in their rates of development with regard to these linguistic concepts and that their conceptual growth was observable during the year. He concluded:

The differences in the responses of the faster, intermediate, and slower developing children are more readily described in terms of the varying degrees of success which they had in solving the problems posed by the novel tasks involved in learning to read. These differences also are more readily explained by their varying levels in the development of cognitive clarity for the more progress they had made towards general cognitive clarity (1) the better the children understood the communication purpose of the written form of language, (2) the clearer was their conception of the symbolic function of writing, (3) the better they understood the processes of decoding and encoding which relate written to spoken language, (4) the further advanced was their development of linguistic concepts, and (5) the better was their command of the technical terminology for such abstract units of language. (p. 19)

Francis (1973), is a study of primary school children in another part of England, reported: "It was as though the children had never thought to analyse speech, but in learning to read had been forced to recognize units and subdivisions. The use of words like *letter, word,* and *sentence* in teaching was not so much a direct aid to instruction but a challenge to find their meaning" (p. 22). Thus, under current conditions of reading instruction, children learn this technical vocabulary "in the course of learning to read" (Francis, 1975, p. 152).

Several studies of children's metacognitive and metalinguistic development related to reading have been reported from English-speaking areas of *Canada.* Downing and Oliver (1973–74), in more extensive experiments on children's conceptions of "a word" in a cross-sectional study of different age groups, confirmed the results of the earlier study in England. They noted that children even up to 6.5 years of age considered nonverbal sounds, phrases, sentences, and phonemes as "words." Subcultural groups also have been compared in Canadian studies. Downing, Ollila, and Oliver (1975) found that Canadian Indian beginners from a cultural background with no tradition of literacy were less mature in their development of concepts of the functions and features of written language than were non-Indian beginners. In another study, Downing, Ollila, and Oliver (1977) discovered that the development of these concepts was related to socioeconomic levels in Canadian city children of kindergarten age.

Also in Canada, two reports of a longitudinal study of the language awareness and related reading achievements of some three hundred children have been published. The first (Downing, Ayers & Schaefer, 1978) showed that cognitive development was more related to reading readiness than to perceptual development. Then Ayers and Downing (1982) reported a high level of predictive validity of tests of language awareness in kindergarten for reading achievement in grade 1. These tests were subsequently published as *Linguistic Awareness in Reading Readiness (LARR) Test* (1983). Another type of language awareness research conducted in Canada has consisted of experiments in training children's ability in segmenting spoken words into their component phonemes. Ollila, Johnson, and Downing (1974) found that children who had such training developed greater awareness of the phonemic structure of English than children who had only the more usual type of reading readiness program. Bell (1982) trained kindergartners in phoneme segmentation and showed that the resulting improvement was maintained on a test administered several months later.

In the *United States* a large number of studies has shown the existence of language awareness phenomena and their development in American children. Several of these studies have demonstrated that language awareness is connected with reading achievement. But the exact nature of the causal relationship is a matter of controversy. These American studies are well documented in other chapters in this book (see Yaden, this volume) and by Johns (1984; this volume). Therefore, they will not be reviewed in this chapter. However, it should be recognized that a number of American reading specialists have emphasized the practical importance of metacognition in reading instruction. For example, Smith (1972) argued that "pupils should be fully aware of the purposes of materials they have been asked to read" and that "pupils need to learn how to set their own purposes" (p. 92). Carrillo (1973) too claimed that "the reader . . . must always be *conscious* of *his level of understanding* of the printed passage. . . . All of this means that instruction in comprehension, so *that one knows how much one knows* when reading, is a prerequisite to flexibility" (p. 64).

Clay (1967, 1969) made weekly observations of 100 *New Zealand* children's beginning reading behavior during their first year at school. On the basis of her research, Clay has provided extensive practical assistance to teachers wanting to help children develop language awareness in relation to print. Her *Sand* (1972b) and *Stones* (1979c) tests, along with the diagnostic survey, *The Early Detection of Reading Difficulties* (1979a), pioneered the systematic testing of children's concepts about print. Clay reported a high correlation between beginners' scores on her "Concepts about Print" test at age six and their later progress in reading at ages seven and eight. An important point made by Clay is that reading readiness measures such as letter-name or letter-sound knowledge provide only a "tip of the iceberg" clue to a much more significant and central factor in learning to read. Clay's (1979b) book, *Reading: The Patterning of Complex Behavior*, supplies a systematic set of suggestions for helping children to construct their concepts of the skills of literacy.

In *Australia*, Turnbull (1970) followed similar interview procedures and obtained results with school beginners similar to those in Reid's (1966) original study in Scotland. Austin (1974) developed a more structured measure of cognitive clarity with which he tested school beginners in Adelaide. Their reading achievement was tested four months later. He obtained a correlation of more than 0.9 between the cognitive clarity and reading scores. More recently, Watson (1984) has reported his investigation of the interrelationship between language awareness, learning to read, and general cognitive development. He used a longitudinal method to assess the effects of operativity, oral language, and reading progress on a measure of linguistic awareness—the "Units of Print" test. Watson's results, derived chiefly from path analysis, are consistent with his theoretical position that children's progress in the development of concepts about print depends on matching their general level of cognitive development with appropriate teaching methods.

Another recent Australian study (Downing, 1983) moves the consideration of language awareness factors up to the secondary school level. The study evaluated a new combination of teaching methods designed to improve comprehension and study skills in some Queensland high schools. Teachers spontaneously referred to the way in which the new content area teaching methodology had improved students' *awareness* of their own subskills and strategies in comprehension and studying textbooks. Their understanding of the technical terminology for describing print, text, and books also improved. These advances were considered to be responsible for better standards of reading comprehension.

Thus, in the English-speaking world, the phenomenon of language awareness has been well established by the research evidence. It is clear also that language awareness is importantly related to the development of skilled reading. These findings are consistent across several different cultures that share the use of English as the mother tongue.

French

Studies of language awareness have been conducted in several French-speaking cultures, including *Belgium* and *Switzerland,* by investigators using Piagetian theoretical constructs (Berthoud-Papandropoulou, 1978, 1980; Papandropoulou and Sinclair, 1974; Sinclair, 1980). They provide evidence of the existence of language awareness phenomena in French-speaking children. In the most recent publication on this topic from the Geneva School, Sinclair and Berthoud-Papandropoulou (1984) compared studies of a child's conception of a word in French, Russian, and Spanish, and observed that "there are striking similarities in the results" (p. 83). They conclude that although a clearly established developmental sequence of the growth of metalinguistic awareness at present eludes us, research thus far has shown that "a gradual dissociation of the different observable forms of language (utterances, written words or phrases) from their meaning underlies the progress we have described" (p. 89). Theoretically, their view is that the alphabetic writing system "represents some aspects of sounds and bypasses meaning entirely. To use alphabetic reading and writing techniques, new conceptions where words and their meanings are coordinated and dissociable must be constructed. Exactly how these new conceptions are elaborated is at present unclear, but certainly ideas about language as well as reflections on the written system play a part and interact" (pp. 90–91).

In *France,* Leroy-Boussion and Martinez (1974) and Leroy-Boussion (1975) reported a longitudinal study of children's ability to analyze spoken syllables into phonemes and to synthesize spoken phonemes into syllables. A large sample of children was tested every three months for three years, beginning at age 5 in kindergarten. The children's IQs were also tested. The results showed a gradual improvement in these metalinguistic abilities. The synthesis task was more easily learned than the analysis task. Success in both was related to IQ. A certain minimal cognitive level seems to be a prerequisite for learning these metalinguistic subskills. Leroy-Boussion (1975) compared 145 pairs of children matched in age, sex, IQ, and socioeconomic class. One member of each pair was in a class that received reading instruction in kindergarten. The other kindergarten group did not. The metalinguistic task used for comparison was synthesis of phonemes into syllables. The kindergarteners receiving reading instruction were superior, and they maintained their superiority in grade 1. However, the children in kindergartens without reading instruction did make substantial gains in scores on the synthesis test during kindergarten. Furthermore, this control group had higher scores at the end of grade 1 than those which the children with reading instruction had attained at the end of kindergarten. It was the children with very high IQs who showed the greatest improvement in the reading group. (For more details see the review [in English] by Valtin, 1984).

Spanish

Ferreiro and Teberosky (1979) too have approached this problem in a Piagetian frame of reference. Studying children's conceptions of literacy in *Argentina,* they compared groups of Spanish-speaking children at ages 4, 5, and 6 at two socioeconomic class levels. They also made a longitudinal study of children at the lowest socioeconomic class level. They found that the children went through several conceptual stages before grasping the alphabetic principle in the Spanish writing system. There was also a marked difference between the socioeconomic class subcultures in the rate of this conceptual development. Although all children passed through the same sequence of stages of awareness of written language, the middle class children started earlier and progressed more rapidly in this concept development than did children from the lower socioeconomic class. This is because of the greater exposure to literacy objects and activities in middle class families.

Ferreiro and Teberosky found that children begin to construct concepts of literacy spontaneously long before entering school. This construction seems to follow a logical sequence. The child first establishes a global correspondence between the object represented and the text. During these first stages, writing begins to be differentiated from drawing, but the meaning still depends on the picture. Since the children know only a few letters, if any, they produce similar written representations for different objects. Thus, at this stage, children seem to believe that the intention of the writer is the basis for stating meaning. Later, children look for a physical correspondence between the object represented and the text. They may center on the size of the object. For instance, "whale" needs more letters than "armadillo" because a whale is a bigger animal. Finally, the child recognizes that there is a phonetic correspondence between text and speech and that he or she must find a unit of sound that can be represented by a single grapheme. When children establish a syllabic hypothesis for this unit, they have to confront conflicts with written words which they already know and with other restrictions that children usually invent, such as a minimum number and variety of letters required for a word to be readable. In order to solve these conflicts, the child must search for smaller phonetic units to be represented by single graphemes.

Further research and applications of this line of thinking are found in *Venezuela*, where a team of investigators and educators of the Venezuelan Institute of Audiolinguistics have suggested that teachers adopt a new role in their approach to reading instruction. It should be that of investigators and coordinators of the learning situation. They should promote interaction among children and offer appropriate material which copes with the conflicts children are facing in their effort to construct concepts of literacy (Lerner de Zunino, 1982).

Yánez (1984) recently compared the metalinguistic concepts of Venezuelan Spanish-speaking school beginners with those of Canadian English-speaking children of the same age level. He developed a test with parallel items in Spanish and English which was administered in the appropriate language for the country. There were also parallel Spanish and English questionnaires for the children and their parents. Yánez's results using a different research methodology provide strong confirmatory evidence for the early findings of Ferreiro and Teberosky (1979) in Argentina. Yánez writes: "Children, in fact, create their own system of writing" (p. 78). Yánez found that the Spanish-speaking children and the English-speaking Canadian children were alike in this respect. Also, in both languages, preschoolers below the age of six years did not possess the adult concept of "word," so often employed by teachers in beginning reading instruction.

There was one interesting cultural difference between the Venezuelan and Canadian children. In general, the Canadian children's responses indicated that they "possess a more advanced level of hypotheses about writing than their Venezuelan counterparts" (p. 81). The parents' questionnaire responses showed that the Canadian parents spent more time reading to their children than the Venezuelan parents did. Yánez concludes his thesis with an important practical point:

Children who have already formulated a grapho-phonetic correspondence between the written and oral languages make the best use of the school experience. Children who enter school with less developed hypotheses about the nature and purpose of writing, however, may become confused and even lose the confidence in their own ability to understand the written language. (p. 82)

The importance of the child's understanding of concepts of literacy for progress in learning how to read and write was shown in a recent study in *Mexico* by

Ferreiro and Gómez (1982). They found that among several factors studied, such as parents' educational level, socioeconomic class, and preschool experience, only the child's level of development of concepts of literacy was significantly related to reading achievement.

Dutch

Metalinguistic abilities of analyzing syllables into phonemes and synthesizing phonemes into syllables have been tested also in a large-scale longitudinal study in Holland. As in Leroy-Boussion's (1975) French study, synthesis was learned more readily than analysis. Perhaps the most interesting finding of the Dutch study was that the scores on these metalinguistic tests do not show a gradual learning curve. Instead, there is a sudden leap upward in score. This suggests that the child gained some important insight into how to perform the task (i.e., cognitive clarity). This insight occurred early with high performers and later with low performers. The above findings from these Dutch studies are reported by van Dongen (1979); van Dongen, Bosch, and Mommers (1981); van Dongen and van Leent (1981); van Dongen and Wolfshage (1982); Mommers (1982); and van Leent (1982, in press). A detailed review (in English) is provided by Valtin (1984).

Finnish

Downing has developed a Finnish version of the *Linguistic Awareness in Reading Readiness (LARR) Test* and piloted it in kindergartens at Oulu, Finland. It proved sensitive to phenomena of language awareness and cognitive clarity (Luukkonen, 1979). The Finnish *LARR* test's predictive validity has been studied in a longitudinal study by Luukkonen (1984). The LARR test was administered to preschoolers aged 6 and 7 years in kindergarten. (Grade 1 begins in September after the seventh birthday in Finland.) These same children's reading achievements were studied for five years in grades 1–5. There was only slight fluctuation in the predictive power of the *LARR* test over these five years. It explains about 25 percent of the variance in reading. The subtest that provided the best prediction of later reading attainment was the one measuring metalinguistic concepts of print.

Russian

Interest in language awareness developed very early in Russian education. In the middle of the nineteenth century the Russian educational philosopher K. D. Ushinsky proposed that reading instruction should be a continuous language study beginning with the child studying his or her own speech. The whole history of Russian reading theory, research, and practice centers around this theme of fostering the child's development of language awareness. (For a comprehensive review see Downing, in preparation.)

In recent years this theme has taken the form of the theory first propounded by Luria (1946). It has become popularly known in the USSR as the "glass window theory." Luria wrote that when the child comes into grade 1 (at age 7), he or she "is still not able to make the word and verbal relations an object of his consciousness. In this period a word may be used but not noticed by the child and it frequently seems like a glass window through which the child looks at the surrounding world without suspecting that it has its own existence, its own structural features" (p. 61). Vygotsky (1934) had earlier commented on research showing that school beginners have only a vague idea of the functions of written language and are confused by the abstract features of speech and writing when they are first introduced to reading instruction.

This central theme of language awareness has produced a wide range of studies in the USSR. Examples include: Beliakova (1971, 1973) on the segmentation of speech into words; Elkonin (1963, 1973) on segmentation of speech into phonemes; Karpova (1955, 1975) on awareness of words and phonemes in speech; Orlova (1965) on developing syntactical concepts; and Zhiukov (1965) on the formation of morphological concepts. This theoretical theme has also influenced practical work by teachers and parents. For example, there are published articles on how parents can assist preschoolers in developing language awareness (Bezrukova, 1971); how kindergarten teachers can train a child's concept of the word (Sokhin, 1974); language awareness problems in bilingual situations (Bogush, 1971; Konstandian, 1971); phoneme analysis in children with articulation defects (Maksakov, 1971); and the like. Within the USSR, Elkonin's (1973) method for training "phonematic hearing" is being applied in more than one language. It was adopted in two non-Russian republics before the decision was taken to implement it throughout the Russian republic (Elkonin, 1982). Thus, within the Soviet Union one can observe that in several different languages schools are actively using training procedures for improving children's metalinguistic abilities as a preparation for reading instruction.

Swedish

Lundberg and Tornéus (1978) presented Swedish preschoolers with word pairs—one long and one short. The researcher spoke each word to the child and then showed him or her a card on which the two words were printed, but the relation between the printed word and the spoken word was not revealed. The child was required to point to one of the words nominated by the researcher. The children showed a clear tendency to use a semantic strategy in selecting the printed word. For example, if the spoken word was the name of a larger object, the child pointed to the longer of the two printed words. Lundberg and Tornéus concluded: "A substantial number of children in the oldest preschool group seemed to have poor concepts of the basic principle of our writing system. There is a considerable risk that conventional beginning reading instruction with phonic emphasis starts well before the children have developed necessary metalinguistic skills, with serious educational consequences. The results of this investigation may suggest that prereading programs might focus on development of linguistic awareness" (p. 412).

Later, Lundberg, Wall, and Olofsson (1980) put forward a formal causal model of learning to read: "The main determinant of reading and spelling ability is assumed to be a set of metalinguistic skills measured in kindergarten which includes analysis as well as synthesis of phonemes and syllables. Necessary prerequisites for these skills to develop are assumed to be general intelligence and more specific ability to analyze and decenter in nonverbal tasks. The latter factors may also directly influence the reading and spelling ability" (p. 161). Lundberg et al. (1980) report a longitudinal study of 200 Swedish children followed from kindergarten (aged 6 to 7 years) through grade 2. Testing included phoneme awareness, nonlinguistic decentration, and reading achievement. Path analysis treatment of the data led to the conclusion that "The most powerful determinant of reading achievement in grade 1 is the ability in kindergarten to analyze phonemes and reverse their order" (p. 166). Valtin (1984) has performed a factor analysis on the data of Lundberg et al. (1980) and claims that its results are consistent with her view that phonemic awareness is a reflection of the child's experience with print.

In summary, research conducted in several different languages and in different cultures and subcultures reveals that language awareness is a universal phenomenon. Furthermore, several studies have shown that there is a significant relationship between beginners' level of language awareness and subsequent progress in the acquisition of the skill of reading. In general, these findings fit the cognitive clarity theory. However, the research in Argentina conducted by Ferreiro and Teberosky (1979) showed that children begin to construct concepts of literacy spontaneously long before entering school. This raises a question about postulate number 5 of the cognitive clarity theory, which will be dealt with in the final section of this chapter.

Differences in Orthography and Metalinguistic Ability

Postulate number 8 of the cognitive clarity theory states that the development of cognitive clarity in different languages will be similar in regard to functional concepts, but will vary in relation to the technical coding rules of different writing systems. Conventionally, writing systems are classified into three types according to the units of language represented by their visible symbols. For example, Lado (1957) listed them as follows: "1. *Alphabetic* writing systems in which the characters represent phonemes of the language; 2. *Syllabic* writing systems in which the characters stand for syllables rather than phonemes; 3. *Logographic* writing systems in which the characters represent morphemes—that is, units of form and meaning—rather than units of sound such as syllables or phonemes" (p. 95). Clearly, there will be different metalinguistic concepts needed for the child to understand how these different types of writing systems operate. But the problem is more complex. For one thing, writing systems often have features of more than one of the three types in Lado's list. For example, the English writing system contains symbols for morphemes as well as phonemes, and Chinese has phonetic symbols as well as its morphemic characters. Nevertheless, it is accurate to describe English as mainly alphabetic and Chinese as mainly logographic.

Downing's *Comparative Reading* (1973) compares different languages in regard to the problems that they pose for children trying to comprehend how their writing system operates. Some features of the learner's task were found to be quite different from one language to another. The most obvious difference is the unit of language represented by the basic unit of writing. Chinese has several different types of characters based on different systems of coding (one of which is phonetic), but the major feature of the Chinese writing system is its code for morphemes. Therefore, the task of the learner is primarily to acquire knowledge of the relationships between the characters of the Chinese writing system and the morphemes of the Chinese language.

Japanese, too, has a very different writing system from English and other European languages. Japanese has several writing systems, but the everyday usage in books and other written or printed Japanese materials is a combination of two main types of characters—*Kana* and *Kanji*. Kanji characters are logographic, like the Chinese symbols. The Kana characters represent the sounds of syllables of Japanese speech. It is possible to write Japanese sentences in Kana characters alone. This is done in telegrams and in the first reading materials of young beginners. Thus, the initial task of Japanese children is to relate the Kana characters to the syllables of Japanese speech. Later they must learn more and more Kanji characters for morphemes as they replace the Kana syllabic symbols. English speech also can be analyzed into syllables, but the written characters of the English alphabet were not designed to represent syllables, as were the Japanese Kana characters.

Most other widely used world languages are written in alphabets in which the unit coded is the phoneme. Different languages have different phonemes, although of course there is overlapping. For example, in Spanish, there is only one phoneme for what English speakers recognize as *b* and *v*. *Phoneme* has a precise linguistic meaning, and is quite unlike the ambiguity of the word *sound* as it is often employed in teaching phonics. Another ambiguity which causes difficulty in phonics teaching is in the terminology for describing the units of the writing system. Most English-speaking teachers call these units *letters* of the alphabet. But Spanish teachers, for example, describe *ch* as a letter, although most American reading teachers would say *ch* consists of two letters. This problem arises when the phoneme is coded by a unit larger than a single visible symbol. Certainly the term *letter* is inadequate for understanding the relationship between written and spoken English. Teachers and parents who rely on this unit alone for teaching phonics cannot help but cause confusion in the child's mind. Albrow (1972) states that "it is necessary to distinguish in the description between *letters* and *orthographic symbols*. The alphabet with which we write English consists of twenty-six letters, but these have to be seen as creating a much larger number of orthographic symbols" (p. 11). Albrow gives as examples the letters *t* and *h* employed in the orthographic symbols *t* as in *ten*, *h* as in *hen*, *th* as in *thin*, and the letters *c* and *h* used in the orthographic symbols *c* as in *car*, *h* as in *hen*, *ch* as in *chin*.

Hebrew, Sanskrit, and some other Asiatic languages have writing systems which have a transitional form between a syllabary and an alphabet. But all the modern European languages are written with an alphabet. If the orthographic symbols in these writing systems primarily represent phonemes, then an important task for the learner in these alphabetic languages is to acquire knowledge about the way in which phonemes are related to the orthographic symbols.

To sum up, a universal task in all languages is to learn *how* the writing system represents language. The writing system is the basic tool of literacy, but the tool varies from one language to another. In Chinese, writing mainly signals morphemic units; in Japanese, the initial tool symbolizes syllables; in English, the chief units of the tool represent phonemes. The learner's task must vary correspondingly. Therefore, the agenda of metalinguistic awareness must differ from one language to another. The featural concepts and their labels in the language instruction register needed for thinking and talking about writing and reading will differ accordingly.

Writing systems vary in several other respects. For example, Chinese employs a very large number of characters, and it is commonly supposed that the resulting burden of memorization makes it difficult to learn to read Chinese. However, the *Comparative Reading* study concluded that this burden may have been exaggerated, and that in contrast, the burden of memorization has been underestimated in the alphabetic system. The number of graphemes in English, for example, is far greater than the twenty-six letters of the alphabet. One must take into account, for instance, such alternative graphemes as *ie, y, uy, igh, i* for the single phoneme common to *pie, my, guy, sigh, mind.* Other alphabetic writing systems have fewer alternative graphemes than English. Certainly, the load on memory represents a different task from one language to another for the literacy learner. For example, Finnish children have very few graphemes to acquire in comparison to the large number in English orthography.

Another difference between writing systems is the complexity of the rules linking the written language to speech. For example, Finnish has a nearly one-to-one relationship between its phonemes and graphemes. In contrast, the relationship is more complex in English. Thus, the task of understanding the writing system may be more difficult in English than it is in Finnish.

Yet another interesting difference noted in the *Comparative Reading* study is in the spatial representation of the temporal features of speech. Israeli children must learn to relate the order in which sounds occur in spoken Hebrew to a right-to-left representation in written Hebrew. In English, the direction is the opposite way. In Chinese, the conventional ordering on the page is vertical instead of horizontal. In Japan, about one half of all modern printed books show vertical lines, and the other half horizontal lines. A universal task is to learn the relation between the ordering of speech units in time and the order of written units in space. But the spatial arrangement differs from language to language.

Two other differences noted in *Comparative Reading* are the *complexity of the written symbols* and the *transfer value of their names.* Research cited in that book (especially Kawai, 1966; Leong, 1970) indicated that extremely simple shapes are not ideal. Children seem to discriminate and remember more readily the characters which have more complex features. Simple characters are more readily confused with one another, especially if the differences between them are primarily orientational (e.g., the four stick-with-loop characters of English orthography—b, d, p, q). Thus, although all learners must learn to discriminate visually between the characters of a writing system, it will be more or less difficult according to the design of the characters employed.

Letter names vary in the extent to which they may provide a clue or mnemonic for the unit of speech that they represent. For example, in English "aitch" and "double-you" do not even contain the phonemes that h and w usually represent. In other languages the letter names have more general transfer value in this respect. Research on teaching children letter names (e.g., Samuels, 1971) shows that it has no effect on learning to read in English. Therefore, learning letter names does not appear to be a primary task for the child in the initial stage of literacy acquisition. It is more likely to be a secondary task which is rather easily accomplished once children are motivated to label a symbol which they recognize as significant and useful.

This brief and simplified account of some of the more interesting differences between the writing systems of various languages already has identified some of the tasks of beginners in learning their writing system. They must learn:

1. What unit of speech is coded by their writing system.
2. A number of visually presented two-dimensional shapes.
3. The rules for relating the speech units to the written shapes.
4. The way in which the time order of speech sounds is related to the spatial order of the written shapes.

Even limiting ourselves to the above four linguistic tasks, when the psychological work involved is considered, the task seems much less simple. Task number 1 requires: (a) learning that speech can be segmented into units; (b) the ability to discriminate those units appropriate for the writing system; (c) the ability to analyze a continuous utterance into those units. Task number 2 raises numerous questions about visual perception. The child must learn which differences between written symbols are relevant and which are redundant. Task number 3 requires considerable work in reasoning and memory. Task number 4 needs, additionally, conceptual development regarding time and space.

Thus, in these many ways, the agenda for developing metalinguistic concepts about the features of speech and writing must vary more or less with the characteristics of each language and writing system. This conclusion leads to interesting questions about the relative difficulty of the cognitive phase of the development of the reading skill. Only a beginning has been made to investigating that problem.

Makita (1968) made a comparison of the reported incidence of reading disability in Japan and the United States. He found that "the incidence of reading disability is extremely rare in Japan." His analysis of the differences between the

Japanese and English writing systems led to his conclusion that "the specificity of the used language, the very object of reading behavior, is the most potent contributing factor in the formation of reading disability" (pp. 601–602). Experimental evidence as to the effect of type of orthography on the efficiency of learning how to read was obtained in the studies reported by Gleitman and Gleitman (1979), Gleitman and Rozin (1973), Rozin and Gleitman (1977), and Rozin, Poritsky, and Sotsky (1971). Their experiments compared the relative effectiveness of teaching logographic, syllabic, and alphabetic writing systems to English-speaking American children. They found that "the logography was easier to acquire than the syllabary which is based on the phonological properties of words. But the syllabary is a gross, molar representation of phonology. It was easier to acquire than the more analytic phonemic (alphabetic) script. Thus, the population with poor reading prognosis differed from successful readers most in acquiring the phonemic concepts of an alphabet, and least in acquiring the ideas behind a logography" (Gleitman and Gleitman, 1979, p. 119). In terms of the cognitive clarity theory, featural concepts of literacy are more difficult to acquire in phonemic writing systems than in syllabic writing systems, and they are easiest to acquire in logographic writing systems. This is evidence in support of postulate number 8 of the cognitive clarity theory.

Conclusions

The cross-cultural comparisons made above seem to indicate: (a) that language awareness is a universal phenomenon which is significantly related to success in learning how to read, and (b) that the development of awareness of linguistic features of text may be affected by the characteristics of the writing system in the child's environment. These conclusions are in accord with the cognitive clarity theory as set out formally at the beginning of this chapter. However, the latest research study conducted by the author of this chapter indicates the need to modify his theory in one important respect.

Downing (1984) and Downing and Downing (1983) report a critical test of the cognitive clarity theory which they conducted in Papua New Guinea. Children were tested on modified versions of the *Linguistic Awareness in Reading Readiness (LARR) Test* and the phoneme segmentation test of Liberman, Shankweiler, Fischer and Carter (1974). Two age groups were tested: younger children aged 7 to 8 years and older children aged 9 to 10 years. In each age group there were three categories of school experience: (a) children at school receiving literacy instruction in the writing system of a second language—English; (b) children at school receiving literacy instruction in the writing system of their mother tongue; and (c) children who had never been to school because no school was accessible for their village.

In both age groups the children receiving instruction in the mother tongue were significantly superior to the children in the English medium classes on the phoneme segmentation test. As the cognitive clarity theory predicts, children whose school instruction is related to familiar examples of their own mother tongue develop the concept of the phoneme more rapidly than do children whose school instruction relies on unfamiliar examples from a second language. Mother tongue instruction taps the child's already existent linguistic awareness, whereas instruction in a second language not only fails to exploit the available linguistic awareness but also causes cognitive confusion by introducing exemplars that do not fit the child's already developing concepts of speech elements. These results provide a theoretical explanation for previous research which has found that initial reading instruction delivered in a second language retards the development of skill in reading (Garcia de Lorenzo, 1975; Larson and Davis, 1981; Macnamara, 1966; Modiano, 1973; Österberg, 1961).

Although the children in the mother tongue classes scored higher to the children in the English medium classes on the phoneme segmentation test, this was not the case on the LARR test. The LARR scores of the English medium and mother tongue classes were not significantly different. This indicates that functional concepts of literacy were less negatively influenced by teaching in a second language than were concepts of features of speech. This result would be predicted by postulate number 8 of the cognitive clarity theory which specifies the universality of functional concepts of literacy across different languages.

But one result from this Papua New Guinea study conflicted with the cognitive clarity theory. On the phoneme segmentation test, although the mother tongue instruction children had the highest scores, the lowest scores were in the English instruction schools and not in the villages without schools, as would be predicted by postulate number 5 of this theory (i.e., that "children approach the tasks of reading instruction in a normal state of cognitive confusion . . ."). The test results showed that the children at school being instructed in literacy in English were more cognitively confused than the children who had never been to school. Hence, postulate number 5 is disproved. It was noted earlier in this chapter that the research conducted in Argentina by Ferreiro and Teberosky (1979) likewise conflicted with this same postulate.

Therefore, postulates numbered 5, 6, and 7 of the cognitive clarity theory have been reformulated as follows:

5. Children approach the tasks of reading instruction with only partially developed concepts of the functions and features of speech and writing.
6. Under reasonably good conditions, children develop increasing cognitive clarity about the functions and features of language.
7. Although the initial stage of literacy acquisition is the most vital one, conceptual challenges continue to arise and thus broaden the range of clarity throughout the later stages of education as new subskills are added to the student's repertory.

These reformulated postulates then explain the results of this latest experiment as well as the results of the previous research related to this theory. The Papua New Guinea children in the English medium schools did not increase in cognitive clarity because they were not exposed to "reasonably good conditions." They were confused by the conflict between their own past experiences of the mother tongue and their teacher's presentation of reading in terms of an unfamiliar language. They did not have metacognitive readiness for reading in the second language. In contrast, the children in the mother tongue classes worked under "reasonably good conditions" and expanded their cognitive clarity because their teacher's presentation of concepts of literacy fitted the children's developing metacognitive awareness derived from their own past experiences of their mother tongue. They had metacognitive readiness for reading in the mother tongue.

Cross-language and cross-cultural research will be an important route to follow in the future search for a better understanding of the causal relationship between language awareness and the acquisition of reading skill. Comparisons between contrasting linguistic and cultural environments will eventually uncover the universal human psychological processes in children as they strive to make sense of literacy objects and activities in their environments.

Acknowledgments

I am grateful to Leonardo Yánez for his help in reviewing the data from Spanish language studies.

Chapter 3

Students' Perceptions of Reading: Thirty Years of Inquiry

JERRY L. JOHNS

When asked how he viewed reading, a second grade student said that reading was "stand up, sit down." When the youngster was asked to explain what he meant, he said that the teacher had him stand up to read; he would continue to read until he made a mistake, then the teacher would tell him to sit down. Hence, he perceived reading as a stand up, sit down process. The way in which this student viewed reading is an example of a perception of reading that greatly differs from reading perceptions held by adults.

Goodacre (1971) identified the exploration of students' perceptions of reading as an area for thought-provoking work. Her observation was an accurate prediction of things to come. A casual review of the literature reveals that many studies related to metalinguistic awareness have been conducted throughout the world (see Downing, this volume). Perhaps the most global strand of research in this area deals with students' general perceptions of the nature and functions of reading. It is this strand of research that probably provided the stimulus for much of the subsequent research in metalinguistic awareness.

This chapter focuses on three areas: first, pioneering efforts with disabled readers' perceptions of reading; second, the core of the chapter, studies investigating the perceptions of reading given by students in kindergarten through grade 8; third, studies focused on teaching students about reading. A synthesis of the research and a challenge to future teachers of reading concludes the chapter.

Pioneering Efforts with Disabled Readers

An early inquiry into students' perceptions of reading in grades 2 to 4 was reported by Edwards (1958). He explored 66 disabled readers' perceptions in their approaches to reading by asking them what they had thought "good" reading was when they first started school. Using interviews with groups of four or fewer students, Edwards asked the students to remember what their teachers and parents meant when they described the students' reading as "good." Although no statistical tests were used in this loosely controlled study, a large number of students shared the perception that "good" reading was a matter of speed and fluency. Edwards suggested that this view of reading may promote speed at the expense of reading for meaning. A decade later, Glass (1968) found that poor readers from fourth grade through college placed a similar emphasis on speed of reading.

Edwards believed that disabled readers in his study might have been more productive if the reading process had been taught directly and thoroughly. He concluded that beginning readers who are delayed in understanding that reading is for meaning could develop ineffective reading habits; moreover, these habits could possibly contribute to retardation in reading.

Johns (1970) echoed these thoughts when he found that 10 of 12 severely disabled readers said "I don't know" to the question, "What is reading?" He concluded that one of the contributing factors to students' reading problems may be their failure to understand what is involved in the reading process. Although the investigations by Edwards, Glass, and Johns had the usual limitations of informal interview techniques, it was clear that the students' perceptions of reading did not emphasize meaning.

Studies Involving Beginning Readers

One of the most frequently cited studies was conducted by Reid (1966). Her study involved five-year-old students from a classroom in an Edinburgh, Scotland, school. The study had several purposes, one of which was to explore students' perceptions of reading. The 12 students, 7 boys and 5 girls, were randomly selected and interviewed individually three times during their first year in school. Although a core of standard questions was posed to each student, the order of the questions was varied as each individual interview progressed, and additional probing was done when necessary.

In discussing the findings of the interviews with regard to students' perceptions of reading, Reid noted that although most of the students were aware that they could not read, they had very few precise notions about reading. They were not even clear whether one read the pictures or the other marks on the page. In short, there was a general vagueness about the nature of reading. Like previous researchers, Reid speculated that a conscious and careful effort to develop an awareness of what reading is might make a difference in students' progress in reading.

A replication and expansion of the Reid investigation was conducted by Downing (1970). He selected 13 students, 6 boys and 7 girls, from a school in Hertfordshire, England. In addition to the interview technique that Reid used, Downing used an experimental method and concrete stimuli (e.g., pictures of someone reading and toy buses with different route numbers). Downing's three research methods produced findings that complemented those found by Reid. Specifically, Downing concluded that students had difficulty in understanding the purpose of reading and had only a vague perception of how people read. He also raised the issue of whether or not teachers were making unwarranted assumptions about students' perceptions of the nature of reading.

In 1963 Denny and Weintraub began an investigation in five first grade classrooms in three school systems to explore students' perceptions of reading. The 111 first grade students came from widely divergent socioeconomic backgrounds (Denny & Weintraub, 1966). Each student was interviewed individually and asked three questions about reading. Students' responses were taped, analyzed, and classified into logical categories. The two investigators had a 90% level of agreement in the assignment of student responses to the categories. An independent judge achieved an 82% level of agreement with the investigators' classifications.

In summarizing the responses to the three questions ("Do you want to learn how to read?" "Why?" and "What must you do to learn how to read in first grade?"), Denny and Weintraub (1966) noted that

a fourth of all these entering first-graders could express no logical, meaningful purpose for learning to read and a third of the children had no idea how it was to be accomplished. . . . Most research on learning supports the proposition that it helps the child to learn if he knows the reason for a learning situation and sees a purpose in a task. Inasmuch as reading is not nonsense learning, but a complex mental process, it may be important to identify it as such and to help beginners establish purposes for wanting to learn to read. (p. 447)

In another report, Weintraub and Denny (1965) presented an analysis of 108 first graders' responses to the question, "What is reading?" The analysis revealed that 27% of the responses were of the vague or "I don't know" variety; 33% were object-related (e.g., "when you read a book"); and 20% were of a cognitive nature or described reading as a cognitive act that "helps you to learn things." The remaining 20% of the responses were distributed almost evenly across three categories: (a) value terms—"I think reading is a good thing to do"; (b) mechanical descriptions—"It's words and you sound them out if you don't know them"; and (c) expectations—"It's something that you have to learn how to do." Denny and Weintraub noted that students came to school with greatly disparate perceptions of the reading process. They emphasized the finding that 27% of the students failed to verbalize an intelligible perception of the reading process.

A subsequent study was stimulated by the work of Weintraub and Denny. The study (Johns & Johns, 1971) involved 168 students from kindergarten through the sixth grade. The sample was stratified and randomly selected so there would be 12 boys and 12 girls from each grade. Students responded to three questions, one of which was "What is reading?" The results revealed that over 70% of the students gave vague, irrelevant, or no response to the question, "What is reading?" Only 4% of the students, moreover, defined reading as a process involving both decoding and understanding. Johns and Johns concluded that teachers should make an effort to help students understand the role meaning plays in the reading process. In addition, teachers were cautioned not to assume that the usual methods and strategies used in teaching reading provide a basis for understanding the reading process.

Two other studies are very closely related to the Denny and Weintraub study. The first study involved responses from 182 first grade students in the United States who took part in a larger investigation by Johns and Ellis (1976). The second study, an international survey (Robinson, Lazarus, & Costello, 1983), involved 709 beginning readers from Australia, Belgium, Colombia, England, Japan, Sweden, and the United States. A questionnaire was developed, translated when necessary, and administered to students soon after school began. Results were presented for six of the most discriminating questions, one of which was, "What is reading?" For this question, the students' responses were placed in categories adapted from Weintraub and Denny (1965).

To compare the findings from the three studies (Johns & Ellis, 1976; Robinson, Lazarus, & Costello, 1983; Weintraub & Denny, 1965), the available data were categorized. In some instances, descriptions for the categories were not identical among the three studies and judgments were made.

- Category One: no response, vague, circular, or "I don't know."
- Category Two: responses that were object-related (e.g., reading a book) or that involved classroom procedures (e.g., reading out loud in a circle).
- Category Three: responses that characterized reading as decoding (e.g., words and letters).
- Category Four: responses that referred to reading as a cognitive act (e.g., learning from a book).

From Table 3–1 it can be seen that the first two categories contain the vast majority of the responses. First grade students from seven countries tended to

Table 3–1

Distribution (in %) of First Graders' Responses to the Question, "What is Reading?"

| | Categories for Responses | | | |
Study	One No Response Vague, Circular, "I Don't Know"	Two Classroom Procedures or Object- Related	Three Word Recognition (Decoding)	Four Cognitive Act or Meaning
Johns and Ellis, 1976 (N = 182)	57	25	15	3
Robinson, Lazarus, and Costello, 1983 (N = 709)	42	42	8	8
Weintraub and Denny, 1965 (N = 108)*	27	33	7	20

*Thirteen percent of the responses related to value terms (e.g., reading is a good thing to do) and are not categorized in this table.

have a nebulous perception of reading or related it to classroom procedures or activities. Only a small percentage of students associated meaning with reading—a finding consistent with the previous work of Weintraub and Denny (1965) and Johns and Johns (1971).

The international survey (Robinson, Lazarus, & Costello, 1983) also included results of interviews during the last two weeks of the school year. Unfortunately, attrition and lack of follow-up reduced the number of participating students to 350—less than half of the original number in the sample. In spite of this limitation, the authors indicated that students' responses pointed toward a growing maturity about reading and reading instruction.

Studies Involving Students in Various Grades

One of the largest studies (Johns & Ellis, 1976) undertaken to explore students' perceptions of reading involved 1,655 students from grades 1 to 8. The students were selected from several public elementary and middle schools located near a large midwestern industrial area of the United States. The sample was assumed to represent the generally expected ranges of intelligence and reading achievement. An informal assessment of students' backgrounds revealed socioeconomic status ranging from upper middle class to lower class. There were approximately the same number of boys and girls in the study.

An individual interview format was used to gather students' responses to three questions: 1. What is reading? 2. What do you do when you read? 3. If someone didn't know how to read, what would you tell him/her that he/she would need to learn?

The responses to the questions were recorded on audiotape. After the students' responses were transcribed, they were classified into five categories:

- Category One: no response, vague, circular, irrelevant, or "I don't know."
- Category Two: responses that described the classroom procedures involved in reading or the educational value of reading.
- Category Three: responses that characterized reading as decoding or involving word recognition procedures.
- Category Four: responses that defined reading as understanding.
- Category Five: responses that referred to both decoding and understanding.

In summarizing the responses to the first question ("What is reading?"), Johns and Ellis noted that 69% of the students gave essentially meaningless responses (Categories One and Two). Only 15% of the students gave responses that associated comprehension or understanding with reading; furthermore, over two-thirds of these responses were from students in grades 7 and 8. In addition, there were significant ($p<.05$) sex differences in the students' responses included in Categories One and Five. Boys gave a greater number of vague and irrelevant responses than girls (Category One). In Category Five, girls gave a greater number of responses that defined reading in terms of both decoding and understanding.

Results from the second question ("What do you do when you read?") indicated that 57% of the students' responses were classified as meaningless. Only 20% of the students indicated that they sought meaning when reading; moreover, nearly two thirds of these responses were from students in grades 6, 7, and 8. Significant ($p<.05$) sex differences in the students' responses existed for Categories Four and Five. In both categories, girls gave a greater number of responses that included the element of meaning.

Replies to the third question ("If someone didn't know how to read, what would you tell him/her that he/she would need to learn?") provided the following results: 36% of the responses were meaningless; 8% of the responses referred to comprehension or understanding; and 56% of the responses emphasized word recognition or decoding. Over one half of the students seemed to know that pronouncing words was a part of reading, but they overemphasized this aspect at the expense of comprehension—the heart of reading. Students' responses in Categories One and Five differed significantly by their sex. Boys gave a greater number of vague and irrelevant responses (Category One), while girls gave a greater number of responses that viewed reading as a process of decoding and understanding (Category Five).

Johns and Ellis concluded that while older students had a somewhat more accurate understanding of the reading process than did younger students, the vast majority of students (over 80%) did not include meaning in their responses. Most of the students' meaningful responses described reading as a decoding process or as an activity involving the use of a textbook and occurring in the classroom or school environment.

There were few significant sex differences in the students' responses. When such differences existed, however, boys gave more vague or irrelevant responses than girls. In addition, boys were less likely to perceive reading as a process that involved meaning. These findings take on added significance when one realizes that boys in the United States represent a majority of the severely disabled readers.

Although the Johns and Ellis study is a large one, it has at least two limitations. First, it is quite possible that some students had perceptions of reading and were unable to verbalize them. Reid (1966) notes, however, that the absence of a term in a student's response (such as *meaning*) can indicate that "it is not one of the terms he habitually thinks with" (p. 58). A second limitation may be due to a possible warm-up effect for the three questions. The number of vague, irrelevant, or "I don't know" responses (Category One) dropped from 33% for question 1, to 22% for question 2, to 14% for question 3. It is possible, therefore, that students' perceptions of reading were somewhat distorted or underestimated.

Canney and Winograd (1979) investigated the warm-up effect by asking "What is reading?" after 14 other questions had been posed. The 24 students in grades 2, 4, 6, and 8 were divided into higher and lower comprehenders. The researchers found that the students gave over 80 distinct responses to the question, "What is reading?" All the students' responses were judged to be meaningful; however, the vast majority of the responses had a decoding focus (e.g., saying words, sounding out words). The lower comprehenders in each of the four grades tended to describe reading in terms of a decoding process. Higher comprehenders in the sixth and eighth grades gave responses that placed greater emphasis on meaning. A similar finding with 65 students in grades 4 and 5 was reported by Johns (1974). He found that students reading at least one year above grade placement gave significantly ($p<.05$) more meaningful responses to the question, "What is reading?" than did students reading at least one year below grade placement.

Canney and Winograd argued that the interview format can be useful in gathering valid information about students' perceptions of reading if more than three questions are used. Ample questions allow students time to warm up to the topic. Neutral probing of students' responses was also suggested by Canney and Winograd. Using individual interviews and reading activities, Tovey (1976) obtained perceptions of the reading process from 30 students evenly divided among grades 1 through 6. Tovey found that 43% of the responses to the question, "What do you think you do when you read?" expressed the idea that reading is looking at and pronouncing words. Only 28% of the responses indicated that reading had something to do with meaning, while 29% of the responses were vague or irrelevant (e.g., spelling, breathing). In his interpretation of these and other findings, Tovey argued that students tended to perceive reading as a word-calling process in which unknown words should be sounded out. He proposed that this view needs to be replaced by one in which students think of reading as reconstructing meaning from print.

Teaching Students About Reading

Because many students seem to have perceptions of reading that are vague, suggestions have been given to help beginning readers and older students improve their perceptions of reading. Johns (1984), for example, suggests the language experience approach and direct-teaching strategies to help students realize that print is meaningful. In addition, two recent studies with students in kindergarten and the first grade offer evidence that instruction in the nature and purpose of reading can improve students' perceptions of the reading process.

Mayfield (1983) used a control group and two experimental groups all equivalent in terms of size of group, socioeconomic status, age, and previous instructional experiences. The 82 kindergarteners were pretested with selected subtests on the Canadian Readiness Test, interview questions adapted from previous studies (John, 1974; Reid, 1966; Tovey, 1976), and an author-constructed code systems identification test and contextual picture test based on Davis (1972). One of the experimental groups received intensive instruction with code systems (e.g., pictures representing an object or event; symbols suggesting an idea; whole words) and the vocabulary involved. The other experimental group received similar instruction integrated in a unit (community and school helpers) typically taught in kindergarten. Instruction in the experimental groups occurred for approximately 25 minutes per day for 20 school days. The control group followed the regular kindergarten curriculum.

Like previous researchers (Johns & Ellis, 1976; Weintraub & Denny, 1965), Mayfield found that a majority (52% to 73%) of students' responses to the question, "What is reading?" could be classified as vague, irrelevant, or "I don't know." On the two author-constructed code systems tests, both experimental groups had significantly higher mean gain scores. This was also the case for one of the two subtests adapted from the Canadian Readiness Test. These results, in conjunction with interview data, led Mayfield to conclude that instruction in code systems was related to students' perceptions of the nature and purpose of reading.

Another study that explored teaching understandings about reading was conducted by Buck-Smith (1983). With 60 first grade students from northern Georgia, two groups were formed. An experimental group of 30 students was randomly assigned to three teachers who taught 20 lessons about the nature of the reading act, the purpose of reading, and the language of reading instruction. The other group was randomly assigned to three different teachers who taught an equivalent number of lessons related to skills in using the newspaper. Each group received daily twenty-minute lessons over a period of four weeks.

Following instruction, students were given the *Test of Linguistic Awareness in Reading Readiness* (Downing, Ayers, & Shaefer, 1983) and the *Gates-Mac-Ginitie Reading Test, Primary A.* Significant differences ($p<.05$) favored the experimental group for the linguistic awareness test and the reading attitude test. There were no significant differences between the two groups on the reading survey test. Buck-Smith concluded that a formal orientation on the reading process had an effect on students' knowledge about, and attitudes toward, reading.

Synthesis of Research Findings

As a group, the studies cited in this chapter focused on students' perceptions of reading. Interviews were the primary means used to obtain this information. Some of the interviews were highly structured, while others were loosely structured. Students who participated in the studies came from kindergarten through the eighth grade. They lived in seven different countries and in various areas of the United States.

Generally, the studies relied on interview questions that were usually evaluated and interpreted by only one professional; moreover, some of the questions may not have adequately assessed what the students actually knew about reading. In addition, many of the students were in the early years of schooling and it is quite possible that they knew more about reading than they could communicate orally. Given these limitations and the problems that are often inherent in using the interview technique to explore a process as complex as reading, only the most cautious of conclusions should be drawn. The following conclusions appear to be supported by a careful interpretation of the available data.

1. Beginning readers in various countries throughout the world are frequently confused about the process of reading. Their responses tend to be vague or concerned with only fragments of the reading process.
2. Efforts to teach beginning readers knowledge and understanding about reading have been successful. Unfortunately, the impact of this knowledge on reading achievement has not been supported by research.
3. As students progress through the various grades, their perceptions of reading demonstrate greater emphasis on the meaning-reconstructing aspect of reading. In addition, better readers and girls tend to give more meaning-focused responses.
4. An interview format can be used to acquire information about reading that is not readily available from a standardized or informal reading test.

Challenge to Teachers

From the research presented in this chapter, it is clear that students' perceptions of reading rarely focus on the essence of the reading process: meaning. But what about teachers' perceptions of reading? After asking many teachers to answer the question, "What is reading?" Stauffer (1969) concluded that teachers need to acquire a better concept of reading.

More recently, Tovey (1983) investigated the degree to which 30 elementary teachers understood the reading process. After using stratified random sampling procedures to identify five elementary teachers in each of grades 1 through 6, Tovey used several questions as a basis for the interviews. The responses from 43% of the teachers revealed that they had not thought about what they do when they read. In discussing the findings, Tovey (1983, p. 12) concluded that "teachers need a more explicit understanding of the reading process."

One help for teachers becoming aware of their beliefs about reading is the *Conceptual Framework of Reading Interview*. According to Grove (1983), the interview can help teachers analyze their belief systems and instructional decision making. Although the responses by teachers in the validating study were not always consistent, the teachers expressed a willingness to learn and use those teaching strategies that help students focus on meaning during reading.

Another strategy teachers could use is to consider the assumptions they make regarding the prior knowledge students possess about reading and the technical language or specialized terms (e.g., word, letter, beginning sound) used in teaching reading. Such knowledge (or lack of it) may directly influence the outcome of instruction. To guide teachers, the following suggestions are offered (Johns, 1982):

1. Have students share their perceptions about reading.
2. List the assumptions you make while teaching that students may not possess.
3. Write down terms that you use during teaching that students may not understand.
4. Use an audiotape or videotape to record several of your reading lessons.

Evaluate the lessons and note additional terms or assumptions that were not on your original list.

5. Plan appropriate strategies to help students develop or refine their perceptions of reading and your instructional language.

6. Determine those reading behaviors you emphasize and reward. Assess the behaviors with respect to helping students form a meaningful concept of reading.

When teachers really come to grips with the implications meaning has for reading, they will be much better equipped to guide students through experiences with print. Much of what students will learn about reading depends, to a large degree, upon the knowledge teachers possess and how that knowledge is translated into instruction.

Conclusion

Reading has been regarded as being more than the sum of a group of skills; nevertheless, for many students, reading is perceived as a vague construct or as a task of learning words. Fortunately, the vast number of students learn to read and are thereby enabled to reconstruct meaning from printed materials. Unfortunately, approximately 15% of the students in North America encounter difficulty in reading. For such students, reading often becomes equated with skills and workbook pages. It may be possible for these students to reap the benefits of reading if they are taught the nature and purposes of reading in conjunction with traditional instructional approaches. If an emphasis in this area helps reduce the percentage of disabled readers, research on students' perceptions of reading will have served a valuable end.

Chapter 4

Reading Research in Metalinguistic Awareness: A Classification of Findings According to Focus and Methodology

DAVID B. YADEN, JR.

During the past decade and a half, there has been increasing interest among language and reading researchers in the ability of young children to consciously and deliberately reflect upon and analyze the structure of both oral and written language as opposed to merely reacting to its content. This capacity for what is most commonly known as "metalinguistic awareness" (Gleitman & Gleitman, 1979; Gleitman, Gleitman, & Shipley, 1972; Holden, 1972), or sometimes just "linguistic awareness" (Mattingly, 1972, 1979; Ryan, 1980), is believed to encompass a variety of language behaviors, including the ability to comment upon the grammaticality of certain types of utterances (de Villiers & de Villiers, 1974; Gleitman, Gleitman, & Shipley, 1972), to segment the stream of speech into words (Tunmer, Bowey, & Grieve, 1983), syllables, and phonemes (Liberman, Shankweiler, Fischer, & Carter, 1974), and to understand the conventions of the written language system as well, the latter capability being more specifically described as "orthographic linguistic awareness" (Day, Day, Spicola, & Griffin, 1981). Surprisingly, however, research has disclosed that many young children first learning to read exhibit an inability to think of *language qua language* and oftentimes seem to misunderstand the very nature and purposes of the reading act itself.

While there exist reviews of the literature and critiques of the research regarding the relationship of metalinguistic awareness to language acquisition and growth (Sinclair, Jarvella, & Levelt, 1978; Tunmer, Pratt, & Herriman, 1984), and to aspects of developing cognition (Hakes, 1980), there are fewer such comprehensive treatments touching upon the broad range of metalinguistic abilities and their direct application to the acquisition of literacy behaviors (cf. Downing & Valtin, 1984; Ehri, 1979; Henderson, 1981; Henderson & Beers, 1980). In addition, many reviews fail to distinguish between the findings of studies using spoken language tasks and those using written language tasks, or present investigations in the area such that a comparative analysis may be done on the basis of differing methodologies. A more fine-grained analysis of studies claiming to investigate metalinguistic awareness and literacy acquisition is needed, since the present "state of the art" seems to be that given the range of variations of problem focus, method of data collection, and unit of analysis between examinations of metalinguistic abilities and reading, there is virtually no consensus as to exactly what emerging conceptual abilities, if any, may be crucial in enhancing those first steps in learning how to read.

The primary purpose of the following review, therefore, is to bring together and discuss a broad range of data-gathering studies exploring children's concepts about the reading act, linguistic units, and properties of the written language system under the general rubric of "metalinguistic." The main body of the review is organized into three major sections, each representative of a distinguishable strand of research within the general corpus of the literature: (a) concepts about the nature, purpose, and processes of reading; (b) concepts about spoken language units and terms in the "reading instruction register" (Downing, 1976); and (c) knowledge of print conventions and mapping principles. Further divisions within the major sections have been made according to the varying data collection procedures employed.

To give the reader some sense of the history and cumulative progress of the research to be discussed, studies within each subsection of the review are presented in chronological order, based upon their appearance primarily in English-language journals (see Downing, this volume, and Downing & Valtin, 1984, for a review of studies in non-English-speaking countries). Similarly, the ordering of the three major research strands follows the approximate development of interest in the field, although by the late 60s research was being carried out simultaneously in all three areas delineated.

It is necessary to distinguish at this point, however, between the focus of the following research and related investigations into "metacognition" and reading (e.g., Brown, 1980, Brown & Palincsar, 1982) and "comprehension monitoring" (e.g., Wagoner, 1983). While it may be accurate that metalinguistic abilities are one facet of a general growth in cognition (e.g., Hakes, 1980; Ryan, 1980; Tunmer & Bowey, 1984) that allows a person to "think about his/her own thinking" and to engage in other metacognitive acts where conscious examination of the actual processes of *mind* takes place (cf. Flavell, 1976), research being tagged as "metalinguistic" generally focuses upon preschoolers', kindergartners', or first graders' developing notions of the purposes and processes of literacy acts and structural properties of either their own speech or the written language system. On the other hand, "metacognitive" studies, as a rule, examine the development of comprehension strategies in both children and adults, being interested in such questions as, "What do readers know about what they comprehend and how they comprehend?" (Wagoner, 1983, p. 329). Thus, it can be observed that metalinguistic investigations study behaviors that are developmentally prior to the growth of comprehension processes needed to fully understand the messages in written texts. It is of interest to note as well that there is little overlap, if any, between the reference lists of individual studies in the following body of research and those investigations studying behaviors described as "metacognitive" which have been excluded.

One concluding caveat is perhaps warranted before the review begins. Readers familiar with the more traditional use of the term *metalinguistic* as an adjectival form of *metalanguage* (Burchfield, 1976, p. 909) in the literature of philosophy and logic or as a description of a branch of linguistics which examines "the relation of language to the rest of the culture" (Pei & Gaynor, 1954, p. 135) will note little similarity to the usages of the term in this paper (see Yaden & Templeton, this volume, for a full discussion). In the literature to be cited, at least, the term has taken on as its referent varying states of psychological awareness as opposed to merely being a description of types of statements made in a *metalanguage* about another *object-language* (Cherry, 1980, p. 82). Perhaps the primary insight that educational research in the 70s and 80s has added to the traditional nuances of the term is that in order to speak in metalanguage and use metalinguistic vocabulary appropriately (Sulzby, this volume) one has to also be able to "think" metalinguistically. And this latter capability, as will be shown in the following research, develops slowly and exists in varying degrees among the population of young children learning to read.

Concepts About the Nature, Purposes, and Processes of Reading

Incongruous as it may sound given the long history of teaching reading, researchers have reported that prior to 1960, relevant literature on children's perceptions of the reading act was "virtually nonexistent" (Denny & Weintraub, 1963, p. 363). It is not fair to say, however, that early professionals in reading were unaware of the disparities in children's notions of what the act of reading ought to entail, since Betts (1946) devotes an entire chapter to "Basic Notions About Reading" (although from an adult's point of view) and at least mentions in passing that some children indeed were observed to "entertain some rather weird notions about reading" (p. 281). It can be said, however, that the pervasiveness of these "weird notions" in most children learning to read is a discovery only of systematic research in the last quarter century or so, when the children themselves have been asked directly about these matters.

Since Johns (this volume) has reviewed a majority of the studies dealing with children's perceptions of what reading actually is in the previous chapter of this book, these findings will not be duplicated here. Instead, one early study by McConkie (1959) will be discussed here, since it has served as a prototype for many of the investigations in this area. Information regarding studies of children's ideas about the nature of reading can also be found in Yaden (1984).

McConkie (1959) reported one of the first extensive discussions of children's disparate concepts concerning the functions and processes involved in reading. Interviewing 81 five-year-olds from middle and lower class families, she noted six categories of response to the question, "What do you think reading is?" These responses ranged from definitions such as, "Reading is telling stories," or "Reading is writing," to "Reading is looking at pages and studying them," and "Reading is when you look into books, then you go home." (pp. 104–105). A "frustrating" aspect of the interviews, according to McConkie (1959), was that only a very few children (11%) could express "that they perceived reading as a means of securing information" (p. 107). In addition, across all categories, only about a fourth of the children indicated that reading had anything to do with looking at letters or words. However, among these children, McConkie also included those who thought that they looked at "numbers," "things," and "names" as well.

McConkie (1959) also asked children how they would teach someone else to read. Interestingly, only one child out of the entire sample said that he would teach someone by helping them to sound out words and letters. Other categories included responses such as, "I'd teach him by making him listen," or "He'd talk about the pictures in the book, that's reading." Perhaps the most interesting response was, "I would have him learn the 'elephant'; I know all of mine" (pp. 128–129). In short, most of the children interviewed thought that others learned to read by retelling stories that they'd heard, talking about pictures, or "guessing" at words. One summary observation by McConkie (1959) was that "children have quite different perceptions of what constitutes an ability to read" (p. 115). An interesting finding as well was that children in the upper socioeconomic class provided usually more "adult-like" comments in defining reading, even though the lower class children were similar in intelligence. Thus, McConkie's (1959) earlier findings imply, as do others more recent (e.g., Ferreiro & Teberosky, 1982), that early experiences with books provide children with insights into more conventional notions of reading such as they can expect to be expressed by teachers.

Concepts About Spoken Language Units

Within the general body of metalinguistic research as it relates to beginning reading ability, the studies exploring children's awareness of the components of their speech and their "verbalizable" knowledge (cf. Templeton & Spivey, 1980) of the metalinguistic terms *word, letter, sound,* etc., are by far the most extensive. Underlying the concern with speech segmentation in particular is the belief that unless a child is aware of his speech as being comprised of a temporal succession of sounds (cf. Bradley & Bryant, 1983; Elkonin, 1973), he/she will have less success in understanding the form of written words as made up of sequences of letters. There is, however, a "great debate" carried on in this section and in the field in general, since some researchers (e.g., Ehri, 1975, 1976, 1979) feel that it is rather exposure to the written form of language that provides insight into the fact that one's spoken language includes several kinds of identifiable units. This discussion will be taken up again later in this book (see Ehri & Wilce; Vellutino & Scanlon, this volume).

Studies of children's knowledge of oral language units (i.e., words, syllables) generally fall into three categories distinguished by the methodology used in assessing beginning readers' ability to isolate or identify these units in the speech stream. The most common strategy used is a "word tapping" task in which the child repeats a sentence and counts each word by tapping on the table with a pencil or similar object. A variation of this task has been to have the child point to wooden blocks or poker chips as each word is spoken. A second task used is to ask the general question, "What is a word [letter, sentence]?" These investigations tend to seek out developmental trends in that they not only point out disparities between children's and adults' notions of language units, but also gather information on what exact concepts children possess at different ages. A third strategy adopted by fewer researchers involves selecting a priori categories of verbal and nonverbal "sounds" and training the subjects to respond "yes/no" when they think they hear a single sound (phoneme) or word. A more detailed discussion of investigations in each category follows.

Word, Syllable, and Phoneme Segmentation

One of the earliest attempts to observe children's ability to segment speech into words was Karpova's (1955/1966) study in Russia with a sample of children ages 5 to 7. Karpova asked children to repeat sentences and respond to the questions, "How many words are here?", and "Which is the first . . . second . . . third word?" Karpova (1955/1966) reported that the youngest children (ages 4 to 5) did not isolate words but rather semantic units. For example, a child aged 4.6 years indicated that the sentence, "Galya and Vova went walking" had two words: "Galya went walking and Vova went walking" (cited in Smith & Miller, 1966, p. 370). Under repeated questioning, children approaching 7 were beginning to isolate nouns and began to break sentences into subject and predicate. It is reported also that some of the oldest children in the sample isolated all of the words correctly excepting functors, as prepositions and conjunctions. Karpova (1955) also instituted a training procedure in which children moved plastic counters as they repeated each word. The procedure apparently was quite successful for the children who initially could not segment any words.

Another early study by Huttenlocher (1964), designed to assess word awareness, investigated the ability of 66 children aged 4.5 and 5 years to either reverse word pairs of different grammatical and nongrammatical relationships or to say the first word of the pair, await a "tap" from the researcher, then say the second. The sample was randomly divided into two groups with each group performing only one of the tasks. Huttenlocher discovered that a third of the children in each group were unable to reverse or segment any pairs. For the remaining subjects, the most troublesome categories involved reversing or segmenting common grammatical sequences such as "man-runs," "I-do," or "is-it" (p. 264). Huttenlocher (1964) then hypothesized that children's confusions as to the identification of a single word might particularly come with words not ordinarily used in isolation such as copulas and pronouns.

In another frequently quoted article, Holden and MacGinitie (1972) generally confirmed Huttenlocher's (1964) suspicions that prepositions and auxiliaries were not seen as distinct units by young children. In a tapping task where the child repeated an utterance and simultaneously pointed to individual poker chips to indicate a word, the majority of subjects when presented with the sentence, "You have to go home," either combined "to" with "have" or "to" with "go." Similarly, when the verb "to be" was used as an auxiliary in the progressive form, "Bill is drinking sodas," kindergarteners generally made the combination "isdrinking" and a few chose "Billis." "In general," concluded Holden and MacGinitie (1972), "the greater the proportion of content words in an utterance, the greater the percentage of correct segmentations" (p. 554).

In one of the first attempts to correlate awareness of word boundaries with actual reading achievement, McNinch (1974) found that with pre-established readiness groups (good, average, poor), ability to segment a spoken sentence into words did not significantly differ. However, in a multiple regression with visual word boundary scores, oral segmenting ability was the significant predictor of end of the year reading scores on the *Metropolitan Achievement Test* (Prescott, Balow, Hogan & Farr, 1971). Similarly, Evans (1975) reported that for a sample of 45 kindergarteners and 45 first graders divided into above and below average groups based upon a segmenting task identical to Karpova's (1955/1966), better readers in December as measured by the *Gates-MacGinitie Primary Reading Tests* (Gates & MacGinitie, 1965) were also the better segmenters a few months earlier.

Like Elkonin (1973), Liberman (1973) and Liberman, Shankweiler, Fischer and Carter (1974) also have offered evidence of the existence of a relationship between syllable and phoneme segmentation and instruction in reading. Employing a tapping task where 135 preschool, kindergarten, and first grade children were to identify phonemes and syllables in spoken words, Liberman et al. (1974) found main effects for both task and grade, observing that phoneme segmentation was uniformly more difficult for all groups than syllable segmentation and that first graders performed better than kindergartners, who in turn performed better than preschoolers. While Liberman et al. (1974) did not discount the effects of maturation, they posited that in all probability "analysis of language, even of the most elementary sort, requires instruction" (p. 210).

In contrast to the findings of previous analyses of children's inability to segment spoken sentences, Fox and Routh (1975) claimed that even 3-year-olds were able to segment sentences into words, words into syllables, and in a few cases even syllables into individual phonemes. Fox's and Routh's (1975) task was to have the children listen to a sentence, word, or syllable spoken by the researcher and then respond to the statement, "Say just a little bit of it" (p. 335). This statement was repeated until all the words or sounds were completely analyzed. The results showed that ability to analyze the items steadily increased with age. However, even 3-year-olds segmented over half of the sentences into words, approximately a third of the words into syllables, and a fourth of the syllables into individual phonemes. These findings contradict earlier statements by Bruce (1964) that until a mental age of 7, children are unable to competently perform word analysis tasks. Fox and Routh (1975) also found significant positive correlations between reading comprehension as measured by the *Peabody Individual Achievement Test* (Dunn & Markwardt, 1970) and ability to segment words into syllables and syllables into phonemes.

Ehri (1975), in addition to a word and syllable segmentation measure, also tested children's ability to analyze a sentence for target words and analyze spoken words for specified syllables. Using a sample of preschool, kindergarten, and first grade children, Ehri found that for most tasks, readers' (first graders) mean performance was higher than prereaders (preschool and kindergarten), while the means for the latter two groups did not differ. As a result of their more frequent exposure to printed language, Ehri (1975) stated that "readers, in contrast to prereaders, possess substantial conscious awareness of lexical as well as syllabic constituents of speech" (p. 211). As did other researchers (e.g., Holden & MacGinite, 1972; Huttenlocher, 1964), Ehri (1975) noted that all of her subjects, particularly the prereading groups, failed to distinguish functors such as "the," "a," "to," and "is," as distinct units of language.

In a similar kind of sentence analysis task designed to tap children's lexical awareness, Holden (1977) tested 26 kindergarten and 24 first grade children on their ability to identify the added word in one sentence of a pair of sentences with homophonous words (e.g., "John leaves after dinner; John rakes leaves after dinner," p. 214). Based upon a previous study (Holden & MacGinitie, 1973) which demonstrated that differences between kindergartners and first graders on this same task was not a result of intelligence, Holden (1977) surmised that regular patterns of response should occur if indeed there were developmental stages in young children's evolving awareness of word units. Holden's findings supported this notion, since the first graders made almost twice as many correct responses as did the kindergartners. Further, Holden (1977) demonstrated that short-term memory recall limitations could hardly have been a factor, since for many of the incorrect responses the children repeated the entire verbal stimulus without error. Holden (1977) observed, however, that even the better performing first graders still exhibited an "unstabilized ability to perceive language at both phonetic and semantic levels simultaneously" (p. 206), as their most common error was to isolate the homophonous word which had changed meaning in the second sentence. Holden (1977) concluded, therefore, that the capacity to analyze language "abstractly" apart from its semantic context shows definite developmental patterns (p. 206). She did not discuss, however, how these patterns might be affected by prior experience with books or direct reading instruction.

Another study employing a tapping task examined under this subcategory of speech segmentation was conducted by Leong and Haines (1978). Testing a total sample of 72 children in grades 1 to 3, the researchers had children segment words into syllables and syllables into phonemes by tapping a wooden dowel on the table as they distinguished each unit spoken. In addition, there were also tasks of identifying the number and order of sound patterns in words (cf. Lindamood & Lindamood, 1971) and recall of sentences varying in grammatical complexity (i.e., "high" or "low"). Results showed that while there was a significant difference across grade in ability to segment words into syllables, there was no difference between groups in segmenting syllables into sounds. However, in the "auditory conceptualization" task of recognizing the number and order of sounds in words, there was a significant difference between grades 2 and 3 combined and grade 1.

To further investigate the relationship of auditory conceptualization, word and syllable segmentation with reading achievement, a canonical correlation was computed with the experimental tasks as independent variables and two measures of reading achievement as the dependent variables. The analysis showed that auditory conceptualization or the recognizing and ordering of sound sequences in words contributed most to the correlation with reading scores ($R = .777$). This was followed in the weightings by recall of high complexity sentences, syllable segmentation, phoneme segmentation, and recall of low complexity sentences (p. 402). Despite the finding, unlike previous studies, that phoneme segmentation did not discriminate between grades (cf. Liberman et al., 1974), the authors suggested that for some children "acquisition of verbal skills is facilitated if their understanding is brought to the focal level. . . . This contemplation of words and sentences, which can be taught . . . , will go some way towards helping the child in the learning to read process" (p. 405).

The final two studies reviewed in this subsection have provided some necessary controls over the mechanics of the data-collection task and the nature of the stimuli themselves not included in previous investigations. In the first, Treiman and Baron (1981) included a nonsense sound counting task along with syllable and phoneme counting to ensure that children could indeed perform the mechanical task itself. In addition, they had the first and second grade children move checkers rather than tap to identify phoneme and syllable units, since the former task seemed less affected by rhythmic responses as noted in other studies (e.g., Holden & MacGinitie, 1972). In addition, nonsense words were used as stimuli in order to aid the child in "thinking about sounds" apart from their meaning. Interestingly, Treiman's and Baron's (1981) results closely corroborated the traditional finding that phoneme segmentation is uniformly harder than syllable segmentation for all children. However, with the inclusion of the neutral sound test, the researchers observed that second graders performed better than first graders on simply the ability to count. Therefore, the authors suggested that the older children's apparent increasing awareness of sounds in words might simply be a result of their superior ability to enumerate. Other results reported by Treiman and Baron (1981) included the finding that for some words fricatives were more easily isolated than stops, and that speech segmentation, for nonsense words at least, proceeded in order of difficulty from vowels being the hardest to discriminate followed by final consonants then initial consonants (p. 172). The authors pointed out, however, that previous research indicated a similar pattern for real words.

The last study reviewed in this section, by Tunmer, Bowey, and Grieve (1983), provided additional control in the nature of the stimuli to be isolated.

In five separate experiments where groups of children 4 to 7 years of age were given word strings to first repeat orally, then to tap out the number of word units, the investigators varied such factors as grammaticality, plurality, form class, and stress pattern. Their results showed that while there is an increasing ability to segment speech proportional to chronological age, the effects of varying syllabic congruence (i.e., more syllables than words in stimulus), plurality (presence of plural nouns), word class (adjectives, verbs, nouns, etc.) and grammaticality (grammatical vs. ungrammatical strings) within the stimulus items had little differential effect between age groups. However, in the experiments designed to explore the influence of stress pattern, Tunmer et al. (1983) observed that young children segmented primarily according to phrase and syllable stress; whereas as the older children in the sample (6 to 7 years) began to focus upon morphemic units (p. 592). Even so, the authors noted that "most 5-year-olds and a few 6 to 7-year-olds do not segment meaningful syntactic phrases into their constituent words in the present studies" (p. 590). Interestingly, Tunmer et al. (1983) observed also that "explicit demonstrations and corrective feedback" did little to enhance the 4- to 5-year-olds' notion of an "abstract concept of word as a unit of language" (p. 591). However, the authors concluded by saying that future research must take into account the effects of memory, stress, word awareness, and other factors before it can be decided whether or not children's awareness of units of language can be enhanced by specific training, and subsequently if "lexical awareness" has any direct bearing upon learning to read.

In short, studies in speech segmentation demonstrated that preschoolers as well as first and second grade children have great difficulty isolating linguistic units in their speech, particularly phonemes or "sounds." In addition, contentives are much more easily picked out of the speech stream than functors. It was suggested also that specific training in segmentation may be less productive since approaching the age of 7 children seem to use a variety of stress cues to anticipate divisions in oral language rather than knowledge of discrete language elements. Finally, researchers in general admit a correlation between reading ability and phonological awareness, but the direction of cause is still much under dispute.

Identifying What Is a "Word"

In the next group of studies, the qualitative content of children's notions about words as units of language is explored. The methodology of the following investigations normally involves a researcher posing to a child an inquiry such as, "What is a word?" Hence, the child's verbalizable or "reflective" (cf. Templeton & Spivey, 1980) knowledge is used as the unit of data. The importance of these types of studies, as noted earlier, lies in their ability to discover the evolving stages of a child's concept of word, this time from the learner's point of view.

Testing a group of 50 5-year-olds four times over a two-year period, Francis (1973) asked, "Can you tell me any letter (word, sentence) you know?" Following this task, she also showed them an example of each element on a card and asked the children to identify the particular units. On the first testing occasion, half of the children chose examples of words or sentences when asked to identify individual letters. Words continued to be confused with letters until the last testing at age 7. The results of asking for each concept were very similar to the recognition test. Words were frequently confused with numbers or names, and words were given as examples of sentences. Overall, Francis (1973) noted that from the first to the last testing, letters were mastered before words and words before sentences. She also noted that children generally learned the last two concepts after gaining some facility in reading. In addition, she found that reading ability was positively correlated with knowledge of technical language terms (i.e., word, letter) even with IQ controlled (Kendall $r = .34$). Francis (1973) concluded, therefore, "that factors independent of a general ability to deal with abstract concepts were involved in learning technical vocabulary and that these were closely related to the reading process" (p. 22).

In probably the most well-known study of reflective word knowledge, Papandropoulou and Sinclair (1974), using a list of commonly known words, identified four levels in development of word consciousness as a result of asking children 4.5 to approximately 11 years of age the questions, "Is that a word?" and "What is a word, really?" An analysis of the results showed that most of the children under age 5 answered in level one, which was characterized by the inability to differentiate between a word and its referent (cf. Markman, 1976) as exemplified by responses such as, "Children are words," or "It can be a cupboard or a chair or a book" (p. 244). Level two (5 through 7 years) as characterized by two functions of words: (a) as labels for things, and (b) to express a "topic-comment" relationship such as, "I put the dog in the kennel," in response to the request, "Say a short word." At levels three (6 to 6.8 years), words began to take on the feature of elements which made up wholes but which did not yet have individual meanings; for instance, "A word is a bit of a story," and "A word is something simple, very simple, it's all by itself; it does not tell anything" (p. 246). Papandropoulou and Sinclair (1974) noted that during the fourth and final stage words finally become "autonomous" elements, having meaning of their own, and play a definite role in grammatical relationships. Responses to inquiries at this stage take the form, for instance, of "letters form words . . . a word is something that means something" (p. 247). Based on their findings, the researchers concluded that the concept of a word

> undergoes a long and slow elaboration during the ages studied. Gradually, words become detached from the objects and events they refer to, and it is only late in cognitive development that they are regarded as meaningful elements inside a systematic frame of linguistic representation. (p. 249)

In a series of related studies, Sulzby (1978, 1979) used a different approach to eliciting student's "metalanguage" in a task designed to explore elementary students' thinking about known and unknown words in both oral and written form. In the first of these studies, Sulzby (1978) examined the responses of 30 rural, predominantly black students in grades 2, 4, and 6 to the question, "How does your [student's] word go with my [researcher's] word for you?" (p. 52). On the whole, Sulzby (1978) found that students in all grades tended to give answers indicating a semantic focus rather than structural (e.g., "They both got letters"), although this tendency increased across grades. In addition, students in all grades gave mostly semantic responses even to words presented in written form. A very interesting finding by Sulzby (1978) was that even sixth graders were observed to be using instructional terminology (i.e., "metalanguage") incorrectly when giving the less frequent structural responses. Sulzby noted as well that by fourth grade, students would create "hypothetical contexts" for unknown words more frequently than give structural responses.

Using the same task, but a different population of 28 predominantly white children in grades 1, 3, and 5, Sulzby (1979) found again that all students gave significantly more semantic responses although more so in the oral presentation mode this time. As in the first study (Sulzby, 1978), Sulzby (1979) noted the tendency of children to create meanings for unknown words rather than give a simpler structural response (p. 52). Both of these studies offer from a slightly different angle evidence that the structural aspects of words, even in written form, if not immediately available for reflection, are subordinated to the child's need to create some kind of intelligible meaning.

In an extension and replication of the Papandropoulou and Sinclair study (1974), Templeton and Spivey (1980) asked a sample of 24 children ages 4 to 7.8 years of age such questions as, "Is [blank] a word?" (from a predetermined list); "Why is/is not [blank] a word?"; and "What is a word, anyway?" (p. 268). In addition the children were queried in a similar manner about long, short, easy, and hard words as well. Templeton and Spivey (1980) also grouped the sample according to performance on the Piagetian concept attainment tasks of classification and seriation, and thus were able to describe responses as being characteristic of children at the preoperational, transitional and concrete levels of operation. The results indicated that the preoperational children in particular were unable "to talk about language abstractly" (p. 274), most often refusing to respond. Transitional children, on the other hand, began to give answers which reflected a notion of "wordness" as having something to do with spoken language (i.e., "It comes out of your mouth," p. 274) apart from a specific context.

Interestingly, Templeton and Spivey (1980) pointed out that even the more sophisticated responses to questions like, "What is a word?", characteristic of concrete operational children, most often reflected the influence of exposure to print (i.e., "We have to read them," or "It's something that you write," p. 275). Therefore the authors suggested that while a more frequent referral to the internal structure of words was in general more indicative of a higher level of cognitive functioning, the ability to think "metalinguistically" seemed to be enhanced by mere exposure to the written language itself.

In another study, Sanders (1981) analyzed first grade classroom interactions by video and audio recordings and then interviewed three first grade males as to their understanding of the teacher's use of instructional terms such as "beginning sound" and "word." Sanders discovered that while students seemed to observably understand classroom directives, individual interviews revealed confusion on the child's part. One child indicated in the personal interview that "*Dog* and *God* and *big* and *dig* begin alike" (p. 269). The researcher also noted that the subjects confused the referents of letters and words as well as "a long word" or a "string of words" (cf. Templeton & Spivey, 1980). Interestingly, Sanders (1981) also observed that the interviewees thought that while learning letter/sound correspondences and letter names was useful for first grade, the skills had little to do with reading itself (p. 269). Further, all of the subjects, as noted by the researcher, adhered to the formula of "three letters, plus or minus a letter" (cf. Ferreiro & Teberosky, 1982) in deciding whether a written array was a word or not. In general, Sanders (1981) observed that while classroom activities provided isolated focus upon many metalinguistic aspects of learning about print, accurate notions of what it means to be literate are derived primarily from functional and meaningful interaction with written language.

Exploring children's reflective knowledge of word and other language units with Spanish-English bilinguals separated into reader groups of fair-to-good and non-to-poor, Matluck and Mace-Matluck (1983) elicited responses from 94 students in grades 1 to 4 over a three-year period regarding their knowledge of decoding processes and understanding of the metalinguistic terms "word," "sentence," and "story." Concerning decoding, very few first grade children in either language could explain why they knew how to pronounce a word. By second grade, however, a large majority of the better readers were giving responses which demonstrated some facility using metalinguistic terminology (i.e., "by syllables, by letters—I sound each letter," p. 28). By the third and fourth grades, over 80% of the good readers were giving accurate, adult-like explanations of print deciphering processes while only half of the poor readers could do so.

In response to the statement, "Tell me what a word [sentence, story] is," Matluck and Mace-Matluck (1983) again observed that only a very few first graders, mostly good readers, could give formal definitions of these terms. By second grade, although more of the entire sample attempted answers, again only good readers gave more accurate definitions. Even by fourth grade, a majority of the formal definitions of these terms were still being given by the good reader group. Interestingly, like other studies (cf. Templeton & Spivey, 1980), definitions of the term "word" reflected the influence of increased exposure to print (i.e., "A word is a group of letters joined together to pronounce a word," p. 33). The authors concluded by reiterating the hypothesis of previous studies that "the development of metalinguistic skills appears to coincide with experience with literacy and to be related to exposure to literacy training" (Matluck & Mace-Matluck, 1983, p. 33).

Finally, in an extension of a previous study (Templeton & Spivey, 1980), Templeton and Thomas (1984) tested equal groups of 7 "transitional" and "concrete-operational" kindergarten, first and second grade children on both "performance-based" tasks, as syllable segmentation and invented spelling, and "reflective-knowledge" tasks, as identifying words in speech and commenting upon them in order to verify differences in metalinguistic knowledge between children of differing cognitive levels. However, even though analyses revealed no significant differences between groups on any of the tasks, children within each cognitive stage demonstrated significantly more ability in identifying words than they did in reflecting upon their structural properties. One conclusion advanced by the authors was that "Piagetian stages do not powerfully predict or explain certain aspects of metalinguistic behavior" (p. 145), although it was noted that preoperational children who were not included in the study may have differed in their concepts about "wordness." Templeton and Thomas (1984) also noted that consistent with previous studies (e.g., Templeton & Spivey, 1980), "subjects' first mention of the intraword structure of words was in terms of letters rather than sounds" (p. 145). This latter finding argues for, suggested the authors, an early school environment where the child is immersed in print (see Taylor, this volume).

Briefly summarizing this group of studies, we observe that young children in kindergarten and first grade have an extremely difficult time verbalizing their notions of the metalinguistic terms used in classroom instruction. And when these notions were tapped, the concepts seemed to be inextricably woven to semantic content rather than including structural dimensions. When children did begin to verbalize more adult-like perceptions of such terms as "word," the influence of print was evident. This finding lends support to the notion expressed earlier by Ehri (1975, 1976, 1979) that until children are exposed to the written language, they have little reason to view their speech as being made up of discrete, isolable units. Finally, while it has been observed that an expression of more sophisticated concepts about language often accompanies increasing development in cognition, the relationship is still confounded by prior exposure to print and the influence of classroom instruction.

Identifying Verbal vs. Nonverbal Units

The next small group of studies discussed have generally used the same paradigm to assess children's knowledge of word, syllable, and phoneme units. Initially, Downing (1970) devised a task in which children were presented 25 tape-recorded auditory stimuli of five types: nonhuman noises (bell ringing) and human utterances of a single phoneme, word, phrase, and sentence. Each child was tested twice with the "sounds" of each category and asked first if he/she heard a single word and then if he/she heard a phoneme. Results of the presentation of the stimuli to thirteen English 5-year-olds showed that five children responded "yes" or "no" to all stimuli in all categories, thus evidencing no discrimination even between verbal and nonverbal sounds. In addition, five children responded positively in the word phrase of the experiment to phrases and sentences as well. No child, Downing (1970) reported, correctly identified either a single word or phoneme.

Later, Downing and Oliver (1973–74) extended the categories to include nonverbal "abstract" sounds (i.e., dice rattling), isolated syllables and both long (e.g., hippopotamus) and short words. He also specified in the pretraining task that the children respond "yes" to only single words. Results, however, followed the pattern of the first experiments: all children, across all ages, gave significantly fewer correct responses for both syllables and phonemes than for any other auditory class, while none of the children in the youngest age group (4.5–5.5) recognized that phonemes or syllables were not words. In addition, Downing and Oliver (1973–74) noted that children even up to 6.5 years confused nonverbal sounds, phrases, sentences, and phonemes as words. They stated, therefore: "A more generalized implication of these findings would seem to be that it is not safe for reading teachers to assume that their beginning students understand linguistic concepts such as word" (p. 581).

Johns (1977) replicated Downing and Oliver's (1973–74) study with a larger sample (120 American children ranging in age from 5.6 to 9.5 years) and generally confirmed the latter's results. In Johns' (1977) study almost 40% of the subjects at beginning reading age were unable to consistently identify a single spoken word. In addition, nearly 90% of the subjects in this age group confused single phonemes with words. Johns (1977) surmised that such confusions

> may be due, at least in part, to the fragmentation that occurs in reading instruction. Concentrating on sounds (phonemes) and word parts may only serve to confuse children who are trying to learn what reading is all about. (p. 256)

In a more restricted version of the task, Ryan, McNamara, and Kenney (1977) presented above and below average readers in first and second grades with a word discrimination task in which they were to identify single phonemes, two-syllable words and two phrases as either a "word," "not a word," or "two words" (p. 399). Their results showed that above average readers scored significantly higher than below average readers in correctly identifying the stimuli. Ryan et al. (1977) then administered the same tasks to third and fourth grade remedial readers divided into above and below average reading groups by placement in basal readers. They again discovered that better readers outperformed their poorer reading counterparts in identifying linguistic units.

Finally, in the most recent replication of the study by Downing and Oliver (1973–74), Horne, Powers, and Mahabub (1983) tested 40 male students ages 6.5 to 10.5 on their ability to distinguish from a range of nonverbal stimuli to types of linguistic utterances. Reader and nonreader groups were equated by intelligence and also given pretraining tasks to ensure their understanding of the response required. An ANOVA comparing reader levels, age, and stimulus class showed that the sample of Horne et al. (1983) performed similarly to students in the previous two investigations (Downing & Oliver, 1973–74; Johns, 1977), in that readers outperformed nonreaders in all classes and that there was uniform difficulty among all pupils in identifying phonemes and syllables as opposed to the rest of the stimuli. An important extension of the Horne et al. (1983) study, however, was the inclusion of the oldest group (9.5–10.5) and the finding that nonreaders in this group mastered *none* of the stimulus groups excepting short words (p. 11), thus indicating extensive confusion about linguistic terminology and concepts about language units.

In summary of the major section, regardless of the method of data collection used, most studies indicated that a great number of primary age children as well as some of those with several years of schooling were not able to analyze their speech into units such as phonemes or words, with some even unable to distinguish between linguistic utterances and infrahuman sounds. Further, a tendency noted by several researchers was for children to overlook functions as distinct language entities and primarily focus upon the semantic aspects of words. With the glaring exception of Fox and Routh (1975), whose method of data collection has been questioned (see Ehri, 1979), the majority of studies reviewed consistently reported that children's concepts of their oral language as being comprised of distinct linguistic units were not stabilized, and some implied that these nascent concepts may be resistant even to direct instruction. Finally, it has been commonly observed that children who are better readers also demonstrate greater facility at analyzing their speech into distinct components and verbalizing more precise notions about the nature of words, sentences, and other language units.

Concepts About Printed Conventions

Clay's (1967, 1969) weekly observation of 100 children's beginning reading behavior over a year's period in New Zealand has provided the impetus for numerous investigations into children's specific concepts about printed conventions such as left-to-right/top-to-bottom directionality, marks of punctuation, and especially "space" as a boundary for written words. This latter area has absorbed much of the attention of American researchers, although some have examined the child's gradual development of an accurate speech-print match as well. Studies in the following section, then, will be further subdivided into separate discussions of children's knowledge of visual word boundaries, the correspondence between the spoken and written word, and concepts about directionality, punctuation, and other printed conventions.

Knowledge of Written Word Boundaries

The first American investigations of children's knowledge of printed conventions almost exclusively focused upon recognizing written word boundaries. Meltzer and Herse (1969) provided the basic algorithm by having children first read the sentence, "Seven cowboys in a wagon saw numerous birds downtown today" (p. 4). The instructions then were to count each word while pointing to it and to finally circle each word. With a sample of 39 beginning first graders, Meltzer and Herse (1969) noted a recognizable developmental pattern: (a) letters are words; (b) a word is a unit made up of more than one letter; (c) space is used as a boundary *unless* the words are short, in which case they are combined; or long, in which case they are divided; (d) only long words continue to be divided; and (e) spaces indicate word boundaries except where there is a "tall" letter in the middle of a word (p. 13). As a result of these findings, the authors stated that "a very cursory sampling of the kindergarten seemed to indicate almost complete

ignorance after three months of school of graphic characteristics which define
. . . a letter or word" (p.11). Meltzer and Herse (1969) also made the intriguing suggestion that this knowledge of printed conventions was not directly taught;
"Rather the assumption is made either that the child already has this information or that he will discover it independently from the material presented to
him" (p. 13).

Subsequent replications of the above study, while supporting the finding that
children do not use space consistently as a boundary for written words, have not
confirmed the existence of a developmental pattern, however. Kingston, Weaver
and Figa (1972) noted that the most common error in their sample of 45 first
graders was that of combining two short words, usually when one contained only
one letter (e.g., "andI" or "Isaid"). Kingston et al. (1972) observed that other
combination errors involving longer, multisyllabic words seemed "to be a result
of a failure to perceive any word meaning in addition to the fact that the printer's space was not recognized as a word boundary cue" (p. 95). Such errors were
recorded as dividing at ascenders, descenders, and putting together the end of
one word with the beginning of the next. Kingston et al. (1972) concluded that
"recognizing the printer's space as the separator of words is secondary to perceiving that a particular linguistic unit represents a meaningful entity" (p. 95).

McNinch (1974) also used Meltzer and Herse's (1969) task in conjunction
with an aural word boundary task (word segmentation) with a sample of 60 first
graders. The primary finding was that while performance on the visual word
boundary task discriminated between readiness groups (high, average, low), it
did not appear as a significant predictor of spring reading scores in a multiple
regression. McNinch (1974) did not report any patterns of word division.

Mickish (1974) tested 117 first grade students at the end of the year on their
ability to segment the spaceless sentence "Thecatandthedogplayball" (p. 20) by
drawing vertical lines in between the words. Even though it could be "safely
assumed," according to Mickish (1974), that the term "word" had been referred
to "hundreds of times," 50% of the subjects did not correctly segment the sentence. Mickish observed also that children in higher levels of basal readers performed better than children at lower levels.

Blum, Taylor, and Blum (1979) also attempted to replicate the task and
findings of Meltzer and Herse (1969) with a sample of 54 first graders and 47
kindergartners. Using the same test sentence, "Seven cowboys in a wagon saw
numerous birds downtown today," and having the children count and circle the
words, the authors reported as did Kingston et al. (1972) that the most common
error of both grades was combining two words and that the putative developmental pattern identified by Meltzer and Herse (1969) was not evident. Blum et
al. (1979) echoed Clay's (1967) earlier admonition, however, that "exposure to
'meaningful' print results in clarity about word space. The nature and pace of
this clarity depends on the nature of the child and the quality and quantity of
print exposure" (p.38).

In one of the more descriptive investigations of the nature and development
of printed word boundaries, Sulzby (1981) gathered writing samples from nine

kindergarten children and recorded their rereadings and explanations of their composing processes. Dividing the sample into high, moderate, and low "emergent" reading groups, Sulzby was able to observe alternative ways of segmenting printed strings, such as dots between words, separate lines for each word (i.e., a columnar display), and even circles drawn around letters in order to, as one child put it, "keep the parts from getting mixed up" (p. 14). Interestingly, Sulzby (1981) noted that children in the lower two groups asked many more questions about the processes of writing and when reading their productions than did the children in the high emergent group, who perhaps, as Sulzby surmised, asked these questions at an earlier age. An important point noted by Sulzby (1981) was that although many young children do not use space conventionally, it does not mean that they are unaware of the principle of segmentation itself.

Thus, the few studies reviewed indicated that the convention of "space" as separating word units in print, if not easily grasped by young children, is not used to begin with. While there is less evidence for a distinct developmental pattern, all of the studies indicated that better readers or those having more exposure to print more closely approximated the adult notion of segmentation. Since Meltzer and Herse (1969) pointed out that there is little specific instruction in this area, it can be surmised that children were quite successful in gleaning from their printed environment alone some of the characteristics of written language, albeit slowly.

The Speech-Print Match

Studies in the following section generally assess the oral/visual correspondence in one of two ways. Some investigations have explored the spoken/written word match from the standpoint of either too many or too few words spoken for the number of written words represented (Clay, 1967; Holden & MacGinitie, 1972). On the other hand, several have focused attention on whether or not children understand that long spoken utterances generally are represented in print by words with many letters as well. Reviewed are examinations of both types.

Clay (1967) observed that subjects in her sample went through several stages before correctly matching spoken and written utterances. During the initial stage, children only matched their memorized rendition of a written text by locating the appropriate page, with no reference, however, to the actual written text. In stage two the child was able to find the appropriate line of print, and during the third stage located some memorized words within the line itself. Stage four was characterized by a process which Clay (1967) called "reading the spaces" or "voice-pointing," where the child exaggerated the spaces between words by prolonged pauses between utterances in oral reading. Finally, some children moved into a more fluent stage where oral reading errors were characterized by a "movement-speech" mismatch where there are either too many or too few spoken words for written ones, or a "speech-vision" mismatch in which substitutions for written words were governed by prior language habits.

In a study mentioned earlier, Holden and MacGinitie (1972) tested a subgroup of 57 kindergartners in their original sample on their ability to match written sentences with previously spoken and segmented ones. In the matching task, responses were scored as "congruent" if the child matched the correct number of written clusters with the oral segments he/she had counted, and "conventional" if the number of spoken words matched the number of written ones as normally printed. The written sentences contained both mono- and polysyllabic words, and many were segmented unconventionally (i.e., "Red and green bal loons popped.", p. 555). Even with children instructed in the principles of printing conventions, Holden and MacGinitie (1972) found that only 5 children in the sample were able to correctly count the words in the spoken utterances and match them to their written equivalents. While several children were able to choose a "congruent" written match with the segments they had counted, the authors stated that none of the children consistently picked out the standard written form of the spoken sentences (p. 556). Summarily, therefore, the authors warned that "a first grade teacher cannot take for granted that children will understand her when she talks about 'words' and their printed representation" (p. 556).

Rozin, Bressman and Taft (1974) tested a total of 218 children in kindergarten and first and second grades on their ability to recognize and explain why pairs of words such as "mow-motorcycle" and "ash-asparagus" represented different lengths of spoken utterances. The authors reported significant differences in percentage between suburban kindergarteners, who were able to match the spoken and written forms correctly (43%), and urban kindergarteners, who performed less well (11%). While the urban group improved performance in first and second grades, Rozin et al. (1974) noted that a fair number of urban second graders could still not perform the matching task adequately (76% and 40% in two classes, respectively). Rozin, et al. (1974) did not offer any explanations as to the differences between socioeconomic groups; however, they suggest that

it might be useful for a child to grasp the nature of the writing system before delving into its detailed specifics (letter/phoneme mappings). It appears that partial mastery of the details does not guarantee appreciation of the basic system. (p. 334)

Using the same task with some variations in the nature of the stimulus pairs, Lundberg and Torneus (1978) asked 100 nonreading children, ages 4–7, to match long or short written words with their appropriate oral representation and to explain the reason why. The researchers varied such factors as vowel duration and semantic referent (i.e., long/short written words referring to either large or small objects). While the results showed a steady increase in correct matching due to age, Lundberg and Torneus reported that less than 20% of the entire sample met the criterion of 90% correct responses (p. 410). In addition, only the 7-year-olds were able to give explanations of their choices, which indicated an accurate understanding of the relationship between the duration of spoken utterances and number of written letters. Other trends noted were that children in all age groups seemed to adhere to a semantic strategy when deciding on the word length, while no groups demonstrated reliance upon vowel duration as a cue. In summary, Lundberg and Torneus (1978) stated that even the oldest preschoolers "seemed to have poor concepts of the basic principle of our writing system" [Swedish] (p. 412).

Finally, Evans, Taylor, and Blum (1979) used the same task of Rozin et al. (1974) as a component in the development of their own instrument to measure metalinguistic abilities. Using a sample of 53 first graders, they found that in a multiple regression with reading achievement as the criterion, the "mow-motor-cycle" test was a significant predictor of achievement while knowledge of visual word boundaries was not. They suggested that tasks such as "mow-motorcycle," which require the child to focus on aspects of both oral and written language, are more useful in helping the child understand print, since they enhance "decision making by the child and an active interaction with his language" (p. 17).

It can be observed, then, that children do not immediately understand conventions of spacing between written words as separating lexical units in print. Nor do they, as reported, realize that longer utterances are usually represented by more letters. Interestingly, as demonstrated in other studies, direct instruction regarding these concepts seemed to have little effect; whereas increasing experience with books and interaction with the printed page led to more adult-like notions of how spoken words are represented in print.

Directionality, Punctuation, and Other Printed Conventions

Most of the studies reviewed in this final subsection of concepts about printed conventions have used the few commercially available tests in the area to measure a variety of reading-specific behaviors. Clay's (1972, 1979) *Concepts about Print Test* (CAPT), the *Linguistic Awareness in Reading Readiness* (LARR) *Test* by Downing, Ayers and Schaefer (1982), and Taylor and Blum's (1980) *Written Language Awareness Test* (WLAT) were all developed to give more accurate insight into the child's direct facility with reading behaviors than was possible with traditional reading readiness tests. Among the tests a range of concepts about written language are measured, including knowledge of printed letter and word units, understanding of metalinguistic vocabulary, correct directional movements, the function of punctuation marks, and in some cases, discrimination between different types of script and cognizance of various kinds of environmental message carriers (see Day and Day, this volume, for a complete description).

Clay (1969) noted that habits of directionality varied according to the attained reading level of the child. Better readers usually established accurate line movement and return sweep after seven weeks of instruction, while children in average and low reading groups took 15–20 weeks to develop accurate movements. Clay (1969) observed, however, that some children took as long as six months to establish correct directional habits. In Clay's (1967) view, though, exposure to written forms should not be withheld because a child is judged "immature" (p. 24). She stated that a correct orientation to print is

fostered by contacts with written language. The visual perception of print, the directional constraints on movement, the special types of sentences used in books, and the synchronized matching of spoken word units with written word units will only be learned in contact with written language. (p. 24)

In one of the more recent and extensive analyses of American children's knowledge of printed conventions, Day, Day, and colleagues (1979, 1980, 1981) tested children three times during their kindergarten year and twice during their first grade year with the *Sand—Concepts about Print Test* (CAPT) (Clay, 1972), which attempts to measure not only knowledge of word boundaries, but also directional habits and knowledge of punctuation. From a previous factor analysis, H. D. Day and K. C. Day (1979) identified four dimensions of printed concepts which seemed to develop sequentially. By the end of the first grade, Day, Day, and Hollingsworth (1981) recorded that 80% or more of their sample of 51 first graders at the year's end had mastered basic book orientation habits of directionality and were able to identify upper and lower case letters as well as single words in print. However, roughly only a third to a half of the sample were able to recognize incorrect letter and word sequences or notice when whole lines of print were placed out of order (top and bottom reversed). In addition, while three quarters of the children could identify a comma, only 16% could explain the function of quotation marks. However, K. C. Day and H. D. Day (1979) cautioned in a previous discussion that strong evidence did not emerge supporting the notion that concepts of print are prerequisite to actual ability, since some children whose scores were relatively low on the test (16 out of 24) were observed to be reading by teachers during the first grade year.

Johns (1980) administered the CAPT to 60 first graders ending their first year of instruction and found that above average readers performed significantly better than below average ones on items assessing knowledge of letter and word units and on tasks where the child was to recognize incorrect letter and word sequences and explain the function of various punctuation marks. However, Johns (1980) pointed out that several items on the test might have not adequately directed the child's attention to the print; therefore, the differences found between types of reader in recognizing inverted letter and word sequences may be less qualitative than an artifact of the examination procedure. Despite these limitations, Johns (1980) surmised that "data from this study indicate that above average readers have a greater understanding of print-related concepts than below average readers" (p. 547).

In a further attempt to replicate and extend findings of previous administrations of the CAPT, Yaden (1982) tested 118 first graders in the spring with the most recent edition of the CAPT, *Stones* (Clay, 1979), and obtained a measure of intelligence as well. Using the reading subtests of the *Stanford Achievement Test* (SAT) (Madden, Gardner, Rudman, Karlsen & Merwin, 1972) as measures of reading ability, Yaden (1982) found that in a multiple regression with print awareness scores as the criterion, the subtest of Word Reading was a better predictor of knowledge of printed conventions than that of intelligence, as measured by the *Otis-Lennon School Ability Test* (Otis & Lennon, 1979). Further, all of the reading subtests (Word Reading, Reading Comprehension, Word Study

Skills, and Vocabulary) retained significant partial correlations with print awareness even with intelligence controlled (cf. Francis, 1973).

In general, Yaden's (1982) study supported the findings of previous research that some beginning readers' concepts of letters, words, and marks of punctuation are not stabilized even after one year of reading instruction. Yaden (1982) also discovered that above average readers had better performance on items purporting to measure directional habits with normal and irregular print, and items pertaining to the identification of incorrect letter and word sequences and marks of punctuation. The study did not confirm, however, hypothesized "large" effects of reading achievement and intelligence upon knowledge of printed conventions based upon computation of prior power analyses (cf. Cohen, 1977). Neither reading achievement nor intelligence can be said to contribute substantially to the relationship with print awareness independent of the other. In combination, however, measures of reading achievement and intelligence proved to be useful predictors of knowledge of printed conventions contributing together approximately 40% of the total variance of scores on the CAPT.

In summary, despite discrepancies in the observation of a distinct developmental pattern in the growth of knowledge of printed word boundaries, there is a remarkable unanimity in the findings that beginning readers do not possess firm concepts of printed language units as letters, words, or punctuation marks. Nor do they immediately understand current directional movements. As noted in studies dealing with oral language units, superior readers recognize these linguistic elements in their written form better than do poorer readers. This observation plus the finding that reading ability was a better predictor of print awareness than intelligence (cf. Yaden, 1982; Francis, 1973) lends support to an earlier contention by Ehri (1979) that practice with written language is the best way to enhance metalinguistic growth.

Conclusion

Extant research on children's concepts of the functions and processes involved in reading and their awareness of the units of spoken and written language reveals that beginning readers are largely unaware of the overriding structure of the writing system as well as of their own speech. They have disparate notions as to what behavior comprises the act of reading and the necessary steps that they must take in getting ready to become a reader. Perhaps the most disturbing thing as pointed out by some is that there is little or no instructional time spent in orienting the children to what reading is or what useful functions it may serve (see Mason, McCormick, and Bhavnagri, this volume). As Meltzer and Herse (1969) early on noted, the children are expected to intuitively grasp these conceptual or "metalinguistic" aspects of reading as if the actual learning of the visual symbols was entirely self-explanatory of the higher processes. What research has divulged, however, is that merely learning the code does not automatically give children insight into how print may be used nor how these "bunches of letters," as one child put it, work together to represent the variety of intelligible messages ubiquitous in everyday surroundings. That traditional tests of readiness have overlooked these more global aspects of literacy is a fault. To continue to overlook them in the face of mounting evidence for their existence would be inexcusable.

Vygotsky (1978) in discussing the history of written language has said that "children should be taught written language, not just the writing of letters" (p. 119). The implications here is that to view written language as merely the reproduction of certain isolated graphic shapes is to miss the importance of the printed code altogether. More recently, Ferreiro and Teberosky (1982) have powerfully reiterated this view.

It has traditionally been thought that to learn to read children must possess good language (or a sufficient level of oral language development) evaluated in terms of vocabulary, diction, and grammatical complexity. If we believe that we must consider language awareness, the perspective changes. Rather than being concerned with whether children know how to speak, we should help them become conscious of what they already know how to do, help them move from "knowing how" to "knowing about," a conceptual knowing. (p. 298)

Donaldson (1984) has recently cautioned literacy researchers against the "fashionable" trend of emphasizing "what children *can* [Donaldson's emphasis] do rather than what they cannot do" (p. 174), and ignoring the real differences in the ease of learning to speak as opposed to learning to read and write. She goes on to say that "some things take longer than others to learn and are achieved later or with less universal success. We do no good to children, or to science, by trying to deny it" (p. 174). Thus, while the writer of the present chapter does not claim to have presented an exhaustive discussion of the literature, it is hoped that enough has been examined to ensure that a reevaluation of current reading approaches in terms of children's "conceptual knowing" may be soon in coming.

Acknowledgments

Portions of this chapter appeared originally in David B. Yaden, Jr., "Reading research in metalinguistic awareness: findings, problems and classroom applications," *Visible Language* 18 (1980), 5–47, and are reprinted by permission of the publisher.

Section 2

Literacy, Metalinguistic Awareness, and the Alphabetic Principle: Theoretical Considerations

Chapter 5

Understanding Children's Knowledge of Written Language

EDMUND HENDERSON

To understand how children learn to read one must step back and consider human speech and written language in broad perspective. This is necessary because learning to speak and learning to read are different from learning history or learning science. Language is deeply fixed in human behavior, and like walking upright it emerges in its season. Written languages are determined by speech, which is to say their specific forms must meet a criterion of resonance with spoken utterance. Written languages thus have by reflection a dynamic quality, a certain organicity and life of their own. It is this characteristic that allows children to learn to read a written language long before they can consider how it was that they did so.

Origins of Language

Phillip Lieberman (1975) argues that human language emerged at least one million years ago and is coterminous with the species homo. Lateralization of function is entailed in language as it is also in the making of tools and the discovery of self (Van Der Vlugt, 1979). So armed, man strayed from his ecological niche and grew ever more dependent for survival upon the growing brain as it directed the hand and tongue. That these matters have long been intuitively understood is clearly shown in the remarkable parallel between the evolutionary and biblical accounts of our origin.

In Lieberman's analysis it appears that the compressed and very rapid speech of modern man became possible about seventy thousand years ago with the evolution of a superlaryngeal structure capable of multiple vowel production. At approximately the same period, toolmaking became more abstract and efficient and man began to draw pictures and use graphic records. By 50,000 B.C. the slow-talking Neanderthal race faded from the scene, and the fluent speakers commenced their ascent toward literacy.

Between the first abstract use of graphics, probably hatch marks denoting a moon calendar (Marshack, 1972), and the emergence of a true written language about forty-five thousand years intervene. The achievement was not a hasty one. Count markers, pictures, stylized pictures or pictographs, thence pictographs adapted syllabically to personal names—these appear to have been the building blocks that our ancestors experimented with over the centuries. The language historian Gelb (1952), however, makes a sharp distinction between these pre-written languages, which he calls semasiography, and true writing. The latter he insists must be independently accessible by a speaker of the language. The Egyptian hieroglyphs (5000 B.C.), like early Chinese (3500 B.C.), served to record ideas; they could remind the reader of what he knew was written, but they failed to offer accessibility by sound. Not until syllable representation was mastered could a true written language be achieved.

Gelb credits the Sumerians with this accomplishment and notes the fact that their particular language was well suited to this task. Its syllable structure was simple, consisting of a regular consonant-vowel-consonant pattern in which vowel changes served a functional role. A CV_1C pattern, for example, might be present tense, while a CV_2C pattern might signal past tense for that word. Given such an oral language, a limited number of symbols could represent sufficient sound properties to allow a reader to construe a novel text.

Syllabic characters were soon borrowed by the Egyptians, who used them both independently and in combination with their contentive hieroglyphic symbols. Worlds apart in China, contentive characters were combined to provide a phonetic representation which allowed independent access to text as well. Modern Chinese, much simplified in the complexity of character forms, preserves this combination of phonetic and contentive elements. Contrary to a lingering misinterpretation by many Europeans, modern Chinese is both a true and a highly efficient written language (see French, 1976, for example).

Our own alphabetic system for writing did not emerge until about 600 B.C., when syllabic characters were adapted to vowel representation by the Greeks. It was a brilliant stroke, well suited to the genius of that remarkable culture, but it was, like most inventions, also born of necessity. Unlike the neighboring Near Eastern languages, spoken Greek employed a complex syllable structure, just as does modern English. We use the patterns CV as in *ma*, CCV as in *try*, VCC as in *asp*, CCVCC as in *tryst*, and so on. The number of syllabic characters required to represent this variation would overwhelm the capacity of human memory. For the Greeks as for us a syllabary would not work.

The solution to the problem lay, of course, in adapting characters, i.e., the alphabet, to each phonemic constituent of spoken words. It is worthwhile to conjecture about how this insight was attained. Did some wild Hellenic perched upon a mountainside suddenly perceive the phonemic structure of speech and set it down in letters? Certainly none did that. Instead, the Greek people enjoyed centuries of intercourse with literate neighbors and learned from them how the words of their language were represented. Thereafter the concrete application of syllabic symbols to Greek words yielded a perceptible dissonance. Vowels required representation, and a limited set of symbols were borrowed and applied to that need.

Concept of Word and Phoneme Awareness

Children who learn an alphabetic language are not faced with the task of selecting a new set of letter symbols. These are given them directly. Still, one should expect that children will follow a concrete rather than an abstract route to phoneme awareness. If they do so, they must first discern "word" as a concrete unit to which letters apply. From thence the phonemic segments should emerge to consciousness quite as they must have done for the Greek inventors.

Contemporary research in written language acquisition paints a somewhat ambiguous picture of this sequence of events. One group of scholars tends to hold that children should first be taught phoneme segmentation in order to learn an alphabetic writing system. A second group argues that a knowledge of alphabet letters and a concept of written word are the primary steps from which phoneme awareness follows naturally. A clear account of these different conclusions is given by Morris (1983), who aligns himself firmly with the concept of word position. I am convinced he is correct to do so and that a contemplation of language history supports his view.

Of this much I am certain: Adults in nonliterate cultures do not have a clear concept of word as a concrete unit of speech (Malinowski, 1965). Illiterate adults fail phoneme discrimination tasks (Morais, et al. 1978). It is notoriously difficult to teach prereading children phoneme segmentation (Gibson & Levin, 1975). Preliterate children who know alphabet letters use them as syllabary symbols as they attempt to represent speech (Bissex, 1980). When children attain a concept of word, they represent phonemes with an accuracy that far exceeds the discriminate judgment of a naive though fully literate adult (Beers & Henderson, 1977; Read, 1975). These findings suggest forcibly that a concrete concept of word is the event that precipitates phoneme awareness.

I have come to believe that our ability as literate adults to perceive phonemes consciously has blinded us to the natural compatibility of spoken and written languages. It is this, too, that has disposed us to the notion that writing is a cypher to be decoded, and that reading is a skill that can be taught mechanically. This same perspective has led to the view that English, which is highly irregular in phoneme representation, is difficult to learn and ought to be reformed. When English is examined historically and compared to other efficient writing systems, a very different perspective of these issues is gained.

Language Comparison and Spelling Reform

No true written language has ever represented the phonemic structure of speech sounds exactly. Many languages operate by hint, or suggestion, providing the minimum of sound information that is necessary for access and no more. A significant weight of language representation in every written language is borne by contentive or meaning symbols. The early adaptations of syllabic cues by the Egyptians and Chinese attests to this phenomenon. In alphabetically "regular" written languages, however, the contentive functions of letter groups is obscured.

Modern Spanish is judged to be quite regular in letter-sound correspondence. Nonetheless, Spanish children commit spelling errors which are exactly comparable to those of kindergarteners learning to spell English (Temple, 1978). In addition, the progress of Spanish children from nonfluent to fluent oral reading and from a limited vocabulary to mastery of abstract terms does not differ from other literate cultures. I am forced to conclude from this that in Spanish, which is a relatively stable language derivationally, alphabetic regularity does not interfere with meaning representation. On the other hand, it is clear that when letter-sound correspondence does interfere with meaning representation, alphabetic regularity will bend to meaning's demand. Such has in fact been the case with English, whose spelling system has resisted the efforts of reformers for five hundred years. Written languages require a homeostatic balance between sound and meaning. They will not endure the hand of the tinker who would change them to a code.

Another way to observe this principle is to reflect on the course that was followed as a written language was developed by the Japanese. The syllable structure of Japanese is wonderfully simple, being composed, with a single exception, of the CV open pattern (Toyota, Subaru, for example). As a consequence it is possible to construct a nearly perfect phonetic rendering of Japanese with a forty-six syllable characters. Two such syllabaries have been adopted which are called the Katakana and Hiragana.

To those who feel concern about the irregular sound system of modern English, the apparent advantages of the Japanese syllabary must seem altogether ideal. Interestingly, however, the Japanese make only partial use of this phonetically regular system. They use the Hiragana to write function words, Katakana to write borrowed foreign words. For the rest, the contentive vocabulary, they use borrowed Chinese characters called Kanji. A repertory of about 1,700 of these meaning symbols is gradually learned by children over the elementary and high school years.

No one today will think that the Japanese people are backward and inefficient; to the contrary we know them to be paragons of forward-looking efficiency. Their written language reflects this posture. Contentive characters were borrowed because they were available, and they are learned and used because they provide an unambiguous and powerfully efficient written language for that culture.

A very similar pattern was followed by the Koreans, whose written language was formally constructed by linguists in the fifteenth century (Taylor, 1981). Unlike Japanese, Korean has a complex syllable structure. To adjust to this condition a phonemic alphabet was designed with letter elements that reflect the actual articulatory shape of the phoneme. These in turn were composed into syllable patterns. Thus Korean enjoys nearly perfect phoneme-grapheme regularity which the reader meets in chunked visual units. To this was then added some twelve hundred contentive characters which children learn over the school years.

Learning to Spell English

The analogy between these Eastern languages and the meaning-based spelling system of modern English should be apparent to all. Old English enjoyed considerable letter-sound regularity when the Roman alphabet was first applied to this German dialect. Over a period of about one thousand years foreign terms from Danish, French, Latin, and Greek were borrowed and intermixed with the Germanic base. Over the same period English spelling patterns fused to meaning and progressively sacrificed large segments of an earlier letter-sound consistency. Modern English requires such a compromise, for, as Bradley (1918) demonstrates, English spelling reform would necessitate a fundamental alteration of the spoken language itself. Spoken language, needless to say, cannot be changed by edict. Thus the resistance.

As a consequence of this amalgamation of languages, English has become difficult to learn to spell. Initially young children spell words phonetically, mapping each letter as closely as possible to the phonemic segments perceived in sequence for each word. The result is an interesting rendering which one can learn to read with practice but not easily or fluently, for it does not suit the spoken language. Not only are homophones undifferentiated, but strange homographs abound. When the same strategy is applied to an adult text, near total confusion results (see Figure 5-1). Children's initial strategy for spelling English

Figure 5–1

Phonetically Regular "Letter-Name" Spelling of "Jack Be Nimble" and Selected Adult Vocabulary

```
JAK BE NEBL, JAK BE KWEK
JAK JOP OVR THE KEDL STEK


          sign   =   SIN
        signal   =   SEGNL
 insignificant   =   ENSEGNEFAKAT
        resign   =   RAZIN

       propose   =   PRAPOZ
   proposition   =   PRIPAZESHN

        social   =   SOSHOL
       society   =   SOSIATE
```

Source: Henderson, E. H. (1984). *Teaching Spelling.* Boston, Mass.: Houghton Mifflin Company. Reprinted by permission of the publisher.

is as dissonant to the spoken language as was the application of a syllabary to Greek, not for want of sound representation but for meaning.

Fortunately, children do not have to reinvent a new system. English words are there to be examined as they are acquired. Children learn the patterns of syllable representation and the pattern-to-meaning plan that governs this spelling system. Time, of course, is required. It is a task that is accomplished over the school years, but in this English really does not differ from most other written languages. Certainly it is true that the incidence of error is troublesome to the English learner, but the source of that trouble lies more with the misunderstanding of our spelling system by adults than with children themselves. If we understood better what it was they were doing when they erred, we could credit their efforts and help them on their way. Ironically, most schoolteachers over the centuries have castigated children for misspelling, taught them systematically to distrust their natural discriminations, and to distrust the spelling system itself. Through such distractions we have compounded a problem that would otherwise answer itself quite naturally over time.

The Paradox of Literacy

Oral language, which has been almost fully mastered by the child of six or seven, is altogether sealed to introspection. Written language is overt, concrete, and fully open to inspection, but it is for the beginner a novelty. Learning to read thus demands the conjunction of a known behavior that is not directly knowable with a knowable behavior that is initially unknown. This is the paradox of literacy and it explains why we cannot tell a child how to read.

Adults do not differ from children in their want of direct knowledge about language. All that we know has been indirectly gained through the examination of written text and the application of abstract models. Psychologists, linguists, even brain physiologists are theory-driven in their quest for knowledge of an essentially inscrutable phenomenon. Nearly a century ago Huey (1908) termed reading "a miracle"; he was right to have done so and those conditions have not changed.

This is not to say, of course, that scientific search is futile or that what we have learned is nonsense. We have learned a great deal; we are approaching an understanding, but we have not yet arrived. Our knowledge is clearly limited and viable only as those limits are acknowledged. As things now stand, we cannot make reading happen artificially. We can, however, observe the process and facilitate it. In addition we can talk about language, and about reading and writing with children. But we can only do so as their experience with text gradually allows them to form some concept of these behaviors.

The key to understanding reading instruction is to recognize that the source of information is overt literate behavior and that no aspect of that behavior can be manipulated pedagogically until the learner has examined reading and writing and formed a functional concept of its office. Put bluntly, we must make reading happen if it is to be learned. That so simple a directive works, as well as being the only thing that will work, stems from the fact that written language is time-forged to resonate with spoken language. Children can learn to read because written language fits the tongue robustly.

Developmental Aspects of Learning to Read and Write

If children are not exposed to literate behavior at all, they will not learn to read and write. If, on the other hand, they are so exposed, if the model is there and they explore it, the likelihood is high that they will learn. Benjamin Franklin reports in his autobiography that he could not remember a time when he could not read. He was reared, as we know, in a printing shop.

Environment and Method

Many researchers today are exploring the childhood environment in various settings and attempting to describe what they term "literacy events" (Otto & Sulzby, 1981; Sulzby, 1983; Teale, 1978). They would concede, I think, that Franklin's circumstance was singularly rich in the experiences it provided with written language. I suspect, however, that the possibilities for a felicitous exposure to reading and writing are well-nigh infinite, and that the search for the ideal "parenting model," though interesting, is not really necessary. Exposure there must be, and an active exploring child as well. To know that these two conditions are essential is sufficient.

Regarding methods of instruction, I have grown increasingly catholic over the years. Gross deprivation is intolerable; beyond that there are certainly hundreds of ways to skin the reading cat. What clearly does make a difference, however, is whether parents and teachers understand what the child knows about written language and the steps and stages by which that knowledge elaborates to a mature literate competence. Only through such understanding can we avoid talking and acting at cross-purposes. As a consequence I pin my hope for improving literacy in English on that research which illuminates these developmental events and on those strategies for instruction which are guided by them.

A multiplicity of disciplines have contributed to this store of developmental knowledge about written language. No single scholar can hope to know these fully or be able to synthesize them perfectly for everyday use. In what follows I will attempt merely to unearth a few principles and sketch in those benchmark events that lead to reading achievement.

Language Acquisition

The literature of oral language development expanded rapidly during the sixties and seventies (Brown, 1973). The universality of the early babbling efforts, the adjustment of these articulations to the mother tongue, and the predicative quality of the first utterance at about one year of age are now widely recognized. Recognized also is the fact that the rapid acquisition of vocabulary and syntax in the ensuing years is cognitive behavior for which there is a unique genetic endowment (Chomsky, 1968; Lenneberg, 1967). In all cultures oral language is largely mastered by age four to seven.

In literate cultures formal reading instruction typically has begun at the close of the oral acquisition period—age four to seven. The tradition seems a sensible one, though it frequently clashes with parents' understandable desire that their child learn to read as soon as possible. Current work in the areas of oral language delay and childhood aphasia (Haber, 1980; Rapin & Allen, 1982) suggests strongly that a reasonably full command of language is necessary for learning to read. Language development that is late, though altogether normal, is almost invariably associated with difficulty in learning to read when instruction is arbitrarily set at age five or six.

I take it as a principle that formal reading instruction should be paced to the language competence of each child. To do so we will need to refine our screening tests for kindergarten and first grade so that language assessments are carefully made. Parents will need much education on this topic, and the administrative design of the primary grades will require careful readjustment.

The studies of oral language acquisition have also influenced our concept of how written language is learned. The notion that children come to kindergarten like blank slates on which the teacher must print letters has been challenged and found wanting. Gibson (1975) and her students, for example, have shown the early fascination that scribbling holds for children as young as a year and a half. Piaget and his colleagues have given close attention to the developmental characteristics of children's drawing and have derived therefrom a systematic account of human symbolizing (Ginsberg & Opper, 1969). These are matters of the greatest importance for an understanding of literacy.

Picture and Print Perception

Human beings are the only creatures who speak, and they are also the only ones who draw pictures, though it appears that some of the higher primates can recognize pictures. I have always found it interesting to observe that young children are initially uncertain about the two dimensionality of a simple illustration. While looking at a picture of a lamb, for example, they will suddenly flip the page over and show surprise at not seeing the other side of the figure (Henderson, 1976). In this quaint event we recognize that picture perception is a very complex activity and one that requires a good deal of experience. Learning to represent reality must precede the even more complex task of learning to represent speech. I take it as a principle that experience with picture books and drawing is a prerequisite for written language acquisition. The pedagogical implications of this principle are I think obvious.

About twenty years ago Geschwind (1974) reviewed a report by the French neurologist Dejerine in which a relatively pure case of dyslexia was described. The patient could identify pictures and geometric forms but not print. This phenomenon has since been recognized both in cases of specific brain injury and in congenitally dyslexic subjects (Henderson, 1981). There is in fact a vast difference between picture perception and print perception.

Print, whether in characters, syllabary symbols, or in alphabetic writing, represents spoken language, including its meaning components, abstractly. It does so by ordering graphic elements in sequenced units that correspond to those phonemic, syllabic, and morphemic units implicit in the speech stream. Written language achieves this featural compatibility by constraining these graphic units to a filled space which flows directionally and proportionately with the temporal flow of speech. In a grand sense the relationship is mathematical.

The significance of this condition for the learner is clear. First, there is no other earthly context for learning about print than print itself. This holds for every written language. Second, the constituents of print must be modeled for the learner as he or she inquires about their properties.

Specifically, if a child wonders how one goes about reading, the behavior must be modeled by speaking and pointing left to right across the line of text. If a child inquires about a particular unit, be it letter, or character, he must be shown how it is made. Because these are not pictures (a fact that the child is busy discovering) the sequence of strokes and relative size element to element must be demonstrated. Thus the seemingly simple task of "teaching children their letters" (which we do quite successfully in most cases) is, in fact, a profoundly complex event. It should be done with attention and care when the child is searching for understanding.

We must indeed wonder about the special capacities that human beings have in order to respond to these abstractions. The probable answer lies in the nature of space perception itself. We do not see in the natural world high-speed pictures frame by frame as the camera presents them to generate an illusion of reality. Instead we interpret the ever changing gradients of intersect that are recorded in ambient light as it falls about objects (J. Gibson, 1975). That we can identify the single frame picture at all is an artifact of a memory that can hold a fragment of visual data and a cognitive ability that can project meaning from these fragments.

It is this same remarkable ability that operates upon a systematic concatenation of graphic symbols and projects from these the temporal flow and form of speech. Reading thus is not at its base a high-speed linear match of letters to sounds or symbols to meanings. It is instead a resolution of abstract graphic relationships with a compatible set that hold for and define speech. We can read only because we have the motoric and mnemonic capacities to do so. The various analyses that we make of the written language surface are but crude approximations of the deeper event. They are not in themselves what the child must learn, but rather what the child must transcend in order to read.

Pedagogically, the critical point to recognize is that the primary data of written language knowledge are relational events which, if arrested in time and space, can but disintegrate into picture and noise. This is the deep reason why reading has to be modeled, be made to happen, if it is to be learned. Nor is this principle disconfirmed by the fact that children can and do learn to deal with letters, sounds, and words in isolation. Human beings can deal with static images. For print, however, their vital meaning lies in the spatial-relational plan from which they are abstracted. This meaning must be realized tacitly before an analytic scrutiny can avail any useful purpose. Thus children who "can't learn their letters" in most cases cannot do so because they do not yet know what letters mean.

Beginning to Write and Read

There is a fundamental bond between reading and writing, the production and recognition of text, both at the beginning phases of learning and throughout the full maturational process. This is not to deny that one can become a reasonably proficient reader and yet spell badly, or read a good deal and compose indifferently, or even spell well, identify words readily, and yet comprehend text poorly. Such variability of achievement is clearly possible though not perhaps desirable. The common base lies instead in that amalgam of motoric features that is the meaning of both.

Children perceive the world. They construct and elaborate symbols for its representation. They identify pictures and test their limits. Each behavior interacts with and nourishes the other. In a similar vein children comprehend that text is the stuff from which reading is done. They begin to learn the peculiar prosodic form of oral reading, its special syntactic structures, and the conventions of organized text. At this point children's principal mode of communication is drawing, but now they will attempt to write. What emerges typically is a scribble that is very different from the random strokes of the two-year-old. It shows direction and spatial delineation; it resembles cursive writing.

An anthropologist's observation of her three-year-old son pinpoints this interesting developmental event.

James has a new game of writing out a squiggly line of imitation writing, while sounding out to himself the syllables of a word. The first one was "he-li-cop-ter." I found this particularly interesting, because I had never tried to teach him that letters represented sounds, but only that letters represented meanings in words. (Carrier, 1984)

These writing attempts reflect what has been learned from an examination of print and from seeing adults write. These attempts exercise and extend this knowledge. They lead inevitably to the question "How do I write my name?", and, in our language, the quest for letters. To satisfy the information needed, alphabet blocks or pictured letters are not sufficient. The letter formation must be modeled for children, and they must attempt their construction. Only then may the picture of a letter affirm the effort. This interaction of production and recognition is essential.

As letters are learned and childrens' apprehension of text is further differentiated, their writing attempts change. Scribbles give way to letter and letter-like symbols. Orientation is usually not consistent, but direction, again in our language, moves toward the left to right order. At this stage many precocious children make the leap to syllabary writing. Letters are used singly as in R =

ARE, U = YOU. They are also used in combination without the vowel, DF = DEAF (Bissex, 1980). The strength of this plan as a strategy for representation is shown in the following curious transition. At the prereading stage the word *pink* is frequently spelled PNK. But when vowels are represented literally, as children do later, the spelling PEK is selected. In the first strategy the letter N is required. In the latter (because it is enfolded with the vowel) children deem it not needed and they leave it out.

These two distinct writing strategies are separated by the discovery of the word unit in text. This is the "concept of word" phenomenon researched by Morris and discussed earlier. At first children write syllabically and without word spaces. Afterwards they write alphabetically by letter name and in word units. The analogy to the Greek invention of alphabetic language is striking.

Certainly no one taught these children to spell *pink* PNK or PEK. In each there is evidence of natural sound discrimination. In the one the strategy is syllabic; in the other the strategy is alphabetic. Between these two attempt modes stands the discovery of word units as examinable objects. In effect, children *find* a better way to use alphabet symbols to map the *words* of their language.

English children, moreover, must find an even better way to spell English, and they do. The change of strategy that they make is necessary because their first alphabetic plan does not work efficiently for English. FED, for example, spells *fid, feed,* and *finned.* Children discover next that the vowel nucleus is spelled by pattern, with the vowel and what follows functioning as a unit. The evolution of this concept in memory for word features has now been clearly demonstrated by Invernizzi (1984). And so the process advances over the school years as meaning and derivational constraints are gradually learned and applied. Thus, word knowledge unfolds from crude scribblings and attention to cloth books to a full command of written language automated and ready to serve the purpose of young adults.

Tacit Knowledge and the Teaching Art

In one sense, children know perfectly well what they are trying to do as they learn to read and write. Their attempts are conscious attempts to write and spell, and they learn, and learn consciously the names and forms of the surface of these events. On the other hand, children do not have a conscious knowledge of the deeper sources of their understanding—of the strategies they employ or the steps and stages by which these advance to full competence. Knowledge of this kind is realized tacitly and can be brought to awareness only by adults who work backwards through theory and observation to construct its properties.

As a consequence, naive adults and children stand on a common ground in their apprehension of reading and writing. Common sense clings firmly to the surface, and it is at this surface level that most methodologies for instruction are advanced and defended. Teach them letters; teach them sounds; teach them words; teach them whole language. Each emphasis makes common sense and each will answer children's needs provided that reading and writing are demonstrated and attempted by the learner. Failure occurs only when methodological extremism destroys either the part or the whole or when a surface operation is demanded of a child before he or she can make sense of it.

Unfortunately there is a good deal of failure. We are not sufficiently sensitive to the developmental properties of written language acquisition. There is much forced instruction of letters and words before children are able to deal with them. There is a considerable neglect of word study in the middle and high school years. In many school systems today there is a shocking overemphasis upon "skills" which works to the detriment of actual reading and writing experience. Worst of all as failures mount, a naive public is ever more easily stirred to embrace yet another extreme solution advanced by some equally naive adventurer.

Fortunately, most teachers do care about their pupils. Teachers want children to learn, and teachers are often keen observers of children's learning. Thus teachers, time and again, do find sound ways to help children learn. Charles Hoole in 1656 had no theory of letter knowledge as we have today, but he did know and recommend that beginning reading instruction be paced to the abilities of different children (1966).

The traditional and conservative basal reading programs that have evolved over the past century are in the main a good approximation of the path that children follow as they learn to read and write. To be sure, these materials are easy to criticize on a variety of counts. They are too gaudy. They often lack taste. They are too prescriptive and claim an infallibility that they do not merit. They are too littered with skills and gimmicks, and over stuffed with right answers. They are deficient in the purposeful exercise of reading and writing that every learner requires. Still, they do reflect with considerable accuracy many empirical needs of teachers and children.

I dream of the day when all teachers may see beneath the surface of language learning. Then they will be able to use whatever materials are at hand and use them wisely. I also feel confident that as that day arrives, most teachers will be doing things with children that have been done for centuries. The only real difference will be that teachers will know when to do those things and why, and they will not give up so easily when children falter.

I have decided to close this essay with an account of beginning reading instruction that was presented to me twenty-five years ago by Russell Stauffer (1970). He recommended the use of group-dictated experience charts to demonstrate written language. The procedure was essentially the same as that followed by Flora Cook in the 1890's and thought by Huey (1908) to be remarkably sound. My paraphrase of Professor Stauffer's rationale will show that while my studies in the intervening years may have taught me a little that is new, they have also forced upon me the profoundest respect for what is old.

Paraphrase of Stauffer's Rationale

If story charts are dictated by the children about an experience the teacher has helped them examine, the sentence structure and the continuity of the account will show the degree to which the children have come to understand written English. First they are likely to dictate in single words and phrases; next come simple sentences, and finally a full report will emerge with a beginning, middle, and end. Such charts provide useful practice for children as they learn to order events to the form they will meet in books. We should not expect children to learn to read easily until they have attained a functional knowledge of the language to be negotiated. A collection of these charts over the weeks provides the teacher with a valuable language record of their pupils' progress.

Teachers should read these charts back to the children, pointing to each word as they do so. Then the teacher should encourage the children to choral-read the story. Finally individual children should be asked to attempt lines from the story and later the whole story by themselves.

As children do this supported rereading, the teachers must observe children's behavior carefully. At first they will depend fully on the teacher's voice. Later they will be able to follow the pointer with little voice support. When children first begin to read alone, they may begin the line correctly but then be unable to keep the pointing and reading together. That happens because they do not yet understand what the spaces are; that is, what words are in running text. One should not expect pupils to learn sight words before they know what words are.

At first children will be able to identify only the first and last word in a line and an occasional very salient word like *umbrella*. When, however, they are able to point and read consistently, they will be able to identify most of the words in the text when asked to do so. At first their response will be delayed as they reread the sentence to find the word that has been pointed to. Later they will be able to identify more and more words on an immediate basis. When they have attained this control of text, their sight vocabulary will begin to build rapidly and permanently.

Stauffer's ideas as paraphrased show a true mastery of reading pedagogy. He was not unaware of the complexity and essential miracle that must occur beneath the surface. But he knew with the strength of extended study and careful observation how to make reading happen. This knowledge freed him to concentrate upon another far more important issue—the purposes for which reading is done and the uses made of reading by responsible students. I dream also of a day when our citizens, too, will feel free to care more for the intellectual honesty and rigor of thought that is applied to reading than for the simple act of reading itself. We are equipped by nature to read if society permits it. The goal of education should be to see that we learn to use this gift wisely.

Chapter 6

The Visual Face of Experience and Language: A Metalinguistic Excursion

DON HOLDAWAY

Introduction

Research in the field of language acquisition, largely focused on the learning of spoken language, has illuminated many aspects of literacy learning in the past twenty years. However, the preoccupation with oral language learning may have obscured some questions arising from specifically *visual* aspects of reading and writing as they impinge upon early development. This paper attempts to define and explore some of these questions in the belief that they provide clues to many of the most intransigent problems in our attempts to understand and to teach reading and writing. We also face the responsibility of explaining consistent research findings which contradict common assumptions—findings such as the early preference for alphabetic or visual strategies over phonetic ones, and for the real simplicities which arise from wholeness and meaning-making rather than the false simplicities of fragmentation.

There are good reasons why such an undertaking is likely to prove difficult and confusing, involving as it does a fundamentally metalinguistic inquiry, but there is no question about its practical importance and urgency. Over the generations, and particularly in the past decade, the phonics vs. meaning debate has produced great harm and little light, debasing early reading materials and turning writing into one of the most arduous, threatening, and painful skills we ever learn. Both normal schooling and remedial intervention have been deeply deformed over the years, regardless of which way the pendulum has swung in the "Great Debate."

We seem to have lost the assured and sane insights which guide us as we support our infants in mastery of speech and many other complex developmental tasks. What are the peculiar relationships between oral and written language which account for our confusion and comparative failure in presenting reading and writing to young children as intelligible and rewarding human skills?

Visual Experience

We tend to image and organize our world in distinctively *visual* ways. This is so especially in modern Western scientific cultures, in which the dissecting of reality into things and their parts (rather than, say, feelings and actions) forms the dominant organization of experience. It would seem that our dependence on print has added a further visual dimension in disposing us to a *linear* presentation of thought, which is another visual form of organization. The computer takes this strategy of working with reality through linear, sequential, static bits a massive step forward. Although not obvious at first sight, this is a rationalization from our visual experience of the world. Such marvels as a symphony orchestra analyzed into digital terms make the original links with visual strategies rather too tenuous for ordinary understanding. What remains clear is the strategy of treating continuous change as though it were made up of static, timeless particles. (The cinematograph film and modern TV are forms of the strategy open to mundane intelligence.)

When we look at something closely our eyes make a marvelously rapid excursion of fixations all over the subject in order to build a view of it. When engaged in *seeing* something, it is easy to stop at a detail and explore it more carefully. It is easy also to point out the detail to someone else, or to talk about it without anyone being confused as to what is being talked about. The relationship between part and whole is easily distinguishable at the *surface* of our perception.

Furthermore, when we analyze things in our strongly visual, scientific manner into even smaller bits, we put *time* to one side for the convenience of the moment in order to concentrate better on space and dimension. The image or the picture or the thing does not go away; it remains stable, and in a most important way *available*. (When we have the appropriate explanatory purpose, of course, we bring time back into the picture and begin to think in terms of "causes," but our most immediate everyday visual experiences are those of recognition.) My point is that visual perception often plays with "things" as if the time dimension were not important. If we make our perception of something as, let's say, a ball, the ball remains in attention at pleasure as a ball—not part of a ball, not a fleeting image of a ball, not the memory of a ball, not something whose edges get mixed up with other visual experience before the brain—but simply a ball. Hence, we can refer to the visual perception of the world in comparative terms as both static and stable.

Auditory Experience

When we *hear* something, or attempt to hold an image or memory of it in mind, we are in a very different position. (Notice how in this, my first sentence about auditory perception, two visual metaphors, "image" and "position," are used quite naturally—there is no comparable auditory term available to use in "placing" what is being talked about.) If we hear, and maybe recognize, a tune, we need to hear several different notes in relationship to each other before we know what it is we have heard. It is impossible to point to a detail and study or talk about it in any simple way. In the first place, each part, meaningless in itself, disappears immediately. It is retrievable only in memory, not in actual perception. Each of these fleeting parts is like an eye-fixation in vision, except that it lacks stability—it has gone.

To compensate for this remarkable difference, we *listen* in small time chunks, each of which has an internal complexity and organization which gives it "shape." Note here our use of the term "phrase" in both music and oral language—one of the few purely auditory concepts in our ordinary language. Now the interesting thing about the entity we call "a phrase," or that we call an oral "word," is the presence of internal complexity—several very different sound items go together to make up a phrase or a word. Even a note does not clearly identify itself in splendid isolation and without reference to other tones. (This is not to say that a note cannot be scientifically analyzed in terms of its own internal complexity. We are talking here about ordinary perception and memory, not about the actual composition of entities in reality.)

We engage in auditory perception with a very different grasp of cognitive organization than is available to us in seeing and touching. Auditory perception is subject to a number of differences vital to our present concerns in the teaching of reading and writing. Because our behavior at the perceptual level is so deeply habituated, these differences are subtle and difficult to analyze, but they may be crucial to an understanding of relationships between spoken and written language, and to a clarification of metalinguistic concerns.

Fundamental Differences Between Visual and Auditory Perception

Perceptual Availability

Auditory perception lacks the moment-by-moment stability of vision. Some of its parts must be brought into the perceived whole from immediate short-term memory—they are not available to continued experience as in vision. We could call this "the problem of perceptual availability."

As an example of possible relevance in early literacy learning, take the difficulty experienced by young children in holding in mind and analyzing the bits or phonemes in a spoken word (see Downing; Yaden: this volume). They "know" the phonemes in an undeniable and functionally effective way, but the analysis and identification of parts presents a problem distinctive in both kind and difficulty from analyzing visual experience. They can see letters and study their order, and even associate a sound with each visual form; but just what exactly does that have to do with the sounds in words, which cannot be so studied?

Holistic Perception

Auditory experiences cannot be handled statically as is possible for the elements of vision. Auditory perception is necessarily more constructive in terms of perceiving the relationship of parts within a phrase. In auditory perception of reality, then, we tend to organize data more holistically into intelligible "processes" or "events" or "acts" rather than into the shape of "things." The relationship of the different and contrasting parts determines, much more fundamentally than in vision, the nature of what we are perceiving. A note can never be a tune in the way that a visually perceived leg may be either part of a table or a thing in itself. Because of the way perceived sound tends to get put together into something with a beginning, a "shape" and an end (or "home note") spread in time from past to present, let's call this necessary wholeness of auditory perceptions "event awareness" or "holistic perception." An example of relevance to early literacy here might be the difficulty experienced by many children in recognizing the whole, real word as being anything like their attempts to put the static parts together by the mysterious process of "blending"—which is, of course, another visual metaphor.

The most serious difficulties, however, arise in interpreting just what it is that written language means: Does it "mean" the sounds of speech—those static bits—or does it "mean" in the same way as spoken language "means the world"? The distinction may be clear enough to us, but the whole rationale that is put to young children must be highly ambiguous for many of them. Is their task to see *this* meaning or *that* meaning? However it is put to them, they are attempting to manipulate their auditory experience in ways which are both strange to them and out of harmony with the nature of auditory experience.

Time and Entity Differences

Spoken words are as real as things, but by comparison they are very strange and slippery entities, hard to grasp and hold, and we have difficulty in giving them the clear parameters of things. An aspect of this difference is the fact that an auditory event occurs fundamentally in the time dimension rather than the space dimension. The entities of auditory experience are quite differently organized and bounded. What are the boundaries of a spoken word, a tune, or even a cough? Unlike the objects accessible in visual or tactile perception, the "things" or entities or auditory experience lack physical shape and mass. Yet we talk about them in a language designed for a world of "things." We could refer to this as the "time and entity" problem. (In this respect, the comparative assurance of visual learning is also enhanced by tactile and kinesthetic confirmations. "Meanings" and their speech tags, on the other hand, float in an infuriatingly undifferentiated time warp which has no crisp edges.)

It is much more difficult for young children to grasp the concept "word" as applied to speech than it is for them to grasp the concept as applied to print. Spoken words cannot be held in front of attention, cannot be studied, cannot be pointed to in any direct way. Furthermore, the auditory junctures between words in normal speech are subtle and blurred. This is no easy insight for a child. There is good reason to believe, and sound research to support, the notion (Clay, 1972; Doake, 1981) that experience with visual language or print in the very early years may facilitate understanding of this subtle concept, "word" (see Sulzby, this volume).

The Visual Metaphor: Talking of Sounds as if They Were Things

These differences are reflected in language and thought by the fact that we must normally use the dominant vocabulary of visual experience to talk or think about auditory experience. We are dominated by a visual and tactile view of the world as distinctively "thingy" and our language reflects that bias even when dealing with entities which lack "thinginess," such as sounds and feelings or sensations. The central linguistic principle of *naming* reflects our visual experience of "things," whether or not what we name has the character of a thing. For much of our discourse about auditory experience we are reduced to using spatial metaphors, such as a "soft voice" or a "full-bodied sound."

Not that this is an insurmountable problem, provided we are aware of it. We make some sort of sense in talking about our feelings, thoughts, and sensations through a similar use of visual metaphor—we "under-stand" and have "in-sight." But the danger with auditory experience is that because it is a part of sensory experience, we are likely to treat it quite inappropriately as actually having the characteristics of "thinginess," or be impatient with young children because they cannot so directly and unambiguously determine the boundaries or parts of spoken words as they can with things, nor talk about them with the same clarity. Furthermore, many an apparently simple and innocuous explanation or request made to young children begins to look suspicious in the light of this problem. How do you spell the second syllable of "enough"?

This matter will be taken up more fully below, but it could be noted at this point that putting parts together into auditory wholes is quite unlike either visual experience or anything that young children have attempted to do in making sense of the world before facing print. It requires holding auditory memories which have disappeared from immediate experience in short-term memory until they cohere. It is likely that the processes by which we make sense of a flow of sound in time are very different from putting blocks together to build a castle. The metaphors of "word-building" and the procedures of "blending" derive from visual strategies and are clearly inappropriate to understanding auditory input. The strategies we actually use of following syntactic and semantic probabilities, of attending to the context in which the speaking occurs, of watching speakers and listening to their general intonations, are essential to auditory interpretation.

The Double Symbolic Confusion

As if all this were not enough, we have in language all the additional complexities of dealing with symbols rather than with things. Here again, we would be advised not to treat symbols as if they are things in the classic visual mode. (One of the classic problems of philosophy from Plato to Wittgenstein revolves around this confusion—it is a perennial mind-teaser.)

Spoken words represent reality in purely conventional ways, and words are in no way like what they refer to—"a rose by any other name." Written symbols stand in a strange, ambivalent relationship to their spoken counterparts. Not only are they expressed in a different mode—linear and spatial—but they may be regarded as either representing spoken words themselves *or* representing the same meanings as spoken language represents. We speak to children at different times implying one sense of "means" or the other, without always being clear about *what* we mean. Many children must be deeply confused about their purposes in using written language. During crucial, early stages of development they often lack any clear criterion for judging whether or not "reading" or "writing" has been achieved.

Implications for the Teaching of Phonics

In teaching the phonetic principle, it should be clear that we are asking children to find an appropriate way of associating two different classes of phenomena: (a) *Sounds in a time series:* Here "beginning" means, "What I heard first and now remember"; "end" means, "What I last heard and remember as being last"; and "After" means "heard later than" etc. (b) *Letters in a conventional left to right (or right to left) space series:* Letters can be seen and not heard; they are always silent. "First" means "first on the left after the space," and last means, "last on the right before the space".

To match these two modally different series, it is first necessary to recognize, and be able to isolate from the flow of speech, the contrastive elements which merge and flow so rapidly and automatically across the tongue. Such competence is *implicit* in the ability to speak. However, it is difficult to become *explicitly* aware of those contrasts. Solution of such problems as these requires the development of "metalinguistic awareness," or an ability to reflect upon linguistic processes rather than simply use them. This is both a developmental and an instructional problem. It is developmental in that reflection on self, reversible operation, and abstraction develop slowly and late. It is instructional in that an attempt to promote such development from an adult, visual postliterate view of the world, instead of a child-oriented, initially auditory, and preliterate view, may be counterproductive for many children.

Several of the most seductive fallacies about literacy spring from misconceptions about these relationships. Most of the public and many of the profession conceive of reading as recognizing and saying spoken words—a strange twisting of a responsive skill properly related in function to listening. How do we know that *listening* has been achieved? Certainly not by checking off the speaking of each word, let alone each phoneme. The alphabetic strategy has proved startlingly successful in ways we cannot begin to analyze here, but the disarming simplicity of the system, taken at face value, suggests dangerous practical applications. ("Dangerous" is not an overstatement when we consider the new, disabling "diseases," such as dyslexia and "learning disability," which have become an accepted part of modern schooling.)

The Alphabetic Strategy

These critical differences between visual and auditory modes of perception are complex and far-reaching. They deserve to be worked through in some detail even at the risk of some initial confusion in attempting to achieve clarity. What are the relationships between parts of spoken language and parts of written language, and how are the perceptual strategies of constructing intelligible wholes in the two modes to be reconciled during learning? Are we justified in thinking that the sounds of language, treated as though they were building blocks out in the spatial dimension, can be associated with letters in the uncomplicated way suggested by the metaphor? Or does the brain find some special problems in crossing such an important modal barrier to make the association? Much that we know of the confusions of young children suggest that this is the case. Psycholinguistic and developmental studies of written language processes suggest that special strategies calling on syntactic and semantic awareness are required to make the leap across the gap. These strategies display the holistic characteristics of auditory perception; they use meaning, expectation, and cross-reference to glue the fleeting bits of passing sound into intelligible perceptions. It almost seems as though in learning to read and write it is necessary to compensate for the fractionating techniques of visual perception by adding the glutinous strategies of auditory experience.

We need to deal with these misconceptions frontally, not because they are centrally important issues in literacy development, but because of the way they dominate both instructional and public assumption. What seems on the surface a wonderfully simple and logical system of representing language turns out to be very different at the level of process or function—like a minefield under a beautifully peaceful terrain.

The Process of Integration

In alphabetic writing it looks as though graphemes stand in a simple relationship to phonemes, or ought to, and that to know and apply these relationships is to read and write. However, even if a perfectly phonetic script were designed, in the manner of ITA, we are still unable to explain reading and writing, or render them significantly more easy to learn. True, the grapheme/phoneme strategy has enormous power, and applies readily to any language, but it will not yield linguistic outcomes if it is taken literally. We may be able to decipher written language, even a foreign language, painfully after a fashion without being able to make sense of it: i.e., to read it. The most dangerous fallacy about literacy is to confuse deciphering with reading, or copying with writing. (For a fine statement, see Ferreiro & Teberosky, 1982, pp. 272–86.)

Alphabetic writing provides the potential for linguistic action, but it is not language, just as the phonemes of speech provide the potential for oral language, but segmented provide a nonlinguistic sequence of noises. We would no sooner teach our babies the segmented phonemes of our language than fly. Certainly, spoken language depends on an implicit classification of contrastive speech sounds, but they function only through the integrating strategies of *time*. They become the internal structure and complexity of phrase, tune, word, or sentence. Only then are they linguistic. From the phonemic flow the brain produces suprasegmental forms.

Normal visual experience also depends on a time-spanning, integrative strategy which gives a picture or a scene its integrity, but we are not aware of *doing* this. In an important sense we must perceive alphabetical language as *picture*, i.e., using the visual, integrative strategy which puts many eye-fixations together into a meaningful whole *in terms of our conceptual organization of the world.*

Responding to letter-sound relationships in a conscious and complete way would entail a linear matching of a temporally ordered sequence of sounds with a spatially ordered sequence of letters, somehow producing identifiable words. That is something which the brain simply cannot do at normal linguistic speed, or anywhere near it. Since we *are* able to read, the brain must do something else.

A prime fallacy in this respect is to assume that knowing the likely sound relationship of each letter gives access to words in print. In fact, it is quite possible to know the sound associations of every letter and be quite unable to handle the sequencing metaphor (i.e., the phoneme last heard in speech appears on the "right" of the phoneme previously heard). Failure in this ticklish application of spatial knowledge often leads to a judgment that the pupil "does not know his sounds." He is then likely to be subjected to a reteaching of the *static* associations without informed concern for how the associations actually work. In such cases, it is not surprising that a child who is being retaught something he already knows but can find no use for, begins to believe that he must have something terribly wrong with him. In desperation, he is likely to attempt alternatives at random until even what was originally learned becomes hopelessly confused. Such a child will produce the strange and apparently irrational responses characterized as the classic symptoms of dyslexia.

Even more difficult to explain in rational terms is that the associations of letter and sound are taught in phonics as if they operated only in one direction—from visual to auditory, from letter to sound. "Look at the letters, say the sounds, and blend them together." Reason suggests that associations are not one-way roads. In fact, there is increasing evidence to suggest, especially in the recent upsurge of fine research into the development of writing, that associating from sounds in words heard or thought to letters that are expected in print may be (a) developmentally prior (e.g. Read, 1975); (b) intrinsically easier or more "natural"—moving from the known to the unknown, rather than vice versa as in standard phonics (Holdaway, 1979, pp. 94–6); (c) more consistent with what we know about the actual processes of problem-solving in reading and writing (e.g. Smith, 1978, pp. 134–150); and (d) of more immediate utility for writing (e.g. Temple, Nathan & Burris, 1982, pp. 59–83). A whole word can be held in the mind with ease because that is the strategy used in auditory perception, but the mangled pieces of a word being "sounded" rapidly dissipate, become confused, or refuse to cohere–because that is an inappropriate visual strategy.

The Process of Naming

Children come to print knowing the spoken language, although they can't express its rules or segment it with any ease. It is the written forms and their principles of organization which are unknown. As they approach print in early childhood, they are likely to try to discover in it a manipulable *object* nature; i.e., they quite naturally begin by using visual strategies to discover how the "things" of print operate (Ferreiro & Teberosky, 1982). This is a fruitful strategy in important respects. It induces exploratory activity, which is basic to all complex learning. It also serves to keep the search focused on meaning or significance—the integrative strategy is kept constantly active.

As children become increasingly aware of relationships between language and print, many of their problems center around strategies for segmenting and matching—words, phrases, syllables, letters as words—relating quantity of print to amount said. Not surprisingly from our earlier analysis, determining juncture, or finding the sharp, "thingy" edges, forms a central problem. Where do the things of print begin and end? Young children are unlikely to discover relationships at the phonemic level either easily or early since they are unaware of them in any explicit way in speaking or listening. They will rather (a) use focal letters as symbols for words or syllables; (b) use their strong grasp of syntax as a possible clue to organization; (c) use their semantic knowledge of language and the world to predict possibilities; (d) use elements of prosody or intonation as segmenting clues; and (e) use important clues from pictures in concert with any of the above (the parameters between print and pictures take time to establish).

In a literate environment, they are likely to hit upon the phonetic connection without direct instruction, and by a route that seems irrational to us but is eminently logical in these modal terms. They begin to recognize letters as distinctive visual forms and learn their conventional names as things. (Only "things" have names, and sounds are *not* "things." (This is what we called earlier "the entity difference.") They now have a marvelous resource to the sound structure of language, and they begin to apply these names as phonic-like operators in both writing and reading. They do this without abandoning earlier strategies, especially the crucial, meaning-driven intention which coordinates perception in integrative ways.

There has been much speculation as to why alphabetic learning normally precedes, and somehow facilitates, phonetic learning developmentally. And because this is thought to be a clumsy, inefficient, erroneous, or even stupid strategy, instructional measures are often taken to discourage it. This, too, is a fallacy in principle and a mistake in practice. Visual print makes language "available" and the marvel of this is not lost on children, who go directly for the obvious strategy. The phonetic connection is much more subtle and obscure—it is not "available." By following the "thingy" nature of print, the children introduce themselves to the phonetic principle, via a visual strategy, in the most cognitively direct way. To name is to grasp.

The Fiction of Permanence

The alphabetic system represents one of the most advanced and abstract of the dissecting strategies of visual organization. The strategy allows the putting aside of time at convenience, so that things can be studied and measured as if they were not changing and in flux.[1] This works with tremendous power in the physical sciences, where things can be "frozen" into a passing millisecond, in contrast with the flux of passing time which gravely limits oral language as observable. The still camera is a central symbol of this strategy. It works less powerfully as the central concern of knowledge becomes one of processes, like growing, acting, intending, feeling, or thinking. (A good example in the physical sciences would be weather forecasting, which has something of the complexity of cognitive and linguistic processes, and of human behavior generally.)

What has become the central strategy of modern knowledge involves the most convenient fiction of all fictions—"Let's pretend that time has stopped." This cutting of reality into static bits stands behind our linear formats of mathematics, formal logic, and, of course preeminently, the computer. Strangely, language itself embodies all of these "as/if" strategies by the overriding linguistic principle of *naming,* which produces a convenient fiction of permanence. After all, who *is* "President Reagan" as a permanent entity? However, it is not until language is visualized in writing that these potentialities are powerfully developed.

In alphabetic writing, each *letter,* rather than each word or name, is regarded as an irreducible entity, like the original concept of an atom. These bits have no internal structure or complexity. Unlike a tune or a cadence or a spoken word they have no internal relationships, no form or structure. That is the convenient and powerful myth which makes visible language in its linear, alphabetic form possible. Now, as we saw earlier, this internal formlessness is unnatural to auditory experience in which the internal relationships of what is perceived often define *what* is being perceived. Young children have no experience of perceptions which have been reduced or abstracted into ultimately contrastive bits, such as letters. Indeed, even mature writers and readers seldom regard letters in this elemental way, although they have the competence to do so, and their competence represents a powerful stratagem when *properly* applied. Normally, however, they attend to complex wholes which have been integrated by the brain from the suggestively spaced and punctuated bits.

The actual difficulties experienced by young children, especially under the influence of naive and oversimplified instruction, strongly support the contention that the great modal leap from auditory to visual language presents predictable problems. It is not surprising that an awareness of the phonetic principle in written language develops rather late in the development of literacy, and that early confusion is rather the rule than the exception (see Downing; Yaden, this volume). For to understand phonics is to become explicitly aware of a very sophisticated stratagem by which the passing moments of continuous and flowing speech are cut up into "things" and laid on paper in linear file. Flexibility viewed by a reading brain, this file of bits forms a generally adequate bank of cues from which language may be recreated. By no stretch of the imagination is the print *language*; it is merely the *potential* for language—a highly suggestive husk.

It is not surprising that the brain must provide much of the information from its own experience of language and the world in order to make the system yield sense. Successful *early* experience in literacy depends even more crucially on integrative and constructive strategies than does mature reading and writing. The "inside-out" strategy so clearly documented in reading (e.g., by Ken and Yetta Goodman, and by Frank Smith) makes its appearance at the earliest stages of emergent literacy (Ferreiro & Teberosky, 1982, pp. 148–9; 263–86). Unless we help children to see how the known is manifested in the unknown, we break a very general and fundamental educational principle.

Natural vs. Artificial Learning

The common practice of explaining the difficulties of reading and writing in terms of their artificiality in comparison with spoken language draws on many plausible arguments. The ancient character of speech; its mastery during infancy; the late appearance of literacy historically; the need for schools and instruction; the complex etiologies suggested for literacy failure: all of these suggest the comparative artificiality of reading and writing.

Considering that language depends on a system of quite arbitrary symbols, there is an important sense in which all language is marvelously artificial, as there is a sense in regarding *all* human culture as artificial. If we are to use the term "natural" for any human behavior, we must use it to imply the distinctively human and enabling activities such as language and the learning of language without which the species would not *be* human. Certainly, even historically recent skills, such as riding a bicycle or using a computer language such as LOGO, appear to be mastered most easily and efficiently by the same principles as apply in learning to speak (Papert, 1980). That kind of learning may properly be called "natural." Recent research of the ethnographic kind demonstrates unequivocally that literacy *may* be learned in this natural manner (e.g. Clark, 1970; Doake, 1981; Taylor, 1983).

It would appear that the differences between learning spoken and written language may be accounted for most correctly and usefully in terms of their modal differences than in terms of a spurious unnaturalness or artificiality. Certainly, there are distinct differences, and learning will be different in terms of the characteristic strategies of visual knowledge. But there is no evidence to suggest that the principles of "natural" developmental learning do not apply to literacy, or will not operate efficiently if applied. Nor is there evidence that the teaching of literacy needs to be as curiously artificial as it has become, particularly in the last decade or more. The tendency for artificiality in literacy instruction appears to spring from two sources: (a) the temptations to formalism and abstraction generic to the visual mode, and mistakenly applied to a process based on symbolic meanings, and (b) the institutional impulse of organized schooling towards artificiality—an impulse which has virtually nothing to do with learning.

"Natural learning," as eminently displayed in the mastery of speech, encompasses the great complexity of language, cognitively, emotionally, and neurologically. Just as natural health and healing are to be preferred to the organic clumsiness of drugs in dealing with the chemical balance of the body, so the inducement to natural learning is to be preferred to the clumsiness of direct instruction. We cannot perfectly explain how we learn or engage in language, but the brain can be trusted to do it well when human curiosity and interactiveness are sustained in natural ways (Goodman and Goodman, 1978; Butler, 1980; Taylor, 1983; Holdaway, 1983).

Bonuses for Written Language Deriving from the Visual Mode

Up to this point our comparison of visual and auditory modes has largely emphasized the type of difficulty likely to be experienced by young children in moving from familiarity with the auditory mode into the visual processing of their linguistic competence. However, this is only half the story. It now becomes necessary to consider more closely the remarkable new powers brought to language by adapting it to the world of vision—by making it possible to use the powerful strategies of "thinginess" not available in the manipulation of auditory entities. If young children can be turned on to these new powers of the visual language and find significance in using its outstanding strategies, new sources of motivation and satisfaction become available in solving what we have seen to be the intrinsic difficulties of the task in the early stages.

Bonuses for the Reader—Availability and Concreteness

Visual experience normally leaves a permanent track or trace behind it, like the LOGO turtle: it is reversible in a Piagetian sense. In geological terms, something of the track remains even after four and a half billion years. Auditory experience leaves no trace or trail: it is like the LOGO turtle in the PENUP mode. Visual tracks can be seen as *linear in time*. Auditory experience is encompassed and swallowed by time, and is therefore linear only as it remains in *memory*, not as it leaves its mark on the world. Written language actualizes the linear potential of oral language, so that it becomes open to cognitive reversibility with startling results in the history of knowledge. The only scientific and nonspeculative knowledge we have of the origins or early forms of language rest on the permanence of early *written* language—there may be more than a million years of un-retrievable history of oral language.

The outstanding advantages of visual operations spring from the qualities of "thinginess" which are not shared by the fleeting and disappearing character of auditory realities. Visual experience is perceptually *available*. A picture does not disappear as we study it but remains stable and accessible, whether it is viewed as a whole or in terms of its parts—the entire thing is there in front of the eyes for as long as necessary. Print shares all the advantages of this perceptual stability.

Auditory experience can provide nothing quite comparable. Speech comes and is gone. Print transcends. True, the strategies we learn as listeners compensate in some measure for the maddening invisibility and impermanence of sound. (Most of our arguments and miseries center around exactly who said what, when, and in what manner.) Auditory perception, dominated as it is by passing time, depends on holding sensory impressions alight in experience (after they have gone) long enough for them to cohere into meaningful wholes. The brain also helps to form the perception by anticipation or prediction—it straddles time in both directions. As we have already seen, this strategy must be moved over into written language if a genuinely *linguistic* experience is to be accomplished.

In film, and in the operation of the TV screen, visual technology has achieved control over time, change, and movement by an analogous strategy.[2] In film, the static bits of visual experience are preserved and then represented at a speed which establishes the illusion of movement. (Of course, a somewhat similar strategy of cutting current into wave or frequency bits is used in radio and telephone, but the principle is not so accessible to ordinary understanding because it is *not* visual.) In the TV screen, rather closer in principle to auditory strategy, the luminescent rear surface of the screen acts as a short term memory and holds each tiny electron impulse alight after it has passed on across the surface. The integrity or wholeness of the picture, its stability, arises from the afterglow.

The leap from still to moving pictures was received as some sort of magical marvel. The leap from competence in oral language to competence in written language also constitutes a marvel of transformation, more than equal in scope, although not nearly so sensational. Pages of print don't reflect triumph over movement and time in their surface form. Normally produced in the stark, maximum contrast of black and white that the eye often finds painful, print itself could almost be said to be ugly. Indeed, there is evidence that some children experiencing reading difficulty greatly prefer moderate contrast (Mears, 1980). Print represents the analytical and reductionist visual strategy without apology. The illuminated manuscripts of the Middle Ages are interesting in this respect. Little wonder that bare pages of print repel and mystify children who don't know how to function. But the new *processes* they make possible—writing and reading—embody all the power of visual strategies as expressed in science and technology.

Print overcomes the major limitation of auditory language by making it perceptually "available" and therefore capable of fulfilling distinctively visual strategies, such as those of verification, formal analysis, correction, the display of structure and its reorganization, dissemination, and what I will call the "work of perfecting" at both the level of form and of detail. The assimilation of visual strategies into the function of spoken language also provide new and powerful ways of doing old things, such as the examination and expression of self. How powerful writing can be in this respect, especially for children, if expression is warmly valued (Graves, 1983).

Even in very early childhood the impact of visual language can begin to fulfill some of these wonder functions: the comforting *concreteness* of books; the feeling of *permanence* in returning to a favorite story which will be perfectly preserved by the miracle of print over time; the fascination of structure in story, poem, and song; the awareness of signs as both message and thing; the power of a pencil; the feeling of self in completing the first notes and letters; the emulative model of parent as powerfully literate and full of skill. . . . In these and in many other ways, written language may make an early call (Butler, 1980).

If we are to use and enrich these positive early experiences, which so nicely begin to straddle the two modes of perception, we need to understand where children are coming from and where they are going to in terms of perceptual strategies. As indicated above in our analysis of phonics teaching, we also need to understand the dominance of exclusively visual strategies, visual metaphors and visual explanations over the forms of early instruction, which veer dangerously towards the visual temptations of abstraction, analysis, and formalism.

On the other hand, children *naturally* explore print in visual or object ways, and feel its special powers. Print is more open to the interactive and manipulative style of early developmental learning and offers cognitive returns to children by being approached in that way. But this is a very different matter from the abstract attempt of early instruction to associate letter "things" with sound "nonthings," which invites deep confusion because it does *not* maximize visual advantages but rather sacrifices them immediately to the disadvantages of auditory process.

Unfortunately, this is a complex matter and a contentious one. The power of visual strategies at the adult level of abstract, reversible operations is so obvious that instruction tends to go overboard in that direction. From a developmental point of view, however, it is the outstanding facility that visual language provides for *concrete operations* which should be maximized in emergent literacy. As has been noted in earlier references, this perspective is being increasingly supported by developmental, psycholinguistic, and ethnographic research. The problem has no simple answer such as that suggested by a naive and abstract visualism. Linguistically, the familiar, known world of young children is auditory, but they maintain cognitive clarity by an uncompromising closeness between concrete operations in the real world and their language development. Their style of learning is concrete and demands "hands-on" interaction with the real world. Our task is to help them see a reflection of those forms of intelligibility in the visual display of print.

Bonuses for the Writer—Orchestrating Meaning

The writer, in comparison with the speaker, has much to gain from visual language, and this has often been celebrated by authors down the ages. However, the process of writing is not easy, the learning of writing appears unduly difficult, and the number of active writers seems surprisingly small. Furthermore, the value placed on the pursuit of writing over the past hundred years demands some explanation. In comparison with the attention given to reading, research has neglected writing to a puzzling degree until quite recently (see Dyson, this volume). Indeed, perhaps the most destructive modern fallacy about literacy has been the separation of reading and writing, the glorifying of the former, and the downgrading of the latter.

Schooling has seen to it that a large proportion of the community will avoid writing at almost any cost for the rest of their lives. Writing is used as a major form of punishment in most schools and seems to be adequately painful for these punitive purposes from an early age. Writers get themselves tortured and imprisoned around the world more readily than any other group. Many of those who *must* write for a living avoid the opportunities that writing provides for clarity and precision by producing mountains of print in the form of bureaucratic nonsense, offensive officialese, and obfuscating, quasi-academic jargon. As Bormuth (1978) pointed out, much of the print which dominates our lives requires unnecessarily sophisticated reading skills—even to determine that it is not even worth decoding. Why has there been so little concern to improve the general clarity of writing? Why do all of these paradoxes center around writing?

We have no technical invention which models the processes of writing as closely as film or TV embody the integrative processes of reading. This is one of those human skills which the most sophisticated computer balks at.[3] What near miracle is required to translate language meanings into contrastive bits on a page? Even when a computer is ultimately programmed to isolate and record the phonemes of speech, this will not constitute writing. The really *linguistic* task will have been carried out by the speaker.

In many central respects writing constitutes a visual form of speaking, although it has distinctive features of its own. It uses essentially the same lexicon, the same syntax, and somewhat the same prosody as speaking. It uses a very small and economic set of contrasts, as does speaking, in the segmentation of the language, and in this respect models the principle which is developed to its limit in the binary system of the computer. However, print presents to the human brain opportunities to leapfrog the grapheme-by-grapheme presentation, which the brain would find absolutely unmanageable. Actual perception groups the linear data of letters and spaces into unique wholes of a startlingly varied kind. These complex perceptions are analogous to the patterns of speech in word, phrase, idiom, sentence, and prosody. They have holistic form.

This integrative strategy opens all the economies of perception in spoken language to written language, including the perception of whole words and phrases through distinctive features—what Frank Smith (1978) calls "feature analysis."

More than this, however, it gives immediate access to meanings through print forms; i.e., without analysis into sound. This is not to say that reading does not usually entail a strong component of sound (just as literate people are often aware of written forms as they speak and listen). It would be remarkable if this were not so, considering the cognitive content shared by the two processes. In mature writing, it also appears to be normal for the writer often to think meanings and produce letters without direct access to sounds.

What is absent from the computer and its printer is the orchestrating facility of the brain of the writer, whether aspects of the total performance are conscious and deliberate or preconscious and automatic. The brain, conducting its own performance and extemporizing without a score, considers *sense units* in the context of the text and responds to syntactic rules. It deals with whole lexical items, segments the ordered items within an overriding prosody, and spins them out through pen or keyboard at a rate defying conscious control—at least, control of every letter or segment. At the level of producing the bits or segments in fluent order, the brain of the writer closely patterns the automaticity of a speaker, who produces speech without a thought for phonemes.

Perhaps we should clarify this "orchestrating" metaphor. An inexplicable characteristic of thought is the awareness of self as thinker, and we all know that conscious awareness of self. It seems, however, that the brain has meticulous oversight of even the unconscious or automatic understructure of a skill. The brain acts as a sort of overseer, rather like the author writing in the third person who expresses a "God's-eye-view" of the world. Virtuoso playing of the piano displays the same sort of powerful oversight and control. The pianist (at least as expressed by Dudley Moore in an interview for *The Body in Question*) does not consciously determine the action and touch of each finger, but from an awareness as overseer of the entire execution, unmistakably "controls" them. (Now this introduces the crucial matter of feedback, which we have ignored in the scope of this paper. See Holdaway, 1979, pp. 94–8.) The elusive function of the brain as "overseer" may be captured in the metaphor of orchestration.

In accounting for reading within the framework of visual strategies, we found it necessary to postulate that the integrative, meaning-directed processes of listening were necessary to proper linguistic functioning; i.e., a time-preserving extension of the visual mode, similar to that achieved by TV, seemed logically necessary for reading. In writing, also, some transfer of strategy from the original auditory mode seems to be called for if we are to explain how a writer can possibly operate. Another way of stating this condition would be to say that it is of the nature of language, although physically segmented into bits, to operate out of integrative strategies whether in spoken or written modes. The perception or prediction of meaningful wholes, which is so much more natural to the auditory mode, remains an enabling condition for reading and writing.

A problem of the *learning* writer is to achieve some degree of automaticity at *every level of development*. In oral language learning this is provided by two undeniably dominant strategies: (a) approximating, and (b) chaining of highly familiar sequences. Invented spelling provides the possibility of using these same strategies for writing as the complexities of the detail are gradually mastered.

Perhaps, in abandoning this metalinguistic exercise, I may be permitted a personal anecdote, not as evidence but as exemplification.

After more than thirty years of two-finger pecking or bashing of typewriters, I was induced by the gentleness of the keyboard of my new electronic typewriter and computer to undertake the learning of touch-typing. This was my first radical relearning of a language skill, and I was convinced that the undertaking would be painful, drill-bound, and time-consuming, especially considering the unlearning of very skilled bad habits which would be involved. In fact, the process was fascinating and in the main enjoyable. Following a surprisingly brief period of learning to locate most keys by kinesthetic means (with the aid of computerized instruction), the pleasure of creating real text sustained me into a development of automaticity so rapid that I was hardly able to track its stages.

One of the many insights about language performance which was strongly confirmed by this process was the indirect way in which automaticity developed. If I tried to think where a key was located, in all probability I missed it. If I relaxed and trusted my fingers, they were almost invariably right. In defiance of assumptions about being careful, "trying hard," and giving conscious control to the task, I found such self-consciousness counterproductive. As soon as I became taken up and lost in what I was writing, automaticity developed rapidly. To find control at the level of detail (i.e., at a level of so-called "subskills") you must lose it. Of course, you lose it to a higher level—to the "overseer role" of the brain. The nervous system seems to be its own person in this way: if it is trusted, it learns and performs; if it is doubted and harried by an overbearing master, it mis-operates, or to use the phrase which children understand so well today, it "mucks up." The resultant behavior of the brain is bizarre and unpredictable.

The task of language learning is not dominantly one of learning to distinguish the bits and pieces which characterize its set of symbols at the surface level, nor to produce them as acceptable calligraphy. The task is rather to master the strategies of integration and orchestration under the direction of meaning and function. It is necessary to learn the bits and pieces, and to learn them with great automaticity. Paradoxically, when approached from a strongly visual point of view, they are best learned when they are least noticed in a self-conscious manner, i.e., when self-consciousness is linguistically engaged with meanings. They do, of course, have an interest to us in themselves, and our awareness of them, or their availability to consciousness from time to time is necessary to performance (just as the ability to modify the touch of a finger is from time to time necessary to the pianist). But this is a complex matter in its own right, and beyond our current scope. For our purposes at this point, it is only necessary to note that this type of control is not generated or learned by passing through a previous stage in which every detail is deliberately manipulated. In language, that is an impossibility, despite the advice usually given to young readers and writers—"Be careful!"

Conclusion

The Visual Impact of Print

Print is enlarging its hold on ordinary life, despite, or in collusion with, TV. The ordinary world of advertising, commerce, and leisure gains our attention by color, enlargement, and design in print. The school has always been slow to reflect the society that supports it. Seldom until recently have the black and white dullness of pencil, pen, and chalk been relieved by the physical pleasure of print that advertising has exploited.

Especially with very young children who lack fine muscle coordination, large, bold print and color may facilitate control of eye and hand, while assisting to capture visual attention at the same time. Spoken language lacks a tactile content, and its kinesthetic relationships in speech production are often left undeveloped. Written language, although it lacks the strong tactile alliance of most visual experience, has clear possibilities for kinesthetic experience. If enlarged print is used, the kinesthetic qualities of large body movement may be associated with reading and writing. There is also a social meaning in the enlarged print of signs and advertisements which tend to be supportively cradled in their real world social context—they *belong.*

Some very effective and beautiful presentations of print for children have been designed by Bill Martin, Jr. and his team (1972). In use, these formats have proven extremely effective in associating visual pleasure with the deadly formalism of print as object. The procedures of warm, communal teaching which have grown up around "big books" have also taken advantage of these factors of large body movement, visual impact, and social satisfaction in early literacy (Park, 1982; Holdaway, 1983).

Visual Analogies—Naive and Sophisticated

Written language, and particularly the act of writing, offers a temptation to become self-conscious about mechanics. We talk about the "mechanics of reading" or the "mechanics of writing"; but we seldom talk about the "mechanics of speaking" and virtually never about the "mechanics of listening." The mechanical metaphor is a compelling visual stratagem which has proved enormously powerful since the time of Descartes, but it can be highly distorting when naively applied to human perception, cognition, and language learning.

The suspicion is that a naive or superficial or literal response to the visualness of written language overwhelms us with inappropriate strategies and teaching methods. Its letters regarded as the "things" of print, its permanence, its easy correctibility, its identities which lack tolerance for variation, its compellingly binary distinctions of right and wrong—indeed, its apparent invitation to be quasi-scientific, make misleadingly desiccating suggestions about how to proceed linguistically.

Visible language can best be understood in terms of that higher-order, visual strategy embodied in film and TV. By adding the time dimension in the presentation of movement, film and TV conquered the intrinsically static nature of analysis which is so open to the visual mode and so closed to the auditory mode. In this way, what we have called "thinginess" is transcended, and we are transported into the living world of action and event. The wholeness of which we are aware in our immediate perception of the world and of language depends on *internal relationships within* the subjects of experience, whereas mechanical entities are understood in terms of *external relationships alone* in order to render them accessible to mathematical and logical operations in which internal relationships are systematically irrelevant.

Although the sensational accomplishments of science spring directly from visible language, and would dissolve without it, perhaps the outstanding triumph of writing has been the enabling of self-consciousness in the proper sense. "Self" is not an awareness of all the petty bits of response which the brain so blithely handles at an automatic level. Above all, print represents a marvel of integration, a continuity of experience and personal history, and an intention to *mean*— for we are all linguistic. It is in the embodiment of these intricacies that the visual accessibility of print displays its distinctive and intrinsic power. This is the face of visible language which can be *looked at* with awe as transcending the impalpable passingness of sound. And it has the integrity of a face because it is directly open to meaning through the integrative strategy lifted from speech.

Notes

[1] Scientists are quite self-conscious about this strategy of "freezing" a moment in reality. D. P. McKenzie in his article "The Earth's Mantle," writes:

> The familiar map of the world is therefore a snapshot of dynamic processes that have their origins in the mantle. The snapshot does not, however, reveal much about the deeper circulation. (*Scientific American*, September, 1983, p. 67)

An attempt to use the same strategy in accounting for the reading process was made by Gough (1978) in an article entitled "One Second of Reading." The dynamic data did not render itself particularly amenable to this statement.

[2] An interesting scientific metaphor is provided by Jean Francheteau in an article "The Oceanic Crust:"

> Mapping techniques that enable geologists to identify the position of these transverse features (tectonic plates) can therefore serve as the basis for reconstructing the history of the plates, by a method analogous to projecting a reel of motion-picture film in reverse. (*Scientific American*, September, 1983, p. 114)

[3] How is it that the human brain can recognize the letter A in any of its many forms (surely an elementary reading task) when the computer boggles at the task? The new directions in artificial intelligence represented by Douglas Hofstadter (*Godel, Escher, Bach: An Eternal Golden Braid*, Basic Books, 1980) throws light on the complexity of the simplest linguistic processes. In teaching, we have no alternative but to trust the enormous complexity of the young brain. Instruction, like the computer, can never completely mirror that creative complexity as Skinner would have us believe.

Section 3

Metalinguistic Awareness and Reading Ability: Experimental Investigations of Causal Connections

Chapter 7

The Influence of Spellings on Speech: Are Alveolar Flaps /d/ or /t/?

LINNEA C. EHRI

LEE S. WILCE

When do children acquire the idea that their language is comprised of a sequence of discrete sounds? Very likely, most children pick up this metalinguistic notion when they learn to read. Figuring out that phonemes are strung together to form language is unlikely with only an acoustic model and with no special instruction, since there are no boundaries separating phonemes in speech. In contrast, this is just how printed language is organized. The subunits (letters) representing sounds are discrete, separate, and sequentially ordered. Prior to reading instruction, there is little reason for children to pay much attention to the phonetic structure of their speech, since this has little functional value. In contrast, acquiring metalinguistic awareness of phonetic units has much adaptive value when children begin learning to read, since print maps speech at a phonetic level.

In previous papers (Ehri, 1984, 1985) we have reviewed evidence indicating that printed language works various effects on spoken language competencies. Learning to read and spell shapes children's conception of the sound structure of words (Barton, Miller & Macken, 1980). Illiterates have much greater difficulty analyzing words into phonetic constituents than people who have learned to read (Morais, Cary, Alegria, & Bertelson, 1979). Research on children's invented spellings reveals instances where print experiences alter learners' analyses of segments in speech (Beers & Henderson, 1977; Ehri, 1984; Read, 1971, 1975; Skousen, 1982). Whereas novices analyze preconsonantal nasals such as in "bump" and "tent" as a single nasalized vowel phoneme, experienced spellers consider the vowel and the nasal to be two separate phonemes. Whereas novices consider the initial consonant blend in "truck" to be one affricated sound /č/, mature spellers analyze it as two sounds /t/ and /r/. In addition, printed language has been found to influence the way speakers pronounce words (Reder, 1981). It may be responsible for teaching dialect speakers Standard English pronunciations (Desberg, Elliott, & Marsh, 1980). It performs a mnemonic function, enhancing speakers' memory for spoken words and nonsense syllables (Ehri & Wilce, 1979; Sales, Haber & Cole, 1969). Knowing the spellings of words influences a listener's speed to decide whether sounds heard are nonsense or real words (Jakimik & Cole, 1980) and to decide whether pairs of spoken words rhyme (Seidenberg & Tanenhaus, 1979). Interestingly, having a written orthography appears to inhibit phonetic drift; that is, change over time in the way words are pronounced in a community of speakers (Bright, 1960; Bright & Ramanujan, 1962; Gelb, 1952).

Two processes are thought to mold children's metalinguistic awareness of phonemes when they learn to read and spell: (a) learning how the general print-speech mapping system works, and (b) learning the spellings of specific words. The first process teaches children phonetic regularities of the general system; for example, that preconsonantal nasals and vowels are separate sound segments. The second process teaches learners about the phonetic structure of particular words (Kerek, 1976). This is a result of the way that word spellings are thought to be retained in memory, by being interpreted as symbols for sounds detected in pronunciations (Ehri, 1980). Because spellings sit in memory as visual symbols for sounds in words, they continue to influence spoken language processes involving those words even after the spellings have been learned.

An experiment was performed to demonstrate directly that learning word spellings shapes children's conceptualization of sounds in the words (Ehri & Wilce, 1980). It was reasoned that if when spellings are stored in memory, letters are interpreted as symbols for sounds, then some variation ought to be apparent in learners' conceptualization of the phonemic structure of words depending upon how the words are spelled and which sounds are represented by letters. For example, the spelling of "pitch" should cause readers to think it has four phonemes including /t/, whereas the spelling of "rich" should suggest only three phonemes, with no /t/. In this experiment, fourth graders practiced reading five pseudo-words. Half of the spellings included letters symbolizing extra sounds, while the other half did not (i.e., Banyu—banu; drowl—drol; simpty—simty; tadge—taj; zitch—zich; extra sounds underlined). The words were pronounced identically. After the reading task, subjects segmented the words in phonemes by positioning counters in a row, one for each sound. Results confirmed predictions. Subjects who had seen the extra letters were the only ones who found these extra sounds in their segmentations.

The purpose of the present study was to obtain further evidence that acquisition of spellings influences spoken language development in children. Of interest here was the development of children's perception of intervocalic alveolar flaps, which lie in stressed syllables between two vowels (e.g., middle, little). Although the flap phoneme is acoustically closer to /d/, it is sometimes spelled T and sometimes D. We reasoned that learned spellings may lead speakers to believe that the "true" sound in the word is the one specified in its spelling. In previous studies (Read, 1971, 1975; Beers and Henderson, 1977), a developmental sequence has been noticed in children's invented spellings of flaps. Initially, beginners select the letter *D* based on acoustic criteria. Subsequently, as they experience conventional *T* as well as *D* spellings of words and realize that /t/ is closely related to the flap sound, they may shift to *T* in their spellings. Finally, as their memory for the spellings of specific words grows, they choose *T* or *D* according to the spelling.

The present study was intended to obtain more direct evidence for these three phases of development. First, second and fourth graders listened to several familiar words containing intervocalic flaps and judged whether the flap sound in each was /t/ or /d/. It was expected that the youngest readers would perceive flaps as /d/, more experienced beginning readers might shift to perceiving flaps as /t/, while the most mature readers would perceive flaps as /d/ or /t/ according to spellings.

Two types of words containing flaps were selected for the study, derived words with roots ending unambiguously in /d/ or /t/ but pronounced with an intervocalic flap because of an inflectional suffix (e.g., ho<u>tt</u>er, sa<u>dd</u>er), and nonderived words containing flaps in the root word (e.g., le<u>tt</u>er, la<u>dd</u>er). Sentences accompanied all words to insure that the roots were recognized semantically. It was reasoned that if lexical processing involves analyzing a word into its morphemic constituents, then derived flaps should be judged accurately by all subjects, young as well as old, regardless of their knowledge of spellings, since the flap is unambiguously represented in the root. This prediction follows from lexical representation theories (Chomsky and Halle, 1968; N. Chomsky, 1970; C. Chomsky, 1970) in which phonetic forms of words are processed by deriving deep structure morphemic units each with its underlying phonological form. Alternatively, if sounds in words are processed more superficially, then judgments for derived and nonderived forms should exhibit the same error patterns.

Experiment 1

Subjects

The subjects were middle-class native English-speaking children in first grade ($N = 17$, mean age 82.2 months), second grade ($N = 20$, mean age 92.4 months), and fourth grade ($N = 33$, mean age 115.7 months). There were 31 males and 39 females.

Materials

Derived and nonderived sets of words containing medial alveolar flaps were selected. These are listed in Table 7–1. There were 10 derived words (5 with flaps spelled *T*, 5 spelled *D*), and 20 nonderived words (11 with flaps spelled *T*, 9 spelled *D*). Sentences depicting the meanings of the words were created (e.g., "I wrote a *letter* to my Grandma"). These were randomized and recorded on audiotape. For each item, the sentence was uttered, then the target word was pronounced alone. The speaker was careful to produce a flap rather than a clear /d/ or /t/ in her pronunciation of each target word on the tape.

Table 7–1

Proportion of Incorrect Responses Across Grades for Each Word

Words	First (N = 17)	Second (N = 20)	Fourth (N = 33)	Mean
Derived (T)				
sitting	35%	20%	11%	
hottest	41%	30%	8%	
smarter	53%	35%	11%	
fatter	59%	25%	8%	
writing	71%	45%	22%	
Mean	51.8%	31.0%	12.0%	31.6%
Derived (D)				
reading	0%	0%	0%	
riding	6%	0%	0%	
harder	6%	0%	0%	
sadder	23%	10%	8%	
maddest	29%	5%	5%	
Mean	12.8%	3.0%	2.6%	6.1%
Nonderived (T)				
cotton	12%	5%	0%	
little	18%	5%	8%	
center	23%	20%	5%	
rattle	41%	60%	32%	
party	47%	15%	11%	
pretty	47%	10%	5%	
spaghetti	59%	25%	13%	
pattern	65%	50%	24%	
sweater	71%	45%	24%	
letter	76%	40%	8%	
attic	82%	60%	40%	
Mean	49.2%	30.4%	15.4%	31.7%
Nonderived (D)				
wonder	0%	0%	0%	
sudden	12%	5%	3%	
modern	18%	10%	3%	
odor	18%	15%	5%	
meadow	23%	0%	5%	
already	35%	0%	3%	
needle	35%	15%	0%	
ladder	35%	30%	8%	
middle	41%	20%	8%	
Mean	24.1%	10.6%	3.9%	12.9%

Source: Ehri, L. C. (1984). How orthography alters spoken language competencies in children's learning to read and spell. In J. Downing & R. Valtin (eds.), *Language awareness and learning to read*. New York: Springer-Verlag. Reprinted by permission.

Procedures

Children were tested individually. They were told they would hear some familiar words, each spelled with a T or a D in the middle. Their task was to "say the word carefully and then tell me whether you think it has a T or a D sound in the middle." After practicing with two unambiguous examples of medial /d/ and /t/ sounds ("Sundays," "between"), they judged the 30 target words. They responded by naming the letter T or D. Because all subjects had undergone at least some reading instruction, they were familiar with the idea that letters stand for phonetic units and so understood that they were to identify letters that symbolized the sounds /t/ and /d/, not the sounds "tee" and "dee." If they inquired whether they were supposed to be identifying letters in spellings or sounds, they were told to attend to sounds.

Results

To determine whether older children judged the flaps according to their spellings more frequently than younger children, performances across grade levels were compared. The proportions of incorrect judgments occurring at each grade for each word are reported in Table 7–1. Developmental patterns are clearly present. First graders made more errors than second graders on 15 out of 16 T-flap word spellings, and on 12 out of 14 D-flap spellings. According to a matched-pair sign test, both differences are significant ($p<.01$). Second graders made more errors than fourth graders on 15 out of 16 T-spelled flaps ($p<.01$) and on 7 out of 14 D-spelled flaps ($p>.05$). According to matched-pair sign tests, the former but not the latter difference is significant. These data indicate that children's judgments of flap sounds become more like the sounds represented in spellings as they grow older, presumably because they are acquiring familiarity with spellings which shape their conceptualization of the sounds.

The reason for weaker effects in the case of D-spelled flaps was that acoustic cues were influencing choices and boosting scores for these words. To determine whether such a response bias was operating, erroneous responses were examined. Our criterion for identifying bias was whether at least 67% of a subject's errors favored one letter choice. Only the responses of subjects making more than four errors were considered (i.e., 50% of the sample). Results confirmed that a bias to judge sounds acoustically as /d/ was operating in the majority of the subjects (83%). A much smaller proportion (14% or 5 out of 35 subjects) exhibited a /t/ bias, all but one of these subjects being first graders. Only one subject exhibited no bias. Detection of a /t/ bias in younger subjects constitutes some evidence for a transitional phase of development in which children shift from primary use of /d/ to /t/ in their perception of alveolar flaps. The small number of subjects may mean either that the phenomenon occurs infrequently or that it lasts for only a short time.

Performances across word classes were compared to determine whether flaps in derived forms were judged more accurately than flaps in nonderived forms. Based on lexical representation theory, it was expected that fewer errors would occur with derived forms (e.g., "writing") because subjects would recognize the phonological identity of the root word (e.g., "write") and its final unambiguous sound. In this comparison, attention was limited to *T*-spelled flaps, since a response bias to guess /d/ obscures the meaning of correct scores for *D*-spelled words. From values in Table 7–1, it is apparent that contrary to expectations, the mean proportions of errors for derived and nonderived *T*-words were almost identical: 31.6% vs. 31.7%. This pattern was verified in the scores of individual subjects. Among children making any errors on *T*-words ($N = 58$), the pattern of a smaller proportion of errors for derived than nonderived words was evident in the responses of only 46% of the subjects which is no greater than chance ($p > .05$). These results fail to support the lexical representation hypothesis. Apparently children did not spontaneously analyze morphemic roots when they heard inflected words.

Discussion

To summarize, results of the present study were consistent with the hypothesis that learning spellings shapes metalinguistic beliefs about sounds. Older subjects more familiar with correct spellings made fewer errors than younger subjects. Also, erroneous responses were more often perceived as /d/ than /t/, indicating that acoustic cues were used when spellings were unfamiliar. The possibility that beginners would shift temporarily to a /t/ bias in their judgments received some support: 25% of the first graders favored /t/ in their erroneous responses. However, the majority of first graders and all of the second graders favored /d/. Response patterns did not support the lexical representation hypothesis. Subjects were not any more accurate in judging inflected than uninflected words spelled with *T*. This indicates that they were not deriving root phonological forms to make their judgments.

Although results are suggestive, the present study has several weaknesses limiting its conclusions. First, the evidence presented is correlational and hence insufficient to support the causal inference that spellings shape learner's perception of sounds. Second, there was no direct verification that knowledge of spellings was superior for words judged correctly. Third, the task may have biased subjects to consider spellings in making their judgments, since they responded by naming letter symbols for the sounds they heard in words.

Experiment 2

A second experiment was conducted to show more directly that learning spellings influences subjects' metalinguistic perception of flap sounds. The study was designed to insure that in making judgments, subjects analyzed sounds rather than letters. Second graders were selected. The experimental group was taught to read a set of words containing medial flaps spelled with *D* and *T*, while the control group heard and pronounced the words but never saw spellings. Then both groups were given a rhyme judgment task to assess whether experimentals perceived flap sounds according to spellings, whereas controls judged the sounds acoustically as /d/. In order to minimize the influence of letters on sound judgments, the rhyme task was conducted with pictures. Subjects were taught to remove and pronounce the first syllable of target words so that the flap consonant was the terminal phoneme of the syllable (e.g., "party"—"part"). This was in order to force subjects to resolve the flap as /t/ or /d/. Then they decided which of two picture names (e.g., "heart" or "yard") rhymed with the syllable, and they pointed to the correct picture. It was this choice that revealed their conception of the flap as /t/ or /d/. Components of this task were practiced first with several nontarget words until it was clear that subjects understood what to do. They then judged rhymes for target words. At the end, a spelling production test was given to verify that experimental subjects knew target word spellings better than control subjects.

Subjects

The subjects were 18 second graders from a middle-class elementary school, 8 females, 10 males, mean age 89.9 months. Subjects were matched according to scores on the Slosson (1963) word reading test and a 22-item spelling test, and pair members were assigned randomly, one to the experimental group, one to the control group. There were 4 males and 5 females in each group.

Materials

The 12 target words containing medial alveolar flaps, half spelled D, half spelled T, are listed in Table 7–2. Flaps were created in three of the words by adding inflections to root forms (e.g., "cheating"). Flaps in the other words were part of the root word. Meaningful sentences containing the words were written, for example, "Would you like to have a fancy gold Cadillac for a car?" Also, pairs of picturable nouns rhyming with the flap-terminal syllables were selected, one noun rhyming with a final /t/, the other a final /d/ pronunciation. For example, the rhyming nouns selected for the first syllable of "Cadillac" were "dad" and "hat." These pairs are listed in Table 7–2.

Additional materials were developed for the purpose of teaching subjects to perform the rhyming task before they were given the target words to judge. This preliminary instructional phase was conducted with 27 nontarget words. First, 17 monosyllabic words all ending in D or T were judged with the seven pairs of pictures to be employed later with target word syllables. Next, 10 multisyllabic words were presented to teach segmentation and judgment (e.g., upwards, weasle, rifle, struggle). The critical syllables to be segmented and judged (see underlined letters) all ended in sounds other than /d/ or /t/ to avoid biasing subjects in their subsequent judgment of target words. Picture rhymes for these practice syllables were "cup-tub," "piece-keys," "knife-hive," "sock-dog," "duck-bug."

Table 7–2

Target Words and Number of Correct Response
Rhymes in Each Training Group (Maximum Correct = 9)

Target Words[a]	Response Rhymes[b]	Groups Experimental (Read)	Control (Pronounce)	Differences
Flap Spelled T:				
Gretel	jet-bed	9	4	+5
meteor	feet-seed	8	3	+5
glitter	mitt-kid	8	5	+3
attic	hat-dad	7	4	+3
notice	boat-road	8	6	+2
cheating	feet-seed	9	7	+2
	Mean	8.2	4.8	+3.4
Flap Spelled D:				
Cadillac	dad-hat	7	3	+4
huddle	mud-nut	8	8	0
pedigree	bed-jet	8	6	+2
modify	rod-pot	8	8	0
shredding	bed-jet	9	9	0
forbidden	kid-mitt	8	6	+2
	Mean	8.0	6.7	+1.3

Source: Ehri, L. C. (1984). How orthography alters spoken language competencies in children's learning to read and spell. In J. Downing & R. Valtin (eds.), Language awareness and learning to read. New York: Springer-Verlag. Reprinted by permission.

Note: There were 9 subjects in each group.

[a] Flap-terminal syllable is underlined.

[b] Response which rhymes with flap-terminal syllable is listed first.

Procedures

Training was conducted with individual subjects. On Day 1, the target words were practiced. Experimental subjects read each word, named its letters, and heard the word in a sentence on a tape recorder. Two test trials followed where the same procedure was repeated except that subjects recalled the sentences. Control subjects performed similar study and test trial activities but they were never shown spellings.

On Day 2, subjects' conceptualization of the flaps in these words was tested with the rhyme selection task. Procedures were identical for both groups. First, subjects were taught to name 12 pairs of pictures. Next, subjects learned to judge which of two picture names rhymed with a designated word. Subjects named the two pictures (e.g., road, boat); they heard the to-be-judged word (e.g., goat) pronounced and defined (e.g., goat: The goat eats grass); they repeated the word and pronounced it with each picture name to decide which pair rhymed (e.g., goat-road; goat-boat). Subjects practiced making judgments with 17 monosyllabic words and then with 10 multisyllabic words (e.g., buckle, private). In the latter case, the experimenter first taught subjects to segment and pronounce the initial syllables of the words (e.g., buck-, priv-) before they judged the rhymes. Practice items that were incorrect were corrected and repeated at the end of the trial until correct. If subjects failed to segment the syllable correctly, they were prompted to "say a little bit more" or "say a little bit less" until the correct syllable length was achieved. This corrective step always preceded the rhyme judgment.

When the rhyming task had been mastered, subjects were given the 12 target words to judge. For each item, subjects first named the pair of pictures; next they listened to the target word on a tape recorder, repeated the word, segmented and pronounced the first syllable (the second syllable in "forbidden"); finally, they repeated the syllable with each picture name and judged which pair rhymed by pointing to that picture. Correct syllable pronunciations were always prompted before the rhyme was judged. The experimenter never pronounced target words or syllables for subjects. The words were always presented on a tape recorder and the syllables were always elicited through prompting. The position of the correct picture (top or bottom) was varied across trials. The target word rhyming task was administered twice in succession to check on the consistency of subjects' judgments. The words were presented in a different order each time.

At the end, a spelling task was given to measure subjects' knowledge of target words. They listened to the words on tape, repeated each, and wrote it.

Results

Subjects were matched according to reading and spelling scores, and pair members were assigned randomly, one to the experimental (Read) group, one to the control (Pronounce) group. From the mean values reported in Table 7–3, it is apparent that the groups did not differ significantly in their ability to read or spell words. Further evidence that the groups were comparable is found in scores on the training tasks. As evident in Table 7–3, the groups performed similarly in recalling sentences containing the target words, in segmenting syllables from multisyllabic words, and in judging correct word-picture rhymes on practice items. It might be noted that very few errors occurred on the latter two measures, indicating that subjects did not have trouble learning components of the rhyme judgment task. Also, errors were few on the syllable segmentation post-test (see Table 7–3), indicating that subjects did not have trouble extracting flap-terminal syllables from target words.

To determine whether learning the spellings of words influenced how children conceptualized the medial flap phonemes, as /t/ or /d/, the number of picture choices that rhymed with spellings of the flap-terminal syllables in target words was counted for each subject, and scores were subjected to an analysis of variance. The independent variables were: word learning condition (read vs. pronounce words); flap spelling (T vs. D); test trial (1st vs. 2nd). The latter two variables were repeated measures. Results revealed a significant main effect of

Table 7–3

Mean Performances of Read and Pronounce Groups on Pretest and Post-test Measures

Measures	Read	Pronounce	Difference	Test Statistic[a]
Pretests				
Word Identification	99.1	99.2	−0.1	<1 n.s.
Word Spelling (22 max)	13.2	14.0	−0.8	−1.50 n.s.
Training				
Memory for Sentences (12 max)	9.1	10.9	−1.8	−2.03 n.s.
Rhyme Choice Errors (27 max)	0.7	1.1	−.4	−1.16 n.s.
Syllable Segment. Errors (10 max)	2.9	3.2	−.3	<1 n.s.
Post-test (Target Words)				
Rhyme Choice: -T (6 max)	5.6	3.3	+2.3	
Rhyme Choice: -D (6 max)	5.2	4.4	+0.8	
Mean	5.4	3.9	+1.5	23.00[c]
Rhyme Choice Consistency (12 max)	10.9	10.6	+0.3	<1 n.s.
Syllable Segment. Errors (12 max)	1.2	1.0	+0.2	<1 n.s.
Spelling: T/D Letters (12 max)	10.1	7.7	+2.4	3.05[c]
Spelling: Words Correct (12 max)	3.7	1.6	+2.1	2.13[b]

[a] Matched-pair t-test values with $df = 8$ in all cases except Post-Test Rhyme Choice, which is F-value with $df = 1,8$.

[b] $p < .05$ (one-tailed test)

[c] $p < .05$ (two-tailed test)

condition. Means and the F-value are given in Table 7–3. Subjects who read the words selected more picture names which rhymed with flap spellings than did subjects who did not see spellings. This supports the hypothesis that spellings shape subjects' conceptualization of flap sounds. No other main effects or interactions were significant in this analysis (all $ps > .05$).

Since there were only two possible answers in the rhyme task, subjects would be expected to get about half of the items correct by chance. To identify the number of subjects in each group performing significantly above chance, the binomial test was applied ($p < .019$ that as many as 10 out of 12 judgments would be correct given that the probability of a correct response $= \frac{1}{2}$). With this criterion, 7 out of 9 subjects in the Read group scored above chance, whereas only 3 out of 9 subjects in the Pronounce group performed above chance. These results are consistent with those above indicating that exposure to spellings influenced metalinguistic awareness of sounds.

Subjects' ability to spell the target words was checked. Matched-pair t-tests confirmed that the group who read the words knew the spellings better than the control group. Means are presented in Table 7–3.

To determine whether subjects exhibited either a /t/ or a /d/ response bias in the rhyme selection task (i.e., bias criterion: at least 67% of their errors favored one letter), the proportions of errors which involved each letter choice were calculated. Only subjects making more than three errors on Trial 1 were included (i.e., 2 Read subjects, 6 Pronounce subjects—all those performing at chance level). Results revealed a /t/ bias in responses of the two Read subjects but a /d/ bias in the responses of 4 out of 6 Pronounce subjects. (One Pronounce subject showed a /t/ bias, the other no bias.) This constitutes some evidence that experience with T spellings of flaps may produce a transitional shift to the perception of flaps as /t/.

To verify that the superiority of the Read over the Pronounce condition held for the majority of words as well as subject pairs, the number of correct choices was tallied for each word in the two conditions. Values reported in Table 7–2 reveal that the Read group outperformed the Pronounce group on every T-spelled flap. In contrast, among D-spelled flaps, the pattern of more correct responses by the Read group held for only half of the words, most likely because scores in the Pronounce group were boosted by a /d/ bias.

Results in Table 7–2 help to rule out an alternative interpretation for present findings, the possibility that Experimental subjects were judging rhymes according to spelling similarity of the vowel-consonant segment in the two words rather than phonetic perceptual similarity. Vowels in three of the flap-terminal syllables were spelled differently from vowels in their response rhymes: meteor-feet, cheating-feet, notice-boat. However, the pattern favoring experimentals over controls was no less evident for these items than for the others.

Four of the target words contained root words ending in an unambiguous /t/ or /d/: notice, cheating, shredding, and forbidden. It was reasoned that if subjects analyze words morphemically, then they should select correct rhymes for these words more often than for the other words. Only the responses of subjects in the Pronounce group were considered, since Read subjects' judgments were very accurate and were influenced by spellings. From Table 7–2, it is evident that "notice" and "cheating" were correct more often than all the other T-spelled words lacking such a root. Likewise among D-flap words, "shredding" was judged more accurately than all the other words. However, "forbidden" was somewhat less accurately judged. The fact that three out of the four words exhibited the expected pattern offers some support for the hypothesis that root words were recognized and influenced flap judgments. Very likely morphemic analysis occurred here because the rhyme task required subjects to pronounce the flap-terminal syllable alone, and this drew attention to root words.

The extent to which subjects judged the flap sounds consistently across two administrations of the rhyme judgment task was also evaluated to verify that uncertainty about flap classifications and haphazard responding were at a minimum. The numbers of rhyme choices which remained the same from Trial 1 to Trial 2 were compared across groups. As evident from the means and matched-pair t-test statistic in Table 7–3, both groups were equally consistent in their responses, with 88% to 91% of the answers remaining the same.

Discussion

Results of the second experimental study confirm results of the first correlational study, both indicating that when children process the spellings of words, they interpret letters as clarifying the word's phonological identity, in this case, whether the medial alveolar flap is /t/ or /d/. In Experiment 2, even though letters were not mentioned in the sound judgment task and subjects merely decided which of two word pairs rhymed, the formative effect of spellings on sound was still clearly evident in subjects' responses. These findings along with those of Ehri and Wilce (1980) document experimentally the impact of spellings on readers' metalinguistic awareness of speech at the phonological level. In the earlier study, spellings were shown to influence the number of phonetic segments thought to be present in pronunciations (i.e., "pitch" having 4 phonemes vs. "rich" having 3 phonemes). In the present study, spellings were shown to influence the identity of sounds in pronunciations. These findings serve to broaden the demonstrated effects of spellings by showing that they are not limited to speech tasks that closely resemble spelling tasks. In the previous study, a phonemic segmentation task was used in which sounds were represented spatially with a row of blank markers, whereas in the present study, a rhyming task bearing little similarity to a spelling task was used.

Present findings are interpreted as further support for our theory of printed word learning (Ehri, 1980, 1984, 1985; Ehri & Wilce, 1979, 1980, 1982). The reason why spellings are thought to exert an impact on speech has to do with the way that spellings are learned. According to our theory, spellings are stored in memory when letters are analyzed as maps for the sound structure of words. When there is ambiguity in pronunciations, letters can resolve the ambiguity by declaring what the "true" sounds really are.

Present findings offer support for three phases of development in the perception of flaps: (1) perception of flaps as /d/ based on acoustic criteria; (2) transitional shift to /t/ when learners first become familiar with spelling conventions; (3) perception as /t/ or /d/ according to the spellings of individual words when they are stored in memory. Evidence for Phase 3 was apparent in both studies. In Experiment 1, the judgments of older readers conformed to spellings more frequently than the judgments of younger readers. In Experiment 2, those subjects who learned spellings were much more likely to judge sounds according to spellings than subjects who did not see spellings. Evidence regarding Phases 1 and 2 emerged from analyses of errors. Phase 1 was found to be much more common than Phase 2. In Experiment 1, a large majority of older as well as younger subjects exhibited a /d/ bias. Only a few subjects, mostly first graders, exhibited a /t/ bias, indicating that Phase 2 is either temporary and short-lived or is optional. The fact that in Experiment 2 a /t/ bias characterized the errors of Experimental chance-level subjects but not control subjects supports the idea that experience with spellings is responsible for this transitional phase.

One other purpose of the present experiments was to determine whether children spontaneously analyze words into constituent morphemes. To find out, two kinds of words were included in the sound judgment tasks. Results of Experiment 1 were negative. Subjects were not any more accurate in perceiving the flap as a medial /t/ in inflected words (e.g., sitting, fatter) where the root signals an unambiguous /t/ than in uninflected words where the flap remains ambiguous. Results of Experiment 2 were more positive. However, this probably occurred because the rhyming task in Experiment 2 required subjects to pronounce the flap-terminal syllables (root words) separately before judging them, and this drew attention to the morphemes. Although several other studies have reported positive evidence for componential processing of morphemes (see Poizner, Newkirk, Bellugi, & Klima, 1981, for a summary), not all have been positive (Simons, 1975). It may be that morphemic analysis occurs under certain conditions but is not a routine operation performed spontaneously in all tasks or by all age groups. Since morphophonemic analysis may play an important role in learning to read (Venezky, 1970), more research on this process in beginning readers is needed.

One source of uncertainty must be acknowledged in our interpretation of present and previous findings. This involves our concept of phonological information about words possessed by learners and influenced by printed language. A variety of terms has been used to describe this information, including references to the pronunciations of words, the phonological representations of words in memory, the perception of, awareness of, and beliefs about sounds in words, and learners' conceptualization of the phonetic structure of words. Specific tasks have suggested the appropriateness of one rather than another term in some cases. For example, performance in a phonetic segmentation task has been regarded as revealing how subjects conceptualize the sound structure of words. Differences we have detected using this task are not apparent in a word pronunciation task. Although the words "pitch" and "rich" are segmented differently, "-itch" and "-ich" are pronounced identically. It may be that the terms listed above reflect different tasks varying in sensitivity but all tapping one underlying phonological knowledge source. Alternatively, it may be that subjects possess multiple types of phonetic information about words. Another possibility is that the terms refer to phonological capabilities that vary in the extent of metalinguistic involvement and control, ranging from very little in the case of word pronunciations to quite a bit in the case of phonetic segmentation skill. Additional research is needed to clear up this uncertainty as well as to clarify whether the effects of printed language are general or limited to certain aspects of phonological knowledge or performance.

Present findings bear on the issue regarding the relationship between phonological skills and learning to read (Ehri, 1979; Yaden, this volume). Results add to previous evidence indicating that learning to read alters aspects of a reader's phonological knowledge. However, findings do not thereby rule out alternative causal relationships (see Vellutino & Scanlon, this volume). There may be other ways to acquire a phonetic conceptualization of language besides learning to read. The Auditory Discrimination in Depth program developed by Lindamood and Lindamood (1975) provides an effective way to make nonreaders aware of phonetic segments in words, by having them monitor articulatory gestures in their mouths. Also, present findings do not mean that children cannot learn to segment words into phonemes before they learn to read, or that phoneme segmentation training will not help prereaders learn to read. The evidence shows otherwise. In a study with prereaders, we were able to teach them to segment CVC blends into phonemes by having them represent the sounds either with tokens or with alphabet letters (Hohn & Ehri, 1983). Downing (personal communication) has been able to teach this skill to unschooled, nonliterate children in New Guinea. Also, there is evidence that if children are trained to segment before or while they are learning to read, reading acquisition will be facilitated (Bradley & Bryant, 1983; Rosner, 1972; Wallach & Wallach, 1976; Williams, 1979, 1980).

Although metalinguistic awareness of the phonemic structure of language can be developed through instructional intervention before children learn to read, in fact such instruction is not part of most children's prereading experiences. For these children, learning to read very likely becomes the primary cause of improvement in phonemic awareness and segmentation skills. Beginning readers learn how to interpret spellings as visual maps for the pronunciations of words. It is in analyzing the spellings of familiar spoken words that beginners learn how sounds in language are structured and which sounds are "really there." Exploration of speech through spellings can even provide surprises when children discover that familiar words contain sounds they never before noticed or pronounced (e.g., "bicycle" pronounced /bay·sI·ko/; "didn't" pronounced /dInt/). Although it is possible to teach prereaders to analyze phonemes before the spelling system is introduced, studies indicate that including letters in the training procedure improves not only the sound learning itself (Hohn & Ehri, 1983) but also the process of learning to read and spell (Bradley & Bryant, 1983). In fact, there may be sound segments that are difficult if not impossible to teach young children without the aid of spellings to clarify the constituent sounds. For example, children who believe that the initial sound in "truck" and "train" is /č/ may be difficult to convince that the sound is really a blend of /t/ plus /r/ until they can see and analyze the spelling. Children who believe that "bump" has only three sounds may not understand how the vowel can be further divided into /ʌ/ plus /m/ until they see the spelling. Since spellings are essentially sound pictures to the tutored eye, they may be worth a thousand spoken explanations.

Acknowledgments

This research was supported by a grant from the National Institute of Child Health and Human Development, Grant No. HD-12903-01. Gratitude is expressed to Davis Joint Unified School District students, parents, and personnel for their cooperation in the conduct of this study.

Chapter 8

Linguistic Coding and Metalinguistic Awareness: Their Relationship to Verbal Memory and Code Acquisition in Poor and Normal Readers

FRANK R. VELLUTINO

DONNA M. SCANLON

The present chapter provides documentation for the view that reading disorder in severely impaired readers is largely attributable to inadequacies in the use of language as a coding device. The basic premise motivating this view is that poor readers have prominent difficulty in processing the structural and formal properties of spoken and printed words, and that such difficulty is causally related, not only to observed ineptitude in acquiring foundational reading skills such as word identification and reading comprehension, but also to ineptitude on any task that entails the use of words and other units of language to code information; for example, spelling, listening comprehension, and verbal memory tasks in general. A corollary assumption is that poor readers are especially deficient in processing spoken and printed words when their linguistic components are themselves the objects of analysis, an attitude that some have termed metalinguistic awareness. Thus, they can be expected to be more attuned to the semantic (meaning) than to the phonologic and syntactic (structural) components of the words and sentences they encounter, and will therefore have difficulty in negotiating tasks that require sensitivity to these latter attributes.

In the sections which follow, we present evidence to support these assumptions, highlighting selected findings from our own laboratory. The first section defines the hypothesized relationship between linguistic coding and reading disability, while the second section provides documentation for this relationship based on our research. The third and final section summarizes the ideas presented in the main body of the paper and makes brief reference to work done elsewhere.

115

Reading, Linguistic Coding, and Metalinguistic Awareness

Broadly defined, linguistic coding refers to the use of language to code or symbolize information. More specifically, it refers to the functional use of the semantic, syntactic, and phonologic attributes of given units of language (e.g., free and bound morphemes, phrases, sentences) in storing and retrieving both the information encoded in those units and the units themselves.

Semantic coding may be conceptualized as the process whereby given meanings become attached to and conveyed by particular components of language. Thus, a word or free morpheme is imbued with interrelated meanings taken from nonlinguistic referents and comes to exist in an increasingly complex network of associated and elaborated meanings. Words arrayed in phrases or sentences also code and convey meanings and types of meanings (e.g., denotative versus connotative), and different arrays of words may code essentially the same meanings. In contrast, the meanings that are coded in bound morphemes—for example, the prefixes and suffixes of words—are invariant and more abstract (e.g., "ed" signifies past tense) and are used in conjunction with free morphemes to qualify the meanings of given words in given grammatical contexts.

These latter distinctions allude to the definition of *syntactic coding* which, in general, refers to the acquisition and application of syntactic "rules" for ordering words in the language, for representing structural differences in given sentences (e.g., active versus passive, declarative versus question, grammatic versus ungrammatic), and for comprehending phrases and sentences. In reference to individual words, syntactic coding can also be defined as the ability to represent and assign syntactic descriptors to free and bound morphemes to aid in making fine-grained distinctions between and among them. The ability to store information about the critical differences between content and functional words, between and among parts of speech, and between root words and derived or inflected words exemplifies what is meant by syntactic coding used in this latter sense.

Finally, *phonologic coding* can be defined as the acquisition and application of phonologic and morphophonemic rules for ordering the phones and phonemes that comprise the words of the language. Phonologic coding also refers to one's ability to represent and assign phonetic descriptors to spoken and printed words, parts of words, and word strings to help in distinguishing and remembering them. When used in connection with printed words, phonologic coding is to be distinguished from *orthographic coding,* the latter more accurately referring to the structural regularities in these words, as represented by the visual system.

It should be clear that whereas semantic coding has reference to the substantive properties of the objects and concepts represented by given units of language, syntactic and phonologic coding have reference to the structural and formal properties of these units, or, more generally, to their "purely linguistic" properties. Thus, semantic coding depends more on one's experience with and knowledge of the things to which language refers, while syntactic and phonologic coding are more dependent on one's experience and facility with language itself. Another important distinction is that semantic coding, as typically used, refers (albeit loosely) to the variable and often ambiguous meanings conveyed by a word or sentence, but syntactic and phonologic coding refer more precisely to the invariant properties of these items—properties that are germane to language. Semantic coding, then, relies heavily upon associative learning and becomes an increasingly complex enterprise as the child acquires knowledge about real world referents and codes this knowledge syntactically and phonologically. Syntactic and phonologic coding rely heavily upon rule learning and are therefore more generative than associative in nature. In addition, their complexities are tied more directly to the structure and nature of language itself than to the structure and nature of the concepts or objects represented by language. Thus, as cognitive enterprises, they are inherently more demanding at earlier than at later stages of development—that is, more so during the acquisition of phonologic and syntactic rules than after the acquisition of these rules.

In accord with the foregoing conceptualization, we suggest that reading disability in otherwise normal children is due in large measure to difficulties they encounter in using language to code information. Either because of basic constitutional deficiencies that serve to impair language development or because of inadequate environmental stimulation, these children seem to be linguistically less mature than are normal readers at the same age and grade level, and have not internalized the units of language and linguistic structures in general to the same level of sophistication. Such lack of sophistication is especially prominent in the difficulty encountered by poor readers in learning to read and spell, but should also be evident on any verbal processing task that requires fine-grained analysis of particular linguistic units. Thus, it has been observed that while poor readers generally perform below the level of normal readers on tasks that make significant demands upon one's linguistic capabilities, reader group differences are typically much greater and more consistent on tasks involving precision in recall of given words and sentences (i.e., verbatim memory) than on tasks involving recall of the concepts or ideas that are coded in these units (Perfetti & Lesgold, 1979; Vellutino, 1979).

These and other findings have led us to speculate that poor readers may not be as facile as normal readers in representing and coding the purely linguistic attributes of printed and spoken words, but may be closer to normal readers in coding their substantive features. They would therefore be expected to be less sensitive to the structural and formal components of words than to their meanings. Implied in this distinction is the likelihood that poor readers would not be as well equipped as normal readers to engage in the type of metalinguistic analysis that many believe is critically important for success in beginning reading and especially important for code acquisition (Downing, 1971–72; Elkonin, 1973; Liberman & Shankweiler, 1979; see Yaden, this volume, for a comprehensive review). These investigators suggest that if the fledgling reader is to acquire a functional knowledge of spelling-sound rules, he/she must develop a conscious awareness that spoken words are comprised of individual phonemes that often correspond invariantly with printed letters or combinations of letters. They also suggest that the failure to develop this processing attitude fosters *total* reliance on a whole or "sight" word approach to word identification. It is therefore of some importance that poor readers have often been found to be less proficient than normal readers in segmenting spoken and printed words into constituent phonemes (Liberman & Shankweiler, 1979).

If these speculations are correct, then certain testable hypotheses logically emerge. For one thing, hypothesized differences between poor and normal readers in linguistic coding should be apparent in the processing of both printed and spoken words and should be manifested in reader group differences on both word encoding and word retrieval tasks. It might also be expected that sensitivity to purely linguistic codes would be greater in older than in younger poor readers, given more experience of the type that promotes such sensitivity—for example, the metalinguistic analysis typically promoted by school learning and by reading itself (Ehri, 1980). Thus group differences on verbal processing tasks that rely heavily on linguistic coding ability should be greater at younger than at older age levels.

Finally, if it is true that success in beginning reading, and code acquisition in particular, are directly and causally related to phonemic awareness and attendant ability to analyze the internal structures of spoken and written words (Liberman & Shankweiler, 1979), training in phonemic awareness should have a salutary effect on this enterprise.

In the section which follows, we discuss several studies conducted in our laboratory that have evaluated these hypotheses employing a variety of experimental paradigms. The particular studies discussed employed procedures that more directly evaluated semantic and phonologic coding processes, but only indirectly evaluated syntactic processes. However, reference is made to other studies, not detailed here, that more directly evaluated syntactic processes.

Subjects in all of the experiments described were poor and normal readers from middle to upper middle class school districts selected on the basis of reading achievement, intellectual ability, and certain exclusionary criteria. Both poor and normal readers were of average or above average intelligence, having achieved an IQ score of 90 or above on a standardized test of intelligence. Poor readers were severely impaired and typically scored between the fourth and tenth percentiles on an oral reading test. They were also extremely deficient in phonetic decoding. Normal readers were randomly selected from those schools recommending poor readers for inclusion in our studies. Subjects in both groups attended school regularly and were free from severe neurological, emotional, and social disorders, and from (uncorrected) vision, hearing, and speech problems.

Research Evaluating Linguistic Coding in Poor and Normal Readers

Encoding of Meaning Versus Structural Features of Printed Words

If poor readers are more attuned to the semantic than to the phonologic and orthographic attributes of printed words, then they should be more inclined to detect similarities in the meanings of these stimuli than to detect similarities in their structural characteristics, and should more closely approximate normal readers in detection of their meanings. If it is also true that older poor readers are more attuned to structural codes than are younger poor readers, then the older poor readers should be more sensitive to the structural similarities in words than should the younger poor readers.

These hypotheses were initially tested in three separate studies using printed words as stimuli. In the first of these studies (Vellutino, Scanlon, DeSetto & Pruzek, 1981), a free sort procedure was used with poor and normal readers in grades 1 through 6, as well as with randomly selected ninth graders and college students. Subjects in each group were presented with 16 sets of words that could be categorized either on the basis of taxonomic similarity or on the basis of orthographic/phonologic similarity (e.g., *duck, moose, goat; caboose, truck, boat*—meaning; *duck, truck; goat, boat; moose, caboose*—structure). Words in each set were arrayed randomly and subjects were simply asked to put together the words that they thought went together. Scoring to determine processing attitude was based only on those words in respective stimulus sets that were correctly identified, and testing to assess ability to identify stimulus words was conducted after the experiment proper. The dependent measure was proportion of words that were actually categorized on the basis of meaning, relative to the number of words in a stimulus set that could have been categorized on this basis. Thus, meaning and structural categorizations were reciprocals of one another.

Figure 8–1 presents scatter diagrams depicting this relationship for poor and normal readers in grades 1 through 6. The first thing to note is that meaning was the dominant processing mode in all subjects. But more important for present purposes, normal readers at the lower grade levels (between first and fourth) were more variable in their use of meaning and structural categories than were normal readers at the upper grade levels. Particularly striking is the fact that a sizable number of normal readers at each grade level made extensive use of structural categories, some making primary use of these categories. In fact, it was not until sixth grade that subjects in this group categorized the words they could read almost exclusively on the basis of meaning. And while the data are now shown in Figure 8–1, ninth graders and college sophomores also categorized almost exclusively on the basis of meaning.

Poor readers, on the other hand, appeared to be much less variable than normal readers, and were generally inclined to categorize the words they could read on the basis of meaning rather than on the basis of structure. This was true at all grade levels at which they were able to identify a substantial proportion of these words (grades 4 through 6). Thus, the relationship between the *actual* number of words categorized on the basis of meaning and the number that were *potentially* available for such categorization was stronger in poor readers (r = .96, p<.05) than in normal readers (r = .80, p<.05).

Moreover, when poor readers *did* make extensive use of structural principles of categorization—which occurred when they were able to identify very few of the words in a given set—the structural principles they employed were rarely based on the orthographic/phonologic similarities built into that set. This was

Figure 8–1

Scatter Diagrams Depicting the Relationship Between the Number of Words Potentially Available for Meaning-Based Sorts and Those Actually Sorted on the Basis of Meaning

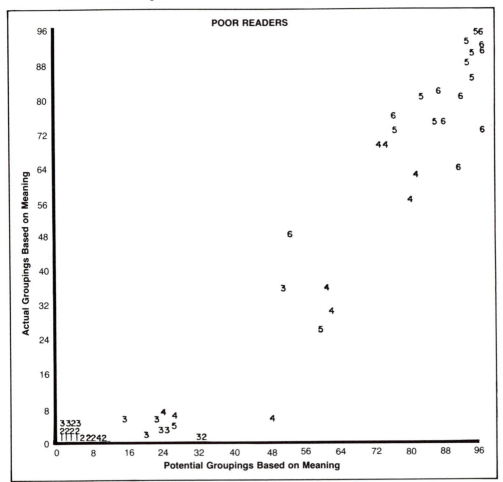

Source: Vellutino, F. R., Scanlon, D. M., Desetto, L., & Pruzek, R. M. (1981). Developmental trends in the salience of meaning versus structural attributes of written words. *Psychological Research, 3,* 131–153. Reprinted by permission of the publisher, Springer-Verlag New York, Inc.

Note: Numerals within the diagrams represent the grade level of each subject plotted.

especially true of the poor readers in the lower grades. For example, these children were as apt to put *goat* and *truck* together as to put *goat* and *boat* together, presumably because they all contain the letter "t." In such instances, higher order structure was apparently ignored. This tendency was much less evident in normal readers, who by no later than third grade made exclusive use of higher

Figure 8–1   Cont'd.

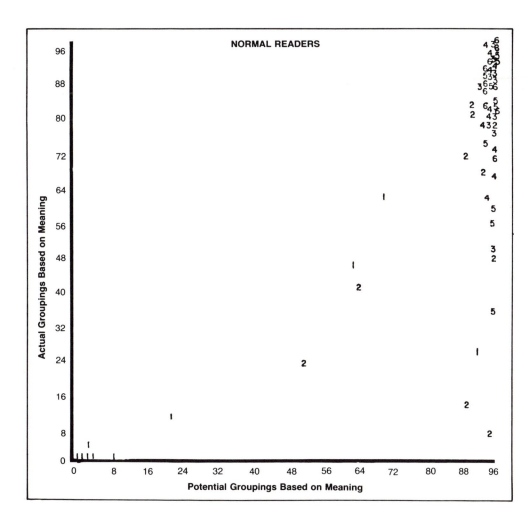

order orthographic principles to classify those words that they *did* place in structural categories. On the other hand, consistent with the suggestion made earlier,
the performance of poor readers in fifth and sixth grade more closely approximated that of the normal readers at this level, indicating that older poor readers
are more sensitive to word structure than are younger poor readers. The data
depicting these developmental changes appear in Table 8–1.

The results of this study provide substantial evidence that poor readers at
the beginning stage of skills development are generally more attuned to the

Table 8–1

Means and Standard Deviations for Percentages of the Total Number of
Structural Categorizations Based on Higher Order Orthographic Principles

Grade	Normal Readers			Poor Readers		
	X̄	SD	N	X̄	SD	N
1	66	23	20	58	19	10
2	92	16	18	71	20	19
3	100	0	17	77	15	19
4	99	2	18	85	17	19
5	99	6	17	93	11	11
6	100	0	6	100	0	7
9	100	0	9	—	—	—
College Soph.	95	14	6	—	—	—

Source: Vellutino, F. R., Scanlon, D. M., Desetto, L., & Pruzek, R. M. (1981). Developmental trends in the salience of meaning versus structural attributes of written words. *Psychological Research, 3,* 131–153. Reprinted by permission of the publisher, Springer-Verlag New York, Inc.

meaning than to the structural codes embedded in printed words, and less attuned to structural codes than are normal readers. They also suggest that normal readers are especially sensitive to the internal structures of words during the period of time that they can be presumed to be heavily invested in code acquisition. These inferences are given additional support by the second study we conducted (Vellutino & Scanlon, manuscript in preparation-a) which found essentially the same results.

Subjects in this second study were poor and normal readers in the second, fourth and sixth grade, comparable, in terms of selection criteria, to those evaluated in the study just discussed. A randomly selected group of first graders were also included in the research sample. Each subject was presented with a forced choice rather than a free sort procedure, wherein one could group *two* of three words in a set, on the basis of either similarities in meaning or similarities in structure (e.g., *room, goose, duck*). In addition, respective stimulus sets were comprised of words that were more easily identified than those employed previously.

The patterns evident in the first study were replicated in the second study (graphs not shown) insofar as normal readers were more variable in their attendance to word meanings than were poor readers. And, as in the first study, such variability was especially evident in the lower grades. These differences are reflected in the actual/potential correlations computed for respective groups (r = .89, p<.05 normal readers including first grade group; r = .22, p<.05 normal readers excluding first grade group;[1] r = .90, p<.05 poor readers). Thus, we can be reasonably certain of the reliability of group trends.

Encoding of Orthographic vs.
Phonologic Features of Printed Words

While the first two investigations contrasted poor and normal readers on their sensitivity to the semantic versus the orthographic/phonologic attributes of printed words, the third compared the two groups on their sensitivity to the orthographic as opposed to the phonologic attributes of these stimuli (Vellutino & Scanlon, manuscript in preparation-a). The procedure employed in this experiment was identical to that employed in the second experiment, except for the fact that word sets could be categorized *either* on the basis of orthographic *or* phonologic similarity and were devoid of similarities in meaning (e.g., *paid, said, made*). Subjects were poor and normal readers in fourth and sixth grade selected in accord with the sampling criteria used in the first two studies. The dependent measure was the proportion of the total number of word sets categorized on the basis of phonologic similarity. Proportions were again based only on those words that the subject had identified correctly. The central findings from this study are presented in Table 8–2.

It can be seen that the normal readers at both grade levels categorized a much larger proportion of the words they could identify on the basis of their phonologic similarities than did the poor readers at these grade levels. In fact,

Table 8–2

Means and Standard Deviations for Poor and Normal Readers in
Fourth and Sixth Grade for Categorization Principles Employed on the
Orthographic Versus Phonologic Forced Choice Task

	Potential Phonologic[a]	Actual Potential[b]
Grade 4 Poor		
X̄	5.47	.10
SD	1.92	.22
Grade 4 Normal		
X̄	9.53	.45
SD	.64	.33
Grade 6 Poor		
X̄	8.13	.24
SD	1.68	.36
Grade 6 Normal		
X̄	9.87	.44
SD	.35	.39

[a] Means represent the average number of complete sets read correctly and therefore potentially available for phonologic sorting (total possible sets = 10).

[b] Means and standard deviations for the ratio of number of sets actually sorted phonologically to those potentially available for phonologic sorting.

the normal readers utilized both orthographic and phonologic similarities in approximately equal measure, whereas poor readers made primary use of orthographic similarities for categorizing words in a given set. These findings provide rather strong support for Liberman and Shankweiler's (1979) suggestion that poor readers are not as sensitive as normal readers to the phonologic attributes of printed words, and add weight to the idea that poor readers are generally less conversant than normal readers with the structural characteristics of these words.

Noteworthy, however, is the fact that the sixth grade poor readers demonstrated greater sensitivity to a word's phonologic attributes than did the fourth grade poor readers. This, of course, reinforces our suggestion that older poor readers are more sensitive to the structural attributes of printed words than are younger poor readers.

The results of the studies just discussed provide considerable support for our contention that poor readers are more attuned to the meaning than to the structural components of printed words. Moreover, the data from the third study conducted suggest that even when poor readers are forced to attend to the structural similarities in these stimuli, they are more attentive to their orthographic than to their phonologic similarities. The results therefore support the linguistic coding hypothesis under consideration. And, insofar as older poor readers demonstrate greater sensitivity to structural codes than do younger poor readers, they also support the developmental hypothesis advanced earlier.

Our findings also have implications for the hypothesized relationship between metalinguistic awareness and reading ability mentioned earlier (Liberman & Shankweiler, 1979). While the data do not constitute direct evidence for this hypothesis, they are at least consistent with it. That is, if children who are identified as deficient in both whole word identification and phonetic decoding are also implicitly insensitive to the orthographic and phonologic regularities embedded in printed words, then it seems reasonable to infer that they are neither conversant with nor explicitly aware of the structural characteristics of spoken and printed words, and that such lack of awareness may be causally related to their difficulties in learning to read. On the other hand, some researchers suggest (see Ehri, this volume) that a deficiency in metalinguistic awareness is a *consequence* of reading disorder rather than a contributing cause of such disorder, and would no doubt hasten to point out that the present results could be interpreted either way. Thus, more direct evidence is needed to resolve the issue.

Nevertheless, we are inclined to believe that the failure to become conversant with the structural regularities inherent in spoken and printed words is partly responsible for the poor reader's difficulty in learning to read, and we suggest that linguistic coding deficits of the types we outlined earlier lie at the root of both problems. However, in order to sustain this position, it would be necessary to demonstrate that poor and normal readers at the early stages of skills development do, indeed, differ in the processing of spoken language, and that such differences are related to metalinguistic awareness. We turn now to studies which have attempted to provide such evidence.

Linguistic Coding and Recall of Spoken Words

If the linguistic coding explanation of reading disability is valid, then coding deficits should be apparent not only in the processing of printed words, but in the processing of spoken words as well, and should be especially prominent in poor readers at younger age levels. These conjectures were tested in a second series of studies conducted in our laboratory presenting poor and normal readers with tasks involving memory for auditorially presented words.

These studies evaluated the linguistic coding hypothesis by comparing poor and normal readers at different grade levels on memory for spoken words that were systematically varied with respect to their lexical attributes. Our results are convergent and generally support the hypothesis. However, because of space limitations, we will describe only one of the experiments we conducted.

In this investigation (Vellutino & Scanlon, 1985) the lexical attribute varied was degree of abstractness. Previous research evaluating semantic memory (Paivio, 1971) has consistently demonstrated that abstract words are more difficult to remember than are concrete words, and the most popular explanation for this discrepancy is that abstract words do not as readily generate referential images that can be used to assist recall. However, several studies have provided compelling evidence (Paivio & Begg, 1971a, 1971b) that abstract words are more difficult to recall than are concrete words, not only because they are less imbued with (or totally devoid of) imageable referents, but also because they are linguistically more complex. Thus,

some abstract words derive their meanings primarily from their relationship with other words (e.g., *is, but, there*), while others are derivatives from concrete words or other abstract words (e.g., judge → justice → judicial). Many also necessitate a working knowledge of complex syntactic rules for comprehension and correct usage, as with morphological prefixing and suffixing (judicial → prejudicial; judge → judgment). Abstract words are consequently more diffuse and less easily discriminated than are concrete words and facility in encoding and retrieving such words would seem to imply a high degree of linguistic sophistication. (Vellutino & Scanlon, 1982, p. 232)

If, then, poor readers are less proficient than normal readers in using linguistic codes to store and retrieve information, they should perform significantly below normal readers on recall of abstract words. On the other hand, given the likelihood that poor readers are as well equipped as normal readers to utilize imagery to aid storage and retrieval (Vellutino, 1979), they should be closer to the normal readers on recall of concrete words.

These hypotheses were evaluated in two separate experiments comparing poor and normal readers in second and sixth grade on free recall of the two types of words. The first experiment used a random presentation procedure, with concrete and abstract words commingled, while the second presented these words in homogeneous blocks, counterbalanced for order of presentation. The two word sets were initially dichotomized on the basis of normative data gathered in pilot study, using randomly selected children in second and sixth grade. In order to control for conceptual complexity, the two lists were also equated for denotative (definitional) and connotative meaning. The results of these studies are presented in Figure 8–2.

It can be seen that in each investigation, poor readers at each grade level performed below the level of normal readers on both concrete and abstract words, but the hypothesized interaction between reader group and word type was evident only at the second grade level. That is, while poor readers in second grade were closer to normal readers in recall of concrete words, as predicted, poor readers in sixth grade were as far below their normal reading peers on recall of the concrete words as they were on recall of the abstract words. This disparity was not anticipated, but it is *not* inconsistent with our suggestion that linguistic coding deficits may be more readily observed in younger than in older poor readers. Thus, it may be inferred that poor readers at the second grade level had more difficulty than the normal readers at this level in remembering the abstract words because they were not as well equipped to utilize the phonologic and syntactic components of these words to aid recall. This inference is, of course, based on the assumption that the processing of abstract words requires greater facility in coding and cross referencing linguistic attributes than does the processing of concrete words. Moreover, the fact that these two groups were more disparate on the abstract than on the concrete words cannot be attributed to group differences in knowledge of the meanings of these words, because the two word sets were equated for meaning.

However, a deficit in linguistic coding could not be as readily inferred in the case of the sixth grade poor readers, because this explanation could not adequately account for the fact that these subjects performed well below the level of the sixth grade normal readers on the concrete as well as on the abstract words. A plausible alternative is that the older poor readers, in part because of longstanding reading disorder, had a less well developed vocabulary than did the older normal readers and a less elaborate semantic network generally. These characteristics could result in comparatively poor performance on recall of a given word list, regardless of whether its components happened to be concrete or abstract words.

This interpretation is given additional support by results derived from a qualitative analysis of the different types of intrusion errors made by respective reader groups. In this instance, a frequency count was made of errors that appeared to be prompted by either the meaning or the structural components of given word stimuli. Thus, substitution errors, such as "prince" for "queen" or "thinking" for "thought," suggest that the subject was more attuned to the semantic than to the phonologic and syntactic attributes (respectively) of stimulus words, while errors such as "fought" for "thought" or "though" for "thought" reflect the tendency to be (respectively) more attuned to their phonologic and orthographic components than to their semantic components.

Consistent with our speculations, we observed second grade poor readers make more meaning than structural type errors, while the errors made by second grade normal readers were more evenly distributed across both categories. However, poor readers at the sixth grade level were inclined to make as many or more

Figure 8–2

Trial Means for Reall of Concrete and Abstract Words
under Random and Blocked Presentation Conditions

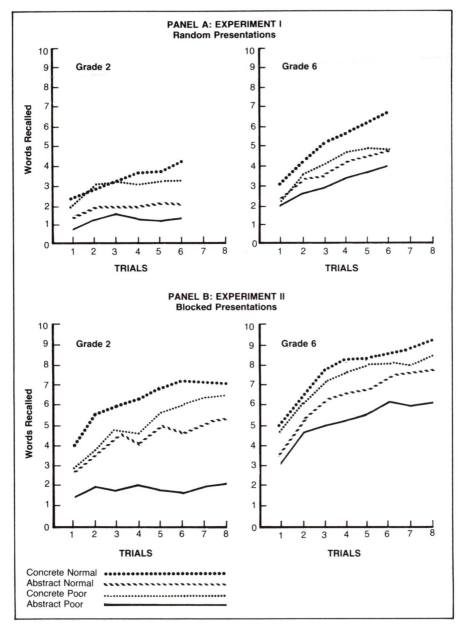

Source: Vellutino, F. R., & Scanlon, D. M. (1985). Free recall of concrete and abstract words in poor and normal readers. *Journal of Experimental Child Psychology, 39,* 363–380. Reprinted by permission.

structural type errors as the sixth grade normal readers and, in fact, the normal readers were somewhat *more* inclined to make meaning errors than were the poor readers.

These results are entirely consistent with the results of the studies discussed earlier, reporting group differences on the encoding of printed word features. They are also consistent with the results of several other studies conducted in our laboratory, evaluating recall of spoken words in poor and normal readers (see Vellutino & Scanlon, 1982, for a comprehensive review of these studies) and the combined data sets constitute strong support for our position. If poor readers have difficulty in processing spoken words and if such difficulty is due, in significant measure, to deficiencies in storing and retrieving the linguistic components of these stimuli, the readers would quite likely have difficulty in explicating the internal structures of printed words and thus in learning to decode them. In short, deficiencies in linguistic coding lead to deficiencies in metalinguistic analysis, which in turn lead to deficiencies in learning to map alphabetic symbols to sound.

Yet it could still be argued that while these results have demonstrated a probable connection between reader group differences in the encoding and decoding of spoken and printed words, they have not demonstrated a definitive and causal connection between metalinguistic awareness and printed word decoding. A final study (Vellutino & Scanlon, 1979) we wish to discuss provides documentation for this connection.

Training in Phonemic Segmentation, Phonologic Memory, and Code Acquisition

This study addressed the question of whether or not training in metalinguistic awareness would have a salutary effect on the processing of spoken and printed words. As indicated earlier, previous research has provided suggestive evidence for a positive relationship between phonemic awareness and reading ability (e.g., Liberman & Shankweiler, 1979), and there is extensive evidence that severely impaired readers are especially deficient in decoding printed words phonetically (Vellutino, 1979). Thus, we were particularly interested in determining to what degree training in phonemic segmentation would influence performance on tasks evaluating phonologic memory and code acquisition.

Subject and procedures.   The investigation itself was rather complex and involved three different phases. In the first phase, poor and normal readers in second and sixth grade[2] were given a test of phonemic segmentation ability to evaluate the reliability of previous findings. This test used both spoken and printed words and pseudowords as stimuli and included several subtests designed to assess the child's ability to discriminate and vocalize individual phonemes in given units.

The second phase was the experiment proper. In this phase, respective reader groups were compared on verbal response learning as well as on code acquisition tasks with or without training in phonemic segmentation. There were five different treatment groups, and poor and normal readers at each grade level were randomly assigned to one of the five.

In one condition—the phonemic segmentation training and response acquisition condition (PSTRA)—subjects were given five or six consecutive days of training in segmentation analysis (one-half hour each day), which consisted of several different exercises designed to attune them to the phonemic composition of spoken and printed words and pseudowords. Such training also included practice in analyzing and remembering phonemically redundant nonsense syllables *(sij, duj, dif, suf)* presented auditorily. Training in segmentation analysis was culminated with extensive practice in detecting grapheme-phoneme correspondence in printed pseudowords (see Figure 8–3A) in order to foster structural analysis of these stimuli. The task used for this purpose simulated code acquisition and consisted of both training and transfer learning sequences. Our primary objective was to teach subjects to abstract invariant units to assist in learning whole words. Thus, the paired associates were, for the most part, presented as whole words. However, to attune subjects to the invariant units embedded in stimulus pairs, they were intermittently presented with the individual characters contained in the trigraphs and were encouraged to articulate the grapheme-phoneme associations.

After a two-day hiatus, each subject was given 20 free recall trials using phonemically redundant nonsense syllables *(goz, gov, zab, vab)* that were different from those used in segmentation training. This task was designed to evaluate the subject's ability to discriminate and remember nonsense words that were subsequently employed as responses on visual-verbal association tasks. Because these stimuli were essentially meaningless, performance in remembering them was largely dependent upon phonologic coding ability.

Following a short break, the same subjects were given 15 trials of paired associates learning, wherein the same nonsense syllables presented on the free recall task were paired with cartoon-like animal pictures (see Figure 8–3B). The intent of this task was to provide subjects with meaningful associates to the nonsense words. It also allowed us to compare poor and normal readers on the type of visual-verbal association learning involved in object naming.

On the next day, subjects were given the training subtest of code acquisition. During this phase, subjects were presented with the same nonsense syllables presented on the free recall and object naming tasks, paired with graphemically redundant pseudowords (trigraphs) consisting of novel graphic characters. The graphic characters were different from those used in segmentation training (see Figure 8–3C), and each corresponded invariantly with respective phonemes comprising the nonsense syllables. Each of these pairs was presented for 20 acquisition-test trials, requiring that subjects produce whole word responses. The use of a different set of pseudowords and the use of whole word responses allowed us to evaluate whether subjects had acquired the analytic attitude we hoped would be fostered by segmentation training.

Subjects were presented with the transfer subtest of code acquisition on the day after presentation of the training subtest, using the same experimental procedures used for training. The transfer subtest was designed to evaluate the degree to which subjects could generalize the grapheme-phoneme units picked up

Figure 8–3

Stimuli Used in the Study of the Effects of Phonemic
Segmentation and Response Acquisition Training on Code Acquisition

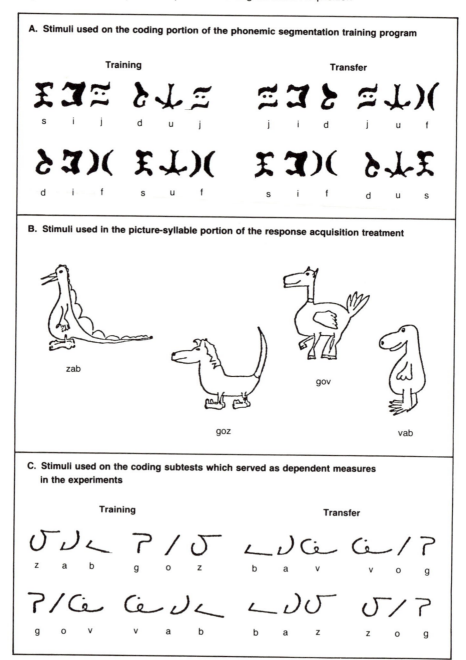

A. Stimuli used on the coding portion of the phonemic segmentation training program

B. Stimuli used in the picture-syllable portion of the response acquisition treatment

zab

gov

goz

vab

C. Stimuli used on the coding subtests which served as dependent measures
in the experiments

on the training subtest to aid in identifying a "new" set of pseudowords that were created by permuting these units (*baz, bav, zog, vog*).

The primary objective of the PSTRA condition was to evaluate the combined effects of phonemic segmentation training and verbal response learning on code acquisition. It also allowed us to evaluate the effect of segmentation training on free recall of the nonsense syllables.

A second treatment condition—phonemic segmentation only (PST)—presented subjects with the training and transfer tasks, after they received practice in phonemic segmentation. This condition was designed to evaluate the effects of segmentation training on the code acquisition subtests, with no prior exposure to the verbal responses used on these subtests.

A third condition—response acquisition only (RA)—presented subjects with the response learning (free recall and object naming) and code acquisition subtests, but they received no training in segmentation analysis. This condition was designed to evaluate the influence of verbal response learning on code acquisition, but also allowed us to compare poor and normal readers on response learning without the influence of segmentation training.

The fourth and fifth treatment conditions were control conditions. One (C-1) presented respective reader groups only with the training and transfer subtests of code acquisition, and the other (C-2) presented them only with the transfer subtest. A schematic outline of respective treatment conditions is presented in Table 8–3.

The third and final phase of the study presented all subject groups with an alternate form of the phonemic segmentation test that was administered, prior to initiation of the experiment proper. The intent here was to evaluate the degree to which exposure to the various treatment conditions influenced phonemic segmentation ability.

Table 8–3

Order of Tasks Administered to Subjects in Each Condition of the Study and of the Effects of Phonemic Segmentation Training and Response Training on Code Acquisition

		Response Acquisition		Code Acquisition	
Condition	Phonemic Segmentation ⟶ Training	Free ⟶ Recall	Picture Syllable ⟶ Association	Symbol- Syllable ⟶ Training	Symbol- Syllable Transfer
PSTRA	X	X	X	X	X
PST	X	N.A.	N.A.	X	X
RA	N.A.	X	X	X	X
CONTROL 1	N.A.	N.A.	N.A.	X	X
CONTROL 2	N.A.	N.A.	N.A.	N.A.	X

Note: N.A. = Not administered. Filler activities unrelated to the experiment were substituted in order to control for time spent with the examiner in the testing situation.

Results. The major findings that emerged from this study are presented in Tables 8–4, 8–5, and 8–6. First, at both the second and sixth grade levels (Table 8–4), poor readers performed significantly below the normal readers on both the pre- and post-experimental test of phonemic segmentation ability. This, of course, replicates previous results (Fox & Routh, 1980; Helfgott, 1976; Liberman & Shankweiler, 1979); it also documents the fact that subjects in our sample were significantly impaired in phoneme analysis, which was the major cognitive skill addressed by the segmentation training program. Secondly, poor readers at both grade levels performed below the level of normal readers on the free recall and picture-syllable subtests (Table 8–5), suggesting that poor readers are quite basically impaired in phonologic coding ability. Finally, poor readers at both grade levels performed significantly below the normal readers on both the training and transfer components of code acquisition (Table 8–6), consistent with previous findings (Vellutino, Harding, Phillips & Steger, 1975).

However, in line with the developmental hypothesis advanced earlier, the magnitudes of reader group differences were, in most instances, found to be greater at the second than at the sixth grade level. The only exception to this general pattern occurred on the phonemic segmentation tests, where the two reader groups were as disparate at the sixth as at the second grade level (Table 8–4). This is not surprising, given that the majority of items on those tests were real words that the normal readers may have already learned to segment. All other measures of phonologic processing involved new learning and, on these, the sixth grade reader groups were closer together than the second grade groups. Indeed,

Table 8–4

Means and Standard Deviations for Percentage Correct on
Pre- and Post-Treatment Measures of Phonemic Segmentation Ability

		Grade 2 Poor		Grade 2 Normal		Grade 6 Poor		Grade 6 Normal	
		Pre	Post	Pre	Post	Pre	Post	Pre	Post
PSTRA	X̄	43.46	53.21	63.21	76.05	57.78	75.55	76.05	88.27
	SD	(10.98)	(10.64)	(14.31)	(15.26)	(18.00)	(11.23)	(14.22)	(6.05)
PST	X̄	46.05	54.81	57.65	69.75	62.35	76.79	70.99	85.55
	SD	(6.71)	(10.54)	(18.77)	(18.72)	(14.66)	(11.69)	(15.96)	(8.32)
RA	X̄	45.31	45.43	57.41	60.00	60.25	61.23	75.43	80.74
	SD	(8.28)	(9.72)	(15.53)	(13.03)	(11.48)	(16.38)	(12.59)	(16.00)
C-1	X̄	41.98	44.81	56.54	64.32	59.26	65.80	75.55	86.18
	SD	(7.69)	(6.31)	(15.82)	(13.74)	(14.24)	(12.40)	(15.27)	(10.28)
C-2	X̄	45.19	51.73	54.32	63.58	59.51	63.58	73.21	78.27
	SD	(11.26)	(12.07)	(12.80)	(13.58)	(11.88)	(13.35)	(12.02)	(12.93)

Table 8–5

Means and Standard Deviations for
Percentage Correct on Response Acquisition Measures

	Second Grade				Sixth Grade			
	Free Recall		Picture Syllable		Free Recall		Picture Syllable	
	Poor	Normal	Poor	Normal	Poor	Normal	Poor	Normal
PSTRA								
X̄	27.08	55.00	24.44	55.89	60.00	72.83	63.56	80.56
SD	(13.13)	(24.13)	(12.09)	(18.21)	(19.85)	(24.28)	(22.83)	(17.10)
RA								
X̄	33.92	55.42	28.22	60.00	53.25	70.58	65.33	68.78
SD	(19.65)	(23.85)	(24.12)	(27.24)	(22.17)	(22.92)	(22.92)	(22.45)

Table 8–6

Means and Standard Deviations for Percentage
Correct on Training and Transfer Subtests of Code Acquisition

		Grade 2 Poor		Grade 2 Normal		Grade 6 Poor		Grade 6 Normal	
		Training	Transfer	Training	Transfer	Training	Transfer	Training	Transfer
PSTRA	X̄	42.92	39.67	85.25	89.08	84.83	79.25	92.92	90.42
	SD	(18.63)	(31.64)	(16.59)	(10.26)	(12.01)	(4.88)	(6.32)	(4.92)
PST	X̄	42.92	51.75	66.00	79.66	63.58	78.25	72.25	88.58
	SD	(21.81)	(29.71)	(18.16)	(25.72)	(16.43)	(6.11)	(18.40)	(4.32)
RA	X̄	37.04	26.50	64.08	49.75	68.42	55.75	81.00	76.42
	SD	(17.49)	(30.64)	(20.17)	(30.12)	(23.70)	(9.33)	(12.07)	(6.18)
C-1	X̄	26.17	24.58	51.67	50.58	52.75	52.58	66.92	65.60
	SD	(17.66)	(25.93)	(21.08)	(25.36)	(20.75)	(11.15)	(19.21)	(8.66)
C-2	X̄	N.A.	33.17	N.A.	45.17	N.A.	59.94	N.A.	62.08
	SD		(21.08)		(23.73)		(4.41)		(5.47)

Note: N.A.: Not administered.

the second grade poor readers had an extraordinarily difficult time in remembering the nonsense words and made very little progress over trials in doing so, both on the free recall task and on the picture-syllable learning task.

As regards the treatments effects, we should first note that phonemic segmentation training (PST) had no apparent effect on free recall and picture-syllable learning, either in the poor or in the normal reader groups.[3] However, segmentation training did positively effect code acquisition and had its strongest and most stable effect on transfer learning, these patterns being evident in both poor and normal readers. In fact, PST subjects performed better on the transfer subtest than they did on the training subtest, which indicates that phonemic analysis has its most profound effect on generalization learning.

But here again, developmental factors were operative. While segmentation training alone did not bring the second grade poor readers closer to the second grade normal readers, it did bring the sixth grade reader groups much closer together (see Table 8–6). On the other hand, those second grade poor readers who received segmentation training performed at least as well as second grade normal readers, who did not receive this training, and sixth grade poor readers who received segmentation training performed better than sixth grade normal readers, who did not receive the training.

Prior exposure to responses presented on the training subtest of code acquisition, received by subjects in the RA conditions, also had a salutary effect, but this was true only on the training subtest (see Table 8–6). In fact, the performance of RA subjects generally declined on the transfer subtest. We suspect that this occurred not only because of all the additional practice they received in learning the responses used on the training subtest, but also because they received no training in structural analysis. That is, since these subjects were not attuned to the grapheme-phoneme invariance embedded in the paired associates used on the code acquisition subtests, their performance on the transfer subtest was disrupted more than that of other subjects, by interference from responses learned on the training subtest.

On the other hand, PSTRA subjects received both segmentation and response training, and these subjects demonstrated very little reduction in performance level on the transfer subtest. In fact, PSTRA subjects generally performed better than subjects in the other treatment groups, on both the training and transfer subtests.

It is also important to note that the different treatments fostered different processing strategies on the code acquisition tasks. Whereas subjects exposed to response training (RA) apparently utilized a whole word approach to pseudoword identification, those who received segmentation training (PST) utilized a more analytic approach. Interestingly enough, those who received both types of training (PSTRA) appeared to have used both strategies, emphasizing whole word learning on the training phase of code acquisition and structural analysis on the transfer phase. These findings suggest that PSTRA subjects were better equipped than subjects in the other treatment groups, to vary their processing strategies in accord with task demands. It is therefore not surprising that they generally performed better than subjects in the other treatment conditions.

Finally, segmentation training also had a positive effect on phonemic segmentation ability, as measured by performance on the postexperimental version of this test (see Table 8–4). However, at the second grade level, the magnitudes of the differences, on the average, were greater in normal readers than in poor readers, but at the sixth grade level the differences were comparable in the two groups. Not surprisingly, response training had no substantial effect on performance on the postexperimental segmentation test.

Discussion.   There are several important conclusions to be drawn from this study, relative to the questions raised earlier, the question of metalinguistic awareness in particular.

It is clear, from the results in general, that basic deficiencies in phonologic processing constitute defining and rather pervasive characteristics of poor readers of the type we have been studying—that is, severely impaired readers who are apparently normal in other areas of cognitive development. Such deficiencies were especially apparent on the tests evaluating phoneme analysis as well as on the free recall test, the latter leaning heavily on one's ability to store and retrieve phonetic descriptions of the nonsense syllables presented.

Moreover, it is quite likely that reader group differences in phonologic processing are intrinsically related to group differences in visual-verbal learning. This is suggested in our observation that results on the free recall test were highly correlated with results on the picture-syllable test at both grade levels. Indeed, when performance on the free recall test was statistically controlled, reader group differences on the picture-syllable test were greatly reduced or eliminated. In addition, results on both the free recall and picture-syllable tests were highly correlated with results on the code acquisition tests. These findings are important, for they provide strong support for the idea that observed differences between poor and normal readers in visual-verbal association tasks (Vellutino, Steger, Harding & Phillips, 1975) are due primarily to group differences in learning the verbal response components of these tasks.

There is also little doubt that differences between poor and normal readers in phonologic coding and phonemic segmentation are directly and causally related to differences between these groups in code acquisition. This can be inferred from the observation that subjects in all groups who received segmentation training performed significantly better on the code acquisition tasks than did subjects who did not receive this training. In this connection, we should also mention that performance on the tests of phonemic segmentation was found to be positively and significantly correlated with performance on the code acquisition tasks, correlations being greater when the transfer task was the dependent measure. This latter finding is yet another indication that segmentation analysis is especially important to success in generalization learning.

Additionally, it is apparent from the treatment differences noted that despite what appear to be basic deficiencies in processing phonologic information, poor readers are able to profit from training that attunes them to the grapheme-phoneme invariance in printed words, to assist in identifying those words. Indeed, it would appear that segmentation training facilitated the development of a processing attitude in these children, that to some extent compensated for their deficiencies in phonologic coding.

Still another conclusion allowed by our results is that the type of training a child receives can foster either a holistic or an analytic processing strategy, and that while each has utility in word identification, the child equipped with both is much better able to alter his perceptual attitude to conform to task demands. A holistic or salient features strategy is functional as long as the printed and spoken words to be associated are highly distinctive and easily discriminated. But when such distinctions cannot be readily made, as is often the case with orthographies based on an alphabet, metalinguistic analysis is a critically important and complementary tool for learning. The importance of segmentation training is demonstrated in the fact that subjects who received this training did not show any decrement in performance on the transfer phase of code acquisition, and performed better than those who did not receive this training on transfer learning. That both holistic and analytic strategies are important to success in word identification is demonstrated in the fact that subjects who received both response and segmentation training were generally our best performers.

Finally, the present results provide additional support for the developmental hypotheses advanced earlier, insofar as reader group differences on most of the measures of phonologic processing were of much greater magnitude at the second than at the sixth grade level. Indeed, these findings indicate that deficiencies in phonologic coding are especially encumbering to poor readers at the early stages of skills development and not quite as encumbering to those at later stages. This is in contrast to results on tasks comparing younger and older reader groups on lexical and semantic memory, where group differences at older age levels are as great or greater as they are at younger age levels.

Synthesis

The results of the studies discussed in the preceding sections provide considerable support for the linguistic coding deficit explanation of reading disability set forth earlier. Moreover, the evidence, while seminal, suggests that the nature of the coding deficits hypothesized and their particular manifestations may vary at different levels of development. Thus, poor readers in the primary and intermediate grades (grades 1 through 4) appear to be more attuned to the meaning than to the structural components of spoken and printed words or, more specifically, to the semantic rather than the phonologic, syntactic, and orthographic components of these stimuli. In contrast, normal readers at these levels appear to be attuned to both meaning and structural components and are especially attuned to word structure during the period of code acquisition, when they are heavily invested in learning symbol-sound correspondence rules.

Sensitivity to a word's constituent features has typically been referred to as metalinguistic awareness, and in young poor readers a lack of metalinguistic awareness appears to be but one manifestation of a more basic problem in linguistic coding. Accordingly, these children have also been found to be less proficient than normal readers on tasks evaluating memory for spoken words, and there is reason to believe that such difficulties are due in large measure to the difficulties they encounter in storing and retrieving the phonetic and syntactic descriptions of given words—what we have termed their purely linguistic attributes. That poor readers at younger age levels are especially deficient in coding information linguistically is suggested in our observation that the differences between second grade reader groups were especially pronounced on free recall of abstract words, a task that relied heavily upon their ability to encode and crossreference the phonologic and syntactic as well as the semantic components of auditorily presented words.

But perhaps the most impressive evidence that young poor readers are deficient in phonologic coding inheres in the finding that our second grade poor readers had extraordinary difficulty, compared with their normal reader counterparts, on response learning and code acquisition tasks involving memory for phonemically redundant nonsense words. Memorizing nonsense words is an enterprise that relies primarily on one's ability to store and retrieve phonetic information, and the second grade poor readers made very little progress in doing so. The same subjects also performed below the level of normal readers on measures of phonemic segmentation ability, implying that there is an intrinsic relationship between phonologic coding and metalinguistic awareness on the one hand and reading ability on the other. That this relationship is causal is suggested in the fact that training in phonemic segmentation had a distinctly positive effect on code acquisition—poor readers as well as in normal readers.

However, the picture presented by reader group contrasts at older age levels is somewhat different than that presented by group contrasts at younger age levels. For one thing, older poor readers (sixth graders in this case) appeared to be closer to normal readers at the same grade level in metalinguistic awareness, insofar as they more closely approximated the normal readers on most tasks evaluating their sensitivity to the structural properties of spoken and printed words, particularly those involving new learning. For another, they appeared to be comparable to the normal readers in their ability to code the purely linguistic attributes of spoken and printed words. This was especially apparent in the fact that their performance level was much closer to the normal readers on tasks evaluating memory for phonemically redundant nonsense words as well as on those evaluating code acquisition.

In contrast, the sixth grade poor readers performed consistently and substantially below the sixth grade normal readers on tasks that relied more heavily upon semantic structure and lexical development; that is, on tasks that evaluated memory for real words. Moreover, qualitative analyses of error patterns on these tasks suggested that they were just as inclined as the normal readers to encode the structural features of the word stimuli, but somewhat less inclined to encode their meanings. Taken together with results from the studies evaluating featural encoding in printed words, these findings support our contention that at older age levels, cumulative deficiencies in semantic coding are more important determinants of reader group differences on word perception and word memory tasks than are deficiencies in phonologic, syntactic, and orthographic coding.

The present view is given additional support by the results of studies conducted elsewhere. That poor and normal readers at younger age levels are differentially attuned to phonologic and semantic codes is supported by a study by Byrne and Shea (1979), who found that the recognition errors made by second grade poor readers in processing semantically or phonetically similar words were almost exclusively occasioned by semantic similarity of target and distractor words, while the recognition errors made by second grade normal readers were occasioned by phonologic as well as semantic similarity of targets and distractors. Similar results were obtained by Mark, Shankweiler, Liberman and Fowler (1977), who used a visual analogue of the task used by Byrne and Shea. In addition, Siegel and Ryan (1984) analyzed the response substitution errors made by poor and normal readers (ages 7 to 14) on oral reading and oral language tasks, and found that young poor readers were inclined to make many more semantic than phonologic substitution errors, while normal readers tended to make a sizable number of errors of both types. These results are, of course, consistent with those we obtained.

Our suggestion that reader group differences in featural encoding are themselves related to group differences in phonologic coding ability is supported by the results of a series of studies conducted by Liberman and her associates (Liberman and Shankweiler, 1979) wherein young poor readers (second graders) performed consistently below normal readers on rhyming and nonrhyming consonant letters presented both visually and auditorily. Deficiencies in phonologic coding were especially apparent in the fact that the normal readers were disrupted more than the poor readers by consonants that rhymed with one another. Similar results were obtained by Mann, Liberman, and Shankweiler (1980), using a sentence repetition task. Phonologic coding deficits have also been interpreted to account for differences between poor and normal reader groups on tasks evaluating verbatim memory for information embedded in connected text (Perfetti & Lesgold, 1979; Waller, 1976). Interestingly enough, these studies also found that the poor readers were comparable to the normal readers in abstracting broader meanings and general themes contained in the same texts, consistent with the idea that poor readers are more sensitive to the meaning than to the structural components of language.

The suggestion that the acquisition of initial reading skills is significantly influenced by metalinguistic awareness is supported by a sizable number of studies in which significant positive correlations were found between tests of phonemic segmentation ability and tests of reading ability (Fox & Routh, 1982; Helfgott, 1976; Treiman, 1976; Zifcak, 1976). Also impressive are the results of longitudinal studies showing strong correlations between segmentation tests administered to children at the pre-first grade level and tests of reading ability administered to the same children after they had begun learning to read (Bradley

& Bryant, 1983; Liberman, Shankweiler, Fischer & Carter, 1974). The results of one of these studies (Bradley & Bryant, 1983) are particularly impressive because some of the children in this study were given training in phonemic segmentation, and those who received this training eventually performed better on reading and spelling tests than those who did not receive the training. This finding, of course, provides direct support for a causal link between segmentation ability and reading ability and reinforces our own findings.

Additional support for this type of relationship is provided by results from a study recently completed by Treiman and Baron (1983) in which pre-first graders, who were trained either to segment spoken syllables or to simply repeat spoken syllables, performed better in learning to identify words containing phonemes that had been embedded in syllables previously segmented than in learning to identify words containing phonemes that had been embedded in syllables simply repeated.

The results of all of these studies are entirely consistent with our findings, but while they directly support our speculations as to the relationship between reading ability and phonologic versus semantic coding, ability, they provide no direct support for the hypothesized relationship between reading ability and syntactic coding ability. Moreover, since these studies were conducted on preschoolers and early elementary grade children, they provide no support for the developmental hypotheses we have advanced.

As regards syntactic coding, there is at least suggestive evidence from work done elsewhere, but the studies are few in number. Thus, Brittain (1970) and Vogel (1974) have reported research demonstrating reader group differences in knowledge and use of inflectional morphemes, and we have obtained similar results (Vellutino & Scanlon, 1982). In addition, there are several investigations that have demonstrated differences between poor and normal readers on tests evaluating receptive and expressive language, and it is significant that most of these studies evaluated children in the primary and intermediate grades. Space does not permit extensive discussion of these data, so it will suffice to point out that poor readers at these age and grade levels have been found to be less proficient than normal readers at these levels on a variety of measures, including judgments of grammaticality, sentence imitation, comprehension, and use of complex syntactic constructions (e.g., embedded sentences), detection of ambiguity, ability to paraphrase, and ability to use syntactic structure to recall words embedded in sentences (Bougere, 1969; Flood & Menyuk, 1979; Fry, Johnson & Muehl, 1970; Goldman, 1976; Goldsmith, 1977; Pike, 1977). The results are uniform in their suggestion that poor readers have, at best, incorporated weak representations of the syntactic differences in words and sentences and are therefore unable to make fine-grained distinctions on comprehension, production, and verbal memory tasks that require such distinctions. Thus available evidence, although seminal, is supportive and highly suggestive.

As regards the developmental hypotheses of interest here, we can only state that there has been very little research systematically contrasting poor and normal readers at different age and grade levels on featural encoding and verbal memory tasks. Indeed, so far as we know, no other investigators have reported results, derived from developmental contrasts, comparable to those we have reported here, with one notable exception. To be specific, Olson and his associates (Olson, Kliegel, Davidson & Foltz, 1984) compared young (ages 8 to 10) and older (11 to 15) poor and normal readers on a false recognition task similar to that used by Mark et al. (1977), and found that while the young poor readers were less apt to be confused by rhyming words than were the young normal readers, the older poor readers *did* manifest this type of confusion and, in fact, behaved more like the young normal readers. On the other hand, the older normal readers were not so inclined to be confused by rhyming words, suggesting that they were more attuned to word meanings than to word structures. These results, of course, are consistent with the results we reported earlier, and are in accord with the developmental hypothesis under consideration here.

Finally, as pointed out by Yaden (this volume), there is *not* uniform agreement as to the importance of metalinguistic awareness in learning to read, and one especially prominent point of view is that of Ehri (Ehri, 1976, 1979; see also Ehri, this volume), who contends that metalinguistic awareness is an inevitable by-product of successful reading; and that training to facilitate metalinguistic awareness would therefore have limited utility. The implication of this point of view is that deficiencies in metalinguistic awareness are a consequence rather than a cause of reading disability. However, Ehri's contentions are contrary to our observation and that of other investigators (Bradley & Bryant, 1983; Treiman & Baron, 1983) that training in phonemic analysis has a direct and facilitative effect upon code acquisition and thus word identification. Furthermore, while there is little doubt that learning to read is catalytic and itself promotes the type of analysis that heightens metalinguistic awareness, we think that existing evidence favors the preeminence of deficiencies in linguistic coding and metalinguistic awareness as basic causes of reading disability in many children, particularly those in the early stages of skills acquisition. The present chapter has attempted to document this point of view. However, we admit that our results are preliminary and the hypotheses we have advanced need to be evaluated more thoroughly. We hope that our account serves to stimulate such research.

Notes

[1] The actual/potential correlation for normal readers, exclusive of the first grade group, may be spuriously low, due to restrictions in range created by near perfect performance in identifying the words included on the forced choice test (i.e., the potentially available word sets).

[2] The reader may be wondering why, in almost all of the studies reported herein, we have consistently compared poor and normal readers in second and sixth grade. Aside from the economy derived from studying reader groups at a limited number of age and grade levels, we have elected to study second and sixth graders because we have consistently observed in previous research we have conducted that second grade normal readers perform at a level comparable to sixth grade poor readers on measures of reading ability.

Thus, we are able to compare reader groups matched for both chronological age and reading ability on various experimental measures.

[3] The finding that segmentation training had no apparent effect on free recall is of interest, since it suggests that phoneme analysis is not normally adopted as a perceptual attitude in processing linguisitic information, except under extraordinary instances wherein the learning task prompts one to adopt such an attitude, as in alphabetic mapping where discovery of grapheme-phoneme invariance is functional. It should also be noted that this result is consistent with the theory of speech perception articulated by Liberman and his associates (Liberman, Cooper, Shankweiler & Studdert-Kennedy, 1967) who suggest that the syllable is the basic unit of perception in processing language.

Acknowledgments

We wish to thank the administrators and teachers of the public and parochial schools in the Albany, Schenectady, and Troy metropolitan areas for their cooperation in conducting the research reported in this paper. We also wish to thank Melinda Taylor and Veronica Carney for their assistance in editing and typing the manuscript. Finally, the studies discussed and the paper itself were supported in part by a grant to the senior author (#1R01HD0965801) from the National Institute of Child Health and Human Development.

Section 4

The Influence of Home and School Interventions on the Development of Metalinguistic Awareness

Chapter 9

Issues Related to Home Influences on Young Children's Print-Related Development

ELFRIEDA H. HIEBERT

A shift is evident in the perspective of what constitutes prereading and when this development occurs. Researchers have moved from an emphasis on acquisition of written language forms, such as letter naming and visual discrimination, to a view of reading acquisition as also involving an understanding of the purposes and processes of using print. With this shift has come the recognition that preschool children are acquiring such knowledge about print as part of their everyday experiences. This changing view is reflected in descriptions such as Goodman and Goodman's (1979) "learning to read as natural" and Smith's (1976) "learning to read by reading."

Even though the home environment has long been viewed to be an important influence on children's success in beginning reading instruction (Almy, 1949; Sheldon & Carrillo, 1952), this recent emphasis on naturalistic learning has directed even more attention to influences of the home environment on preschool children's print-related learning. Evidence of this renewed interest is the proliferation of articles on what parents should be doing to further their young children's print-related learning. Information on what parents actually do and the effects of these home influences on preschool children's print-related learning is less abundant.

The purpose of this chapter is to discuss several of the more important questions related to home environment influences on young children's print-related learning. While there are undoubtedly many more questions, three have been chosen that appear particularly pressing. The first considers the influence of individual child and parent differences in print-related experiences. This discussion encompasses both the influence of parents in creating or responding to child differences and to differences among children in how they initiate or respond to different experiences. The second issue relates to the characteristics of successful home learning experiences. Specifically, the degree to which experiences are si-

145

multaneously informal and directed will be discussed. The final issue considers the appropriateness of home intervention programs, and if intervention programs are to be conducted, the structure and content of such programs. In discussing each issue, relevant research will be reviewed. Based on this discussion, directions for research to provide answers to pressing questions will be suggested.

Of particular interest in addressing these issues is the influence of the home environment on what will be called metalinguistic knowledge. Smith (1977) identified knowing about the uses of print and beginning to participate in the process of using print as part of reading acquisition, even though the child is not formally reading. Others have identified book handling skills, recognition of words in their environmental context, and concepts of the processes used in reading as important aspects of early print-related development (Clay, 1972; Downing, 1970; Goodman, 1983; Harste, Burke, & Woodward, 1982; Smith, 1976). In the present context, the term "metalinguistic knowledge" will be used to encompass various proficiencies such as context-dependent recognition of words, book handling knowledge, and concepts of the purposes and processes of reading.

Research on children's development of metalinguistic knowledge is quite recent. Thus, it is understandable that much of the research on home environment influences has examined acquisition of the forms of written language (e.g., letter naming, visual discrimination). Often these studies provide the only available insight into the mechanisms of print-related development within young children's home environments. Consequently, some studies of home environment influences that have used conventional reading readiness performances as criterion measures will be discussed.

Individual Parent/Child Differences

Differences among children as a result of socioeconomic status have long been recognized. Overall, children from middle income homes perform better than children from lower income homes in beginning reading instruction (Dean, 1965; Fleming, 1943). Even among middle income children, however, differences in print-related knowledge have been found to be extensive. Hiebert (1981) and Mason (1980) each reported an extensive amount of variation in middle income preschool children's knowledge of print. Some children could recognize print in various settings and knew all letter names, while other children appeared to be oblivious to print. Surprisingly, both studies indicated a high degree of uniformity in the print-related activities that parents reported doing with their children (Hiebert, 1980; Mason, 1980). While the predictive value of parental self-reports needs to be considered in interpreting these results, consideration also needs to be given to the influence of differences among children in their motivation and interest in print. Many parents acknowledge the differences among their children through statements such as "This one is interested in reading but his older brother wasn't," or "We did the same things with both of them but she just wasn't interested in books and writing like her brother is." The nature, creation, and influence of child differences on print-related experiences in the home has received scarcely any empirical attention, although researchers as well as parents frequently mention individual differences as affecting children's print-related learning. There are two aspects to the topic of individual differences in children's print-related home experiences. The first has to do with differences among children in initiating or responding to experiences; the second has to do with the influence of parents in creating or responding to differences among children.

Child Differences

There can be little argument with the statement that parents influence children's development, print-related and otherwise. It is increasingly clear, however, that parent-child influences are reciprocal: children's behaviors and characteristics also affect adults' behaviors toward children (Bell & Harper, 1977; Lerner & Spanier, 1978). Even among infants, different child behaviors have been found to influence responses of adults to the child (Lewis & Rosenblum, 1974).

While research on children's roles in parent-child interaction related to print has been extremely limited, questions related to this topic can be easily identified. One question is how children differ in their initiations of print-related experiences with adults. Another relates to the effects of different child responses on adults' behaviors when adults initiate print-related experiences. One child characteristic that parents identify as influencing their print-related interaction is children's interest. Hiebert and Coffey (1981) found that parents of preschool children strongly agreed with the statement that provision of print-related experiences depended on children's interest. Parents' interpretations of children's interest in print, however, may very well be a function of parents' expectations of young children's capabilities. For example, one parent may judge a child to be interested only if the child asks to have a story read, while another parent may judge a child to be interested if she/he expresses pleasure when the parent says that she/he will read the child a story. Furthermore, children's interest may be a function of the kind of reinforcement that they have received for involvement with print or the kinds of experiences with print that they have had in the past. The bases for parents' judgments of children's interest in print require further study, particularly since parents' perceptions of children's interest may influence the print-related experiences that parents provide for their young children.

Parent Differences

Smith's (1973) "difficult way to make learning to read easy" is for teachers to respond to what the child is trying to do. Similarly, it has been suggested that parents' ability to provide information and experiences appropriate to children's developmental level influences children's print-related learning. Teale, Estrada, and Anderson (1981) hypothesized that the more effective a parent or sibling is at negotiating the child's zone of proximal development in literacy events, the more effectively the child will learn to read and write. The zone of proximal development pertains to Vygotsky's (1978) distinction between potential, or the degree of competence that the child can achieve with aid, and the child's performance on some test measure without assistance. In Teale et al.'s study, one child received more experiences with print than other children but yet was behind in her knowledge of print. Teale et al. hypothesized that this child's experiences may not have been appropriate to the child's level of development.

Some research confirms the idea that parents' responsiveness to children's print-related capabilities relates to children's achievement. Parent responsiveness to children's questions has been cited as a key factor in the success of early readers (Teale, 1978). Studies of early readers, however, do not clarify the degree to which parents' discussions of print depend on children's initiative in asking questions. Durkin (1966) has described early readers as persistent in their requests for information about print.

Although the question-asking strategies of parents of early and nonearly readers have not been compared, Flood's (1977) study indicated that the number of questions asked by parents of nonearly readers related positively to children's performances on a prereading measure. The prereading score was a composite of alphabet recognition, whole word recognition, vocabulary, visual discrimination, and recognition and production of geometric shapes. Four of fourteen components of the parent-child reading episode accounted for 23% of the variation in children's prereading scores—total number of child's words, post-story evaluative questions asked by parents, positive reinforcement by parents, and warm-up questions asked by parents. While interaction patterns were not analyzed to determine the relationship between parent responses and children's questions, these data do support the notion that parents' question-raising influences children's print-related learning.

A recent ethnographic study of the parent-child reading episode indicates that the two children being observed asked at least a thousand questions about print and books over a period of several years (Yaden & McGee, 1984). These children were in a situation where the parents were quite receptive to children's inquiries. Different parental response and question modes appear to influence the kinds of questions that children ask when they enter school (Heath, 1982).

Findings of another study provide support for the importance of parental sensitivity to children's abilities. Adams and Hiebert (1983) administered to a group of preschool children a battery of measures that assessed knowledge of the functions of print (environmental print recognition, storybook orientation, and writing) as well as knowledge of the forms of print (letter naming, auditory discrimination, and visual discrimination). Mothers and fathers of these children were asked to predict their children's performances on the measures. Parents of children who performed well on the measures were more accurate in predicting their children's performances on these tasks than parents of children who performed less well. Also interesting in light of the frequently held view that fathers are less involved with their young children than mothers, was the finding that fathers were as accurate in predicting children's performances as mothers.

Although Adams and Hiebert's (1983) study did not indicate how parental awareness of children's ability develops, data from another study suggest that parents' perceptions of print-related experiences become more appropriate as their children get older. Hiebert and Coffey (1981) found that mothers of three- and five-year-olds did not differ in the activities they viewed as appropriate for their children. However, mothers' views related negatively to children's achievement at age three on a battery of print-related measures (including assessment of children's understanding of the purposes and processes involved in using print), while views of mothers of five-year-olds accounted for a positive, significant amount of variation in children's achievement. While the possibility that experiences at one point are critical but only are manifest at a later point in development cannot be ruled out, another interpretation of this finding is that parents begin with unrealistic expectations of appropriate print-related experiences for young children. The attention span and abilities of young children may render these efforts meaningless. At a later point, however, these same strategies may be appropriate.

Finally, there is a need to look at the contributions of both parents and children in creating print-related experiences in the home. Given the interactive nature of this process, the precise contribution of either participant cannot be singled out. Nevertheless, investigations of print-related experiences need to be guided by an interactive model in which both parent and child are seen to influence the interaction.

Characteristics of Successful Home Experiences

While research indicates that successful home experiences are informal rather than didactic, some characteristics of informal experiences are frequently overlooked. One of these has to do with the directed nature of successful informal experiences. The other has to do with the motivation of parents in utilizing these experiences to assist their children's print-related learning.

Informal Versus Formal Activities

Proponents of a naturalistic perspective in reading development have emphasized informal experiences as the mechanism by which children learn about print in the home environment (Goodman & Goodman, 1979; Harste, Burke, & Woodward, 1982; Smith, 1976). Examples of informal experiences are storybook reading and identifying print on traffic signs, billboards, and television commercials. Support for the idea that children acquire print-related knowledge through informal experiences comes from several sources.

One of the only studies in which the issue of formal versus informal home experiences has been tested directly was part of the Denver Reading Project (Brzeinski, 1964). Three types of parent activities with their preschool children were studied: a control group in which parents were told to continue their normal print-related activities with their children; an experimental group in which parents were trained through a guidebook and series of television programs to teach their children reading readiness skills; and a second experimental group in which parents received guidance in teaching their children reading readiness skills from experienced teachers in addition to the guidebooks and television programs. Children's improvement in reading readiness performances related directly to the amount of time in which they were engaged in the activities, with statistically significant gains in achievement made by children whose parents worked with them for at least 30 minutes or more per week. Interestingly, since parents had been given no guidance or encouragement to conduct this activity, reading to the child was also found to have a significant effect, whether or not the child was in one of the groups in which parents received training in reading readiness activities. While the best performances on the test were made by children who had practiced the beginning reading activities more than 30 minutes per week and had been read to more than 60 minutes per week, even control subjects whose parents read to them for at least an hour a week made significant gains on the reading readiness posttest. Information is not provided in the report to determine if storybook reading accounted for more variation in children's performances than the reading readiness activities. Evidently, young children can be taught reading readiness skills through didactic activities and with some degree of parent effort. An activity such as storybook reading, which many parents normally do with their children, however, appears to be at least as effective as more formal instruction.

Descriptions of early readers' home environments provide further support of the informal character of successful home experiences. In surveying accounts of early readers, Teale (1978) found that parents most frequently cited participation in informal experiences with print as the means by which their children had acquired reading proficiency. In one of the studies on early readers, Clark (1976) described the experiences that facilitated print-related learning as casual rather than systematic.

Taylor (1981) provides evidence that such informal experiences also characterize the home environments of children who, although not formally reading, come to school knowledgeable about print. Taylor conducted an in-depth study of the literacy environments of six children over the course of three years—the years preceding their initiation into school and their transition into the literacy demands of the school. A theme that runs throughout Taylor's account is the informal nature of these children's print-related experiences. The children became aware of the functions of print through meaningful, concrete tasks that were a part of the social interactions of their lives, such as writing letters to family members and reading signs. According to Taylor, the children resisted any attempts of didactic instruction in letter naming, although all learned the alphabet as they used print themselves in their everyday experiences.

One experience within the home that influences young children's print-related learning is viewing educational television programs that are designed to teach children about print. In Flood's (1975) study, ability to name characters on television programs such as *Sesame Street* accounted for more variation on a prereading battery than any other single print-related experience in the home. Similarly, Mason (1980) found that only two home influences were consistently related to four-year-olds' word reading in a significant, positive manner at both the beginning and end of the preschool year—viewing of *Sesame Street* and parent-child discussions of the programs that had been viewed. Other home activities such as storybook reading and library visits were related to children's word reading in only one or another analysis.

Initially, these findings on television viewing appear to contradict the evidence on informal experiences. A television program in which a child is taught about a consonant blend, even if the teacher is a funny puppet, appears more didactic than, for example, a parent pointing out a letter in the child's name as they pass a billboard. Television viewing, however, may permit more flexibility in attending than working with an adult on a reading readiness workbook. Furthermore, as Mason's (1980) results confirm, viewing *Sesame Street* is not the only critical element; parents' discussions of the content of the program with the child are as important.

The Directed Component of Informal Experiences

While research supports the idea that print-related learning results from informal experiences rather than didactic or highly structured ones, the process is not one of children acquiring information about print via osmosis from a print-saturated environment. In one manner or another, children's attention needs to be directed to the print in these informal experiences. The terms informal and directed may initially seem contradictory, but examples of activities that are simultaneously informal and directed can readily be identified. In a story reading episode, a parent points to words that contain letters in the child's name or words that the child might recognize. While grocery shopping, the parent points out words on containers that the child recognizes from television commercials. The directed dimension of informal experiences has frequently been overlooked in descriptions of naturalistic learning, but appears to be an extremely important part of these experiences.

Research on children's identification of print within and outside of environmental contexts supports the idea that successful informal experiences have a directed component. While exposure to connected discourse varies as a function of socioeconomic background of the family (Teale et al., 1981), print on billboards, traffic signs, and television commercials, to name but a few examples, appears with similar frequency in the physical environment regardless of socioeconomic background. Mere presence or salience of environmental print, however, is not sufficient to direct children's attention to this print. Examples such as Torrey's (1969) case study of a child who learned to read from television commercials are exceptions rather then the general rule. A number of studies have shown that children focus on contextual features such as the logo or unique characteristics of the environmental setting rather than the graphic features to give the print meaning (Dewitz, Stammer & Jenson, 1980; Hiebert, 1978; Masonheimer, 1983). Dewitz et al. reported that children produced the word associated with the new environmental setting when words were transposed from their environmental setting to another one. For example, children would say the name of a fast-food restaurant if the word "stop" were placed with the logo for that restaurant. This research suggests that without specific directions to attend to the graphic features of words, many children will not attend to the graphic characteristics. Yet children are capable of identifying specific features of the word when their focus is directed to the word (Masonheimer, 1983). In one way or another, the attention of children needs to be directed to the print.

Studies of the home environments of early readers have frequently been cited as support for the informal nature of successful home learning experiences. These descriptions have been based primarily on retrospective reports by parents and have been rather global accounts of these experiences. In a study that provided a very detailed description of the home environments of early readers, Tobin (1981) compared the personal and home characteristics of early readers, nonearly readers, and children who were being taught to read in a preschool setting (preschool readers). Of the 85 child characteristics and home influences analyzed, Tobin found that two variables had the most power in discriminating among early readers' performances and those of nonearly and preschool readers. These two variables both related to parental assistance. Specifically, parents of the most fluent readers were more likely to engage their children in informal, game-like activities that could be expected to promote mastery of initial phonics skills and to direct children's attention to the relationship between spoken and written words.

A similar finding that learning about print reflects specific experiences with print has been confirmed with children who are not formally reading but who are learning about print. Hess, Holloway, Price, and Dickson (1979) hypothesized that if home experiences that further children's letter naming involve specific experiences with letter naming, a stronger relationship between such specific experiences and letter naming should exist than between more general language activities and letter naming. To test this hypothesis, Hess et al. studied the homes of two groups of children. One group had high letter naming and low vocabulary scores (as measured by the vocabulary subtest of the *Wechsler Intelligence Scale for Children* (WISC), and the other had low letter naming and high vocabulary scores. The three family activities on which the two groups were compared were: (a) activities that encourage a child to name letters; (b) activities that involve nonreading skills—counting, recognizing colors, learning the names of shapes; (c) activities that indicate mother's interest in reading books, magazines, and newspapers. The findings substantiated the hypothesis that letter naming but not vocabulary development reflected specific as compared to general experiences with language, in that children in the high letter naming and low vocabulary group received more assistance in letter naming than children in the low letter naming and high vocabulary group. There was little difference between the two groups, however, in nonreading assistance or parental reading, even when accounting for intelligence.

Parents' Motivation

The informal character of successful print-related learning experiences in the home also needs to be viewed in the context of findings that beliefs about print-related experiences frequently distinguish parents of successful learners from less successful ones. In some cases, these beliefs predict children's print-related knowledge more highly than parents' described activities. Such is the case in Dunn's (1981) study, in which mothers kept diaries of the educational interactions they had with their children as well as similar interactions of fathers and children. Although measures from the diary record, such as how much time parents spent reading to the children, did not relate significantly to children's performances, parents' beliefs regarding their teaching roles were powerful predictors of children's scores. One parental belief in particular predicted children's achievement: Parents who felt that it was their job to teach children letter and number skills had children who performed more highly on letter naming and number measures than parents who did not view these skills to be their responsibility.

In an extension of the study already described, Hess et al. (1979) found that a parent motivation factor accounted for more variation in children's achievement than involvement in print-related activities. Measures of parental "press for achievement" and of relevant experiences were related to children's letter naming skills. The press for achievement measure consisted of mothers' views of age-appropriate times for mastery of school-related tasks and of verbal initiative and assertiveness, child's (hypothetical) progress in school, child's potential for occupational and educational achievement, and the importance of language learning activities in the preschool. The experiential measure consisted of five environmental items that have been identified as providing direct experience relevant to latter naming: hours spent watching *Sesame Street*, hours parents coviewed *Sesame Street*, whether parents checked out books from the library for the child, how often the child listened to educational records, and the amount of time the parent spent reading to the child. Children whose mothers had high scores on the press for achievement measures but below average scores on the relevant experience measure performed considerably better on the letter naming task than children from homes with high experiential scores but low press for performance scores. However, children who had high availability to experiences but whose mothers had a low press for achievement performed better than children from homes with a low press for achievement and few relevant experiences.

These findings on the role of parental beliefs and motivation suggest that parents may have a more intentional reading instruction agenda than has frequently been thought to be the case. Thirty-seven percent of the parents surveyed by Tobin and Pikulski (1983) reported that they were deliberately attempting to teach their nursery school or kindergarten children to read. Parents' intentions to create various activities at different stages in children's development clearly needs attention.

One caveat to this discussion of the characteristics of home learning experiences needs to be stressed. Some of the studies that have been reviewed as support for the directed and parental motivation components of informal experiences have used a conventional reading readiness measure such as letter naming as the criterion for print-related learning (e.g., Hess et al., 1979). Children's metalinguistic knowledge may be a more implicit form of knowledge. Consequently, the process of learning may be different. However, one aspect of metalinguistic knowledge—familiarity with storybooks—has been linked to specific experiences with books. In an intervention study that focused on children's story reading proficiencies, Mason and McCormick (1983) found that the treatment accounted for variation in children's performances on a book handling task but not on a letter naming task. The degree to which experiences in which children develop metalinguistic knowledge are content-specific and the kinds of experiences that facilitate such understanding need particular attention.

Intervention Studies

The Scope of Home Intervention Programs

Many studies of home environment influences have been aimed at identifying activities that further print-related learning so that intervention programs can be designed that facilitate children's learning in homes where such activities do not occur. The idea of home intervention programs, however, has been questioned by some. If the answer is positive to the question of whether home intervention programs should be implemented, an additional question relates to the structure and content of such programs.

Taylor (1981) has criticized the pattern of many intervention programs in which parents are provided with specific "how to's" of reading instruction. One program identified by Taylor specified 37 reading skill activities for parents to do with their young children. In contrast, Taylor found no evidence among the families in her sample that parents specifically taught their children to read. Rather, literacy activities were part of the social processes of family life and "not some specific list of activities added to the family agenda to explicitly teach reading" (Taylor, 1981, p. 167).

Others have posed similar criticisms against the imposition of strategies in the home environment. Scribner and Cole (1973), for example, have noted that requiring parents with little formal education to teach skills commonly delegated to the school, such as reading, may be inappropriate and even dysfunctional, since these tasks may demand modes of learning and thinking different from those needed in everyday life.

The criticisms that have been leveled against home intervention programs are legitimate. Frequently, strategies have been imposed on parents in attempting to increase young children's print-related strategies. A survey of popular magazines and professional journals indicates a host of "how-to" articles that provide many activities that parents "should" be doing to prepare their young children for reading. Furthermore, many teachers of beginning reading apparently conduct their own "home intervention reading programs" by asking parents to assist their children with reading worksheets and word lists (Becker & Epstein, 1982).

Despite these criticisms, however, home intervention strategies should not be dismissed. The didactic mode of previous intervention programs does not mean that future programs need to take a similar tactic. Furthermore, implicit in some arguments against home intervention programs is the idea that parents should be allowed to do "what comes naturally." The status quo, however, appears to represent a type of intervention that creates in parents a notion of what it means to do "what comes naturally." Suggestions to parents in the past have frequently stressed reading readiness skills. The content of the parent intervention component of the Denver Prereading Program illustrates the emphasis on reading readiness that was prevalent several decades ago (Brzeinski, 1964). Parents evidently have been influenced by this conventional view of reading readiness. Tobin and Pikulski (1983) found that a majority of parents of nursery school and kindergarten children felt that their children should learn to name letters and to recite the alphabet in home environments. In contrast, many parents perceived reading common words in the environment as an activity that could wait until kindergarten or first grade. This finding suggests that parents may not be fully aware of the strategies that have been espoused by a naturalistic approach to beginning reading. Parents, indeed, may need guidance to do what has been thought to come naturally.

An Exemplary Home Intervention Program

To date, very few intervention programs have emanated out of the view of reading as a naturalistic language learning process. One exception to this pattern is a study by Mason and McCormick (1983). Mason and McCormick's intervention strategy centered around "little books" which consisted of simple illustrated stories. A procedure for using the books was demonstrated to children during preschool screening, which occurred in the spring preceding their entry into preschool in the fall. Parents who consented to participate in the study were given three books and guidelines for their use. One group received an additional packet of books on two occasions—once during the summer and once in the fall. The second group received the materials only during the preschool screening. Each group was followed through kindergarten, where performances of children who received the books were compared to those of children who did not receive the books. For children who received three installments of the books, performances on word reading and spelling subtests at the end of kindergarten were predicted by treatment and entering language ability, as measured by the Peabody Picture Vocabulary Test (PPVT). The treatment accounted for significant differences on story reading and the PPVT accounted for significant differences in letter name knowledge. For the children who received the books only at the preschool screening, their story reading performances were affected by the treatment and the PPVT. On other measures, however, these children did not perform differently than their kindergarten peers, who had not received any books. Information from a parent questionnaire as to the degree of their involvement in various print-related activities did not predict children's reading performances. While the possible confounding effect of preschool participation on children's learning is a factor that needs to be considered in interpreting these results, Mason and McCormick's study indicates the potential for furthering children's print awareness through very simple home interventions.

Suggestions for the Structure and Content of Home Intervention Programs

The recent research on preschool children's print-related learning and parents' influences on this development provides the basis for suggestions on the structure and content of home intervention programs. Since children appear to learn about print through content-specific activities, techniques and materials designed at furthering children's print-related learning should be content-specific. If furthering children's book-related abilities is of interest, then an intervention program should emphasize book handling activities. Mason and McCormick (1983), for example, noted that the lack of an effect for their treatment on letter name knowledge was not surprising, since none of the materials sent to parents addressed letter naming.

Suggestions should also not require extensive allocations of time by parents. Since an increasing number of young children live in homes with a single working parent, asking parents to do activities that consume large blocks of time seems unreasonable. Indeed, the best techniques for home intervention may be those that can be performed by the child, independently of adults. Mason and McCormick's (1983) activity could be performed by the child without the assistance of an adult. Another activity that can be performed without direct adult involvement and that has proven successful in furthering children's print awareness is viewing of television programs such as *Sesame Street*. This suggestion is not meant to dismiss any parental involvement. Parents in Mason and McCormick's study may have been involved with the children in reading the books or children's participation with the books may have resulted from parental urging. As previously discussed, studies of *Sesame Street* indicate that parental encouragement of children's viewing is an important factor in children's learning from the program, as is parental discussion with the child about ideas seen on the program (Ball & Bogatz, 1970; Bogatz & Ball, 1971). Activities that children can perform independently at times and that parents can also participate in and reinforce at other times seem particularly appropriate as the focus of home intervention programs.

While numerous writers have identified learning about print in everyday activities as crucial to children's print-related experience, no intervention programs to date have provided parents with suggestions on how to use the print in the environment to further children's print-related learning. Print on billboards, packages, and signs is readily accessible to families, regardless of socioeconomic status. Such activities may be very commonplace in middle income homes, but may occur infrequently in lower income homes. The effects of teaching parents techniques to direct children's attention to the print in environmental settings needs to be explored. Continued work with activities that foster familiarity with books and the language of books should be another priority in home intervention programs, since such familiarity is an integral component of print-related success.

Issues Related to Home Intervention Programs

These ideas for the structure and content of home intervention programs have been presented only as suggestions to guide research efforts. A number of issues need to be resolved through systematic research efforts before more extensive implementations of such ideas are initiated.

One issue relates to the points in children's development at which home intervention programs should most appropriately occur. Suggestions have often been globally aimed at "parents of preschoolers." Teale et al. (1981) raised the need to consider the appropriateness of activities relative to the child's level of development. Some activities may be suited to children at a particular developmental level, while others may be appropriate with children at other levels.

Another consideration is how parents translate investigators' suggestions. In studies of classroom instruction, the degree to which teachers actually implement the treatment has been studied as a factor (Anderson, Evertson & Brophy, 1979). Parents may implement some suggestions and translate other suggestions differently. Still other ideas may simply not be suited to the home setting.

Another issue relates to the effects of compatibility, or a lack of it, between instructional techniques or materials in the home and those in the preschool or kindergarten. If parental intervention programs complement the preschool program, the effect may be very different than if the preschool program diverges from what is happening in the home (Winetsky, 1978).

The issue of compatibility between the print-related activities of the home and those of the school relates to a final topic that has to do more with intervention programs in school settings than it does with intervention programs in the home. Home intervention programs may be very successful. If beginning reading instruction in the school setting does not utilize this knowledge, however, the efforts of the home may be rendered ineffectual. As Durkin (1974–75) found, instructional gains of children in a kindergarten program faded when first grade teachers failed to adapt instruction to children's levels. This issue is a particularly important one in relation to the current research in print awareness. Some researchers have attempted to establish the relationship between various measures of children's metalinguistic knowledge and success in beginning reading (Kontos & Huba, 1983). There is no reason, however, to expect this relationship to be high if beginning reading programs are not oriented to the knowledge that young children have. As intent as investigators are in establishing home influences and the creation of more optimal print-related experiences for children in home environments, the ultimate success of these programs is dependent on the instructional programs of the school. A priority in the study of young children's metalinguistic knowledge needs to be the development of instructional programs that build on the knowledge that young children have gained in the home environment.

Chapter 10

How Are You Going to Help Me Learn? Lesson Negotiations Between a Teacher and Preschool Children

JANA M. MASON

CHRISTINE McCORMICK

NAVAZ BHAVNAGRI

Reading tasks for children and lesson suggestions for teachers are based on assumptions that every child can be the typical child, that all materials and lessons can be understood by the children, and that everyone will gain in skill or knowledge by becoming engaged in the learning activities. Of course teachers know this is not true, but there has been less than adequate advice about how to help children who do not seem "ready" to take part in school lessons. Some schools encourage parents to wait another year to enter such children in kindergarten; others advise a second year of kindergarten. Another possibility, the one to be addressed here, is to provide activities in kindergarten classrooms that show the children how to participate in group reading lessons.

Among the many ways to foster successful group reading in kindergarten, one that is seldom discussed is giving children the opportunity to generate verbal statements about what they are reading and learning. Its value can be argued from two perspectives—the child development literature on representational thinking (e.g., Laosa & Siegel, 1982), and the reading comprehension literature on metacognitive strategies (e.g., Forrest-Pressley, MacKinnon & Waller, 1985). Talking about their lesson, a book they are hearing, or a story they are trying to read helps young children because they (a) begin to distance themselves from the topic and treat it more "as an object" of comprehension; (b) begin to use reading strategies of figuring out how to participate in reading activities; and (c) begin to monitor their understanding of the topic.

To make our case, we first need to explain why children who are at risk academically might need alternative instruction in a preschool. Their incoming ability to participate in school reading lessons is affected by *materials in the home environment, parents' motivation and press for achievement,* and *parent-child interaction patterns.* We propose that of these, parent-child interaction patterns is the one least likely to be ameliorated by teacher intervention. The purpose of this research is to show how alternative teacher-child interaction procedures might be established.

Influences on Emerging Literacy

Home Environment Materials

We have known for many years that children enter school with varying knowledge about reading because of differences in the availability of reading materials and activities that foster attention to print (e.g., Callaway, 1968; Durkin, 1966; Flood, 1975). Related to this is exposure to a variety of activities (Miller, 1969, 1970) and parent support for reading (Mason, 1980; McCormick & Mason, in press). Some parents begin reading to their children when they are infants. Later they point out letters, name words, and encourage attempts to read, write, spell, and even give school-like workbook tasks. Other children, many of whom are from lower socioeconomic status families and single parent homes, do not receive these materials and activities at home (Shinn, 1978). As a result, they do not recognize letters when they begin school and have only fuzzy notions about how to read a book or listen to a story. The children can often be recognized in kindergarten by their seeming lack of attentiveness to lessons or reluctance to speak out, and failure to reach the same level of achievement as their more advantaged classmates (Francis, 1977; Kinsbourne, 1976; McCormick & Mason, in press). Kindergarten and preschool teachers often counter with helpful but insufficient actions such as (a) putting books and reading games in prominent locations in the classroom; (b) reading to the children; (c) sending books home for parents to read to the children; and (d) giving direct reading instruction.

Parent Press for Achievement

Another home variable that affects beginning reading achievement is the mother's expectations for school achievement, degree of concern over school progress, and occupational and educational aspirations for her child. According to Hess, Holloway, Price, and Dickson (1982), low parent expectations seem to operate as a depressant to achievement, at least in conjunction with a sparsely supported home environment for beginning reading. Presuming this to affect motivation to learn, teachers try to (a) make reading and listening to stories a pleasurable event; (b) encourage children to work closer to their potential; and (c) point out to them how they are succeeding to learn.

Style of Interaction

Parents' style of interaction with their children can help school learning. Ninio (1980), Ninio and Bruner (1978), and Snow (1982) studied parent-child games and storybook reading between infants or young children and their caregivers. They found that middle class parents structure game or reading events so that the child gradually and successfully acquires knowledge about how to play a significant role in the activity. An important aspect of this type of parent-child interaction is the opportunity the child has to develop and establish a view of self as an active participant in carrying out and construing the meaning of a task.

A related perspective is voiced in the child development literature regarding the enhancement of children's representational thinking. According to Hess, Holloway, Price, and Dickson (1982), the parent is thought to teach "strategies that challenge the child to anticipate outcomes, reconstruct past events, and attend to transformations" (p. 262). Hess et al. find a schooling advantage (higher reading test achievement scores in the lower and middle grades) for children whose parents use directives and questions that require children to generate original responses. Siegel (1982) argues that opportunities to describe, infer, and interpret rather than to observe or label is critical in the development of representational thinking. This aspect of learning has seldom been investigated in the preschool or kindergarten classroom.

Encouraging Social Interactions in the Classrooms to Promote Literacy

Three explanations for differences in young children's early reading knowledge and attitude about learning have been proposed. First, their home environment may not have supported reading activity. Second, their parents may not have encouraged high achievement. Third, social interactions with parents may not have fostered child-constructed verbalizations. While teachers have developed approaches for the first and second mentioned problems, they are not likely to have developed approaches for fostering the third.

How might teachers counter with instruction that could help to encourage social interaction that will affect reading? One approach is to use different social interaction patterns in the classroom that lead children to develop higher-level verbalizations; another is to provide opportunities for children to monitor their own understanding. These are described next.

Interaction Patterns in School Lessons

Teachers often use social interaction patterns that neither enhance representational thinking nor lead the child gradually from dependence on the teacher to self-sustained learning. That is, a common interaction pattern is one in which the teacher asks a question to which the child responds and the teacher comments (Dillon & Searle, 1982; Mehan, 1979; Sinclair & Coulthardt, 1975). One problem with this pattern is that little may be required from children except agreement, choice between two alternatives, or a labeling response (Guszak, 1967). Dillon and Searle comment that teachers almost talk for their students, use an "oral copying" approach, and ask questions for which children need only select among answers already stated. Another problem is that extensive use of this interaction pattern does not give children sufficient opportunity to describe their own personal experiences about the lesson topic, which in turn makes it more difficult for them to understand and remember the topic (Au & Mason, 1981). A third problem is that it does not lead children from dependence on the teacher for information to self-generated activity (Vygotsky, 1979).

Because most four- and five-year-old children are not reading on their own, we suggest that social interaction patterns be built from language games, story reading, and listening tasks. However, as the following study by Morrow (1984) shows, it is not easy to implement.

Morrow had one group of kindergarten teachers read eight stories to children but without discussion or questions (the children drew pictures after they heard each story). Another group of teachers read eight stories and taught children how to ask their own story questions. The instruction was as follows:

There was discussion and questioning related to the story prior to reading. For the first three stories, questions were posed for children to think about while the story was being read. After they had dealt with three stories, children were given guidance in posing their own questions and did so with the remaining five stories. During the reading, pictures were shown to the children. Stories were not interrupted for discussion. After the story was read, the teacher asked questions and encouraged discussion. (p. 15)

Morrow found that teaching children to ask their own questions was effective for high and middle achieving children, but made no difference for low achieving children. We would expect that if the instruction had provided more alternatives or had encouraged discussion about personal experiences, the children could have learned how to ask themselves questions. Techniques for doing this in the classroom, referred to as metacognitive strategies, have been described by Palincsar (1984) and Paris (1983), among others.

Metacognitive Strategies

Metacognition refers to knowledge of the thought processes and to the regulation or control of thought. Knowledge of how one thinks is assumed to be late-developing while its regulation can be initiated by young children. Self-regulation includes planning (predicting, organizing, scheduling, etc.); monitoring (testing, revising, redoing); and evaluating (checking outcomes), according to Brown, Bransford, Ferrara, and Campione (1982).

Sulzby (1981, 1982) and Sulzby and Otto (1983) found that some preschool children were using metacognitive strategies to tell and pretend-read stories. They signaled in a variety of ways for help; they used explicit metalinguistic terms such as "read"; they told the experimenter which part of their discussions should be considered part of the story they were telling and which part were comments about the text; and sometimes they used indirect indicators and direct metalanguage to refer to the created text. In short, according to Sulzby and Otto, "children create a textual entity, separate from the rest of their speech, which they can comment on and treat as an object."

Olson (1983) makes a similar point in his discussion of an "inside-outside" view of text, or an ability to distinguish between what is said and what is meant. This is difficult for young children because "writing preserves the surface structure, what was said, independently of the intention it expresses, what was meant." Before schooling children have only a rudimentary sense of the distinction; with literacy they take on not only an understanding of intended meanings of text, but, in time, an understanding of metacognitive terms such as "thought, belief, knowledge, memory, plan, intent, and imagine." They learn to express metacognitive constructs.

Modeling Metacognitive Strategies in the Classroom

The following study describes a reading lesson in which the teacher modeled the behaviors children were to develop. Verbal statements and comments about easy-to-read stories were encouraged. In so doing, we fostered the beginnings of metacognitive strategies for reading comprehension.

Subjects

A class of four-year-old children from a Headstart Center were taught to recite the print in easy-to-read little books (Mason, 1980), using an approach that had been successful with middle class preschool children (McCormick & Mason, in press). All of the children were from a poor, outlying region of a southern Illinois town. Approximately 50% of the parents were on welfare and 50% worked as farm laborers or other minimum-wage laborers. Almost half were single parent families. Based on prekindergarten screening tests, the children were considered by school officials to be at risk academically.

Procedures and Materials

The children were taught by us in the classroom on three occasions, once in October, once in February and once in April. We separated the children into groups of about five children, since this group size allowed each child to respond individually in each lesson. We repeated the lesson for each of the three groups. The classroom was used so that the regular teacher could observe the procedure.

The lessons were framed around four instructional moves: *open, model(s), tryout(s), close.* We opened the lesson by showing the children the new book they were about to read and tried to engage them in a discussion of the topic. This was followed by modeling story reading in which we read the story aloud, showing the print and pictures to the children. The modeling ended with another brief discussion of the story. The third step was a tryout in which children were encouraged first to recite the story with us as a group and then singly, each saying a portion of the text. The children who were listeners were allowed to insert comments or repeat the recitation of the child whose turn it was to respond. The story was modeled until the children were willing to say it with us; tryouts were repeated until we were sure they all knew most of the story. In the

October lessons the children needed two modelings and two or three tryouts of each book, and in April the children needed one modeling and two tryouts before accurately reciting the story. The last step of each lesson was closing comments about the story by us with elaborations by the children.

Because we had supposed that the children would look at and learn to recite the story materials, we left several copies in the classroom. This approach had been effective in a middle class day care center the previous year where the books had been placed within easy reach for the children; the teachers, who were impressed with the children's interest, had encouraged rereading. However, in the Headstart Center we found, when we visited the classroom in December and again in January to observe the classroom and catalogue children's use of the materials, that the teacher had not read the books to the children and the children were seldom looking at them. Checking an outline of the teacher's program, we found that it featured skill activities of sorting, counting, and classifying, but not early reading. The teacher read a storybook (not ours) to the entire class once or twice a week, but she did not help them talk about stories and did not think she ought to help them identify letters and words. Moreover, the teacher had placed all books in a loft above the playroom. Only one or two children ever climbed up to look at our books or any others.

We realized that our model lessons and materials would have no effect unless books could be made more available and the children more strongly encouraged to look at them. Thus, in effect, we began the study again. We gave a second set of model lessons to all the children in February using two new stories, sent copies home with the children, and asked the teacher to place copies

Figure 10–1

Examples of Text from Several "Little Books"

Ghosts
a happy ghost
a sad ghost
a big ghost
a little ghost
a scary ghost
Boo!

Apples
red apples
yellow apples
green apples
blue apples
red apples, mmm
yellow apples, mmm
green apples, mmm
blue apples, yuk

Funny Farm Family
one baby chick, peep
two baby chicks, peep
three baby chicks, peep
four baby chicks, peep
five baby chicks, peep
and
one big baby duck, quack

To the Park
We walk past
    Jefferson School
Stop
    post office
    library
    one-way
to Kiwanis Park

on the shelves where the children played or worked. We constructed and gave the teacher several copies of two other books: an alphabet book (there were none in the classroom, not even an alphabet poster) and a book we made from photographed signs near the school with the labels from the signs handprinted below each picture. The text of some of these books (Mason & McCormick, 1985) is shown in Figure 10–1.

Findings/Discussion

Analyses presented here concentrate on the model lessons given in October and April. We omitted an analysis of the February lesson because responses were similar to the October lesson. Lesson transcriptions followed the procedure described in Mason & Au (1984).

Lesson Outcomes

A comparison of the October and April discourse statements disclosed that our questions, responses, and comments relative to the children increased substantially in the opening and modeling segments of the lessons. Using an analysis system described in Mason and Au (1984), we found that we were able to ask more questions and give more information. We acknowledged or praised more of their responses and responded to their initiations (Table 10-1).

Table 10–1

Comparison Over Time of Teacher Discourse
with Preschool Children in an Early Reading Lesson

	Average No. of Remarks in a Lesson		Percent of Total No. of Remarks	
	September	April	September	April
Requests and solicits information from children	15.0	28.0	20	25
Gives information about lesson content	20.0	27.0	27	24
Gives information about lesson structure	11.0	11.0	15	10
Evaluates children's responses	3.0	10.0	4	9
Assists, corrects and highlights children's responses	14.0	15.0	19	13
Regulates verbal interactions and responds to their comments	11.5	22.0	15	19
TOTALS	74.5	113.0	100%	100%

The children's responses and comments to us more than doubled. Their discourse became more complex, with their mean length utterance increasing from 1.65 to 2.15. Moreover, their type of speech changed. In October and January it was very limited, consisting almost entirely of responses to direct questions and repetitions of statements made by us. There were few child-initiated remarks and no predictions by them about the text. In April they were initiating appropriate remarks and predictions about the story, responding to our challenging predictive questions, and initiating conversations with the teacher (Table 10-2).

The greatest increase in remarks by the children took place during the opening and modeling segments of the lesson, when the new information was being introduced. This suggests that the discourse change was due not so much to our organization of the lesson, type of question, or comment as it was to the children's greater knowledge about how to read these books and greater confidence that they could participate. Furthermore, we believe that the change was directly related to the children's opportunity at school and home to hear, read, and talk about stories. A comparison of the February lesson with the ones in October and in April showed that the only difference between the October and February lessons was that the children were more willing to repeat the teacher's words from the story. In February, they were still unwilling or unable to speak out or participate unless explicitly directed to do so.

In Figure 10-2 are examples of the opening discourse from one October and one April lesson. Notice how the children were able in April to help us discuss the story topic. They offered their ideas about the story during the opening lesson segment, and when confused, tried to express what they did understand. When wrong, they were helped before trying to read the story.

Table 10–2

Comparison Over Time of Preschool Children's
Discourse with a Teacher in an Early Reading Lesson

	Average No. of Remarks in a Lesson		Percent of Total No. of Remarks	
	September	April	September	April
Initiates lesson information	2.0	12.0	4	12
Initiates conversation with teacher	.5	9.0	1	9
Responds to teacher with new or repeated information	39.5	65.0	86	65
Responds to teacher with prediction	0.0	8.5	0	9
Responds to teacher with conversation	4.0	4.5	9	5
TOTALS	46.0	99.0	100%	100%

Figure 10–2

Example Dialogue from Opening Segment of Lesson

October Lesson, Opening

1. T: We have something special today on Halloween. It's a special little book. Look. What's it about?
2. C: Ghosts.
3. T: Ghosts. Yeah. Just like William, isn't it? Okay, let's see what it's about. *[Begins reading book.]*

April Lesson, Opening

1. T: You get to hear a new story.
2. C: I knew what that yellow was. *[Refers to one of the books the teacher is holding.]*
3. T: Which one, this one? You know this one, don't you? *[Referring to the fact that copies of the book had been given to the children to take home.]* Yeah.
4. C: I already got my two books.
5. T: You did? Did you like them? *[Child nods.]* Did you? *[Speaks to another child.]*
   T: Did you get your two? Your two *[inaudible]*. Are they still . . . Cathy's got ripped up. Who else's got ripped up?
6. C: I don't.
7. T: You don't?
8. C: I don't got mine ripped up.
9. T: Did you take good care of them? *[Children nod.]* All set? *[Gets ready to discuss story.]*
10. C: But, but—
11. T: —Oh, okay.
12. C: I don't know where mine are.
13. T: Ohh, you'll find them again. Now—*[Gets ready to discuss story.]*
14. C: —I know where mine are. They are, they are on my floor.
15. T: Oh, well, that . . . Maybe you can put them on the shelf. We've got a new story for you today. It's about a funny farm family. Huh, what do you think those might be on that first—
16. C: —Eggs.
17. T: Oh you knew. Can't fool you, can we? They're eggs.
18. C: I knew that they was eggs.
19. T: You knew too?
20. C: I knew too.
21. T: Oh, you guys are really good. But look. There's some little ones. And look at that one *[points to a picture of a large egg on the cover of the book they are about to read]*.
22. C: Big one.
    C: Big one.
    C: Big—
23. T: —Big ones. I wonder—
24. C: —I'll show you where the littlest one is.
25. T: Yeah, well I think that these are all about the same size and this one is the big one. Let's see what's going to happen in here, okay? *[The teacher now starts reading the book.]*

Their initial participation affected the continuation of the lesson. Responsive to their more interactive behavior, we were able to modify the succeeding portions of the lesson. We extended the opening by responding to their comments (e.g., Figure 10-2, numbers 3, 5, 6, 8, 10, 14, 20), and asked more questions (numbers 16 and 22) about the picture on the cover.

Our modeling of the story was changed because the children could now answer our requests to predict what would happen next as shown in Figure 10-3, numbers 1, 7, 11, 13, 17, 21, April). Tryouts moved along more smoothly because the children answered our questions and became more involved in reciting. Also, because the children could ask questions about the text or a particular picture, we could clarify and reduce their confusion.

Figure 10–3

Example Discourse from Modeling Segment of Lesson

October Lesson, Modeling
1. T: Okay. This little story is about ghosts. Aah . . . A happy ghost.
2. C6: Happy ghost.
3. T: A sad ghost.
4. C3: Sad ghost.
5. T: You knew it, didn't you?
6. T: A big—
7. C3: —Big.
8. T: Ghost.
   T: A little ghost.
9. C3: Little.
10. T: A scary ghost. Boo.
11. C4: Boo.

April Lesson, Modeling
1. T: Funny farm family. Let's see on page one.
   We've got one baby chick.
   How's it go? Peep.
2. C4: Peep.
3. T: One baby chick—peep.
4. C4: Peep.
   C2: Peep.
5. T: Now here's the next one.
   Two baby chicks peep.
6. C3: Two baby chicks peep [softly].
   C4: Two baby chicks peep.
7. T: Now what do you think is on the next page?
8. C4: Three.

```
 9. T:   You think so? I think . . . Right you are.
         Three baby chicks. Peep.
10. C3:  Baby chicks. Peep.
    C4:  Peep. Peep? [Late.]
11. T:   What's on the next page, you think?
12. C5:  Four.
    C2:  Four.
    C4:  Four.
    C1:  Four.
13. T:   OK, let's see, right! Four baby chicks, peep.
    T:   What's on this page?
14. C2:  Five.
    C4:  Five.
    C5:  Five.
15. T:   Five—baby—chicks—peep.
16. C5:  Five.
    C3:  Baby—chicks—peep.
    C1:  [Hiccups.] Four.
17. T:   Now we are on five, let's see . . .
18. C2:  One.
    C4:  Six [softly].
    C5:  Six.
19. T:   Well, and . . .
20. C5:  Nine [softly].
21. T:   Well, what do you think, we've got one big egg left.
         You think—something's going to be—in that funny, in that big egg?
22. C2:  One . . . one [drawn out].
23. T:   One something, wonder what's that gonna be?
         And—one—baby—duck.
24. C2:  One baby [together but slightly trailing behind].
    C3:  Duck.
25. T:   He goes quack. Who can . . . can you make a quack?
26. C2:  Maack.
    C3:  Quack.
    C5:  Quack.
    C4:  Quack.
27. T:   OK, he was in the big egg. One baby duck.
28. C:   Duck.
29. T:   Quack.
```

Metacognitive Remarks

The children substantially increased their metacognitive verbalizations. The modeling segments of one October and one April lesson shown in Figure 10-3 indicate ways that the children utilized metacognitive constructs about story reading. Unlike their remarks in October and February, in April they became involved in planning and monitoring the activity and began to verbalize their comprehension of the story. They were predicting the story sequence, indicating an ability to construct expectations about the story line. They were asking questions and commenting about story events and printed information from pictures on the page, indicating that they were monitoring their understanding of story and picture information. Challenges to the turn-taking procedure indicated that they had noticed our unspoken rules for turns and were now planning how they might negotiate a change. Examples of each are presented next.

Predicting a story sequence.   There were two ways that story prediction was apparent. The more common was a response to our prediction question, "What do you think is going to be on the next page," which we asked during the story modeling. The other way was unsolicited predictions by the children about the content or the words that might appear on the next page; for example, "There's only one more," "A big," or "Three baby chicks." The children made no predictions in October; one child made one prediction in February; in April there were 28 predictions recorded during the reading of the new story.

Monitoring comprehension.   Evidence that children were using the picture information and our comments to explain the story to themselves appeared in self-initiated comments about the text or pictures. For example, in April children interjected, "Eggs," before we could finish our question about a picture of the eggs; they inserted, "Big one," after we told them to look at a picture that included a large egg; and they said, "I'll show you where the littlest one is," as the group discussed the picture. In the October lesson there were four child-initiated statements, in February there was only one, and in April there were 15.

Monitoring comprehension failure.   Children's greater awareness of text meaning was clearly evident by their expressions of confusion about the text or picture. Below is the one instance (Number 1) of story monitoring in October, but which didn't occur until there had been six tryouts of the story. There were no instances in February; the three in April are listed below as numbers 2, 3, and 4.

1   T: See him yelling. *[Discussing that the ghost said "Boo" in the story.]*

    C: Ghosts don't say that. They go "Wooh."

    T: Yeah, he could go like that. This one goes "Boo."

2   C: That isn't a baby duck. *[Interjecting a comment about the picture of the duck on the last page.]*

    T: Sure it is. See how big it is. The chicks are just little and it's a big, a big baby duck. See its bill and its feet? That's a baby duck.

    C: Ahh. Because it is big.

3   T: One baby duck. *[Reading to another group of children.]*

C: It's a Mama hen. It's a Mama hen.

T: Well, no . . . *[Continues with explanation similar to the one above.]*

4   C: Hey, I didn't see the baby colt. *[Comment about the cover page after the teacher said the story was about a farm.]*

T: Ooh?

C: Because it walked off with the mother. *[We presume that the child was explaining to herself why a picture about a farm did not include horses.]*

Monitoring turntaking.   Although these children to our knowledge had never been asked before to take turns to recite and had not been told during our lessons how they would take turns, when we used the same approach each time, they quickly learned the procedure of listening to us read, reading with us, and then reading one by one in a fixed left-to-right order. So, for example, after we named the child who was to recite and turned the book so the child could see it more clearly, soon nonverbal cues of turning to and looking at the next child were sufficient to elicit a response. Repetitions of tryouts were signaled by us saying, "Let's read it again." In the October lesson, if children did notice the predictable organization, they did not show that they were using the information, for they did not respond to the nonverbal cues and made no comments. In February, after we said, "Let's see if we can do it together," one child responded, "I wanna do it first." In April, there were seven requests to be first or to do it "all by myself," and one challenge of the turn-taking (we had begun with the second person in the group instead of him): "I didn't get mine."

When we gave these lessons in October and again in February we were startled (and disheartened) by the children's passivity. For example, when we asked them in October and February to sit on the rug for lessons, they lined up with their backs against the wall, waiting silently. Although in October they had never seen us before, they did not ask who we were, what we were setting up (videotape equipment), or why we were there; and they had nothing to say when we explained. Although we had brought stories that other groups of children had eagerly discussed, these children were polite but unresponsive, except to repeat what we said when we told them what to do. It was difficult to elicit any verbal comments from them, they would not elaborate on our comments, and they were quite reluctant to perform one by one. Here, for example, is one of the failed interchanges in October. We asked, "Christopher, what's this one? [No response.] A scary ghost. Can you say that? [No response.] A scary ghost. [No response.] Here we go."

Conclusion

Young children who have not been encouraged to verbalize their own ideas at home can learn to do so in school. The approach we demonstrated here, story recitation, is but one way. What was important to the development of these successful social interaction patterns were easy-to-read materials and a lesson structure that led children from listening and watching a teacher perform the task to child-initiated discussion and performance. Children's greater competence in April was observed in their verbalizations about the topic before the story was read, a willingness to predict and discuss its content, and an ability to express confusion about it or a need for clarification. We found that given an activity that is within their grasp and is interesting to them, low performing children can be encouraged to formulate and express their ideas in a classroom setting and begin to regulate their comprehension. In turn, this enables teachers to clarify, extend, modify, or expand on particular aspects of the activity, improving their instruction.

That is, story recitation and discussion not only helps children to regulate their comprehension, it also enables a teacher to construct more appropriate lessons. If children are familiar with the lesson material and procedure, and if a teacher provides an opportunity during the opening of the story reading session for children to talk about their knowledge about the topic, children can negotiate with the teacher to shape the lesson so that it more closely matches their understanding.

When a lesson fosters child-initiated verbalizations, children learn how to negotiate with the teacher about (a) *the flow of the lesson,* by inserting, extending, and modifying the text information and their own ideas, especially during the opening and lesson modeling; (b) *the structure of the lesson,* by commenting about turn-taking rights, their role, and even the role of the teacher; and (c) *the quality of the lesson* by commenting on, challenging, and extending the topic. Although verbalizing puts children at greater risk, as they are now wrong more often—but are also right far more often—verbalizing helps them clarify their lack of understanding. With greater self-confidence that they can construct comments and questions to the teacher, they gain deeper knowledge about how the lesson operates and what they are supposed to do, and they are better able to monitor the lesson by predicting outcomes, voicing a lack of understanding, and explaining what it does mean to them. Even though they are reciting easy text rather than reading, they are developing patterns of thinking and participating that we expect continue to help them succeed in school reading lessons.

Acknowledgments

Portions of this paper were presented at the Society for Research in Child Development Convention in Detroit, Michigan, April 1983. The research reported herein was supported in part by the National Institute of Education under Contract No. HEW-NIE-400-81-0030.

The authors wish to thank the teachers and students in Charleston, Illinois, for making this study possible.

Chapter 11

Developing Beginning Literacy Concepts: Content and Context

NANCY E. TAYLOR

Learning to be literate is a complex task that encompasses psychological, sociological, and linguistic variables. Conceptualizing the foundations of this task has recently begun to concern psychologists, sociologists, linguists, and educators alike. Two facts have emerged from research in this area that have important implications for prereading instruction. First, children who grow up in a literate society know a great deal about print prior to formal schooling (Hiebert, 1980, 1981; Ferreiro & Teberosky, 1982). Second, one aspect of this knowledge involves a metaknowledge—a knowledge about processes, acts, and functions involved in reading—and this knowledge is a factor in literacy acquisition (Ehri, 1979; Evans, Taylor & Blum, 1979; Taylor & Blum, 1981). Unfortunately, there is little evidence that these two important findings have caught the attention of teachers, curriculum developers, or publishers.

In this chapter I will attempt to outline what children need to know if their path to literacy is to be both effective and efficient. More important, I will describe the content and contexts that foster children's acquisition of this knowledge base. Many of the content concepts have been treated in detail in other chapters in this book. They are reintroduced here simply to describe the content of the child's growing knowledge base.

Knowledge Children Need to Acquire in Becoming Literate

If a child has adequate accessibility to written language, what are the aspects of this form of language that need to be discovered? To become skilled users of written language, children need to build a knowledge base in at least four general areas: technical aspects of written language; mapping principles that relate speech to print; functions served by written language; and schemata that characterize the way written language is organized and expressed.

Technical Aspects

Technical aspects refer to the arbitrary conventions that govern written language. In English, we write from left to right and from top to bottom. Technical aspects also include an awareness that in written language words are separated by blank spaces, as well as awareness of the way punctuation functions to mark units and guide information processing. Also included in this category is knowledge of the technical vocabulary used to talk about written language—terms such as "word," "letter," and "sound." These are commonsense understandings for literate adults and so much an intuitive part of our knowledge that it is small wonder that teachers assume children have these understandings prior to formal reading instruction. There is ample evidence, however, that children develop this technical knowledge about written language slowly (Clay, 1979; Day & Day, 1979; Downing & Oliver, 1973; Meltzer & Herse, 1969).

Awareness of these technical aspects of language most likely emerges as children are exposed to and detect the features that characterize print. Progress along this path of exposure, which leads to detection, has important implications for the child's progress in literacy acquisition. The relationship between literacy awareness of technical aspects and successful progress is probably most direct in the child's attempts to construct mapping principles between the spoken and written forms of language. Children's ability to discover the code depends upon their ability to know how and where to look (Smith, 1982).

Marie Clay (1975) provides an exaggerated but wonderful example of the child's novice attempts at knowing where to look:

Suppose a teacher has placed an attractive picture on the wall and has asked her children for a story which she will record under it. They offer the text "Mother is cooking" which the teacher alters slightly to introduce some features she wishes to teach. She writes,

Mother said,
"I am baking!"

If she says, "Now look at our *story*," 30 percent of a new entrant group will attend to the *picture*.

If she says, "Look at the *words* and find some you know," between 50 and 90 percent will be searching for *letters*. If she says, "Can you see Mother?" most will agree that they can but some see her in the picture, some can locate "M" and others will locate the word "Mother."

Perhaps the children read in unison "Mother is . . ." and the teacher tries to sort this out. Pointing to *said* she asks, "Does this say *is*?" Half agree it does because it has "S" in it. *"What letter does it start with?"* Now the teacher is really in trouble. She assumes that children *know* that a word is built out of letters but 50 percent of children still confuse the verbal labels "word" and "letter" after six months of instruction. She also assumes that the children know that the left-hand letter following a space is the "start" of a word. Often they do not. She says, "Look at the *first* letter. It says s-s-s-s" and her pupils make s-noises. But Johnny, who knows only "Mother" and "I," scans the text haphazardly for something relevant, sights the *comma* and makes s-noises! (Clay, 1975, pp. 3–4)

In learning to operate effectively with written language, children must discover the coding rules between the written and spoken forms. These featural aspects involve more than just the relationship between letters and sound. Most children sort out these arbitrary conventions of written language from repeated exposure. Clay's exaggerated example, however, highlights the confusion experienced by young children in the initial stages of learning to make sense out of written language.

Mapping Principles

The way concepts about the technical aspects of written language can lead to the detection of mapping principles between speech and print (i.e., the rules of our orthographic system) influences the second major understanding children must discover about print. This understanding involves the way speech is mapped into print. The rules for this mapping may appear somewhat arbitrary because of the lack of one-to-one correspondence between sound and spelling. This lack of perfect correspondence has led some scholars and educators to advocate either orthographic reform or direct teaching of phonic principles (Chall, 1967). Others argue that there is an underlying structure to our orthographic system that has both phonemic and meaning bases (Chomsky & Halle, 1968) and that both aspects need to be discovered as children learn to read. Regardless of the theoretical position one takes, learning the code ultimately involves learning the orthographic rules that represent the meaning intended in spoken language.

Learning how and where to look probably evolves simultaneously with beginning awareness of code information. Mason (1982) has described a three-stage process of word identification, in which the child at the lowest level recognizes words as whole configurations that are expected in certain contexts (e.g., the child's name on his/her lunch box or a particular word in the page of the child's primer), but does not recognize them in other contexts. At the second stage, the child recognizes the word in any context but still as an object; knowledge about the word itself does not generalize to other words. The child is apparently not sufficiently aware of the orthographic information within the word to use it to hypothesize about other words which contain similar features. This generalizable knowledge characterizes the third stage. By this point the child has developed an awareness of orthographic structure that generalizes to novel situations. Soderberg (1971) provides many examples of these stages in her study of her own child's learning under an adaptation of the Doman method.

Children do not acquire these concepts in an all-or-none fashion. Rather, concepts build up slowly, and at least in the initial stage, generalizations emerge from words that are very familiar to the child. As children become interested in words, many of which they encounter in isolation, they also note technical aspects of written language. This new awareness in turn heightens the opportunities children have to attend to orthographic structure. Emerging knowledge in this area probably promotes the more cognitively based skill of being able to segment oral sentences. Older children and children who are more advanced in literacy skills are better able to operate on language as an object, to think of form as well as function (Karpova, 1966; Hakes, 1980).

The role of cognitive maturation in children's emerging knowledge about written language is of considerable theoretical interest. Hakes (1980) provides a compelling argument that metalinguistic abilities are the linguistic manifestation of the cognitive changes that underlie the development of concrete operational thought. He argues that prior to this time, the child infers heuristic rules or general interpretative strategies as a result of attending to superficial properties that occur with regularity. Some aspects of the child's knowledge base about written language are less likely to be dependent upon cognitive maturity than others. Mapping principles are probably most dependent upon this cognitive change, since they represent generalizable concepts about the orthographic code. Discovery of generalizable orthographic principles most likely requires the ability both to reflect upon the surface properties of language and to employ the controlled processes of comparison and decision.

Functions

The preceding discussion suggests the degree to which exposure to print is important for the discovery of knowledge about written language which leads to literacy. Exposure itself, however, is not enough. There is another factor which is of equal importance: the meaningful context in which children encounter print. Whether children attend to the graphic displays around them depends to a large degree upon the meaning those displays have for them. To be immersed in print has little significance unless children can bring meaning to it.

Making print meaningful to children does not occur by chance. It is highly dependent upon adult interaction. Most of the print children encounter in natural situations is not the print of books but rather the highly contextualized and stylized print used to label and advertise places and products (McDonald's, Coca-Cola, etc.). Except in these stylized situations, children probably have little reason to attend to print unless adults call attention to it. Children's ability to assign meaning to these graphic displays (Harste & Burke, 1978) attests to their natural ability to make meaningful connections between graphics and what they represent. These experiences, however, do not directly lead to the knowledge necessary to learn to code or to deal with the decontextualized nature of written language that characterizes literacy. To accomplish these goals, children must deal with more than the stylized representations of environmental print. Helping children see the functional relevance of print provides the meaningful and motivational context in which literacy acquisition can most effectively take place. This functional relevance is not readily available to children. In natural, non-assisted situations one needs to have a certain proficiency with literacy before print begins to serve useful functions. Perhaps here, more than in any other area, the adult (teacher and/or parent) must engineer the environment to promote the development of understanding.

Schemas That Characterize Written Language

In addition to the orthographic rules and arbitrary technical aspects that characterize written language, this form of language differs from speech in its organization, its decontextualized nature, and the particular expressions that are likely to occur in literate contexts (Olson, 1977; Tannen, 1982). As Rubin (1981) and others suggest, these characteristics may be a source of difficulty in learning to read until the child has enough experiences with the language form to learn the text features that facilitate comprehension. Developing a familiarity with these written language characteristics is essential if the child is to make maximum use of his predictive abilities in reading. This knowledge base is particularly important for young children in the initial stages of reading, since their code knowledge is minimal.

The knowledge base that children build about text characteristics is rich and complex. One aspect of this knowledge is awareness of the structural characteristics of text. Mandler & DeForest (1979), Stein & Glenn (1977) and others have demonstrated that children are sensitive to the schematic structure of stories and use this knowledge to facilitate comprehension and recall. Applebee (1978) has shown that at an early age children recognize certain conventions of stories (e.g., formal opening phrases, formal closings, the use of a consistent past tense). Furthermore, children demonstrate an emerging understanding of these conventions in their told and written narratives (Shatz, 1984). Applebee's work also indicates, however, that the form of the child's concept of story changes with age. The child becomes more sensitive to the fact that story is a restructuring of experience and the child develops an ability to separate the world of story from his/her own world. There are probably other aspects of text schemas that are not acquired as early or as easily as the macro aspects of text characteristics.

How Children Build Concepts About Written Language

All of these knowledge bases interact with one another to promote a well integrated awareness of written language, which forms the basis for the development of future literacy skills. Awareness of these knowledge bases and the processes by which they are acquired are not widely reflected in current early childhood teaching practices. Instruction during these years generally deals with either oral language practice and picture interpretation or direct instruction in phonics and decoding. This is largely because instruction appears to be based on conventional wisdom rather than on a clear conceptualization of what the process of written language acquisition involves.

A careful reading of the literature related to early reading acquisition and the literature in the area of metalinguistics and metacognition provides a basis for an emergent theory of written language acquisition. This literature suggests that three things need to occur as children develop concepts about written language that, in turn, promote literacy acquisition. First, children must develop a broad content knowledge in the areas outlined in the previous section of this paper. Second, this knowledge base needs to be acquired in a manner that leads to flexibility. Third, at some level the child needs to be able to reflect on the system and the use of it, that is, to be able to objectify the acquired knowledge base.

The literature is also clear on the manner in which children build concepts about written language. Children construct theories or schemas about written language from their exposure to print (Ferreiro & Teberosky, 1982; Mason, 1980). Just as in early language learning, these constructed theories are imperfect representations of the "real" or adult model. As children build knowledge and encounter wider experiences with print, they are faced with situations in which their current theories fail to work. Thus, they are forced to modify and extend these theories until eventually they construct a knowledge base that approximates that of an adult.

A critical question underlying a theory of written language acquisition involves the degree to which various aspects of knowledge about written language either need to be or come to be held explicitly, that is, what is known is accessible to the child, and if needed, can be brought to the conscious awareness of the child. Oral language generally operates "out of awareness" (Cazden, 1974b); knowledge of the system is implicit and many aspects are relatively inaccessible. Written language, on the other hand, appears to be much more accessible, perhaps because, as Downing (1984) argues, what is coded in written language are the features of communication and language that were accessible to the creators of the writing system. While the written language system has the theoretical potential of being accessible, it does not automatically follow that all aspects will be characterized by explicit understanding (i.e., conscious awareness of what is known) or the ability to articulate what is known. Thus, it is possible to think about representing the way knowledge can be held along a two-dimensional continuum.

Figure 11-1 presents these dimensions as an awareness continuum that can be characterized at one extreme by implicit understanding of concepts related to written language. As a result of the implicit nature of knowledge these concepts are relatively unarticulated. The other extreme of the continuum is characterized by explicit understanding and articulated knowledge. For example, many first graders, after six or more months of instruction, can be relatively explicit about their knowledge of mapping principles, but would be unable to make explicit their knowledge of narrative structures, although research has shown that they have both developed these structures and use them to guide the encoding, organization, and recall of information.

Clarity about the role of explicit understanding in the development of knowledge about written language is important both for a theory of written language acquisition and a theory of instruction. Explicit understanding is probably facilitated by relatively structured experiences and task-relevant information, whereas implicitly held knowledge most likely requires only repeated exposure to relatively global, unarticulated experiences which contain the knowledge aspects to be abstracted. Figure 11-1 also presents a tentative array of the concept categories discussed in this chapter, an array that needs to be empirically verified. Macro aspects of story schemas, for example, are probably highly intuitive

Figure 11–1

A Hypothetical Arrangement of Concepts About Print Along an Awareness Continuum

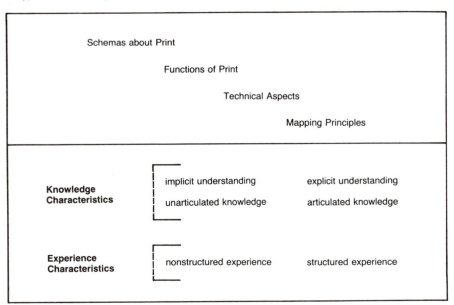

and relatively unarticulated. Wide exposure to texts which embody particular structures may be all children need to develop intuitive schemas that guide and facilitate comprehension. Mapping principles that relate speech to print, however, are more explicit and articulated. This does not mean that story schemas cannot be made explicit and articulated. In fact, there is a trend toward curricula designed to teach these structures in explicit ways to students in efforts to improve comprehension (see Montgomery County Public Schools, 1982). The important question is whether it is necessary to transmit this knowledge in such an explicit fashion. Similarly, the reason mapping principles are so accessible may be influenced by the fact that they are taught that way.

Implications for Instruction

It has been proposed that three aspects are involved in developing competence with written language. These aspects involve building an adequate content knowledge base, building this base in a flexible manner, and becoming able to objectify this knowledge. The problem for early childhood teachers is one of creating an environment which fosters the construction of knowledge in the four areas discussed earlier in this paper: the technical aspects of written language, the mapping principles between speech and print, the functions served by written language, and the characteristic structures that written language takes. The environment must also foster these concepts in a manner that will lead to the development of flexible systems.

Instructionally, this means that children must have a wide array of experiences with written language from which to draw their knowledge base. In addition, children must be free to form their own hypotheses and draw their own conclusions based on the information around them. If children encounter many incidences of the concepts they are developing and encounter them across many contexts, this knowledge base is less likely to be "welded" to specific contexts and thus will be more flexible and accessible when children encounter new and appropriate situations where this knowledge base would be useful (Brown, 1980). Over time, as the child builds content knowledge and organizes it into a flexible system, a metaknowledge will emerge. How explicit this metaknowledge needs to be is not clear, but it is nevertheless clearly of considerable instructional importance.

Several guiding principles can be derived that facilitate the creation of appropriate context for the acquisition of early literacy skills. These principles characterize the type of environment teachers need to create and the way instruction ought to be provided.

General Environmental Characteristics

For children to acquire the understandings necessary for literacy acquisition, teachers must create a "print-rich" environment—that is, an environment full of print that is meaningful to, and serves a function for, children. At least four principles can guide teachers in creating such an environment.

First, in creating a print-rich environment, teachers must provide children with a rich body of written language examples. There must be many and varied opportunities to interact with written language. Print-rich classrooms will contain numerous books: books for enjoyment and books related to things being studied in the classroom. Written language will be incorporated into ongoing classroom activities. Many things that normally are simply discussed will also be put into print. For example, directions for routine activities (e.g., when and how much to feed the goldfish), schedules, and directions become written records that are posted and referred to throughout the day. Print-rich classrooms are well stocked with interesting and motivating materials to use for writing, such as a wide variety of paper and writing instruments. Children's written products are displayed and used. Student-made books and other materials are as abundant as commercial materials.

Second, children's encounters with print must occur in many different contexts. We want the children's theories of written language to be fully developed, flexible, and well integrated. When children's experiences are narrow and restricted to a few contexts, they will have difficulty developing generalizable concepts about written language.

A third principle is that print should be meaningful to the child. Meaningfulness is a controlling factor, but it is very different from the control of word complexity employed by basal readers; the latter is external while the former is internal. The importance of meaningfulness cannot be overstressed. While it is important for all learners, it is critical for young learners. Seeing the connection between what they must do and understand and a goal that makes sense can make the difference between success and failure in learning (Istomina, 1975).

What does it mean to make print meaningful to children? First it means that print must symbolize relevant aspects of the child's life. Ashton-Warner (1971), Soderberg (1971), and others have pointed out the degree to which words high in personal meaning are learned and remembered by children. While there are categories of words common to all children, "high personal meaning" implies highly individualistic vocabularies when these vocabularies reflect experiences outside the school. Some teachers have no trouble building systematic instruction on these highly varied vocabularies, and children's personal experiences outside the school should be a vital part of their school-directed literacy program. At the same time, it is equally important that the classroom become a highly personal and experience-rich environment to which print can be linked. A large part of making print meaningful to children involves making print functional for children. This means creating an environment where one must get information from print in order to know or do something. Traditional activities such as labeling the blackboard, pencil sharpener, and window in the vain hope that children would incorporate these words into their sight vocabularies point out the importance of more meaningful encounters with print. Children have little reason to pay attention to these nonfunctional graphic representations. They must be replaced with situations in which children have to interact actively with print in order to accomplish a child-valued goal. (See Taylor & Vauter, 1978; Taylor, Moeller & Blum, 1982; and Taylor, Blum, Logsdon & Moeller, 1982, for further examples of this environment.)

Teachers' efforts to create such environments, when successful, are guided by insights into the child's experience, the child's point of view, and an understanding of the differences between the functions served by spoken and written language. A major task in becoming literate involves an extension of the child's language competence. This extension includes learning a new code and learning new functions in the broadest sense. Part of this awareness involves developing an understanding that written language allows one to bridge the gap between time and space, to create a permanent record, and to communicate to absent audiences. But written language serves another function. By virtue of its static nature, it also allows one to reflect on what has been said and to build an awareness, not only of how the code can work, but also, of the way ideas can be organized to communicate the essence of thought.

General Instructional Characteristics

In addition to creating an environment rich in print, the way teachers structure children's interaction within this environment also has a marked influence on children's acquisition of literacy concepts.

One very obvious principle here centers on the degree to which knowledge about written language needs to be explicitly held in the early stages of literacy acquisition. Figure 11-1 presents a hypothetical arrangement along an awareness continuum of the four areas of knowledge suggested in this chapter. This arrangement is based, in part, upon an analysis of what appears to be involved in each of these knowledge components as well as observations about the way children demonstrate their knowledge. Perceptions based on children's demonstration of their knowledge might, however, simply reflect the way children have been taught. Nevertheless, certain knowledge bases of written language need to be comprehensively held and explicitly developed by children. The closer a particular aspect of prereading knowledge is to the "explicitly understood, articulated knowledge" end of the continuum, the more the teacher needs to articulate the relationship and make it explicit to the children. This articulation is not the same as teaching rules. Rather, it is a matter of pointing out, or calling attention to, regularities across incidences. Children must discover these relationships for themselves. The environment that the teacher creates needs to be flexible and fluid enough for children to discover for themselves, while providing experiences and feedback that make salient the important aspects of written language.

A second principle governing the way teachers structure interaction involves the necessity of recognizing that "a literate environment is essentially a social rather than physical phenomenon . . ." (Teale, Estrada & Anderson, 1981). In becoming literate, children must make a transition from an oral culture to a written culture. Gumperz and Gumperz (1981) argue that a discontinuity exists between the child's acquisition of language as an oral skill and the acquisition of language as a literate skill. This discontinuity is lessened for the middle class child who experiences a wide variety of literacy events within the home context. For all children, however, teachers need to provide for what Gumperz and Gumperz term the social-cognitive aspects of transition from oral to literacy performance.

This means that teachers must help children integrate literacy experiences into their existing conceptual frameworks. The way teachers use literacy materials, the type of interactions they structure for children, and the practices they use with children in classrooms all influence this transition. In the home culture, language and literacy events are functionally linked to ongoing activities that are highly relevant to the child. In the classroom, a similar linkage can be accomplished by integrating literacy activities into all aspects of the school day. Teachers who are effective at doing this seem intuitively to find ways to link print easily and naturally to regular classroom activities and outlines. Among other things, they have children take their own attendance by checking in on a sign-up sheet each day. They gather children around in a participatory fashion to share written directions, and they leave children special messages via notes (Taylor, Blum, Logsdon & Moeller, 1982).

Another way teachers positively structure children's interactions with written language is to provide for free and interactive access to meaningful written language, access which focuses on attention and use of print. Many classrooms have the trappings of a literate environment, such as well-stocked reading and writing centers, but the classroom day is so tightly organized and controlled by the teacher that children have little access to these materials. If children are to construct theories about written language, they must have both free access to a wide variety of print and ample time to interact with this material. Teachers, therefore, must structure classrooms so that children use written material daily. Such usage occurs best in classrooms where teachers structure the day so children engage frequently and independently in literacy activities. In these classrooms, past written products are accessible to students and serve as references for new experiences. Both the reference products themselves and the way teachers routinely structure independent activities with written language provide a framework which enables the child to operate independently.

Closely related to this accessibility principle in providing interaction with print is the teacher's use of classroom routines. Routines provide structured and highly predictable contexts in which children can encounter written language. They function in much the same way as routines in language interaction between mothers and young children (Snow, Dubber & De Blauw, 1983). Routines are characterized not only by structure and predictability, they also allow for growth in complexity and independence of response. Attendance and activity selection are favorite routines in many of the preschool classrooms we have studied (Taylor, Blum, Logsdon & Moeller, 1982). These particular routines provide a good example of the way teachers initiate children to literacy events by using highly predictable events and increasing complexity and independence as children learn to operate within the predictable structure of the event. Initially, children "sign in" each morning by matching their name card to a name under their picture. Later children "sign in" by placing a name card under their picture. At this point, they no longer need to match to a model. Eventually children move to "signing in" each morning by writing their names under the activity they want to work on during the first segment of the day.

Conclusions

Earlier in this chapter, the contention was made that meaningful encounters with literacy events were dependent to a large degree upon adult structuring. The teacher, like the parent, is the key in creating a literate environment. What is learned will, in part, reflect the teacher's own understandings about literacy and the way written language works. Teachers and parents transmit a literacy tradition to children through the examples of print they provide and the ways they choose to call attention to this print. In many cases, this transmission of knowledge takes the form of assertions about written language, assertions coming from highly authoritative individuals. As Olson and Hildyard (1981) point out, "the truth of the proposition is a function, not simply of the truth conditions, but *also* of the authority of the speaker" (p. 321). Teachers, by virtue of their role and regardless of their ability, carry high authority. What they choose to make explicit to children about print will mediate their perception of the nature of written language and orthographic structure. This places a tremendous ethical responsibility upon teachers and curriculum designers. In our assertions to children, we must reflect what is true about language in both its oral and written forms. At the same time, we must phrase these assertions in ways that are developmentally appropriate for the child.

This chapter has attempted in a very global way to identify areas of knowledge about written language that are both legitimate and necessary to transmit to young children. In addition, some general principles that characterize an optimal learning environment, principles which interact in a highly dynamic fashion, have also been suggested. Currently, neither the content nor the instructional method recommended by these principles are very apparent in young children's preschool and primary programs. Changing this state of affairs should be a major goal in early childhood education.

Acknowledgments

The preparation of this paper was supported in part by the Gallaudet Research Institute, Center for Studies in Education and Human Development, Gallaudet College, Washington, D.C. 20002.

Section 5

Tests of Metalinguistic Awareness

Chapter 12

Tests of Metalinguistic Awareness

KAAREN C. DAY

H. D. DAY

Research of the past fifteen years (e.g., Downing & Oliver, 1973–74; Francis, 1973; Holdaway, 1979; Reid, 1966; and Smith, 1973) has resulted in educators taking a new look at reading readiness. Traditionally, reading readiness has been measured by tasks that allow the examiner or teacher to observe a child's ability to use a pencil, copy geometric shapes and patterns, discriminate between auditorially similar words, identify letter and word reversals, and match identical words (Weimer & Weimer, 1977). The *Metropolitan Readiness Test* (MRT), for example, which is widely used, includes such tasks.

These traditional reading readiness measures enable one to observe how well children can do these tasks, many of which the children will be required to do in school; however, these tasks may not be directly related to the act of reading and do not really allow one to observe exactly how well a child understands what the reading process is all about. The traditional reading readiness tests seem to assess isolated skills that may have very little to do with whether or not a child is able to gain meaning from print in the environment or to understand the purposes and functions of reading. A teacher cannot observe from these tests if the child knows how to handle a book, understands the conventions of print, or understands the specialized language of reading instruction. Findings that many elementary children have little understanding of what reading is all about (e.g., Vernon, 1957) and do not understand basic elements such as vocabulary or terms used by the teachers, how to hold a book, the conventions of print or even the reasons or purposes for being able to read (Clay, 1967, 1979b) have resulted in much recent interest in children's ability to interact and gain meaning from print that goes beyond traditional views of reading readiness.

Early studies involving interviews to learn what prereaders think about the process and purpose of reading (e.g., Denny & Weintraub, 1966; Downing, 1970; Reid, 1966) led to later work using more objective measures of linguistic awareness. Holden and MacGinitie (1972) and Huttenlocher (1964) studied the development of the ability to detect aural word boundaries by asking young children to tap once on a table for each word they heard in a sentence, and reported that many children are either unable to successfully complete this task or at least experience some confusion. In other studies, such as those by Francis (1973) and Papandropoulou and Sinclair (1974), children have been asked to identify or explain a letter, a word, or a sentence. Again, children display a lack of understanding of these concepts and often confuse a word with a sentence or a letter. Downing and Oliver (1973–74) found that a group of 5-year-olds, when asked to identify sounds that were words, often did not discriminate between nonhuman sounds and phonemes on the one hand, and words on the other. Johns (1980b), using a similar task, found essentially the same confusions with a group of children ranging from 5.5 to 9.5 years of age. In the 5.5- to 6.5-year-old group, only 44% of the children were able to identify short words, and 28% could identify long words.

Morris and Henderson (1981) have devised another word-sound matching task that uses a rhyme children can easily memorize. After the rhyme is learned, a copy is shown to the children, and the examiner demonstrates to the children how to finger point as they recite the rhyme. The children are then asked to "read" a word within the rhyme as the teacher points to it. Finally, six words from the rhyme are presented in isolation as sight words to be read, and the children are asked to read the words. Morris and Henderson suggest that this task can help teachers observe the child's awareness of spoken word/written word match or one-to-one correspondence of speech and print in reading. An additional method of observing letter and word awareness was devised by Mc-Cormick and Mason (1981) and is called the *Letter and Word Reading Test* (LWRT). This test consists of six subtests that enable the examiner to observe the child's ability to identify words when given a picture stimulus, spell a common word, name upper and lower case letters, and identify common words. Two subtests use nonsense words to assess the child's ability to decode nonsense words, utilizing long, short, long (final consonant, silent *e*), and *r* controlled vowels.

The practical value of a teacher's knowledge of a child's language awareness and the increasing interest in such awareness as an object of research have led to the development of several classroom-applicable tests of this construct. Although other tests seem to have been developed (e.g., Watson, 1979), the purpose of this paper is to describe four of the more widely known tests of metalinguistic abilities, three available commercially and one experimental edition obtainable from the authors. In the order of their publication, the tests are the *Concepts About Print* by Clay (1972, 1979a), the *Test of Early Reading Ability* by Reid, Hresko, and Hammill (1981), the *Written Language Awareness Test* by Taylor and Blum (1980), and the *Linguistic Awareness in Reading Readiness Test* by Downing, Ayers, and Schaefer (1983). These tests examine the child in various print-related situations and measure aspects of early reading behavior that are more related to the actual process of reading than the abilities assessed in traditional reading readiness tests, such as the child's awareness of the purpose of reading, awareness of what one does when he or she reads, knowledge of how to handle a book, and awareness of other print conventions.

K. C. Day has recently administered these four tests to 60 kindergarten children in a counterbalanced design. Therefore, in addition to describing the stated objectives of the tests, format of the test items, available normative data, and statistical integrity of each test, a more informal comparative evaluation of the applications of each test can be made at this time as a result of observations of the same children performing on each test within a very short period of time.

Concepts About Print

Although Marie Clay has developed a number of tests of early language abilities in children, perhaps the best known is the *Concepts About Print* (CAP), a measure of the child's knowledge of print conventions. The CAP was originally published in 1972 and made use of a child's book entitled *Sand*. The latest edition of the CAP (Clay, 1979a) also appears as one test in a battery designed as a diagnostic survey to detect reading difficulties in early primary children. To facilitate repeated applications of the CAP to the same child, a second book entitled *Stones* (Clay, 1979a) can now be used as the target of questions comprising the CAP.

During the 10 to 15 minutes required to administer this individual test, the child is asked 24 questions as he or she and the examiner read *Sand* or *Stones* together. Concepts observed include how to hold a book to read, the idea that print and not pictures carries the message, the definitions of letters, words, upper and lower case letters, first and last letters and words, punctuation marks, etc. The child is instructed to help the examiner read the book by pointing to certain features in the book, and scores ranging from zero to 24 can occur on the CAP. The only normative data for the CAP is for New Zealand children and consists of two sets of stanine scores, one set for 320 5- to 7-year-olds tested in 1968 and another set for 282 children aged 6 years to 7 years 3 months tested in 1978.

Clay (1979a) reported a split-half reliability coefficient of .95 for 50 5- to 7-year-old children, and similar coefficients in the range of .70 to .90 have been reported by several studies involving American children (Day & Day, 1979; Hollingsworth, 1978; Johns, 1980a). Our study (Day & Day, 1979) is the only one reporting test-retest reliability for the CAP, and temporal stability coefficients higher than .70 were reported for 56 children in five repeated administrations of the CAP over the kindergarten and first grade years.

In 1967, working with 100 6-year-old children, Clay found a correlation of .79 between the CAP and *Word Reading*, and other studies have confirmed the validity of the CAP. Generally strong positive correlations have been found between the CAP and the *Metropolitan Reading Survey, Gates-MacGinitie Reading* tests (Johns, 1980a), reading subtests of the *Peabody Individual Achievement Test* (Hollingsworth, 1978), the MRT (Day & Day, 1979), the *Iowa Test of Basic*

Skills (ITBS) (Day, Day, Spicola, & Griffin, 1981; Day & Day, 1984), and the reading subtests of the Stanford Achievement Test (SAT) (Yaden, 1982).

Yaden (1982) found a correlation of .48 between the CAP and the *Otis-Lennon School Ability Test,* and, moreover, that the partial correlations between the CAP and the reading subtests of the SAT, with intelligence controlled, remained significantly different from zero. Similarly, we (Day & Day, 1984) have found that the correlations between the CAP on the one hand, and the total scores of the first, third, and fourth grade adminisations of the ITBS on the other hand, remained significant and ranged from .32 to .73 with the total mental age score of the *Short Form Test of Academic Aptitude* partialed out. Thus Yaden's and our findings suggest that the CAP is tapping some construct other than just general intellectual ability.

In our (Day & Day, 1984) study of the 56 kindergarten children, six boys and two girls were required to repeat a grade during the five years covered by the study. For each of the five CAP administrations, the mean score for the eight retainees was significantly lower than that of the children who were not retained. Furthermore, the mean ranking for the retainees ranged from 5.81 to 7.18, an indication that on each CAP administration, those children who would later be retained were very close to the bottom of the CAP distribution. These validity studies suggest that the CAP has acceptable predictive validity as an indicator of later performances on school achievement tests, and that the CAP may be a useful measure at the kindergarten level to identify those children who are at high risk of being retained in the early primary grades. Also attesting to the validity of the CAP are the expected developmental changes we (Day, Day, Hollingsworth, & McClelland, 1980) have reported across five administrations of the test to the same group of children, the series beginning in the third month of kindergarten and completed at the end of the first grade. The mean CAP scores across the five administrations ranged from 6.5 to 17.6 (*SD*s from 3.6 to 4.6) for the boys and from 9.0 to 19.6 (*SD*s from 3.5 to 4.2) for the girls. Spanning the period when the children were learning to read, therefore, the children's growth was reflected by a steady increase in CAP performance.

Day et al. (1980) have reported that girls score two to three points (about half a standard deviation) higher on the CAP than the boys. Those differences occurred in each of three different samples involving 56, 80, and 54 children respectively, and the samples were tested independently and by different researchers. Johns (1980a) and Yaden (1982), however, report no such gender differences for their samples. For our sample of 56 children and that of Hollingsworth (1978), we have computed predictive validity coefficients separately for boys and girls, and the correlation coefficients between the CAP and a variety of criterion variables are higher for girls than for boys (Day, et al., 1981; Day, Day, & Hollingsworth, 1981), and in the case of the Hollingsworth sample, some differences are profound (Day & Hollingsworth, 1984). These gender differences in predictive validity occur in the absence of any apparent statistical artifacts that could account for them. Confirmation of gender differences in central tendency on the CAP could mean that separate normative data would need to be made available for boys and girls. Gender differences in predictive validity suggest that the CAP may be slightly less valid as a predictor of later achievement for boys than for girls; however, this criticism of the CAP may not be valid, since Clay's purpose in developing the test was not to predict later school achievement.

Test of Early Reading Ability

The *Test of Early Reading Ability* (TERA) was designed to "(a) identify those children who are significantly behind their peers in the development of reading; (b) to document children's progress in learning to read; (c) to serve as a measure in research projects; and (d) to suggest instructional practices" (Reid et al., 1981, p. 5). The test consists of 50 cards that are presented in 10 to 15 minute individual interviews of children from 4 to 7 years 11 months of age. Administration of the test is facilitated by guidelines suggesting basal levels for various ages of children; beginning with the child's basal level, items are presented sequentially until five items are missed in a row.

The TERA contains items intended to measure three components of early reading behavior. The first component, "Construction of Meaning," assesses awareness of print occurring in environmental contexts, knowledge of relations among vocabulary items, comprehension, and ability to anticipate written language in a cloze task. The second component, "Knowledge of the Alphabet and Its Functions," includes letter and numeral naming, alphabet recitation, oral reading, and proofreading. The last component, "Conventions of Written Language," measures knowledge of print conventions and is similar to Clay's CAP.

The first experimental version of the TERA contained 170 items and was given to 100 children. Using both an index of difficulty and a coefficient of discrimination, this item pool was reduced to 76 items and then administered to an additional sample of 150 children. Subsequent item analyses reduced the number of items to 50, the final version of the test. The TERA was subsequently standardized on 1184 children living in eleven states and one Canadian province. Raw scores can be converted into percentile ranks, reading ages, reading quotients, and other common standardized scores, and normative data from the large sample are provided in the test manual.

For a stratified random sample of 550 children from the normative group, coefficient alphas ranged from .87 to .96 for five age levels, and test-retest reliabilities ranged from .82 to .94 for a two-week testing interval. Criterion-related validity coefficients with the *Metropolitan Achievement Test* (MAT) and the composite score from the *Test of Reading Comprehension* were .66 and .52, respectively. Construct validity was confirmed by demonstrating improvement in scores across the five age levels, low scores for children diagnosed as having reading difficulties, and significant positive correlations with various tests of intelligence and school readiness.

Written Language Awareness Test

The *Written Language Awareness Test* (WLAT) battery (Taylor & Blum, 1980) is individually administered and is appropriate for 4- to 7-year-olds and older children who cannot read. The WLAT consists of four subtests: (a) "Aural Word Boundaries," requiring the segmentation of oral sentences into their component words; (b) Rye-Rhinoceros word cards, designed to test the child's understanding of the relationship between speech and print; (c) "Metalinguistic Interview," an assessment of the child's knowledge of the technical aspects of written language; and (d) "Aural Consonant Cloze," a measure of the child's ability to use initial consonants to supply a missing word at the end of sentences read by the examiner.

In the "Aural Word Boundaries" task, the child is asked to indicate the individual words appearing in a sentence by moving a block or a chip for each word. The child is given several practice trials, and if these are done correctly, four sentences of varying lengths are then administered. Since each sentence is scored on a scale of one to four, a range of zero to 16 is possible on this subtest.

In the "Rye-Rhinoceros" task the child examines eight cards, each of which presents a pair of words starting with the same letter. One word is a very short word, and the other is much longer. The examiner reads the two words and asks the child to point to one of the words. For example, on one card, the examiner reads the words "rye" and "rhinoceros" and then asks the child to point to "rhinoceros." The number of correct responses is scored and this ranges from zero to eight on this task.

The "Metalinguistic Interview" is designed to measure knowledge of the technical aspects of written language. The child is first asked five questions to check his or her knowledge of the alphabet, letters, words, and sentences. Then the child is given a booklet, "I Can Read 'Martha'," and asked a series of questions about how one reads a story. For example, the child is asked to put a red "X" at the place one begins to read, to circle a letter and a word, and to draw a line under a sentence. There are six such questions, and the child can score between zero and 11 on this subtest.

In the "Aural Consonant Cloze" subtest the child is asked to provide an unknown word located at the end of a sentence which the examiner has read, omitting the last word. The child is given three practice items, and if these are successfully completed, 10 additional items are given. The child receives zero points for no response and three points for a response that begins with the same consonant and makes sense; intermediate responses are scored either one or two. Total score on this subtest, therefore, can range from zero to 30.

The WLAT is an untimed test that takes between 15 and 20 minutes to administer. A test booklet and a copy of "I Can Read 'Martha' " are required for each child, and the test kit is completed by 10 chips or blocks, Rye-Rhinoceros cards, sentence strips, and red, blue, and green crayons.

An earlier version of the WLAT consisting of seven subtests was given to

53 first graders during September and May of the school year (Evans, Taylor, & Blum, 1979). The MAT was given in the spring to these same children. Based on the regression of the reading subtest of the MAT on the seven subtests of the WLAT, the current test consists of the four subtests that significantly entered the multiple regression for that sample.

The current WLAT was administered to 267 first graders in 17 schools at the beginning and end of the school year (Taylor & Blum, 1981). Internal consistency reliability for the total test was .92 and .95 for the two administrations, and test-retest reliability was .85. For the subtests, test-retest reliability ranged from .48 for the Rye-Rhinoceros task and .97 for "Aural Consonant Cloze"; internal consistency coefficients ranged from .60 to .96 for the subtests.

Criteria for predictive validity analyses were the September administration of the MRT and the May administration of the MAT. The correlations of the total WLAT with the MRT and MAT were .65 and .64, respectively. The subtest correlations with the MRT ranged from .46 to .59 and from .35 to .59 with the MAT. Additional regression analyses involving the *California Short Form Intelligence Test* indicated that the WLAT exhibits incremental validity over the test of intelligence in predicting achievement.

Linguistic Awareness in Reading Readiness

Downing et al. (1983) state that "The key principle underlying the construction of the *Linguistic Awareness in Reading Readiness (LARR) Test* is the fact that the learner must understand the purpose of the skill to be acquired and must grasp the concepts that are used for talking and thinking about how to perform the skill" (p. 1). The LARR was developed to be used with children during their first two years of school and consists of three parts: (a) "Recognizing Literacy Behavior," a measure of the child's recognition of what it is that one reads or writes; (b) "Understanding Literacy Functions," an assessment of the child's understanding of the purpose of reading and writing; (c) "Technical Language of Literacy," a measure of the child's understanding of such terms as letter, word, number, sentence, etc. Each subtest takes 15 to 20 minutes to administer and should be given on different days if possible; if not, a 30-minute break between subtests should be taken. Each child has his or her own booklet for each of the three parts, and the child is required to draw a circle around a picture or a portion of a picture with a crayon or pencil.

The LARR is unique among tests of metalinguistic awareness in that it is a group test. The authors recommend giving it to no more than 10 to 12 children at a time, however, unless an aide is present to assist. Although there can be problems with a group testing situation of children so young, the authors have argued that the benefits of group testing outweigh the disadvantages, because of the time involved when interviewing or testing children individually (Ayers & Downing, 1982). The LARR is available in two equivalent foms; therefore, it is possible to give one form at the beginning of the year and the second at the end of the year to measure a child's progress. The same directions are used for both forms for Parts 1 and 3; however, different instructions are given for Forms A and B for Part 2.

Part 1, "Recognizing Literacy Behavior," has 22 items, excluding two practice items. Each item consists of a picture cue for the row and then one to four pictures in that row in which children must circle their responses. For example, children are asked to circle the persons who are reading, each part of a book that someone can read, each thing that someone can read, each thing that someone can use for writing, and each person who is writing. Part 2, "Understanding Literacy Functions," consists of 23 items that require children to circle pictures that show a person who is finding out how to bake a cake, who is finding out a telephone number, who is leaving/sending a message, who is reading an advertisement, etc. Part 3, "Technical Language of Literacy," has 30 items and is designed to measure the child's understanding of the reading register (Downing, 1976). In this portion, the children have to identify and circle letters, numbers, printing, writing, words, punctuation marks, first and last letters and words, etc., as they appear in context, for example, as the first word of a sentence.

Downing et al. (1983, p. 26) state that "a weak score on the LARR Test indicates a low level of readiness to profit from formal instruction in reading." Although normative data on this test are not yet available, the authors suggest that a beginning kindergarten child who scores below 50% on Parts 1 and 2 and 30% on Part 3 is weak or below average; by the end of kindergarten these percentages should be 75% for Part 1 and 60% for Parts 2 and 3.

The first version of the test was given to approximately 300 kindergarten children enrolled in 18 classrooms in seven schools during May and June of 1977. Item analysis resulted in a revision of the test that was given twice the following year to 330 kindergarten children. In both samples, half the children were given Form A and half were given Form B. The revised version had subtest internal consistency reliability coefficients ranging from .84 to .92 for the fall administration and .76 to .95 for the spring administration. The published version is a revision of this first revision, and reliability estimates for the latest version are not yet available.

To see if the LARR (given at the end of kindergarten) could predict the children's reading achievement at the end of first grade, the Cooperative Primary Reading Test was given to the first group of 300 kindergarten children a year after the LARR administration, i.e., at the end of their first grade year. Predictive validity coefficients were generally higher for Form A (approximately .60) than for Form B (.44 to .48), a possible consequence of the fact that Form B exhibited lower reliability than Form A. Generally, it was found that Part 3, "Technical Language of Literacy," was the best predictor of first grade reading. In separate analyses for individual classrooms, less than half the correlations were significant for Parts 1 and 2, but the coefficients for Part 3 were significant for all but one group.

Evaluation of the Four Instruments

Although the CAP was apparently developed as a tool to be informally used by teachers to diagnose early reading difficulties (Clay, 1972), by virtue of its originality and early publication, it has been widely used as a research instrument by American investigators. The high internal consistency and temporal reliability of the CAP, coupled with its predictive and construct validity, support the application of the test by teachers to assess children's knowledge of print conventions and by researchers interested in the correlates of early reading behavior. Although the test is limited in its metalinguistic scope, other tests in Clay's (1979) battery would enable the teacher to get a broader view of a child's early linguistic abilities and deficiencies. The CAP is easily and rapidly administered and has the advantage of a target book that can be repeatedly used and procedures that enable the teacher to systematically observe the child's interaction with a book. The principal limitation of the CAP is that only very limited normative data exist, and these data presently occur only for New Zealand children. A teacher without considerable personal experience with the CAP, therefore, would have difficulty identifying children working below expected levels.

From the perspective of a classroom application of the CAP, the principal advantage of the test is that it allows a teacher to observe the understanding a child has of how one goes about reading a book; the teacher can very quickly identify those children who have had previous exposure to books. Children generally respond well to the CAP; the stories are interesting and the questions, for the most part, seem natural and do not interrupt the flow of the story. There are eight items, however, four involving letter, word, or line reversals and four involving punctuation marks, that the majority of children fail to respond to correctly; indeed, even those children who are reading often fail to notice the reversals and are able to read the material as it ought to mean. Johns (1980a) has noted that since some of these questions do not direct the child's attention to the print (many children refer to some aspect of the picture on these items), individual differences on these questions may be more of an artifact of the testing procedure than a real difference in ability or knowledge.

Of the tests reviewed in this paper, the TERA has been the most carefully standardized. It is accompanied by the most extensive and useful normative data and especially helpful guidelines for the interpretation of scores. The use of basal and ceiling levels for administering the test is unique to this type of test and greatly shortens the administration time and makes the test suitable for a wider range of ages. The graphics of the target stimuli are of very high quality, and the stimulus items are reusable. By the presentation of stimuli on cards, several facets of metalinguistic awareness are examined in a variety of linguistic contexts, and throughout the test, the emphasis seems to be on the ability of the child to extract meaning from print.

The TERA is also a test young children seem to respond well to; the variety of stimulus pictures seem capable of holding even the attention of kindergarteners for the duration of the test, and the use of basal and ceiling levels prevents the test from being too long and avoids including many difficult questions that would likely frustrate children achieving at lower levels. In K. C. Day's recent administration of the test to 60 children, only two items seemed to cause enough confusion to be worthy of note. The first item is one that asks, "What numeral is this?" The word "numeral" may not be as familiar as "number" to children of this age, and some of them thought it might be a trick question. Many of the children who missed this item when asked, "What numeral is this?" were able to answer correctly when asked, "What number is this?" Another item that seemed to cause some confusion was one on which several coupons were shown and the child was told, "Tell me about these." Rather than indicating that coupons are used to save money or buy food, many children attempted to name the specific item or brand represented.

The WLAT and LARR are of more recent availability and are also multifaceted tests of metalinguistic abilities. The LARR is distinguished by the fact that it is the only test of these abilities that can be given in a group setting, although three separate testing occasions are required to complete the test administrations. Neither the WLAT nor the LARR currently has normative data available; thus interpretive difficulties could be expected to arise in the application of these two tests. Since in both instruments the child marks on the test, the administration of both the WLAT and LARR would presumably require the purchase of a test booklet for each child to be tested. In spite of these limitations, the diversity of metalinguistic abilities assessed by these instruments should be attractive to the classroom teacher.

The WLAT incorporates many different aspects of reading awareness, and the variety of stimuli seem to hold the children's attention. The test has more materials (chips, cards, crayons, booklet, and sentence strips) for the examiner to manipulate than do the other two individual tests; however, the change of pace may help keep the children involved. Almost all of the 60 kindergarten children recently tested were capable of "chipping" the noun and verb phrases of a sentence; much more difficult, of course, was chipping for each word heard. In order to recite the alphabet, many children resorted to singing the alphabet song and then had difficulty saying one letter, one word, or one sentence. Only one item of the test seems to be ambiguous. In the aural cloze portion, the children are asked to supply a missing word at the end of a sentence. One of the sentences reads, "At the zoo, the children saw a *monkey*" (with monkey not being read); many children inserted the word rhinoceros, which was a target word for the Rye-Rhinoceros subtest the child had just previously taken.

The LARR has the advantage of being able to test up to 10 or 12 children at once and the saving of the teacher's time could be a major benefit. In testing the 60 children, the LARR (Form A) was given to groups that contained no more than six children. These particular children had not had previous experience with standardized tests, and it was extremely difficult to keep them from attempting to see what others had marked or from talking about their responses.

A few children developed a pattern of circling all boxes or only one per row, and no amount of direction altered their response pattern. Even in groups as small as six, there was a wide variety of abilities represented, and some children found the pace to be too slow and others in the same group had difficulty keeping up. A few of the items may assume experiences (i.e., riding a bus) that some children may not have had. Several items appear to cause considerable confusion in these children, particularly the five items in Part 3 that attempt to distinguish written language from a mechanical source (printer or typewriter) and written language that is written by a person (handwriting). This was a difficult concept to explain and the majority of children missed these items.

Summary Statements

The commercial availability of four instruments that measure various aspects of metalinguistic competence now makes possible more extensive studies of criterion-related validity. Subsequent examinations of the convergent and discriminant validity of these tests will no doubt help clarify the meaning of the construct of metalinguistic awareness, and principal component analyses of the tests will perhaps identify subtle complexities of the construct. Organismic relevant variables such as gender differences in both average performance and predictive validity need further attention before widespread adoption of these tests occurs.

Section 6

Young Children's Writing and Metalinguistic Awareness

Chapter 13

Children's Early Interpretations of Writing: Expanding Research Perspectives

ANNE HAAS DYSON

Small children in the home long before they start to school often claim a share in written messages to absent members of the family. It is quite common for mere babies to scribble what they call a letter, in full faith that it will serve the same mysterious purpose as those which the postman brings. (Moore, Betzner, & Lewis, 1927–28)

As the above quote reveals, educators have long known that "mere babies" try their hand at writing. But only recently has young children's writing attracted intense scholarly interest. Beginning most notably in the 60s, researchers acknowledged that, indeed, children did attempt to write. Then they peered at the product, and most recently they have stood back to examine the home and school environments in and through which writing occurs.

As children's stature as writers has grown, researchers have begun to seek their views on the nature of writing as a symbol system—as a way of encoding meaning. After years of literacy experience, it is difficult to communicate with another who is a relatively new user of print. Perhaps that is why researchers have focused most intensely on children who are already operating within the alphabetic symbol system (e.g., Chomsky, 1979; Read, 1971, 1975). Children are described as "able to compose when they know about six consonants" (Graves, 1983, p. 184); that is, they are then able to compose a decipherable message within the alphabetic system.

Before that, though, many children do write. Is there any system to their early attempts? What do they think they are doing? That is, how are they interpreting the writing act? Where do their concepts about writing come from?

These questions are the central concerns of this chapter. I discuss selected studies of young children's writing. In doing this, my aim is to trace the gradual widening of the window through which researchers view children's writing—and to suggest gaps in our own (adult) vision or understanding of their efforts. As we push back the edges of our window on children's writing, we will also uncover more of their own thinking and thus fulfill another purpose of this paper, to highlight children's early interpretations of the written language symbol system (of how meaning is encoded in graphics).

In keeping with the theme of this book, exploring children's views of the symbol system will involve a consideration of "metalinguistic awareness." Here that term refers specifically to children's awareness of language as an entity that is linked to (encoded in) graphics in precise ways. My concern, though, is with intuitive rather than overt knowledge about this link (Goodman, 1984). Thus, to reveal children's thinking, I do not rely exclusively on children's explicit reasonings in interview situations but also on observations of children's spontaneous writing and their talk during and about that writing. (See Cazden, 1975, and Franklin, 1979, for discussions of varied levels of "metalinguistic awareness," including differences between being able to act on the basis of knowledge and being able to explicitly describe that knowledge.)

The Written Language Symbol System

To make sense of children's early written symbols, we might first consider in an analytic way, the nature of any symbolic act. Such an act involves using a distinct form to refer to a separate experience. In Werner and Kaplan's (1963) model, this symbolizing involves the symbol itself (e.g., a graphic form) the symbolic referent (the experience being referred to), the person producing the symbol, and an intended recipient. A symbolic act is guided by the producer's intention—what the person wants to accomplish.

Different symbol systems (language, drawing, symbolic play) are governed by different rules for rendering experience into an observable form (Wolf & Gardner, 1981). Written language is a second-order symbol system—symbols stand for other symbols. To illustrate, consider how one would represent the meaning "house" in drawing, a first-order symbol system, and in writing. As shown in Figure 13-1, in drawing one makes lines that directly denote the house; it is not a language-dependent symbol system. So, one could communicate through drawing to a non-English speaker. The written word *house*, however, is language-dependent; it is a transcription of the word "house." Thus, conventional writing assumes a certain metalinguistic ability—an ability to conceptualize the units of language that will represent thoughts.

Against this backdrop of information on symbolic acts, I introduce Ashley, a kindergartener. Ashley "writes" pictures, letter-like forms, and cursive writing (wavy lines). As he works, Ashley tells elaborate stories about his brothers, friends, cousins, piranhas, and strange fish; at times, though, he simply reports on his behavior: "This how my mama writes [∿]." Figure 13-2 contains an example of Ashley's work.

How is Ashley encoding his experiences? How does he view writing as a symbol system? In the following sections, I selectively review research on children's writing that may allow us insight into Ashley's efforts. His writing will provide a focal point as the window on child writing widens.

Figure 13-1

Symbolizing the Meaning of "House" in Drawing and in Writing

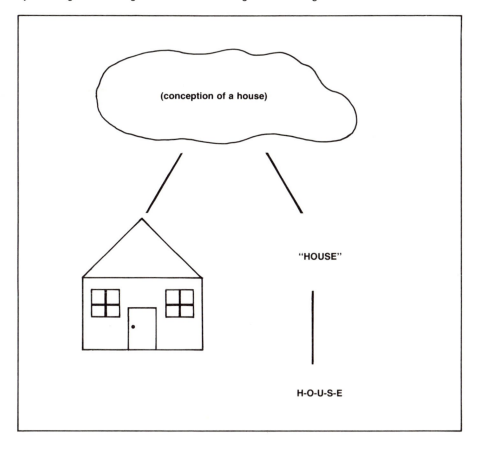

Examining Young Children's Products

Initially, young children's writing was not systematically examined as a complex symbolic act, nor was there an explicit acknowledgment that young children's way of encoding meaning might be different from that of adults. As the opening quote revealed, however, at least some children were acknowledged as attempting to write. Children's interest in writing was mentioned in studies of preschool readers, including those by Durkin (1966), Plessas and Oakes (1964), and Torrey (1969). Children's exploring of letter forms was noted in studies of children's drawing development (Kellogg, 1970), and their efforts to write their own names were examined (Hildreth, 1936).

In a classic study, Clay (1975) focused specifically on young children's message writing. Her analysis centered on written products—on the forms of the

Figure 13–2

Ashley's Written Product

symbols themselves (or potential symbols, if there were no referents). Clay ana-lyzed writing samples spontaneously produced both in the home and in the school by New Zealand children between the ages of 4.10 and 7.10. She studied chil-dren's perceptual awareness of the conventions of written language.

Informed by Clay's work, we now pay close attention to the graphic forms in the upper left hand corner of Ashley's product, under his name:

We note that Ashley has produced an approximation of adult writing. He has made letters and letterlike forms. His letters follow the left-to-right directional pattern of written English. Ashley is apparently aware that letters can be con-tinuously rearranged; he did not, for example, simply repeat the letter *L* but in-termingled it with other letters.

While Clay's work allows us to view Ashley's product with new apprecia-tion, we might still wonder what "sense" his product makes? Is Ashley attempt-ing to communicate a message? To answer that question, talking to Ashley about his product seems necessary.

Clay did not explicitly stress talking to children about their products. She implied its necessity, though, by suggesting that children discover two critical written language principles. These are (a) the *sign* concept: Letters and letter-like shapes carry some unknown message, and (b) the *message* concept: Messages the child speaks can be written down. Does Ashley understand these concepts?

Generally, when I asked Ashley to "tell me about his letters," he dismissed me with, "I don't read 'em; I just write 'em." That response implies an under-standing that letters carry messages (Clay's *sign* concept). When I asked Ashley about his letters on this occasion, though, he gave a more specific response. Ashley had drawn his cousin before writing the letters (see Figure 13-2, section A). He explained that his letters were the "letters of it"—the letters that went with his drawn cousin. Is this Clay's *message* concept? Is Ashley displaying here his un-derstanding that spoken messages can be written down? He did not, after all, say, "This spells 'cousin.' " Clay's work allows insight into Ashley's letterlike forms, but Ashley himself is directing our attention to his drawing—he has made letters that go with his drawn cousin.

To allow further understanding of Ashley's efforts, I turn here to a consid-eration of children's development as symbolizers; the literature on symbolic de-velopment will broaden our view of Ashley's product to include not only his writing, but his drawing as well.

Viewing Children as Symbolizers

In developing as symbol users, children separate more clearly symbols and their referents, producers and recipients, and they learn new ways of linking these elements. As Wolf and Gardner (1981) illustrate, there is no reason to assume that young children and adults follow identical rules as they talk, draw, play—or, I might add, write. Children continually refine their ways of encoding meaning.

Wolf and Gardner (1981) theorize that there is a developmental sequence to children's understandings of how meaning can be represented through symbolic forms. The discovery of new ways of encoding meanings underlies abilities in varied symbol systems (drawing, music, language), although each symbol system has its own unique demands on the child.

For example, during the first two years of life children acquire the ability to symbolize situational roles, such as the agent or the recipient of an action. The ability to encode roles underlies the capacity to acquire the grammar of language, which encodes roles (agent, action, object), and to engage as well in symbolic play, in which children assume situational roles. This understanding of how meaning is encoded affects children's early attempts at symbol systems that demand other ways of encoding meaning. To illustrate, initially children represent meaning through drawing by having their crayon assume the role of agent of an action. A four-year-old, for example, produced Figure 13-3 by quickly moving her marker back and forth over her paper. When asked what she had drawn, the child commented, "I don't know, but it's running fast." Eventually children symbolize objects by representing salient physical characteristics of the referent—they draw simple objects. And later, by five or six, children can make symbols to represent other symbols—they can use graphic symbols (letters) to represent other symbols (spoken words).

Wolf and Gardner do not specifically consider children's development as writers in their discussion. Nonetheless, their theory is suggestive. Between the ages of three and six, children's scribbling gradually develops into recognizable objects (Brittain, 1979) and, similarly, the scribbling gradually acquires the characteristics of print—including linearity, horizontal orientation, and the arrangement of letterlike forms (Clay, 1975). Children control drawing before they control (conventional) writing. They might, then, initially attempt to encode meaning through writing as they do through drawing—by directly representing objects. Their writing may not be written *language* at all.

Although Wolf and Gardner do not directly address writing development, Vygotsky did:

It seems clear that mastery of such a complex sign system [as writing] cannot be accomplished in a purely mechanical and external manner; rather it is the culmination of a long process of development of complex behavioral functions in the child. Only by understanding the entire history of sign development in the child and the place of writing in it can we approach a correct solution of the psychology of writing. (1978, p. 106)

Figure 13–3

Child's Drawing: "I Don't Know [What It Is], But It's Running Fast"

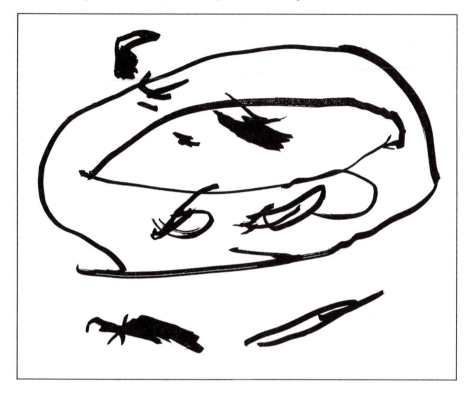

According to Vygotsky, children's first representations of meaning arise as first-order symbolism: Their representations, such as those occurring in play and in drawing, directly denote objects or actions. Children approach writing also as though it were first-order symbolism, like drawing—their first marks are written symbols that directly denote objects or actions. In order to write in the conventional manner, children must discover that one cannot only draw things, but also draw speech: "The written language of children develops in this fashion, shifting from drawings of things to drawing speech" (Vygotsky, 1978, p. 115). Writing must thus become second order symbolism—written symbols must function as designations for verbal ones. Gradually the necessity for language as an intermediate step in writing disappears and written language again becomes direct symbolism (i.e., graphic symbols directly representing meanings).

In the participant observation project in which I met Ashley, children themselves appeared to acknowledge a link between drawing and writing. To elaborate, Ashley was one of five focal children in a study of how young children use speech during writing (Dyson, 1982, 1983). I set up a writing center in a kindergarten classroom that was academically, ethnically, and socially balanced. The children were asked simply to write, according to their own definitions of writing. Observing their spontaneous writing led naturally to an interest in the relationship between drawing and writing. In their written products, all five focal children frequently intermingled drawing and writing, often without linking the drawing and writing thematically.

Certain children, like Ashley, made letters "to go with" objects, people, or events (e.g., Ashley's letters went with his cousin). Others had stable graphic forms they repeatedly wrote, most typically well-known names. Rather than trying to encode speech into graphics, then, most of the children made meaningful graphics about which they could talk, much as they talked about their drawings (e.g., "This is *dog* [a written word] and this is a house [a drawn object]."). Writing, like drawing, was a means of symbolizing significant people and objects in their world.

Further, the children frequently interchanged the terms *draw* and *write*, most commonly using *write* in a situation in which an adult would use the term *draw* or *make*, as in "I'm gonna write him pants." Not only did the children use "write" to refer to symbolizing people and objects through both pictures and letters; they also used it to refer to creating "notes" or graphic objects (including pictures) as gifts for others and to refer to producing graphic forms that had a role in an overriding oral narrative, as Ashley's cousin had a role in an ongoing story (i.e., his cousin was going to be eaten by a soon-to-be-drawn piranha).

The data collected in that study suggested that writing as a symbol system begins as a form of drawing (a graphic representation) that children talk about. Eventually writing becomes a form of language (an orthographic representation): The language surrounding the print takes form on the page.

These developmental inferences about writing and drawing were based on observations collected within a limited span of time. The child's independent production of written language has not, to my knowledge, been included in the study of symbolic development across modes. Nonetheless, the theoretical perspective on symbolism discussed here suggests caution in interpreting Ashley's efforts. Random letterlike forms, such as Ashley's, are often assumed to be children's early attempts to record speech (see, for example, Wood, 1982). But this may not be the case. Have there been any longitudinal attempts to study children's thinking about print? Such work would allow us more confidence as we widen our view on children's writing to include their reasoning as well as their products.

Tapping Children's Reasoning

Using Piagetian methods, Ferreiro (1978, 1980, 1984) and Ferreiro and Teberosky (1982) have focused on uncovering the child's view of written language. Consistent with the Piagetian view of the child as an active constructor of knowledge, their work has illustrated children's gradual construction of the alphabetic nature of the written language symbol system. That is, it suggests that the manner in which children encode meaning—the way in which they link symbol and referent—changes over time, and that initially children do not operate within the alphabetic system.

Recently, Ferreiro (1984) studied a group of 33 children between the ages of three and six in Mexico City. She interviewed them regularly over a two-year period. During the interviews, she asked each child to perform particular reading and writing tasks. She found that regardless of social class, children did not initially conceive of writing as encoding speech. Rather, letters were viewed as "going with" or "belonging to" something or someone, just as Ashley's letters were of his cousin. Eventually letters were seen as referring to particular objects or people or, more specifically, the names of objects or people—which names the child may or may not know. During this early stage, the children believed that only referents for concrete entities are actually written in a written sentence, although one reads the "complete" sentence. Thus, when asked to identify the individual words in the printed sentence "Delfino vendio tres gatitos" ("Delfino sold three little cats"), a five-year-old identified *Delfino* as the first word and the three remaining words as the three little cats. Writing is thus like drawing—only static aspects of the experience are represented. At a later point in development, the children's writing behaviors reflected an understanding that a relationship exists between print and the formal characteristics of speech.

Although Ferreiro examined children's behavior in researcher-directed tasks, she and her colleagues argue that the responses they identified are reflective of the process by which children reconstruct the symbol system itself. One may wonder, then, about the existence or the extent of the existence of such child reasoning outside researcher-structured tasks. Do children engage in such thinking spontaneously, or is the reasoning an artifact of the experimental situation?

Further questions may arise when one considers that Ferreiro provided the children with messages to be written or directed that the children add writing to their drawings. As she was interested in the relationship between oral and written language, the origin of the particular message to be written was of little interest. Her work provides a fascinating analysis of children's evolving construction of written language. Yet the data do not allow us to see how children use and reason about written language as they incorporate it into their daily lives; the data lack the intentional framework within which a symbol system forms.

Recognizing Child Intentions

Ashley's behaviors, then, may have a new significance. His reasoning was similar to that described by Ferreiro but was displayed in a less structured situation. Since Ashley was invited to simply "write," he structured his own writing task. And that structuring was dependent on his own personal intentions. We need, then, to consider not only Ashley's writing, but Ashley himself. We, therefore, will broaden our view yet again and consider Ashley's characteristic way of functioning in school, and also his reasons for writing.

Ashley was an avid talker and, in his teacher's words, a "storyteller." He blended experiences from the television, the movies, and everyday life to create dramatic, imaginative narratives for anyone who would listen.

During the daily center time, in which the children were free to self-select activities, Ashley preferred to enact adventures in the big block center but—when the block center was full, and no one in the puzzle and game area needed a play partner—he would come to the writing center.

For the most part, Ashley drew at the "writing" center. Generally, he told a series of elaborate narratives within which his drawing and writing evolved. He alternated between narrating his story and planning or monitoring his drawing activities (e.g., "Here go Spiderman. I'm writing both of 'em in real life [Spiderman and his unnamed friend].''). As noted earlier, in producing the graphics in Figure 13-2, Ashley drew his cousin and then wrote the "letters of it." Later Ashley drew the object in section B of that figure and again added letters (although these letters were obscured by a later drawing over them). Listen to Ashley's reasoning about his work:

Interaction	Comment
	I ask Ashley about the letters he has written.
Ashley: These is the letters of it.	
Mark: And what is this?	Mark, one of Ashley's peers, is referring to the object in section B of Figure 13-2
Ashley: That's like a piranha.	
Mark: Yeah, but this looks like a chicken.	
Ashley: It snapped my cousin.	
Dyson: What does this spell?	I am attempting to refocus Ashley's attention on the "letters of it."
Ashley: Well, it spells that he snapped my cousin one time and I got mad. And them are his teeth and here goes somethin' else. He have big eyes.	Ashley is adding new details to his picture.
Mark: It don't look like a chicken no more.	

Note that Ashley changed from attributing his letters to the piranha to relating them to a whole event. Ashley represents meaning by relating letters to that meaning as a whole or to concrete entities within that whole. He is attuned to the experience he is narrating, although we, as adults, might focus on his utterances, noting the change in linguistic form from word to proposition. The nature of my question and of his own shifting interest, from the piranha to the piranha's role in his evolving narrative, changed the nature of his response.

I noted this liability in many of Ashley's classmates' responses as well, and developmentally, this is not surprising. Young children's early concepts are labile; various aspects of a concept may be brought to the fore, depending upon the nature of questions posed or tasks assigned (Werner, 1948). Ashley's behavior, therefore, leads us to both find support for, and to extend, the work of Ferreiro. In the most extensive report of that work, Ferreiro & Teberosky (1982) list "developmental levels," referring to specific behaviors, for all of the varied tasks used in their research. The fact that the behaviors are responses to researcher-structured tasks should not be overlooked. While the general trend of children's changing conceptions of written language (from a representation of reality to a representation of language) seems supported, precise descriptions of varied levels of behaviors all children engage in seems an overly ambitious statement.

To further illustrate, Ashley wrote in varied ways, depending on his purpose. In addition to using letterlike forms to represent objects or events, he used cursive-like writing for producing notes (see Figure 13-4). In these notes, there was no attempt at encoding meaning at all; the notes were for his mama to read—not him. At other times, he simply explored the forms of print. At still others, he made specific letters to accurately depict a drawn object, as when he added the S to Superman's shirt.

Ashley, then, focuses our attention on the variability of children's writing processes. Children write differently for different purposes. Observing children's spontaneous writing in the classroom has, therefore, broadened our picture of Ashley and other child writers. Such observations revealed the sorts of reasons why young children might write and suggested relationships between writing processes—more specifically, ways of encoding meaning—and the child's intentions. Different children then might attend to different aspects of the written language symbol system and come to understand writing in different ways.

Allowing for Individual Differences

To clarify this notion of individual differences, we here focus briefly on three of Ashley's peers: Rachel, Vivi, and Tracy (complete case studies available in Dyson, in press). We focus on these three because they had similar knowledge about letter names and sounds (as indicated in structured tasks), but they appeared to have different ways of approaching written language, approaches that made sense when each child was viewed within the context of her own unique interests and styles of functioning.

Figure 13–4

Ashley's Note

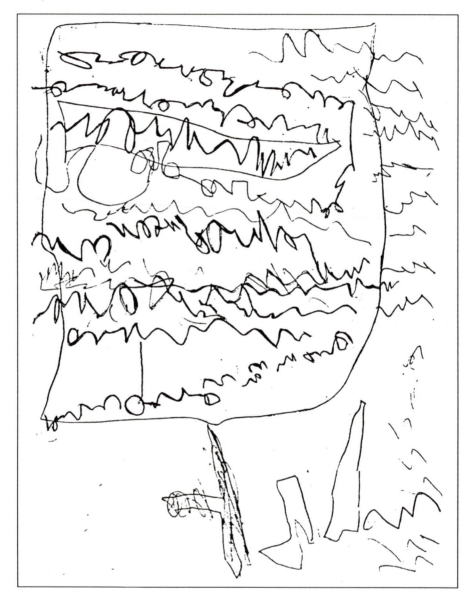

Of all three children, Tracy could spell the greatest number of conventional words, although she did not write for a variety of purposes, nor did she appear interested in understanding the encoding system. She wrote words by memorizing letters and their spatial arrangements and by requesting unknown words from others. Tracy's interests in drawing and in constructive play were to "build" particular entities. Her interest in words as entities was consistent with that drawing and play style.

Rachel did not know many conventional words, but like Tracy she did not appear intent on understanding the encoding system. She wrote by requesting words and also by simply putting down letters randomly, despite her awareness that such writing was not "real." However, Rachel wrote for a variety of purposes; she attempted lists of peers, notes to friends, dialogue for her stories. Her interest in the purposes of writing was consistent with her interests as a person. She engaged often in dramatic, imaginative play—even her drawings took shape within elaborate narrations. Rachel's imaginative narratives, like her informal conversations, generally focused on relationships between people.

Vivi did not write as many conventional words as did Tracy, nor did she use writing for as many purposes as did Rachel. Yet, she appeared intent on figuring out exactly how the written language encoding system worked. She frequently attempted to write words and phrases that served no identifiable instrumental purpose. Vivi's interest in writing was consistent with her approach to other activities; for example, when drawing, she was more intent on exploring varied shapes and colors than producing coherent products. The three children illustrate, then, that as we change our focus from encoding strategies to, for example, writing functions, a different view of a child's competence may emerge.

Even when we focus specifically on encoding behaviors, variable child strategies for exploring the symbol system are evident. Many recent early literacy researchers have appeared to assume that for all children, arriving at the connection between print and formal aspects of speech will initially, consistently, and "naturally" result in alphabetic invented spelling and attempts to "sound out" words. However, this is not necessarily the case. Torrey (1969, 1979), for example, described a five-year-old who wrote using conventional spellings, asking for the unknown spellings of desired words. While clearly understanding that print was a form of language, and capable of using graphophonic information when reading difficult words, sounding out was not his own initial route into encoding words; he appeared to rely instead on visual memory.

The exact strategies a child uses when encoding may vary with what exactly the child is attending to—trying to figure out about written language. To illustrate, Vivi had varied procedures for exploring the link between graphics and speech. Most frequently, Vivi wrote the name of any letter she heard in the spoken word or phrase, and added other letters for each syllable in order to have a sufficiently lengthy text. For example, she wrote PNEDN for "in a minute" (which is pronounced "EN[N] A MEN[N] UT"). She appeared to be attending to how to choose letters to represent spoken messages in print. On other occasions, however, she appeared to attend to how to convert spoken messages into written symbols for words. On those occasions she requested spelling from adults or copied words available in the environment.

To return here to Ashley, we see him now not just as a preconventional writer, but as an individual with a certain style, a way of approaching written language. While the focus here is on his knowledge of the encoding system, we should be aware that, after all, we are examining only one aspect of what it means to be literate. We should acknowledge also that Ashley's future exploration of the encoding system is not entirely predictable—there are varied possible routes.

This consideration of children's varying intentions in writing, though, raises another question: Where do children's conceptions of writing come from? While individual differences may be related in part to individual makeup, certainly the environment has a role to play.

Viewing the Child in Context

Researchers interested in how literacy develops in the preschool years study reading and writing as activities occurring in varied social settings. They speak of the "literacy event," a concept derived from Hymes's (1972) concept of the speech event as an occasion structured by a way of using speech, for example, a debate, a quarrel, a casual conversation, a classroom lesson. Literacy events are activities engaged in by one or more persons that are centered around reading or writing (Teale, Estrada, and Anderson, 1981) and that are also governed by social rules constraining how participants use speech during the activity (Heath, 1982). Researchers study the kinds of literacy events that occur in home and preschool settings. In this way, they gain insight into what children learn about reading and writing before formal school entry.

These researchers have suggested that for young children, literacy events are embedded in familiar daily situations (Cochran-Smith, 1984; Taylor, 1983). Before children have a precise understanding of the nature of our symbol system, they observe or share in literacy events with others. The following description from the parents of a five-year-old are illustrative:

Mom: When I was working on my shorthand a few months ago, she'd sit down and want to write too. So, I'd give her a paper and she'd make wavy lines. She's been doing this for at least six months.
Dad: She's always after me to read to her. She wants to read big books . . . I would be studying and she'd go get a big book so that she could read like me.

Observing and sharing in literacy events may be the foundation for literacy learning. Through participating in family or community literacy events, children come to view literacy as a valued social tool, one that allows them to fulfill varied goals.

In engaging in these reading and writing events, children are, in a sense, on the outer edges of the graphics/speech connection; letters are written and are also read. Beginning with an appreciation of reading and writing as valued social tools, how do children come to grapple with exactly how graphics and speech connect?

The work of both Clay (1975) and Ferreiro (1980) suggested the value of writing for uncovering the nature of the symbol system. In writing, children make explicit their current hypotheses about the written language symbol system, and as a direct result of that process, children may reflect upon and revise their hypotheses. Yet, as illustrated in the previous section, all ways of writing do not appear to cause children to focus on the speech/print connection. It may be in fact that certain children are more apt to consider this connection when they are playing with messages outside of an instrumental context—that is, when the motivation appears to be simply to represent a meaning. Couched within the idea that writing is a way of symbolizing, they play with writing—exploring it, just as they do other media, such as drawing, block building, and sand play.

Consider, for example, this mother's description of her five-year-old's interest in writing:

She started just putting anything. She'd bring it to me and say, "What does this say?"

". . . Errhophf."

"But that's not a word."

"I know it's not, but that's what you wrote."

She'd get frustrated . . . and say, "I want to write a word." That's when it really started, when she realized she wasn't really spelling anything.

Studies of children who have already begun to write within the alphabetic system describe children using, in noninstrumental ways, pieces of print they have extracted from their literacy environments. Bissex (1980) reports, for example, that her son wrote a "Happy Birthday" card for no one in particular, an "out of order" sign for nothing, and a "Paul's telephone booth" label for no known entity. In this regard, recall the earlier example of Vivi writing "in a minute," which message had no recipient. Having acquired a sense, then, of what literacy is and of what its use is, certain children may spontaneously investigate further.

Reports of children's interest in functional language (signs, labels), their writing, and their questioning of others (e.g., "How do you spell ————?" "What does ———— say?") are common in studies of children who read in a conventional manner before school entry (Durkin, 1966; Clark 1976). The studied children were attentive to the written language used in their environment, tried it out themselves, and questioned others to gain needed information, taking a reflective, inquiring stance toward print's potential meanings.

Taking such a stance, however, does not necessarily involve extensive questioning of others. Torrey's five-year-old, John, did not appear to engage in questioning to the degree that other described early readers and writers have. John was also different from other early readers and writers in that his parents did not read to him. John appeared to have learned about print primarily from watching television commercials, which, like often-heard picture books, provide repeated exposure to meaningful print. In Torrey's words, John appeared to have asked just "the right questions of his environment," questions "about the relation between language and the printed form. . . . The key question is 'How does something I can say look in print?' or, vice versa, 'What does that print say?' "

(Torrey, 1969, p. 556). Within the context of meaningful messages, John, like other early readers and writers, reached an essential insight—"that print is a form of language like what you speak and hear" (Torrey, 1979, p. 141).

What seems to be important, then, is a sense of the general purpose and nature of written language, a motivation to produce one's own written meaning (although that meaning may serve no instrumental purpose), a certain reflective stance toward that meaning and one's production of it, and, for most children, a responsive, knowledgeable user of print. Note here, though, that reflection does not precede production; it is use itself—the desire to represent a meaning—that is guiding the child's activity.

Returning here to our consideration of Ashley, we may now appreciate varied aspects of his "literacy event" that were not salient previously. Ashley is in an environment—his kindergarten classroom—filled with print. He observes his teacher reading and writing routinely, and he often participates in this reading and writing, as when his teacher reads to the class or writes class-dictated stories. Within this environment, the writing center provided Ashley with an opportunity to write and access to an adult who was responsive to his efforts.

It may be, then, that if Ashley had been sitting alone he would not have reflected on his writing—nor, perhaps, have actually written at all. Although, as researcher, I did not structure the writing situation by giving children explicit directions, I legitimized writing (by asking the children to "Come write"), and I caused reflection by asking, "Tell me about that." Given exposure to written language, access to pencils and paper, and another person interested in responding to children's writing (rather than in preparing children to write), children might teach themselves a great deal about written language; Bissex (1984, p. 101) argues this point: "The child as teacher is child mind interacting with the information and structures provided by its immediate environment, and guided and supported by the enduring structures of human mind and language which, like a great net, protect it from falling into the abyss of nonlearning."

Viewing the Child as Community Member

We began by noticing that Ashley wrote. Then we peered at his product, and gradually we broadened our vision to a holistic consideration of Ashley's writing behaviors within a particular school context. Ashley's behaviors, though, are based on his experiences with print not only inside but outside the school setting, in his home and community. Vygotsky (1978) is often credited with the concept that literacy is a cultural tool—an instrument for accomplishing valued personal and social ends. Recent early literacy work has examined written language as a cultural phenomenon, one which may vary with different social groups. Since, as already noted, children interact with others in their daily environments to construct literacy events, it is reasonable to conclude that children from varied communities may come with varied concepts about written language and varied ways of approaching literacy.

For Ashley, we do not have access to his behavior outside the school context. He is black and from a non-middle class home, but that does not provide us with any helpful information about Ashley. As Teale, Estrada, and Anderson (1981) have demonstrated, specific demographic characteristics (such as ethnicity or income level) do not allow one to make specific generalizations regarding the kind of literacy experiences children have had. Many interrelated factors affect the nature and frequency of literacy activities in the home, including parental occupation, religious practices, and interpersonal communication patterns. Acknowledging this lack of home data and the perspective such data would allow on Ashley's writing, I consider here selected research on literacy activities in varied social groups.

Schieffelin and Cochran-Smith (1984) discuss literacy values and patterns of use in three different social groups: educated school-oriented parents in a Philadelphia suburb, a family in a traditional nonliterate society in Papua, New Guinea, and a Sino-Vietnamese family in Philadelphia. Literacy classes in the Papuan village appeared to have little impact on the people's everyday lives. On the other hand, a Sino-Vietnamese nine-year-old, whose parents did not speak English, was successfully acquiring literacy in English; although no one in his family could read to him or assist him in his reading and writing efforts, literacy itself was seen as a valued tool within his native culture. Schieffelin and Cochran-Smith demonstrate, then, that viewing literacy as functionally relevant is a prerequisite for becoming literate, a finding supported as well by research cited in the previous section of this paper.

Heath (1983) has examined cohesive communities in the southeastern part of this country, documenting differences in literacy events across communities. She studied black and white mainstream families (who were not considered as a "community"), a white working class community, and a black working class community. In comparing their ways of using written language, Heath draws the sharpest contrasts between the mainstream families and the black working class community. While children in the latter community encountered print in varied situations (e.g., labels on food cans and cartons, price tags at the local store, brands of cars and bicycles), only the mainstream children had extensive book reading experience. In addition while the mainstream children were oriented to identifying and labeling features, not only of books but of the environment (i.e., answering "What's that?" questions), the black working class children were oriented to making general comparisons between whole situations or items ("What's that like?").

It is not clear precisely how these cultural differences would affect how young children came to understand the alphabetic nature of the symbol system. Researchers of early literacy have not, as previously noted, extensively examined variability in children's explorations of written language. Heath does demonstrate, however, that children may come to school with strong concepts regarding the functional utility of print—and, in fact, be competent users of print in everyday situations—and yet be unsuccessful in primary classrooms. Teachers tend to value knowledge of the discrete parts of written language (the names, sounds, and formations of the alphabet) more than knowledge of the uses of print. (See

Dyson, 1984, for an illustration of the senselessness of certain school literacy activities for a child apparently oriented to using, rather than taking apart, print.)

Toward a Holistic View of Child Writers

We come back once again here to Ashley, as he talks, draws, and writes about piranhas, superheroes, and others significant in his world. This chapter has highlighted the many perspectives on his writing researchers might take. As has been discussed, interest has expanded from a curiosity about written forms to questions regarding ways of encoding meaning in writing and in other media as well. Researchers have wondered too about the extent to which a child's behaviors are idiosyncratic or reflections of cultural or universal ways of uncovering the alphabetic nature of the symbol system. Throughout the discussion, the complexity of written language and the limits of this paper's primary focus on the encoding system have been stressed.

For practitioners, the research reviewed here has suggested caution in treating written language as a system of rules (e.g., governing letter formation, meaning encoding) that can be divorced from the intentions of the symbolizer—the child. It has suggested as well caution in implementing curricula organized around sequential skill mastery without, first, a consideration of the child intentions that will organize skills in sensible ways to accomplish ends and, second, without regard for the individuality of each child. The research suggests therefore both the necessity of critical evaluations of literacy programs available to young children and the importance of teacher sensitivity to individual children's ways of approaching writing.

This chapter concludes with a seemingly contradictory message: Researchers and practitioners may benefit from close examinations of individual children operating within the broad contexts of the classroom, the family, and the community. Although individual researchers' efforts, of necessity, focus on only certain portions of that comprehensive picture, the view is a goal to which all may contribute. Such a view, with the child at the center, will lead to a keener insight into not only what the child knows about written language, but also how the child comes to know.

Chapter 14

Children's Elicitation and Use of Metalinguistic Knowledge About *Word* During Literacy Interactions

ELIZABETH SULZBY

This volume brings together two major areas of research: the area of beginning reading/writing and that of metalinguistic awareness. Important changes in assumptions and resulting methodology in research in early literacy (which I have begun to call emergent literacy, or emergent reading and writing) have implications for research in metalinguistic awareness. The changes involve how development is viewed.

Early Reading/Writing Research and Child Development

This decade has brought about a great change of emphasis in the field of early reading and writing (see Teale & Sulzby, in press). The change has been (1) away from defining reading and writing separately and toward defining them more broadly as literacy; (2) away from treating oral and written language as separate systems toward treating them as systems in complex, dynamic relationships within and between cultures; and (3) away from documenting what children know or fail to know about conventional reading and writing toward documenting what children know that leads up to conventional knowledge and performance.

Thus research in early reading and writing has become more developmental. The methodology used in research has increasingly turned from asking children to respond to "prereading" and "prewriting" tasks—like segmenting conventional print, naming letters, or describing what could be read in a picture—toward asking children to perform tasks of reading and writing in whatever way the child conceives of reading and writing. These "production tasks" are designed to be sensitive to and reveal the child's interpretation of the task; thus children's performances vary in terms of the actual tasks performed. This means the results are more difficult to compare with traditional experimental tasks, but the comparisons can lead to important new interpretations (and, hopefully, to more relevant experimental designs). I will return to these tasks, but first I must define what I mean by development.

When I claim that children's emergent reading and writing is developmental, I mean that children hold rule-governed concepts prior to conventional reading and writing, and that these concepts change in a logical manner toward conventional concepts as the child learns more about reading and writing. Many of the concepts are, like those evident in oral language development, not taught by adults, but are hypotheses constructed by the child (see also Ferreiro & Teberosky, 1982; Ferreiro, in press). They are, however, legitimate concepts about reading and writing and I judge these children to be reading and writing. Even though the concepts are developmental, I do not believe that they fit a strong sequential stage model of development; rather, my research (Sulzby, 1981, 1983a, 1983b, in press-b) indicates that there are a number of patterns of development with individual variation within those patterns. Additionally, children appear to keep vestiges of previous concepts as part of a repertoire of understandings and abilities; these vestiges are more obvious prior to conventional reading and writing, but can still be detected through techniques like metalinguistic interviews or posing problematic situations. Two examples of children's concepts about reading and writing follow.

Development in Emergent Reading of Storybooks

Before children are reading conventionally from print, they will read from favorite storybooks while looking at the pictures. My research with two- to six-year-old children (Sulzby, 1983b, in press-b) has revealed patterns of language that develop from labeling and commenting on the content of discrete pictures; retelling the story in language with patterns associated with oral interactive or oral monologic language; to retelling the story with orally delivered language having written language characteristics. This final pattern culminates in children attempting to retrieve verbatim the story they have heard read. All of these patterns lead up to the child's attending to the print as the item of attention for reading. Once this long line of development has been accomplished (by the four- or five-year-old) and the child is attending to print as "what is read," there are further patterns of development in how the child uses the print. I have observed infant children babbling to storybooks in what sounds like "reading intonation" (see Sulzby, 1983b). Clay (1979, 1982) has tracked children's development in attending to print in storybooks for instructional purposes (see also Andrews & Mason, this volume; Holdaway, 1979).

Development in Children's Emergent Writing

Before children are writing in conventional English orthography, they use various systems for writing. They scribble or mark on paper; they draw; they use repeated variations of known letter strings; they use what may appear to be random series of letters with no phonetic basis; they use one letter per phonetic syllable, with or without conventional phonetic basis; they use meager or quite full invented spelling with clear phonetic basis; and, gradually, they use conventional spelling. Ferreiro and Teberosky (1982), working in a Piagetian paradigm, have indicated a sequence of development that at least partially recapitulates the historical development of writing systems culminating in alphabetic writing. My work indicates that children do not all go through the same sequence and that children retain the lower level conceptions in a repertoire, at least up to conventional writing. (These conceptions probably become transformed into more conventional concepts but may be maintained in some form.)

Concept of Word

While all of children's metalinguistic understandings are important, both emergent literacy research and metalinguistic awareness research have raised questions about the nature of the child's concept of word. One major question is descriptive: What is the child's concept of word? Researchers have examined the child's concept of word using numerous techniques: through responses to interviews or judgment tasks (Berthoud-Papandropoulou, 1978; Papandropoulou & Sinclair, 1974; Sulzby, 1978, 1979); through observing reading and writing tasks (Ferreiro & Teberosky, 1982; Sulzby, 1981a, 1981b, 1983a, 1983b); through having children complete artificial tasks like counting or tapping for the number of words in a given oral utterance (Holden & MacGinitie, 1972; Leong & Haines, 1978); and through noting children's prosodic adjustments in dictating, voicing while composing, or in reading attempts (Cook-Gumperz & Gumperz, 1981; Gumperz, 1982; Scollon & Scollon, 1981; Sulzby, 1982, 1983a, in press-a, in press-b).

The second major question has been about the relationship between concept of word and reading. (Writing has been ignored.) Yaden (this volume) reviewed the literature to see what conclusions could be reached about whether children need metalinguistic awareness about such units as word prior to conventional reading and/or reading instruction. Ehri (1975, 1976) has explored the question of whether or not concept of word is prerequisite, a consequence, or a by-product of learning to read, using experimental techniques and conventional adult standards of correctness and treating children as "readers" and "prereaders."

This second question has been difficult to answer because we have not clarified sufficiently what is meant by concept of word and metalinguistic awareness of word. It has been pointed out numerous times that even linguists do not agree about definitions of "word" (Read, 1978; Sulzby, 1978). On the one hand, we could be driven to the position that there is no point at which a child "does not have a concept of word" at some level, even prelinguistically. On the other hand, we do need to address the nature of the child's developing concept of word, particularly as it relates to literacy development and to how word is represented in written language.

I take concept of word to be inherently difficult to define, because it, along with other metalinguistic terms, belongs in the category of "fuzzy sets" (see Sulzby, 1980), rather than finite sets with clear boundaries and specifiable definition. To do research, however, we assume that we must define our terms. If the object of concern is "fuzzy," we seem to be in an untenable position. And here experimentalists and naturalists often separate. I believe, however, that we can begin with a working definition as a heuristic and then observe what children can reveal about the concept. We can compose such a definition for "word" in English: "An entity composed of letters bounded by space according to the conventions of English orthography indicating a meaningful relationship in a stable manner." Then we can observe what children know about that concept. We can also observe what children can teach us about the limitations of such a definition.

My research indicates support for the position that children are learning more about the unit "word" during the process of learning to read and write. However, the issue of how metalinguistically aware a child must be in order to read and write still remains. I have suggested (Sulzby, 1981a, in press-c) that in order to learn to read conventionally from English orthography, the child needs to coordinate three kinds of knowledge: some notion of the word as a stable unit, some understanding of letter-sound relationships, and some notion of the text as a stable entity for understanding, retrieval, and manipulation. This means, by definition, that the child has some metalinguistic awareness. The stress here is on *some* awareness, not complete understanding. Our observations of children becoming conventional readers appear to support the claim that the children do not have complete concepts about word, nor are their concepts and expressions of awareness the same. While awareness seems more apparent in emergent writing, we still observe children writing competently and understandably while still demonstrating nonconventional concepts about aspects of word.

If concept of word is part of reading and writing, then the questions become, more appropriately, what is the *nature* of the child's developing concept of word and *how* does the child's concept of word develop? I cannot answer those questions definitively from my current research, but I can suggest some newer ways of looking. In this chapter, I describe some general findings from my research that affect what can be observed about the child's concept of word; I describe some of the ways that children's knowledges about the concept of word can be observed during reading and writing tasks; and finally, I discuss an extended example from our longitudinal study in which a child is working through problems about the concept of word while doing reading and writing tasks. In this example the child appears to be learning more about reading and writing, as well as using and eliciting metalinguistic knowledge in the process.

Data Base and Method

In 1980–81, as part of a two-year study of children's literacy development (Sulzby, 1983a, in press-c), 24 children in a middle class suburban kindergarten classroom in which reading and writing were not taught formally were interviewed individually about what they knew about reading and writing. From those 24 children, nine were selected for intensive case study scrutiny, including weekly classroom observations and five individual experimentally structured writing and reading sessions.

The overall design of the two-year study coordinated experimental, interview, and observational techniques in order to study children's literacy development longitudinally. Embedded in the design were tasks, situations, and questions designed to tap the child's metalinguistic and metacognitive awarenesses about reading and writing. The basic task design of three of the individual reading/writing sessions was to ask the child to "write a story." Tasks leading to the eventual written story included storytelling to an audience; dictating the story to a scribe; rereading and editing the dictation; and finally, writing the story and rereading and editing it. Three trials of all tasks were collected from the nine case study children in the winter and spring of 1981. Transcripts from the tape-recorded sessions serve as the data base for the examples given in this chapter. (Full details of the method are given in Sulzby, 1983a.) Each of these tasks offered many opportunities to tap aspects of the children's concepts for *word*.

In these sessions, examiners introduced only a selected set of metalinguistic terms (*read, write, story, dictate*). Other metalinguistic terms (e.g. *word, letter, sentence, sound*) were used by the adult only after the child used them. If a child used an "indirect metalinguistic indicator," like pointing or referring deictically (Sulzby & Otto, 1982), the examiner attempted to probe the child's usage indirectly. One of the terms that was not introduced by the examiner but that was studied most intensively in the project was the term *word*.

To produce the "general findings" section, I compared the evidence from the three writing sessions with other sessions of the longitudinal study, as I detail below.

What Children Reveal About Their Concept of Word

General Findings

Three general findings from the longitudinal study (Sulzby, 1983a, in press-c) are particularly relevant. The first overall finding came from a comparison of storywriting trials with beginning- and end-of-the-kindergarten-year interviews and with a group storywriting study conducted in early spring. This finding fits with the other literature in metalinguistic awareness and with previous research with these specific tasks (Sulzby, 1981, in press-c). There are task differences. The two most important tasks differences that I have found appear to be stable to the tasks. This means that the same child performs the same way in repetitions of the same task and differs in the same way in other tasks.

Task differences in choice of writing system.   All of the children had some items of conventional English orthography in their repertoires, and when asked to "write everything you can write," wrote lists. The children primarily used a column display; this display made their notion of word appear to be that of a conventionally space-bounded entity. In storywriting, in contrast, the same children showed other ideas about how space and boundaries operate in relation to word. In this task, the children seemed to use "lower-level" writing systems (scribbling, drawing, various kinds of letter strings, and various levels of invented spelling) to perform the complex task of writing a story. The graphic display of the writing was accompanied by speech that also revealed information about the child's segmenting of the speech flow to accompany composition and to reread from the graphics. These tasks' differences reveal complexities in the child's understandings that we must piece together. The inventory task makes the child's understandings appear more conventional; the writing task makes them appear less conventional; the speech yields yet other information about the child's understandings.

Types of writing and reading. The second overall finding is that there are types of writing and reading to the young child in which the concept of word may be displayed. It is not always clear that children conceive of rereading from their own compositions to be the same kind of reading that storybook reading is. They may fail to attempt to track the print in rereading their own writing but track it in the storybook or vice versa. Children may try to sound out words from dictation but not from storybooks and vice versa.

Variability. The nine case study children were divided into groups of three, each judged to be high, moderate, and low in emergent literacy. The writing from the storywriting tasks reveals stability in use of the writing system for the individual children during the kindergarten year in the storywriting tasks. Yet within each ability level, there was variation that had not been predicted by suggestions that children develop from low level writing systems to the highest level. Overall, it was the case that the low children showed less elaborated concepts about *word;* the moderate children showed more understandings; and the high children showed the most knowledge (see Sulzby, 1981b, for details). In choice of writing system, though, two of the three high children consistently used letter strings as their preferred system even though they began to read conventionally during this period. These children rarely used invented spelling. They were able to explain how the writing system they used worked for them, "for me." Some of the lower ability children did use invented spelling and some used conventional print copied from the environment. This print did not match what they read as their story conventionally, but it was used by them, perhaps as a "placeholder" and a representation of what writing should look like.

Significance of the General Findings

These findings alert us to the complexity of the child's concept of word and to a few of the situations in which it develops. This complexity suggests that we need both naturalistic and experimental designs and much longitudinal evidence from children's activities in reading and writing. In the section that follows I inventory only a few ways of detecting aspects of the child's concept of word from the storywriting tasks.

Observations During Reading and Writing of Children's Concept of Word

Segmentation at the Word Level

By five years of age, children are quite adept at segmenting the speech stream at the word level in oral situations. Syntax requires this ability. In actual situations, when children are conversing or answering interview questions, they may show disfluencies in which they *hmm* and *uh* around as if in search of a word. Or they may pause quite specifically between word units, as if in search of a given word or as if self-correcting a word that did not match their plan.

Noting all instances of these types of disfluencies, pauses, and self-corrections will give evidence of children's ability to isolate words in their speech at some level. They also exhibit this ability, with some important modifications, in using speech to compose, reread, and discuss written language.

There is some evidence that children lower in emergent literacy show more disfluencies with written language situations, a reflection of monitoring at a very local level. As children increase in emergent literacy, they interrupt written language utterances with metastatements that are clearly signaled as standing outside the ongoing discourse (Sulzby, 1983b). (It should be noted that all of the children showed disfluencies at times, often when trying to verbalize metalinguistic or metacognitive understandings; see Example 6 below.)

When Betsy was asked to tell a story in preparation for writing the story, she showed evidence of segmenting her speech stream through pausing as if to think of the precise word, *tricycle* (Example 1.1) and of self-correcting (1.2). These segmentations are important evidence of semantic and syntactic aspects of her concept of word.

Example 1.1:

   Child: Now I want a bike and not a dumb little *[pause]* tricycle.

Example 1.2 [continuing 1.1]: One of the tricycles I used to have is—was blue.

Word as a unit in written language can be inferred from children's segmentation of the speech flow in dictating or in rereading attempts. Children gradually become able to sustain long pauses while dictating, and increasingly time those pauses between single word units. After that point, they may time their pauses at phrase boundaries, but wait a realistic time for a scribe to write. Typically, these more advanced children watch the scribe write but occasionally they seem to be estimating the time needed. Across the trials of our study, including first grade, there was an increase in the time differential between dictating and telling the same semantic content (Sulzby, in press-a). In rereading attempts, children often use a word-by-word prosody with almost a list intonation (cf. Bolinger, 1972; Cook-Gumperz & Gumperz, 1981; Sulzby, 1982; in press-c; in press-e).

Another way children show awareness of word as a unit in dictation is to be interrupted or to interrupt themselves and to begin again, either at the immediate next word or to restate what was said just before the interruption. Typically the children low in emergent literacy are very poor at this and more advanced children are very good.

Even though children low in emergent ability were poorer at these tasks, this did not mean they showed no knowledge that words were segmentable in written language tasks. In Example 2, Mike made a separation of clause-level utterances which he called "word." He was attempting to reread dictation but he was not looking at the print.

Example 2:

>   Child: I can only read that story in my mind—but I can only read one word at a time.

>   Adult: Okay. Well, let's do it one word at a time, but let me hear it, too. . . .

>   Child: The first word is: He did it in space. [*Stress on* **is** *followed by a long pause and indrawn breath on* **he.**)

He continued to isolate clause-level units as "first word," "second word," "next word"; however, the prosodic cues he used were those appropriate for someone saying "word-as-word." That is, the intonation is similar to someone repeating an unclear word in a conversation: "Not *cat!* I said *hat!*"

Word-internal Segmentation

Another concern in metalinguistic research is whether or not children can segment words into phonemes prior to conventional reading. Evidence of this ability to segment can be detected when children "voice" (Graves's term, 1979) during composing. This voicing can include word units and also letter names and phonetic utterances. In Example 3, Douglas is writing, "He wanted it." The example begins after Douglas has written *he* (HD) which he composed after saying the letter names, *H* and *E*. The section of interest is the first syllable of *wanted* and how he retraces the segmentation of the surrounding syllables while working on it.

Example 3:

>   Child: [*Laughing.*] I can't think.

>   Adult: What are you doing now—what part of it?

>   Child: *He.*

>   Adult: Uh-huh, that's good. What now? [*Long pause.*]

>   Child: Wan—ted. [*Long pause.*]

>   Child: W.

>   Adult: Sure. [*Pause to turn audiotape over.*]

>   Child: He—/wə/ [*short pause*] he, he [*short pause*] /t/ [*short pause*] he [*short pause*] he [*short pause*]. [*Long period of writing, then rereading at adult's indirect request.*] He—wan—ted—it.

The kind of retracing of the segmentation that Douglas uses is quite common. Children sometimes look at the print, but often they do not. It is as if they are rechecking their segmentation hypotheses phonetically but without reference to the print. Other children operate quite linearly, without retracing. Once a unit has been composed via internal segmentation, these children reread it or resay it with word units that are signaled prosodically.

Richard showed low understandings of word boundaries and internal segmentation overall at midyear, yet in the same session that he showed low understanding, he also demonstrated very competent oral segmentation of the words *big wheel*. His low understanding is discussed in Sulzby (1981b). Example 4 contains his competent "sounding out." While there are errors in the segmentation and match with letter names from a conventional standpoint, we can see that he could segment and solve segmentation problems quite well, including eliciting aid from the adult.

Example 4 (taken from near the end of a longer sequence):

Child: /bə/   /I/.

/wə:/   /wə:/   /wə:/.

/i-ə/.

/I/, /I/, /w/, /w/.

/i-ə/, /hwiəl/

Wh-at's /hwi-əl/? Oh, /hwə/! Y.

/i-əl/

/I/, what's—/I/, what's /Ig/? Oh, yeah! T. right?—I mean, I. *[He had confused T and I visually earlier in the session.]*

Segmentation in Graphics

Advanced children often use linear sounding-out and write in invented spelling but still omit spaces to show word boundaries. One way of further detecting these children's concept for word is to note whether or not the invented spelling is discrete and nonoverlapping. Example 5 is taken from Sulzby (in press-c) and is midway through a long story written in very full invented spelling in which most units were exclusive. In this example the three words *have, a,* and *big* are not nonexclusive units; instead, HB was written as *have,* the A operates as the article *a* and also as the vowel in BAG (*big*); finally, the B from *have* and the A join with the G for *big*. When the child reread the sections with nonexclusive units, she tried to sound them out as if they were nonsense words rather than the words she had said while composing. Other parts of the composition were read easily, with the child tracking the print with finger and eye.

Example 5:

Line 6 *[And she wanted to have a big wheel.]:*

ANQSEWATHOHBAG-WEL

Children also show their concepts about word in the act of writing, whether or not the writing system they are using is conventional. In Sulzby (1981a) I found one child who composed three pages of scribble-like marks. When finished, he turned to the second page and struck the page with a pencil near the bottom between two of his marks. He was asked why he did that and he explained that it was "a dot," "to split the word," "when it comes to make a new word."

Children who used invented spelling often begin to list words in column fashion, to insert large dots, dashes, or boxes between words, or to use abbreviations for words (Sulzby, 1981a, in press-d). These devices appear to be inventions and not anything that children are taught or could observe in this form (see Clay, 1975; Ferreiro & Teberosky, 1982; Ferreiro, in press).

Examples 1–5 give a few glimpses of ways that children demonstrate aspects of their concepts for "word," using the tasks in our study. They do not, however, reveal the larger context of how children were learning more about the concept of word. Subsequently, in example 6, we will observe Douglas, as he works through a problem of matching his understandings, metalanguage, and print.

Working Through Problems About the Concept of Word

Douglas, the child in this extended example, was one of the children judged to be "moderate" in emergent literacy. Even though he was not reading or writing conventionally, he showed many of the characteristics reported in the literature (Clark, 1976; Durkin, 1966; Read, 1975) about precocious readers and writers. Socially and academically, he showed characteristics that Blank (1973) calls "well functioning," or competent. He was lively but rather quiet. He got along well with other children, both boys and girls. They sought him out as a playmate, fellow worker, and helper. He was able to stand up to the class bully calmly until the child left him alone (observation from field notes).

. In the sessions of the study, the examiner assigned to Douglas stated that she enjoyed his company. Enjoyment of a child's company has been noted (Clark, 1976; Durkin, 1966) as typical in the parent-child relationships of young fluent readers. In spite of not being a precocious reader, he showed yet another characteristic reported about them: *the ability to ask questions and elicit aid from an adult.*

In the example that follows, the examiner was instructed not to introduce linguistic terms or to assume that she knew what the child's concept was for a given term. Hence, she volunteered less information than a parent might in the same situation.

As the example begins, Douglas is trying to reread a story which he has just dictated to the examiner. The story is about himself and how he learned to ride a "big wheel" (common child's vehicle similar to a tricycle). The story is presented in Example 6a in the manuscript of the examiner to illustrate the kind of writing the child was reading and the placement of words on the page.

Example 6a:

line 1   My mom and dad
line 2   were with me when
line 3   I did it and my
line 4   sister and brother
line 5   were with me, too.
line 6   I wanted it cause
line 7   I wanted fun. So
line 8   I got one. And
line 9   another reason why
line 10   I want one . . . .

Douglas began to attempt to reread, using his memory for the dictated text as an aid. He pointed to line 1 and recited the first sentence as he had dictated it; then he pointed to line 2 and gave the second full sentence. He then had a problem because he had already recited, "My mom and dad were with me, too," and, "Al–so—my sister, my brother, they were with me, too." He evidently was expecting the third line to read, "I wanted it 'cause I wanted fun," but he detected a problem. Up until this point, Douglas had not used letter/word information to confirm his speech. At this point, he noticed the *I* which appears consistent with his expectations about the speech, but not from Doug's point of view. In this part of the transcript, the examiner has just asked Doug what he is pointing at (line 3).

Example 6b:

135 Child: The *I*. Thought I knew—I /I/—I thought I knew, knew what that was, uh, knew it what, that was gonna say. [*The following discussion is about line 3:* I did it and my.]

137 Adult: Uh-huh.

138 Child: But I don't. But I forgot [*under breath* "what it was"]

138 Adult: OK.

139 Child: [*Louder, as if finishing above statement.*]—say.

138 Adult: OK. So—you knew what it was gonna say—

139 Child: Yeah.

140 Adult: Yeah, but you got here *[pointing]*, and what's that?

140 Child: I ↓ *[distinctly]*

141 Adult: What'd ya think?

141 Child: Huhh. *[Pause to 144.]* Hmm. *[Pause, 144–145.]* I don't know it.

145 Adult: *[Chuckling]* OK. Well—you were sort of pretend-reading it, huh?

146 Child: *[Says something covered by adult comment.]*

146 Adult: A little bit? Uh-huh.

The examiner next offered one of a number of structured encouragements, telling him that she could help. This encouragement usually ends with, "What do you want me to do?" to elicit the child's ideas, but Douglas voluntarily began to explain his predicament. His explanation indicates a problem having to do with word boundaries and minimum units in words. Notice that in this section he does not use any metalanguage but refers to "this" and "that," "that thing," and then finally calls it *I*. By the use of indirect metalinguistic indicators he is able to show *where* his problem is but not *what* it is. Since the examiner cannot be certain that the child means the *I* to be a letter name or the word (or some other notion), she tries to get Doug to explain further.

Example 6c:

148 Child: Hhh. *[Short pause.]* I don't really know if that thing goes—uh, if this goes with that. *[I did, Example 6a, line 3.]*

149 Adult: OK. It does. Uh-huh, sure does.

150 Child: Uh. *(Pause, 150–152.)*

152 Adult: Well, what'd ya mean, "goes with"? I'm sorry, maybe I didn't answer you right. *[Child begins answering while adult is saying "didn't answer."]*

152 Child: That Iiii (elongated)→

152 Adult: Yeah→

152 Child: Did it go with this?

153 Adult: You mean, d'—what'd mean "go with"?

153 Child: Thought it could—does the *I* go with that?

154 Adult: This *I* is all by itself.

155 Child: Yeah.

155 Adult: Uh-huh, and this over here is all by itself. *[Indicating I and did, line 3.]*

156 Child: Yeah.

156 Adult: Uh-huh. Yeah.

156 Child: So does this go *with* that?

In the section that follows, Douglas asserts that one letter cannot be a word, consistent with the findings of Papandropoulou and Sinclair (1974) and Ferreiro and Teberosky (1982). Then he decides that the *I* can only be the letter name *I*, "that's the only thing it can make," "the only thing it spells." Finally, after deciding it is *I*, Douglas begins to laugh in delight, as he realizes that it can be the word *I* that he was expecting to match his speech. Notice the increasing specificity in his requests: earlier he had stressed the deictic words (*this* with *that*, 148), then the relationship *with* that (156), but here he becomes more and more specific with metalanguage being used appropriately (*letter, spells, word,* 161–169):

Example 6d:

157 Adult: Hmmm. *[Short pause.]* If it went with it, what would it be?

158 Child: I don't know.

159 Adult: Oh, OK. Hmm. I don't know exactly how to answer your question, 'cause I don't know what you mean.

161 Child: See, like, this thing's one letter.

161 Adult: Yeah.

161 Child: And th—and that doesn't spell anything, just one letter.

162 Adult: I see.

162 Child: 'n, I'm wondering if *this* thing goes with, with these letters. *[Indicating I and did.]*

164 Adult: Uh-huh. To do what?

164 Child: To, like—'cause this one's all alone, and it can't make a w— and it ca—and it can't make a word.

166 Adult: I see. *[Pause.]*

167 Child: The only letter it, the only thing it can make is, uh, *I. [Said with extra stress.]*

169 Adult: Yeah.

169 Child: That's the only thing it spells, *I. [Pause.]* Yeah.

170 Adult: OK, uh—

171 Child: *[Interrupts, excitedly.]* Oooh! Iiiiee—

171 Adult: —I! *[Child claps.]* OK! *[Both begin to laugh extendedly.]*

The laughter marking this incident seemed to indicate high affect by the child and adult at this moment of discovery. Holdaway (1979) suggests that discoveries supported by positive affect between child and adult are important in the development of what he calls self-regulation in emergent reading. Similarly, the early reading and writing studies that used retrospective interviews (Clark, 1976; Durkin, 1966; Read, 1975) also describe the positive affective relationship between parents and children.

In this instance, after the child and adult laughed and then discussed the discovery that there is a time when one letter can be a word, Douglas went back to his pursuit of the reading attempt and was able to give the appropriate semantic interpretation to *I*. He was expecting the next clause to be "I wanted it," rather than "I did it," but as he read the line, he treated the *I* as being correct and questioned his miscue with *wanted*, continuing to monitor the print cues.

Douglas showed disfluencies in this example; these disfluencies are probably due to his discussing a new problem. His metalanguage appears not to be automatic but to be developing. Immediately after this example, the examiner used an echo reading technique with pauses for Douglas to continue alone. Douglas asked numerous questions, including six in which he wanted to be told a word; four of those times, he asked first, "What's that letter?" and then clarified himself, "What's that word?" The final two times he asked for information using the word "word" appropriately. What I suggest from these incidents is that Douglas was illustrating conceptual problems but he was also showing how at least one child tests out his hypotheses and learns more about the concept *word*.

Discussion

I have illustrated ways of observing children's concepts of word during reading and writing tasks. While observations such as these are best used to generate hypotheses, they can also be used to confirm or question the validity of conclusions of other kinds of studies. For example, finding that Douglas had difficulty in treating *I* as a word is a confirmation of reports by Papandropoulou and Sinclair (1974) and Ferreiro and Teberosky (1982). Yet we learned the further information that this unit remained a problem rather late in the hypothesized development of writing systems, after Douglas was writing phonetically. Thus we see vestiges of earlier problems, the kind of problem that Blank (1982) contends remain with all readers, but particularly with poor readers.

Second, while the larger study revealed an increase in knowledge with variation within ability groups, these examples also revealed a wealth of knowledge even in children lowest in metalinguistic understanding, Mike confused *word* with *sentence*, implying that the unit of importance to him was the semantic whole. Yet both he and another low child, Richard, showed some ability to sound out words during writing tasks and both (not discussed above) encoded fewer of the sounds into letters than they voiced while composing. This finding is consistent with Ferreiro and Teberosky's (1982) claim that what is written is a conceptual judgment on the part of the child not limited by the child's phonetic awareness.

Finally, the study revealed that children can and do learn more about linguistic entities, such as *word*, during literacy interactions. This is consistent with other findings from the research project, such as the analysis of pausing during storytelling and dictating (Sulzby, in press-a), of separation of asides from text during storyreading (Sulzby & Otto, 1982), and of use of "reading intonation" in storyreading attempts governed by pictures (Sulzby, 1983b, in press-b).

The methods used in this study do not give children equal opportunities to respond to a given set of items, as is typical in more traditional experimental studies, but they do put each child into a consistent task environment and observe the child's interpretation of that task. Furthermore, the findings are interpreted in light of longitudinal data from case studies based on interviews, observations, and experimentally structured tasks. From such methods, researchers may be able to devise more valid and informative experimental tasks delving into children's metalinguistic awareness during literacy acquisition.

Acknowledgments

I wish to thank the schools and children involved in the studies mentioned herein along with numerous students from Northwestern University. Additionally, I thank but do not hold responsible for my statements the funding agencies that supported various parts of the project, the Research Foundation of the National Council of Teachers of English, the National Institute of Education (NIE-G-80-0176), and the Spencer Foundation. Finally, I thank Marcia Farr for her helpful comments on an early draft.

Chapter 15

Metalinguistic Awareness in Writing and Reading: The Young Child as Curricular Informant

DEBORAH W. ROWE

JEROME C. HARSTE

Metalinguistic awareness has been receiving considerable attention lately. Like many of our colleagues, we have been fascinated by the implications of this work. Given the intellectual tenor of these times, it seems to us that at least four major questions have to be addressed in order to deal with the topic of metalinguistic awareness: (1) What is it? (2) How can we recognize it? (3) What kinds of metalinguistic awareness do young children demonstrate? And (4) Why is it important—that is, what practical application does it have for our understanding of literacy and the improvement of instruction?

In this chapter we will discuss our current thinking about metalinguistic awareness as we introduce you to some of the young readers and writers who have pushed us to these conclusions. Said more formally, we will present those insights which we developed as we looked for evidence of metalinguistic awareness in the data collected in several research projects (see Harste, Burke, & Woodward, 1981, 1983; Harste, Woodward, & Burke, 1984; Rowe, 1982; Rowe & Cunningham, 1983).

What Is Metalinguistic Awareness?

We are not the first to observe that the term "metalinguistic awareness" has been used in the literature to refer to a variety of concepts, strategies, and behaviors (e.g., Paris & Jacobs, 1984). It is important to note, however, that most discussions of metalinguistic awareness have focused on language as an object. An example is Ehri's (1975) definition of metalinguistic skills as "the conscious awareness of and ability to manipulate language as an object," or the "awareness of these [linguistic] structures apart from their meanings" (p. 204). While these concepts are certainly part of a reader's knowledge about language, they do not comprise the whole of it, or perhaps even the most interesting and important parts of it.

If we take a broader perspective, metalinguistic knowledge can be viewed as only one aspect of metacognition. From this vantage point, it is easier to see what else might be involved. Flavell's (1979) definition and discussion of metacognition have been quite influential in our thinking about the nature of metalinguistic awareness.

Metacognitive knowledge consists primarily of knowledge or beliefs about what factors or variables act and interact in what ways to affect the course and outcome of cognitive enterprises. There are three major categories of these factors or variables—*person, task,* and *strategy.* (p. 907)

He goes on to state that the "person" category includes beliefs and knowledge about oneself and others as cognitive processors. The "task" category includes awareness of information available during a cognitive enterprise, as well as a conscious understanding of what implications this information may hold for the management of the cognitive task. (An example of task knowledge might include the awareness that you have little information available on the subject of auto mechanics and are therefore unlikely to achieve your goal of repairing your car alone. The task category also includes knowledge about the task demands of auto repair which allow you to make this judgment.) The "strategy" category consists of procedural knowledge about those strategies which are likely to be effective in achieving the goal. (In the case of your clunking and chugging auto, you are aware that the only strategy likely to get you on your way is a social act, namely calling the nearest auto repair shop.) While our choice of illustrations may not be entirely eloquent, it is important to recognize that metacognitive knowledge consists of much more than awareness of the task as an object.

In the same way that metacognitive knowledge goes beyond object, so metalinguistic knowledge consists of much more than information about the structures of language (e.g., words, letters, sounds). It consists, in addition, of beliefs about oneself and others as language users, knowledge about the demands of different literacy events, a repertoire of language strategies, and knowledge about orchestrating this complex of concepts and strategies in the face of particular literacy events. Given this definition, we proceed to make the bold claim that young readers and writers frequently demonstrate metalinguistic awareness. The issue, we will argue, is not whether they are metalinguistically aware, but whether or not we are.

How Can We Recognize Metalinguistic Awareness?

Two insights gained in the original analysis of data from the National Institute of Education (NIE) studies (Harste, Burke, & Woodward, 1981, 1983; Harste, Woodward & Burke, 1984) have helped us recognize the metalinguistic awareness of young children. Essentially they entail our realizations that (1) reading and writing responses are context-specific literacy events, and (2) convention is not a good yardstick for measuring young children's language knowledge.

To illustrate the metalinguistic acumen of our young informants, we introduce Abigail, a 5-year-old kindergartener, and her sister Becka, who is in the first grade. Nancy Vargus (1981), their mother and a research assistant on our project, recorded the following interchange as Abigail was reading a book to Becka:

Becka: Abigail! The word is *fetch,* not *get.*

Abigail: Yeah, well, *get* works.

Becka: That kind of reading is okay at home, but it doesn't work in school!

In this brief exchange both girls provide us with well-verbalized evidence of their conscious awareness of language. In correcting Abigail's reading, Becka demonstrates that she makes a sharp (and most likely accurate) distinction between the reading strategies appropriate for home and those for school. Abigail, on the other hand, provides us with evidence that she has purposefully employed a "making sense" strategy as she reads the story. Their ability to recognize situational constraints and to orchestrate language knowledge accordingly is no small accomplishment! They not only perform this feat, but in the heat of conversation demonstrate a heightened awareness of the process itself.

Conversations like the one between Becka and Abigail have helped us to realize that we must *expect* literacy responses to vary depending on the context of situation. This means that we have learned to expect metalinguistic knowledge to be demonstrated in a variety of ways depending on the context in which it is observed.

When we look at the reading of Abigail and that of our other young informants it is clear that many of these children produce nonconventional responses. In the NIE studies, children sometimes recognized this themselves and would comment, "That doesn't look right!" or "What does that say?" Other children were more paralyzed by convention and responded, "I can't read." While convention is obviously a necessary part of written language, it is not an appropriate yardstick by which to measure language knowledge, or metalinguistic awareness. It is only by looking at awareness of both language products and processes that we can begin to get a more accurate picture of metalinguistic knowledge.

This brings us to the second insight which our young friends have forced us to develop; that is, convention is not language. As we have come to view it, the ability to produce conventional spoken or written language is simply an artifact of one's experience as a spoken or written language user in a community of other language users. Conventions are not prerequisites or criteria for judging language use. The amounts and types of experiences children have had with written language largely determine how conventional their reading and writing responses will appear. The conventionality of children's responses does not, however, determine the amount of metalinguistic awareness which they demonstrate. It is clear that we can begin to explore the metalinguistic competencies of young children only if we look past the language forms produced to see the language functions being explored.

These two insights have been important in helping us to fully appreciate young children's metalinguistic awareness. They have allowed children to convince us of an important point—their responses to print are intentional. As we have come to the understanding that children alter their responses according to the situational context and that even unconventional responses may be evidence of planfulness, we have discovered that children possess a great deal of metalinguistic awareness. Many of our best insights have come from the asides made by children as they attempt reading and writing tasks. Claire Golomb (1974) has reported a similar experience in her studies of young children's representational art. When children comment on their actions we have direct evidence of their metalinguistic awareness. However, we can also be reasonably sure that metalinguistic awareness is involved when we see them self-correct, make judgments about linguistic structures, play with linguistic units, or alter their strategies in response to a new situation or problem (Clark, 1977). Morris (1981) has called such behavioral indicators "indirect" measures of language knowledge. The young child's oral fascination with rhyme, jump rope jingles, and even with Dr. Seuss, is strong evidence that metalinguistic awareness is not something endemic to written language or written language learning. This assumptive error in thinking runs wanton in the literature on metalinguistic knowledge.

We have chosen to discuss in this chapter instances where children provide us with direct and indirect evidence of metalinguistic awareness. Elsewhere (Harste, Burke, & Woodward, 1981, 1983; Harste, Woodward & Burke, 1984) we have presented evidence of the intentionality of young children's responses to print. We expect that some amount of conscious awareness of language is involved in most instances of language in use. However, even with a stricter definition, our informants look amazingly aware of language as both an object and a process.

What Kinds of Metalinguistic Awareness Do Young Children Demonstrate?

Our discussion in this section will focus on children's (a) awareness of language as an object composed of graphophonemic, semantic, syntactic, and pragmatic cues, and (b) awareness of language as a process including strategies for language use. Since we realize that in the end all dichotomies fail, we will close this section with an in-depth look at the complexity of one child's metalinguistic knowledge as demonstrated during a single literacy event.

Awareness of Language as an Object

Much research and discussion has focused on children's awareness of written language structures and conventions (e.g., words, letters, directionality of print). Perhaps this has been the case because young children's nonconventional responses to print are so obvious that adults seldom attempt to understand the thinking which produces them. Even if language is viewed solely as a product, focusing only on the graphophonemic features of written language is overly simplistic. Readers and writers also make use of the semantic, syntactic, and pragmatic cues which are part of every literacy event. Our young readers are no exception, and under certain circumstances they demonstrate their awareness of the variety of cues available in written language.

Graphophonemic awareness. Patty is a 3-year-old who participated in our study of children's responses to environmental print (Harste, Burke, & Woodward, 1981, 1983). Briefly, in Stage 1 of that study Patty and the other participants were asked three questions about items of environmental print: (1) "What do you think this says?" (2) "Tell me some things that help you know what this says," and (3) "Tell me some of the things you know about this." Obviously the second question provides a direct invitation for children to talk about the cues they attend to during reading. When Patty was presented with a cup from McDonalds, she responded, "It say Coke in it. Drink." While this is not a conventional response, it certainly is in the semantic ball park! In response to Questions 2 and 3, Patty pointed to the golden arches which circle the cup and said, "It got a name on there." On many other items Patty's responses were similar, but she also sometimes named letters in response to Question 1, while continuing to use her "It got a name on there" strategy for answering Questions 2 and 3. She often pointed to some part of the print during these answers.

Obviously Patty knows that print is very important in signing the messages on these familiar items. She points to the print, and uses "name" as a kind of generic term to indicate it. It is interesting that only the youngest children who participated in the study chose "name" as their personal term for print. The 4-, 5-, and 6-year-olds in the study chose other metalinguistic terms (e.g., word, letters, numbers). For example, Alpha, age 5, typically responded to Question 1 with names such as "McDonalds" and to Question 2 with the phrase, "The word." Other children demonstrated more conventional uses of metalinguistic language and more conventional notions about language structures, such as words, letters, and numbers. It seems reasonable to hypothesize that for some 3-year-olds, "name" may be the most salient metalinguistic term in their experience, while many older children have had more exposure to other terminology commonly used to talk about print.

Benjamin, a 4-year-old, provides interesting evidence that he understands that language structures can be talked about as objects, but that they also carry meaning. He was shown a For Sale sign, which also included the words: Bill Morrow Realtor. In response to the question, "What do you think this says?" he pointed to the B and responded, "A b. It says stop and the B says Go". Benjamin is aware that letters have names but also that letters "say" something.

These examples corroborate studies (Carswell, 1979; Clay, 1966, 1972, 1979; Day & Day, 1978; Johns, 1980) which show that young children do not use metalinguistic terms conventionally. However, we feel this emphasis on convention actually obscures children's metalinguistic capabilities. It seems more important to emphasize that even 3-year-olds understood the message function of print and were able to talk about print as an object.

Najeeba, a 4-year-old from Saudi Arabia, provides us with striking evidence that young children are consciously aware of the form of written language and also that particular life experiences may help to determine which language cues one becomes consciously aware of. Figure 15-1 is a story that Najeeba wrote. When she finished it she commented, "Here, but you can't read it, cause I wrote it in Arabic and in Arabic we use a lot more dots than you do in English!" Though Najeeba's script is not conventional Arabic, it does have a distinctly Arabic form, especially when compared to the story written by Dawn, a child from the United States (Figure 15-2). Obviously, Dawn has abstracted much of the form of written English as well. Whether she would be able to make a statement about English similar to Najeeba's insight about Arabic is not known. However, it is possible that because young children are exploring the form of written language, they may be especially sensitive to such matters. Judging from our own reaction to Najeeba's comment, her life experiences have encouraged her to take a metalinguistic perspective which is different and also richer than our own in this matter. Her need to become literate in two languages, using different alphabets, has created the contrast and thus the awareness of a key difference between English and Arabic scripts.

We also have evidence that children were consciously dealing with the concept of "wordness" in their writing, though they had not yet reached conven-

Figure 15–1	**Figure 15–2**
Uninterrupted Story Writing—Najeeba (Age 4)	Uninterrupted Story Writing—Dawn (Age 4)

Source: Harste, J. C., Woodward, V. A. & Burke, C. L. (1984). *Language Stories & Literacy Lessons.* Portsmouth, NH: Heinemann Educational Books.	*Source:* Harste, J. C., Woodward, V. A. & Burke, C. L. (1984). *Language Stories & Literacy Lessons.* Portsmouth, NH: Heinemann Educational Books.

tional conclusions. Another task used in the NIE studies, the uninterrupted writing task, asked children to write their names and then to write anything else they could write. Figure 15-3 is 4-year-old Charvin's final product. He wrote his name (the leftmost mark) and then produced three dense sets of markings in response to "Write anything else you can write." When asked to read his writing, Charvin read, "Tree, bear, dog," as he pointed to each blob right to left. He demonstrates that his current concept of wordness involves one concept per mark.

We have also encountered children consciously separating word units by means other than white space (see also Sulzby, this volume). Virginia Woodward (Harste, Burke, & Woodward, 1981) provides us with the example seen in Figure 15-4. In kindergarten Megan wrote the following message, separating words by the use of lines: "Hi, I like to eat because I'm so hungry. I could eat a whole elephant." Seven-year-old Matt used carefully darkened squares when he wrote his own version of *The Three Little Pigs* (see Figure 15-5). Similar observations have been made by others, including Marie Clay (1981), so we will not dwell on this issue. However, the point is that children would not spend time, care, and effort in producing these divisions if they were not consciously expressing their current concept about words.

Like Clay (1979), Morris (1981), and Rowe (1982), we also observed children's awareness of the match between speech and print, and of the correspondence between the lengths of spoken and written words by watching as they pointed to words during reading. Alison, age 4, verbalized this awareness when

Figure 15–3

Uninterrupted Writing—Charvin (Age 4)

Figure 15–4

Message—Megan (Age 5)

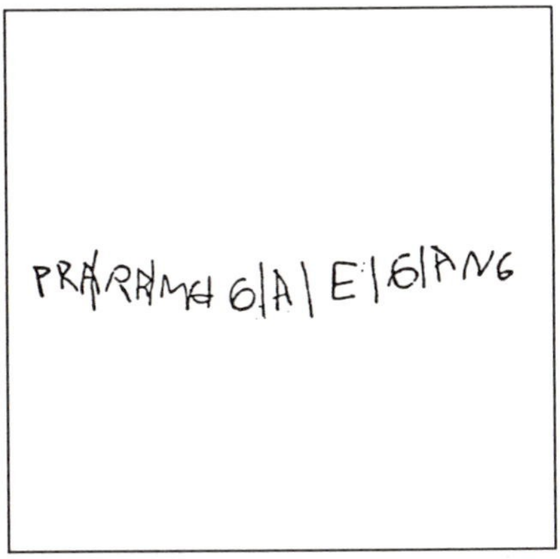

Source: Harste, J. C., Woodward, V. A. & Burke, C. L. (1984). *Language Stories & Literacy Lessons.* Portsmouth, NH: Heinemann Educational Books.

Figure 15-5

"Three Little Pigs" Story—Matt (Age 7)

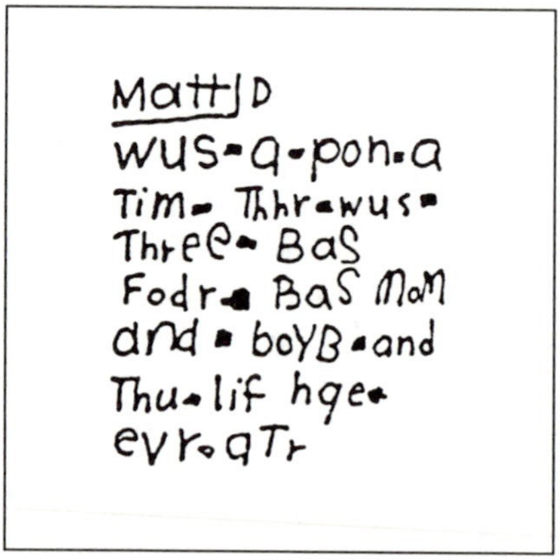

Source: Harste, J. C., Woodward, V. A. & Burke, C. L. (1984). *Language Stories & Literacy Lessons*. Portsmouth, NH: Heinemann Educational Books.

she was shown a soft drink cup from Wendy's and asked, "What do you think this says?" Running her finger under the word "Wendy's," she responded "Wendy's," and then running her finger under "Hamburgers," said "cup." After a brief pause she added, "That's a long word with a short sound!" As has often been the case in our work with young children, Alison talked about the structure of language in the context of a specific literacy event—when doing so was a natural expression of her most current language discovery. When language users encounter features or events which are anomalies in light of their current hypotheses about language, they are likely to spontaneously mention or at least demonstrate their awareness of language. It seems that when a difficulty or a specially highlighted contrast occurs, metalinguistic awareness is most likely to be expressed. As Goodman & Burke (1980) put it, "As long as reading goes as expected, there is no need to consider the process. There is only the need to make use of it. It is only when reading does not go as expected that the reader has a need to shift the focus from ends to means" (p. 28). Our experience with young children suggests that they experience metalinguistic awareness for just these reasons.

Dorothy Watson (in process) and her graduate students at the University of Missouri are studying literacy use and learning among the deaf (see also Andrews & Mason, this volume). One of the very interesting things they found is that deaf children embedded the physical features of their language in their writing. For example, "cookie" is made by forming a C with the fingers of the hand and moving it in a circular fashion around the palm of the left hand. When a deaf child in their study was asked to write "cookie," his product contained a series of four C's embedded in it.

In American Sign Language, "I love you" is made with an extended hand, the middle fingers tucked in. One child wrote, "I love my family," by drawing around the hand sign and then adding pictures of his family.

The literacy lesson in these language stories suggests that particular language situations have particular semiotic potentials which set up relationships in need of exploration. Working with hearing children, we are inclined to mark the child's exploration of how oral language maps onto written language as a major breakthrough. Yet these language stories suggest that what we see as a major breakthrough is but a potential highlighted in settings where oral and written language occur simultaneously. In settings where sign language and written language occur a different semiotic potential exists, and children actively explore its possibilities.

Before leaving this discussion of youngsters' awareness of the graphophonemic features of written language, we would like to note that a number of the older children did attempt to "sound out" words when they were asked, "What do you think this says?" This was more frequent in Stages 2 and 3 of the study when the children were shown the logo cut from the product and printed in mixed primary type. As the other naturally occurring cue systems were eliminated, some children resorted to using what they knew about sound symbol relationships. This comprised the most frequent communication decision made by 5-year-olds in Stage 3, while 3- and 4-year-olds more frequently called off names of products which they had seen in Stages 1 and 2. Obviously the older children are aware that there is a connection between letters (or syllables) and sounds. Jake, a 6-year-old, explains his own strategy, which seems to involve working with chunks of words. For example, one of his responses to "What things do you see that help you know what this says?" is "Cause I put 'sto' and I put P in it and it says stop." He points to the letters involved as he speaks.

Like Read (1971, 1973), Beers & Henderson (1977), and others, we have collected considerable evidence that children consciously make use of their knowledge of the relationship between sounds and symbols to produce functional spellings in their writing. However, as we have suggested elsewhere (Harste, Burke, & Woodward, 1981) this is not the only strategy which children use in functionally getting their meaning down. It is not necessary to review all the evidence which indicates that young children consciously use their knowledge of sound symbol correspondences in their writing. Let it suffice in this context to point out that these observations serve as further evidence that young children consciously reflect on the structures of language in the process of language use.

Syntactic awareness.   In our data we do not have much direct evidence of children's awareness of the syntactic structure of language. That is to say, we just didn't hear children making comments about syntax. However, we have collected indirect evidence that children understand which syntactic patterns are appropriate in different settings. Probably the clearest examples are the differing syntactic patterns children used for different written genre. Figures 15-6 through 15-9 illustrate a birthday list, a letter, a map for birthday guests, and a story. All were written in the space of two days by Stephanie the summer before she entered first grade. It is clear that she understands the syntactic structures which are appropriate in each case. Her birthday list reads, "Melisa, Laura, Tic-Tac-Toe, White Cake, Balloons." On it she has written the names of two guests, a game to be played at the party, and two other items sure to be present there. She does not mark syntactically the relationship between these items (nor would an adult listmaker) because the list context helps to perform that function. In contrast is Stephanie's letter. She opens it with the greeting, "Dear Mom," and continues, "I hope you come back Love Steph." For the map, the text includes labels with appropriate graphics to sign relationships. It reads, "My bedroom, Hallway, Door to come in." Finally, we see that Stephanie's story does indeed contain story-like syntax as she switches to the past tense and a narrative tone not present in any of the other pieces. The contrasts between these texts indicate that syntactic differences were intentional. How explicitly aware Stephanie was of this feature we do not know.

Further evidence of young children's attention to the syntactic systems of language comes from an activity in which we asked children to dictate a story, read it, and then reread it the next day (Harste, Burke, & Woodward, 1983).

Figure 15–6	**Figure 15–7**
Birthday List—Stephanie (Age 5)	Letter—Stephanie (Age 5)

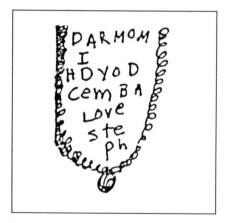

Source: Harste, J. C., Woodward, V. A. & Burke, C. L. (1984). *Language Stories & Literacy Lessons.* Portsmouth, NH: Heinemann Educational Books.

Source: Harste, J. C., Woodward, V. A. & Burke, C. L. (1984). *Language Stories & Literacy Lessons.* Portsmouth, NH: Heinemann Educational Books.

We analyzed the data from this activity to determine what types of relationships (syntactic coordination) existed between the syntactic units produced by children in their story dictation and during their first reading. Four categories emerged from the data: (1) No Apparent Coordination; (2) Generalized Coordination (Text: *Fall Down. A Block*; Reader: "Grey Block"); (3) Available in Text (one to one syntactic correspondence between text and reading); and (4) Mixed (Text: *And we read a book*; Reader: "And we read books"). This last category accepts minimal changes in meaning as illustrated above.

When the children's first readings were compared to their dictated stories only our last three categories proved useful. We found that 18.9 percent of all units produced demonstrated a Generalized Coordination between the text and what was read; 51.4 percent represented a one-to-one correspondence between syntactic units (Available in Text category); and 29.7 percent represented a Mixed syntactic correspondence. There was also a trend for one-to-one correspondences between the text base and what was read to increase with age; we found that 28.6 percent of 3-year-old, 40.0 percent of 4-year-old, and 54.5 percent of 5-year-old responses fell in the Available in Text category.

Because we suspected that some of what the children had dictated was not meant to be part of their stories (even though we had written it down), we used their first reading as the text base for further comparisons. In comparing their rereading of their language experience stories one day later to the surface text of their first reading, 5.4 percent of all response units showed No Apparent Coor-

Figure 15–8

Map for Birthday Guests—Stephanie (Age 5)

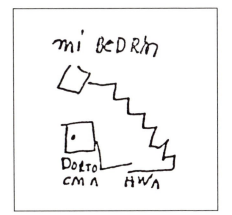

Source: Harste, J. C., Woodward, V. A. & Burke, C. L. (1984). *Language Stories & Literacy Lessons*. Portsmouth, NH: Heinemann Educational Books.

Figure 15–9

Story—Stephanie (Age 5)

Source: Harste, J. C., Woodward, V. A. & Burke, C. L. (1984). *Language Stories & Literacy Lessons*. Portsmouth, NH: Heinemann Educational Books.

dination; 16.2 percent showed a Generalized Coordination, 48.6 percent represented a one-to-one correspondence (the Available in Text category), and 29.7 percent showed a Mixed correspondence. The age trend for the Available in Text category indicated that 42.9 percent of 3-year-old, 45.5 percent of 4-year-old, 40.0 percent of 5-year-old, and 66.7 percent of 6-year-old responses showed a one-to-one syntactic correspondence.

These data provide evidence that even 3-year-olds operated within the syntactic constraints of this reading situation. The reason this effect is more pronounced in the rereading data than in the data from the first reading is that the asides which the children made to researchers during story dictation were no longer being considered part of their texts. In this sense, the set of figures quoted for rereading represents the degree of predictability of children's second readings given their first readings. As can be seen, the syntactic correspondence is universally high across all age levels. These findings provide indirect evidence of children's knowledge of syntactic constraints and their ability to predict and generate a syntactically successful text when reading.

Semantic awareness.   Because the semantic system is not in reality separable from the other cue systems, we have already had reason to include both indirect and direct evidence of children's awareness of semantic cues. In our discussion of children's responses to reading and writing tasks, it should be evident that while the surface form of their responses was nonconventional they were responding conventionally to meaning cues. The consistency with which children produced responses falling into the appropriate semantic field is indirect evidence of their semantic knowledge.

Dan, a 5-year-old we worked with, rarely gave a conventional response in Stage 1 when we asked, "What do you think this says?" However, he always responded with identification of the referent ("toys" for Lego), a functional description; ("playing" for Toss Across Game), a description related to the immediate context of the print; ("egg carton" for Kroger Eggs), or an attribute of the referent ("Strawberry" for Jell-O). All of the semantic relationships listed above are at one time or another used by advertisers and sign makers on items of environmental print; that is, the print on signs and commercial products falls into the same semantic categories which emerged from our analysis of children's responses.

One of our research items, a box of Jell-O, illustrates this point particularly well. The print on the box includes: Gelatin Dessert (the referent identification), Taste the Quality (a functional description of what you are to do with the product), Jell-O (the product name), Recipe (a related concept to Jell-O), Nt. Wt. (a contextual description of the box), and Strawberry (an attribute of Jell-O). When the semantic categories underlying both the print and our informants' responses are compared, it is clear that these children are responding appropriately to semantic cues. In fact, 99.97% of all responses had obvious semantic intent and were codable within the categories outlined above. Evidently the awareness that written language should be meaningful is a natural part of language learning.

Children also provided us with indirect evidence of their semantic decisions in writing. When we asked DuJulian, a 3-year-old, to read what he had written during the uninterrupted writing task, he responded: "Me, and my daddy, and my grandma, that's my granddaddy, that's boy—boy, that's my grandma, that's Ricky, that's too Ricky." (See Figure 15-10.) His response reflects a concern for semantic unity as he produces a text which coheres around the semantic field of "family members."

At times, however, our informants also directly demonstrated or commented upon their awareness of semantic cues in language. A case in point in Benjamin's response to the For Sale sign discussed above. In order for him to respond, "A b. It says stop and the B says Go," he must be consciously aware that written language structures represent messages. This is perhaps the most basic and important form of semantic awareness.

A wonderful example of conscious attention to the semantic unity of a text is provided by Beth, a 5-year-old. While we will describe her uninterrupted story writing more fully below, one aspect of this literacy event is particularly relevant here. As she was writing her story, Beth wrote the name of one brother, David, and then proceeded to write the name of her other brother, Jeff. Because she was dissatisfied with her J she decided to delete Jeff from the story and tried to erase her attempt at his name. Later, after adding a picture of David, she started to draw Jeff. With an exclamation of "Oops!" she stopped midway and decided not to finish his picture. Evidently she feels the semantic cohesion of her story

Figure 15–10

Uninterrupted Writing—DuJulian (Age 3)

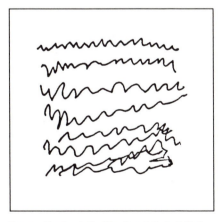

Source: Harste, J. C., Woodward, V. A. & Burke, C. L. (1984). *Language Stories & Literacy Lessons.* Portsmouth, NH: Heinemann Educational Books.

would be violated if she failed to relate Jeff's picture to his name in the same manner used earlier for David.

Meaning is what language use is all about, and we have found that 3-, 4-, and 5-year-olds are no less aware of this than adults. In fact, they may have a stronger meaning focus where written language is concerned. A final example is the exchange between the two sisters Becka and Abigail, also described earlier. The younger girl, Abigail, adamantly believes that using a word that "works" (i.e., makes sense) is an appropriate reading response. Becka has, however, learned other criteria in first grade (e.g. identifying words correctly). In the NIE data we also see a trend for children 5 years and older to begin to abandon their meaning focus for a print focus. One thing that seems certain, however, is that young children first approach written language with an awareness of semantic cues. When they later abandon this strategy, we suggest that instruction is likely to be the culprit.

Pragmatic awareness.   When children are observed in a single language setting, the chance to note their awareness of the pragmatics of different situations is often missed. As mentioned above, we have noticed that it is often the contrast between language settings which prompts children to comment (or otherwise demonstrate) that they are consciously aware of the need to suit their responses to the context of situation. In the NIE studies it is clear that children consciously used their knowledge about the research setting to direct their responses as the print stimulus changed. In Stage 1 children were shown the actual item of print (e.g. on a box of Jell-O). In Stage 2 they were shown the item's logo which had been extracted from the product, and in Stage 3 they were shown a 3×5 card containing the most salient words from the logo in mixed primary type. Therefore, by Stage 3 of the project, children had had a chance to develop strong expectations about the print and questions they would encounter when one of the researchers came to work with them. When they were shown the typed logos in Stage 3, several children responded randomly with names of items which had been presented in Stages 1 and 2. Once again when the normally available cues had been purposefully eliminated, readers responded by using their knowledge of the pragmatic cues which were still present and highly familiar. These children demonstrated that they were consciously making use of the context of the research setting to guide their responses.

The accomplishments of these young language users in tailoring their reading responses to the situations at hand seem at the time ordinary and amazing. Anyone who has spent time with children has observed that they begin quite early to use cues from the environment to predict appropriate language responses. In fact, this aspect of language knowledge is so pervasive that it is often taken for granted, obscuring the complexity and centrality of pragmatic cues in both oral and written language. It is this tendency which allows many adults to convince themselves that they respond solely to print when they are reading. One important outcome of asking children to serve as informants rather than subjects in this research has been the raising of our own metalinguistic consciousness. It is quite remarkable that 3-, 4-, and 5-year-olds not only use pragmatic information in conjunction with graphophonemic, syntactic, and semantic cues, but also are capable of demonstrating conscious awareness of pragmatic constraints.

Awareness of Language as a Process

We have already attempted to show that young children have more metalinguistic knowledge than is usually assumed, and that their knowledge may potentially include awareness of all the cue systems. What is perhaps more exciting to us are demonstrations of children's ability to reflect on some of the strategies they use to make decisions about written language. Sometimes these decision points are accompanied by verbalizations, but other times only by visible shifts in activity such as self-correction, or a move from a "sounding out" to a "making sense" strategy. We will only present a few exemplars of the many types of language strategies which our young informants have demonstrated—as once again our intent is less to catalogue all existing strategies than to show that youngsters are capable of thinking in this manner and seem to do so as a matter of course.

Hank. Though only three years old, Hank, is quite articulate in describing the strategy he uses to produce his signature, H-A-K. This was not the expected signature, since he had been signing his name H-A-N-K, with only an occasionally inverted N. On this particular day when the researcher questioned, "Are you done?" Hank's response was, "Yep, that N is giving me too much trouble so I decided to leave it out." Two weeks later his signature once again contained an N. Hank uses a keep-going strategy when he finds the letter N troublesome.

Beth. Beth's uninterrupted story writing is accompanied by verbalizations which help to demonstrate her awareness of writing strategies, including a monitoring and correction strategy. She first drew a picture of a sun and a house (Figure 15-11A). Figure 15-11B shows where she wrote her name, first near the top of the page and then in the center as she announced, "I can write my name another way." Obviously, Beth is demonstrating conscious awareness that at least in her own name, different combinations of capital and small letters can sign the same meaning.

Near the bottom of the page she writes David Dansberger and announces it to be her brother's name. Shown in Figure 15-11C is her attempt to write her other brother's name, Jeff. She decides her J doesn't look right and says so— "That doesn't look right!"—as she tries to erase it with her finger. Obviously, Beth is both monitoring her success and applying self-correction strategies to her work. Further down the page she draws a picture of David and announces "This is David." Next she begins to draw a picture of Jeff, but remembers she didn't finish his name, and decides not to finish his picture either. She stops the drawing and says, "Oops!" Once again Beth demonstrates that she is monitoring her writing, not just at the point of production, but also against the piece as a whole.

Figure 15–11

Uninterrupted Story Writing—Beth (Age 5)

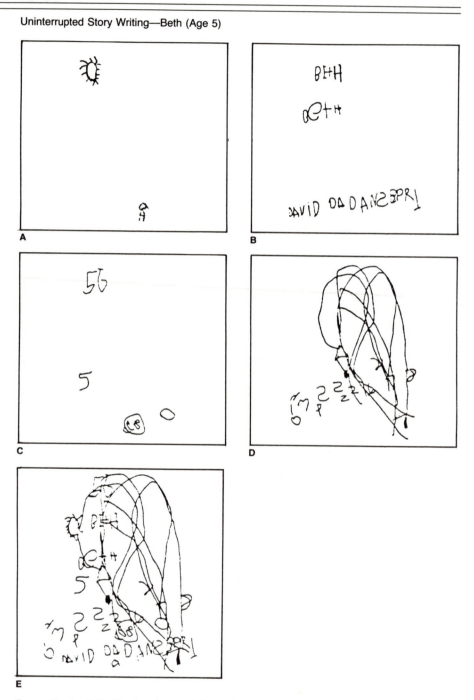

Source: Harste, J. C., Woodward, V. A. & Burke, C. L. (1984). *Language Stories & Literacy Lessons.* Portsmouth, NH: Heinemann Educational Books.

Since she has decided to abandon writing her brother's name because of difficulty forming the letters, she also alters her overall plan and eliminates his picture as well. Beth decides to write her age, 5, near the top of the page and is dissatisfied with the product. So she immediately produces the 5 located in the middle of the page.

After a pause, Beth begins saying and writing her numbers backwards: "8," "7," "6," "5," (Figure 15-11D). Once again she is not pleased with her "5" and says "5," "5," "5," "5" as she makes a series of forms in an attempt to produce one which she can accept. Finally, she shrugs her shoulders and continues by saying and writing "4," "3," "2," "1," "0," "Blast Off!!!" At this point Beth draws the rocket seen in the center of the page complete with plumes of smoke and accompanied by sound effects, "Varoom! Varoom! Varoom! Varoom!" Beth reads her story: "Well this is a story about what me and my brothers do at home, play rockets and things like that." It would have been difficult to recover this sequence without the aid of videotape, since Figure 15-11E illustrates her final product which contains the overlapping print and drawings.

Beth's actions and in-process verbalizations let us see that it is her metalinguistic awareness of form, strategies, and task demands which guide her at points where the process becomes difficult. We expect that her demonstration of the "two ways" to write her name may also demonstrate one of her new discoveries about written language. It is not only young writers who, having discovered a new word or turn of the phrase, manage to find an opportunity to try it out in their next piece of writing. This is not just an amusing trait which we happen to share with Beth. Rather, we suspect that this tendency to find arenas in which to test our newest language discoveries is an important part of written language learning in which metalinguistic awareness plays a vital role.

Her self-corrections indicate that Beth is monitoring her writing according to some internalized standards of form and pragmatic acceptability in the research setting. In this sequence, when her "5" does not meet her own standard, she engages a "try again" strategy, and then finally a "skip it and let's get on with the meaning" strategy signaled by a shrug and her return to writing. It is also interesting to note that she has abandoned the unsuccessful "erase it" strategy which she used earlier in an attempt to correct the J. Beth's behavior is planful and she demonstrates conscious awareness of language strategies as well as language structure and form.

The self-monitoring strategy exhibited by Beth in her writing is also characteristic of the reading of many children. One way children demonstrated this in the environmental print tasks was to respond, "I don't know," or to give no response. A "don't know" response obviously could mean a variety of things, but one interesting finding is that most children chose to answer the great majority of questions asked. Since this is the case, we tend to interpret these responses as real instances in which children consciously reviewed the demands of the task and the relevant information available to them, and decided they "knew they didn't know" (Brown, 1977).

LaShell. LaShell, age 6, is a good example. Out of the 20 items of environmental print in Stage 1, she only responded, "Don't know," to one item. On other items she usually confidently produced the conventional response, and her only nonconventional responses were clearly well within the appropriate semantic field (e.g. "building toys" for Lego). When LaShell's overall pattern of responses is compared with her response to Dynamints, it is clear that she truly is indicating that she doesn't have enough information to respond. To Question 1 she responds, "Don't know," followed by no response to Question 2. When the researcher asks, "Tell me some of the things you know about this?" she answers, "I don't know the word. I had tasted it before." LaShell seems to have some information about Dynamints but not enough to generate a name for the product. Like other children in the study, her "don't know" responses seem to indicate monitoring of the match between task demands and available information.

These descriptions of three literacy events involving Hank, Beth, and LaShell characterize our observations of young children as they read and write. It is true that not all children verbalize their strategies to the same extent as Beth and Hank, and that planful behavior is more easily seen in their writing than in LaShell's reading. But the data indicate that at least under certain circumstances, children can and do use their conscious awareness of strategies to direct their reading and writing.

Metalinguistic Awareness as Stance, Not State

Metalinguistic knowledge goes far beyond "language about language." Children are aware of the multimodal nature of cues presented by written language and also possess a repertoire of strategies which they orchestrate to suit particular literacy events. We would like to conclude this section by taking a closer look at one child's responses to Stage 1 of the environmental print task. We have chosen a 5-year-old named Frank because in the space of this one task he demonstrates his awareness of a variety of language cues as well as the ability to verbalize some of the strategies and questions he poses for himself when he encounters a troublesome item of print. Frank's responses are not unusual, but we also resist the temptation of calling them "typical." Actually, it seems that after looking at each child's responses to a number of research tasks, and also at the responses of many children to a single task, that what we see is not a common pattern of responses but a common pool of language strategies and concepts which individual children express uniquely according to their own experiences and needs in a particular situation. However, we do feel that taking a close look at Frank will allow us to demonstrate the complexity of the metalinguistic knowledge that is orchestrated by individual children in the space of a few minutes.

When Frank was presented with an item of environmental print he usually responded to Question 1 ("What do you think this says?") with a name such as "mints" for Dynamints, "Kroger" for Kroger Eggs, or "blocks" for Lego. When he was asked Question 2 ("What things do you see that help you know what this says?") he usually drew his finger from left to right under the print on the logo. In addition, after pointing to the print on the Jell-O, Coca-Cola, and Crest containers, he added the following verbalizations: "Cause I had some of that before" (Jell-O), "I drink that before" (Coca-Cola), and "I've got some tooth-paste and it's Crest" (Crest). His responses to the third question were more often than not a list of attributes or experiences he had had with the product. Through these responses, Frank demonstrates that he attends to the semantic cues pro-vided by the products' containers as well as the print. He also demonstrates an awareness that graphic cues are important in signing meaning and that English printing conventions dictate left to right directionality.

However, the character of Frank's responses changed when he encountered the three items which were color photographs of signs in their natural contexts. When he was shown the For Sale sign he answered, "I don't know" to Question 1. In answer to Question 2 he said, "This," and pointed first to the words which are the name of the realtor, Bill Morrow, then continued unsure, "or this," pointing to the words For Sale. He continued by examining the background of the picture and commenting, "I can't see nothing. I can't see nothing good."

The For Sale sign is obviously problematic for Frank. His "don't know" sig-nals that he is employing a self-monitoring strategy but he feels he does not have sufficient information to respond. He then begins a search for information as he points tentatively from one item of print on the For Sale sign to another. Evi-dently he does not find the cues he needs in the print, because he then moves to a search of the background of the picture. In this instance Frank not only shows us the variety of cue systems which he uses to make sense out of print; he also demonstrates his conscious control of strategies used when he "knows he doesn't know."

After seeing the picture of the stop sign, Frank paused and then responded to Question 1 first with, "What is this? Dirt?," and then whispered, "P-o-t-s" as he pointed to the letters. Question 2 elicited only silent pointing to the word Stop in the picture, and Question 3 a tentative, "I think it says 'Don't pass the sign.' " All of Frank's responses to the No Parking This Side sign were also ten-tative. To Queston 1 he responded, "I think they are going fishing out there," and to the last two questions, "I don't know." Once again Frank lets us eaves-drop on his self-monitoring strategies, and then his search of picture and print cues. It is interesting that this time he uses picture and print cues in the oppo-site order from the previous item. Frank shows us that he is not only aware of language structures, but also language processing strategies. He shows us that he is capable of using the richness of language to support his literacy learning.

New Directions: Why Is Metalinguistic Awareness Important for Literacy?

One of the important goals in undertaking this look at our informants' meta-linguistic awareness has been an attempt to determine what role such awareness might play in literacy learning and subsequently what implications these findings have for curriculum. We would like to present three major insights which have developed during our examination of young children's responses to print.

Insight 1: There are no particular forms of metalinguistic awareness necessary for successful engagement in the process of reading and writing.

Our exploration of the metalinguistic awareness of young children indicates that it is not a monolithic entity. Especially in the case of young children, metalinguistic awareness is sometimes discussed as if it were an all or none proposition—either they have it or they don't. Our young informants have already shown us that they possess a diverse array of metalinguistic concepts and strategies, and that the nature of this metalinguistic knowledge depends on their interests, experiences, and purposes for using language.

Children's responses to the environmental print tasks have provided potent evidence that metalinguistic knowledge consists of a wide variety of insights about language as an object and as a process. They have also served to remind us that in any literacy event there is a wide array of possible demonstrations of the way language works, but that the "demonstration potential" differs according to the particular needs, experiences, and purposes of the language user. This can be clearly seen by noticing the variety of demonstrations to which children attended. Even though an attempt was made to present participants with the same task (including the same stimuli and questions), they obviously attended to and commented on different demonstrations available in that setting. For some children the salient demonstration was the match between picture and print cues, while others responded instead to the speech/print match, syllabication, sound/symbol relationships, or the pragmatics of the research setting. Because children are in control of the demonstrations to which they attend, each literacy event is unique—even when attempts are made to standardize the research setting.

We have repeatedly observed children testing out their newest language hypotheses with great intensity across a series of literacy events. Each new encounter with print becomes a means of exploring the significance of their newest discovery. We have seen children like Beth find at every turn an opportunity to test the limits of conventional orthography as they try to see just how much variation is acceptable before a particular graphic sign (e.g., *Beth*) comes to mean something else (e.g., *Bath, Both*). After a time they seem to arrive at an internal consensus about their question and move on to test other more interesting hypotheses. The demonstration potential of each literacy event changes as the language user moves through cycles of interest, and these interests are likely to be influenced by past experience as well as current situational constraints.

Language users are never aware of all possible demonstrations; in each language event only a few of the available demonstrations are highlighted. But neither are they, nor should they be, aware of all the cues which they control as they use language. While children may focus and comment on the match between their oral reading and the printed text, they are simultaneously orchestrating syntactic, semantic, and pragmatic cues. When Alison realized the discrepancy between her oral reading response, "Wendy's cup," and the printed display, Wendy's Hamburgers, she was also using the other cue systems to produce her response. Though language users may be aware of some of the cognitive activity involved in their use of language, they cannot—nor do they need to—attempt to reflect on all that goes on as they use language.

Since even the youngest language users we studied were able to demonstrate some metalinguistic awareness, it does not seem fruitful to attempt to judge the adequacy of that knowledge against a conventional standard. It is also evident to us that metalinguistic knowledge is potentially unlimited because it is dependent on the experiences of the language user. Suffice it to say that every instance of language use provides the participants with opportunities to learn language, learn about language, and learn through language (Halliday, 1980). This is as true for adults as it is for children. Clearly, written language is not the only way metalinguistic features are highlighted, or there would be no way to explain all the oral language play children engage in. While it may be the case that certain types of metalinguistic knowledge are highlighted in written language and that our society particularly values these, the extreme emphasis on phonics and "sounding out" which so characterizes early literacy instruction certainly ignores other facets of language knowledge.

Insight 2: Metalinguistic responses are a naturally occurring option within all language events.

This hypothesis stems from a more general notion that metacognition is an integral part of cognition, not a second order process. For young children, opportunities to reflect on the adequacy of their language use are frequent, and invitations to verbalize their knowledge about language occur naturally in the course of their interactions with others. Such an invitation occurred for Alison when she was 3 years old. On a trip with her parents to get ice cream at Baskin Robbins she searched for a trash can to deposit her napkin. When she located the can her mother asked her what she thought the letters PUSH etched in the flap said. She responded, "Push." Her mother, a little surprised, asked, "How did you know that?!" to which Alison replied, "Cause it's got all the right letters."

Because both printed and spoken forms of language are present in children's environments they begin to explore them as a means to understand their world. Sometimes language events call for them to verbalize their understandings about language, but children also spontaneously comment on the discoveries they are making. Our observations lead us to believe that language awareness is a natural result of situations which cause language users to shift perspective. Often it is the result of confronting what the language user perceives as an anomaly. Awareness of language as object and process is just one part of the general metacognitive awareness which occurs when evaluation of one's thinking is necessary. We contend that this is not a "style" of thought brought on only by schooling, but a more natural and integral part of human cognition.

Insight 3: A conducive language learning environment enhances opportunities for language users to experience moments of conscious awareness of language and language strategies within the context of real language use.

Our final insight addresses the role of metalinguistic awareness in school curricula. We agree with Sanders (1981) when she suggests:

> Not all aspects of metalinguistic awareness advance literacy. Rather, isolated bits of metalinguistic awareness which are learned through instructional programs designed to teach that awareness outside meaningful texts may result in misfocusing a child's attention during literacy instruction to highly segmented, skills-oriented aspects of literacy learning. Such an over emphasized awareness of the many threads of literacy may hide the patterns inherent in the whole cloth of learning to read and write. (p. 271)

Metalinguistic awareness is not an end in itself. Instead it is a means by which language users come to evaluate their own language use, and make decisions at points of uncertainty. It is only valuable in use. It may be actually detrimental to literacy learning if it becomes separated from its use in meaningful literacy events.

For this reason, we believe it is essential that instruction remain focused on using language. As a result of using language, learning about language naturally occurs. Through conscious reflection on the use of language, language users are provided opportunities to take a new perspective on their knowing.

What this means is that teachers must be careful observers of students as they read and write in order to come to understand what demonstrations they currently perceive as interesting. Our studies lead us to conclude that if students are actively engaged in using language to learn for purposes which they select and therefore understand, they will naturally encounter the novel and uncertain situations which bring language concepts and processes to conscious awareness. In one sense the richness and complexity of language in use has built within it its own self-corrective potential.

Seeing metalinguistic awareness as a potential rather than a prerequisite in literacy can be quite liberating. Given our data, the real issue cannot be whether metalinguistic awareness is prerequisite to successful written language use and learning. Our informants clearly demonstrate that it is not. Metalinguistic knowledge developed as they were actively engaged in the reading and writing process.

So, if there is a metalinguistic issue, that issue rests with us, and a lineage of instructional approaches to teaching reading and writing which make concepts like "word," "vowel," and "consonant blend" prerequisite to learning to read. The children you met in this paper gained access to reading and writing without the ability to control these concepts in a conventional manner. The real question, we suppose, is: "Can we conceive of the teaching of reading and writing without making metalinguistics what real literacy—to say nothing about school literacy—is all about?"

Section 7

Alternative Symbol Systems: Metalinguistic Awareness in Braille and Manual Language Systems

Chapter 16

Visually Impaired and Sighted Children's Emerging Concepts About Written Language

GAIL E. TOMPKINS

LEA M. McGEE

In an effort to provide insight into reading processes, researchers have increasingly focused their attention on describing the knowledge that young children bring to the reading act prior to or at the initiation of formal reading instruction. Of particular interest has been the emergence of young children's linguistic awareness and the relationship between this awareness and reading achievement (see Yaden, 1984, for a review). Studies have documented the development of one aspect of linguistic awareness, concepts about the conventions of print, and demonstrated a correlation between these concepts and reading proficiency (Day & Day, 1979; Day, Day, Spicola & Griffin, 1981; Johns, 1980; Yaden, 1982). Day and her colleagues conducted two studies investigating children's developing "orthographic linguistic awareness." In these studies, children's knowledge of such print conventions as directionality, book handling, word boundaries, words used in instruction, and the print to speech match were measured by the *Concepts about Print Test* (CAP) (Clay, 1972). Day and Day (1979) reported that children's knowledge of these concepts increased during kindergarten. However, even at the end of kindergarten, the mean score achieved was 10.8, less than half of the possible score of 24. Day, Day, Spicola, and Griffin (1981) followed 51 of these children as they progressed through first grade and found that they continued to improve their performance on most concepts measured by the CAP. In a related study, Johns (1980) reported that first graders scored least well on CAP items measuring advanced print concepts (e.g., recognizing inverted word or line sequences) and letter-word concepts (e.g., locating one word or identifying first/last letters in a word). Further, he demonstrated that above average readers have more knowledge of advanced concepts about print and letter-word concepts than below average readers. Using a larger sample, Yaden (1982) replicated John's (1980) findings and also demonstrated that measures of reading achievement and intelligence together are better predictors of print awareness than either measure alone.

These studies support Downing's (1979) cognitive clarity theory of learning to read. According to this theory, children approach the task of reading "in a normal state of cognitive confusion about the purposes and technical features of language" (p. 37). They gain cognitive clarity as they discover both the functions and the coding rules of written language. In other words, as children gain linguistic awareness, they use this knowledge to discover how written language works.

Downing maintains that the theory of cognitive clarity applies to learning all written language systems. To date, however, research supporting his theory has detailed the emergence of linguistic awareness for only one form of written language, print. Yet, there are many forms of written language which readers can understand. For example, musicians read musical scores, secretaries read shorthand, choreographers read Lebanotation, and the visually impaired (VI) read braille. The present study was an initial attempt to extend knowledge about linguistic awareness of one of these other forms of written language, braille. The emergence of concepts about braille in VI youngsters was investigated. In addition, differences between VI children's emerging concepts about braille and sighted children's emerging concepts about print were examined. In contrast to sighted children, who are immersed in a world of written language as preschoolers, young VI children often lack opportunities to naturally interact with written language. They may have little experience with braille prior to schooling and may begin formal reading instruction without awareness of the functions and processes of reading (Lowenfeld, Abel & Hatlen, 1969; Mangold, 1978; Scott, 1982). Therefore, it was predicted that VI children would be more likely to approach reading instruction having fewer concepts about written language than would sighted children.

Braille: A Written Language System

The braille written language system for finger reading was developed by a young Frenchman, Louis Braille, and published in 1829. The code Braille developed was based on Charles Barbier's *l'Ecriture Nocturne* (night writing). Barbier, a captain in Napoleon's army, invented his code in order to receive and read messages in the dark. Braille simplified and refined Barbier's code for use with VI children and adults (Kugelmass, 1951). Acceptance of the braille written language system was slow, however, due to controversy known as the "battle of the dots" (Lowenfeld, Abel & Hatlen, 1969). The controversy concerned alternative writing systems using embossed dots as well as raised print letters which would be read by both sighted and VI readers. Braille's embossed dot code proved to be quicker and easier for the visually impaired to read, and eventually braille became the universally accepted system.

Braille is an alphabetic system with one character representing each letter of the alphabet. The braille characters consist of one to six embossed dots arranged in a six-dot cell matrix. Each of the dots has a specific number and location in the cell. Figure 16-1 presents the braille six-dot cell and the braille alphabet. Note that there is no relationship between the dot configuration of the braille letters and the shape of the corresponding print letters. Braille used a logical sequence in developing his written language system (Scott, 1982). The first ten letters of the alphabet (the first line in Figure 1) are composed of varied combinations of the top four dots. The next ten letters (the second line) use the dot configurations of the first ten letters with dot #3 added to each letter character. Dot #6 was added to five of the six letters in the third line. Because the letter *w* is not included in the French alphabet, Braille did not include a character for the letter in his code. The *w* character was added later. The braille characters for the letters *a* through *j* also represent the numbers *1* through *10*, and additional characters were also developed for punctuation marks.

The letter by letter reading of braille proved to be slow and laborious. To make braille reading faster and to make braille books less bulky, a complex system of 189 contractions and abbreviations known as signs were developed. Two types of signs are written language signs and word signs (Ashcroft & Henderson,

Figure 16–1

The Braille Six-Dot Cell and Alphabet

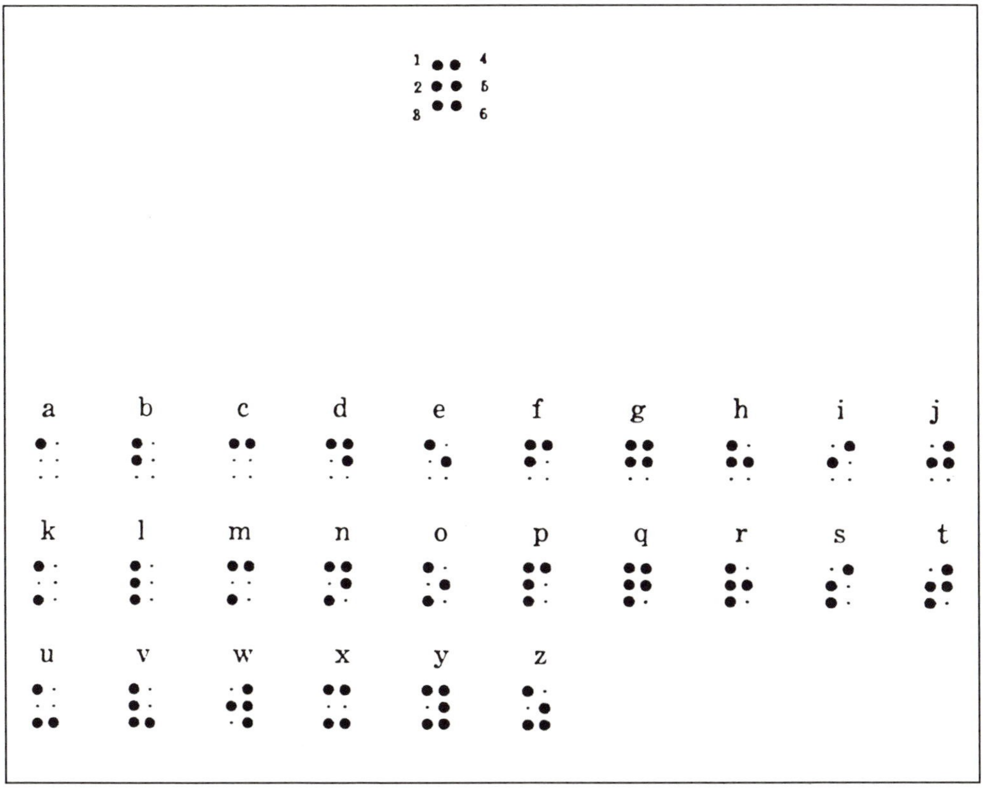

1963). One written language sign is the capital letter sign (dot #6) which is placed before a letter to indicate that it is capitalized. Word signs include whole word signs, short form word signs, and part word signs. A whole word sign is a letter character that can be used independently in a phrase or sentence to represent a whole word (e.g., b = but, y = you, c = can, p = people). A short form word sign uses two or three letters to represent a whole word (e.g., bl = blind, tm = tomorrow, ll = little). Part word signs use the signs for short words such as *and, for, the, of,* and *with* to shorten the spelling of long words containing these short words (e.g., h*and*iwork, ga*the*r). Kederis, Siems, and Haynes (1965) found that 26.5% fewer characters are needed when signs are used than when every letter in the word is spelled out. While signs effectively reduce the number of braille characters needed to spell words, the use of signs also poses additional constraints for students learning to read braille because of the complex rule system involved.

There are three levels of braille, and they are graded according to the number of contractions used (Scott, 1982). In Grade 1 braille, no contractions are used, and there is a one-to-one correspondence with English spelling. Grade 2 braille, known as Standard English Braille, uses the system of 189 signs. It is the most commonly used level, and textbooks are usually published in Grade 2 braille. Grade 3 braille is a very abbreviated form, similar to shorthand.

Braille is read by lightly passing the fingers over the braille characters embossed in horizontal lines, left to right, on heavy paper pages. Proficient VI readers use the fingers of both hands to read the page. They begin by centering their fingers at the midpoint of the top line and then pass the fingers of their left hand to the left margin and back across the left half to the midpoint of the line. The fingers of the right hand pick up at the midpoint of the line and pass over the right half of the line. As the right fingers are moving across the right side of the line, the left hand moves down to the left margin of the next line and the procedure is repeated (Ashcroft & Henderson, 1963).

In summary, while braille is based on our alphabetic writing system, two special problems confront young VI children as they learn to read. One problem is the use of signs. In addition to learning the dot configurations for the characters representing the letters of the alphabet, braille readers must also learn the complex system of signs. A second problem facing young VI children is learning the hand movements necessary for braille reading. After learning the left to right progression of text, these children must also learn how to locate the top line on a page and to move their fingers across and down the lines of braille characters on a page.

Method

Subjects

Thirty-one students, grades kindergarten through third, participated in the present study; thirteen children were visually impaired and eighteen were sighted. The VI children were students in a state residential school for the visually impaired and were receiving or would receive instruction in reading braille. According to school authorities, these students were ranked average or above average in intelligence. Of the thirteen VI students, four were kindergartners, five were first graders, and four were third graders. Third graders were included in the present study to provide a comparison group of mature readers, and they were selected as the comparison group because there were no second graders who were reading braille at the school.

The eighteen sighted children who participated in the study were selected from students in a rural elementary school. Thirteen were matched with the thirteen VI students on the basis of grade level, sex, and reading or listening capacity level. The remaining five children provided a comparison group and will be discussed later.

First the reading levels and listening capacities of the VI students were determined. The *Classroom Reading Inventory* (CRI) (Silvaroli, 1976) was selected as the reading achievement measure. This instrument, despite its limitations, was selected because authorities at the School for the Visually Impaired considered it to be the reading assessment least influenced by visually related content. Therefore, it was expected that performance of the VI and sighted students would be most comparable on this measure. A brailled copy of the CRI, Form A, was used to assess reading comprehension levels. Since the kindergartners were not reading at all and the first graders were only reading at the preprimer level, Form B of the CRI was also read to the kindergarten and first grade students to measure their listening capacity. The reading and listening tests were administered individually at the time of the study (April) by a VI tester.

At the kindergarten level, three children had preprimer listening capacity levels and one child had a first grade listening level. Four of the five first graders were reading at the preprimer level. Of these preprimer readers, one had a third grade listening capacity, one a second grade capacity, and two students had first grade listening capacities. The fifth first grader had a primer reading level and a first grade listening capacity. Only the reading levels of third graders were assessed. Three third graders tested at third grade reading level and the final third grader tested at the second grade reading level.

Sighted children were also individually administered Forms A and B of the CRI at the time of the study. All kindergarten, first grade, and third grade students at the elementary school were tested. At each grade level, same-sex children were matched with VI children on the basis of reading level and listening capacity scores. When more than one sighted student's scores matched a VI student's scores, a sighted student was selected at random.

A third group of five sighted first graders reading on grade level was also included in the study. This group was used as a comparison to the VI and sighted first graders who were reading slightly below grade level at the preprimer level.

Materials

In order to compare sighted children's concepts about print to VI children's concepts about braille, Clay's (1972) *Concepts about Print Test* was modified to develop a *Concepts about Braille Test* (CAB). Each of Clay's twenty-four test items

Table 16–1

A Comparison of the Concepts About Print Test and the Concepts About Braille Test

Dimension	Concept Description	Item Number Concepts About Print Test	Item Number Concepts About Braille Test
I Book Orientation Concepts	Orientation of book: Child identifies front of book.	1	1
	Text, not picture, carries message: child points to text.	2	2
	Left before right: child recognizes that a left page is read before a right page.	11	14
II Print Direction Concepts	Directional rule: child points to top left line of text.	3	3
	Directional rule: child shows that text is read from left to right.	4	4
	Directional rule: child shows return sweep.	5	5
	Word by word pointing: child points to each word as it is read.	6	9
	First and last: child points to first and last parts of text.	7	10
	Inversion of print: child shows how inverted text should be read.	9	13
	Period: child names or explains the function.	16	18
III Letter-Word Concepts	Inversion of picture: child points to bottom of upside-down picture.	8	12
	Capital/lower case correspondence: child locates corresponding lowercase letter when shown an uppercase letter.	19	22
	Letter: child shows one and two letters.	21	24
	Word: child shows one and two words.	22	25
	First and last letter: child identifies first and last letters in a word.	23	27
	Capital letter: child points to a capital letter.	24	19

were replicated with the exception that the two items on letter order were collapsed into a single item. Also, four items measuring concepts specific to reading braille were added. Three of these items related to directional hand movements and the fourth item required children to identify a whole word sign. Table 16-1 presents a comparison, item by item, between Clay's test and the CAB.

There were two major concerns in developing the CAB. First, the pictures used in Clay's test could not be used with VI children; they had to be replaced with objects. Accordingly, common household objects with strong tactile qualities were chosen to replace the pictures on each page of the test booklet. Then new text was written which directly related to the tactile objects. It was anticipated that the tactile objects would stimulate the VI students' interest in the

Table 16–1   Cont'd.

Dimension	Concept Description	Item Number Concepts About Print Test	Item Number Concepts About Braille Test
IV Advanced- Print Concepts	Line sequence: child recognizes that bottom line is read before top line.	10	11
	Word sequence: child recognizes that word sequence is incorrect when text is read as if it were correct.	12	15
	Letter order: child recognizes that letter order is incorrect when text is read as if it were correct.	13	16
	Reordering letters: child recognizes that letter is incorrect when text is read as if it were correct.	14	
	Question mark: child names or explains the function.	15	17
	Comma: child names or explains the function.	17	20
	Quotation marks: child names or explains the function.	18	21
	Reversible words: child identifies given word from pair of reversible words.	20	23
V Braille Concepts	Hand movement: Child places fingers of both hands on top line of text at the middle of the line.		6
	Hand movement: Child moves left hand across line of text from the left side to middle and right hand from the middle to the right side.		7
	Hand movement: Child sweeps left hand down to the left side of the next line and the right hand to middle of the next line.		8
	Signs: child points to a whole word sign.		26

Source: Adapted from Johns (1980).

test booklet as well as being necessary for the completion of two test items. Specifically, picture replacements were needed to measure the concept that print, not pictures, carries the message (Clay's item #2) as well as the concept of inversion of text and pictures (items #8 and 9). In Clay's test, the inversion items were presented early in the test, while they were presented later in the braille test because it was determined that it would be more difficult for VI students to identify the inversion of a common tactile object and braille text than it would be for sighted children to identify the inversion of a picture and print text.

The second major concern involved differences between print and braille. The metalinguistic concepts specific to reading braille were identified and four additional test items were constructed to measure these concepts. In addition, differences between print and braille required changes in other test items as well. Because signs are frequently used in familiar words, special care was required in choosing words without signs for test items on letter order (Clay's item #13), matching upper and lower case letters (item #19), letters (item #21), words (item #22), first and last letters of a word (item #23), and capital letters (item #24). In choosing words for the reversible words test item, words with reversible braille characters had to be selected rather than words with reversible print letters. Also, one punctuation mark, the period, required special care. The period can be confused with the letters "dd" and "dis," and braille readers depend on the context of the sentence to distinguish among the alternatives.

The CAB was constructed by typing the braille text in Grade 2 braille (Standard English Braille) and attaching the tactile object to each page. The test was then bound in a looseleaf notebook. Figure 16-2 presents a sample page from the test booklet.

A print version of the CAB was also prepared for use with the sighted students. This version was identical to the CAB with the exception of having printed text instead of brailled text.

Procedures

The CAB was administered individually to the VI students by a VI tester. Prior to beginning the test, children were given samples of the common household items included in the test to feel and talk about. Clay's procedures for administering the CAP were modified to adjust for a tactile approach to written language. Before reading the text on each page, children were instructed to feel "all over" the page. The examiner asked the children if they had felt everything on the page and encouraged them to identify the object on the page. Since the test was designed to be administered by both VI and sighted examiners, several procedures were modified. Instead of instructing students to show the examiner a target item (letters, words, capital letters, etc.), students were instructed to put the examiner's finger on the target item. Similarly, the children's fingers were placed on target items when asking for identification or explanation of the items. To assess whether children understood the concept of one or two letters, a card was not used as in Clay's test. Instead, children put the examiner's finger on one or two letters. If the examiner was unable to determine if the children had actually identified only one or two letters, she had the children count the letters in an unsigned three-letter word to assess this concept. The print version of the CAB was administered individually to the sighted children in the same manner by a sighted tester.

Results

In order to examine differences between the VI and sighted students at each of the three grade levels, several analyses of variance were conducted. Scheffe tests at the .05 level were used to determine significance of mean differences.

Total scores (excluding braille items) were calculated. Table 16-2 presents

Figure 16–2

Sample Page from the Concepts About Braille Test

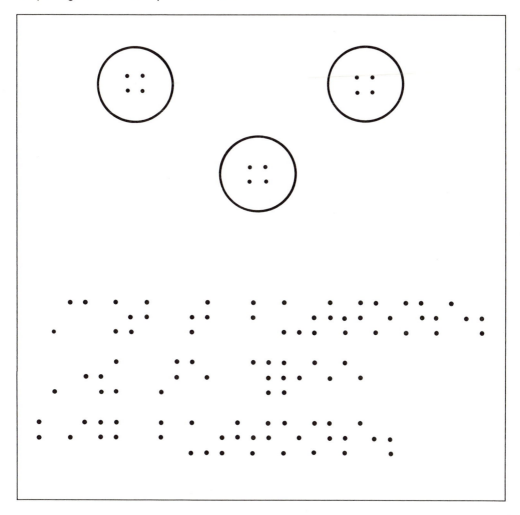

means and standard deviations of VI and sighted children's scores as a function of grade level. A 2 (group) × 3 (grade) analysis of variance revealed significant main effects for group ($F_{1,20} = 42.215$, $p < .0001$) and grade ($F_{2,20} = 94.121$, $p < .0001$). The interaction between group and grade was also significant ($F_{2,20} = 7.59$, $p < .01$). Figure 16-3 graphically displays this interaction. As shown in this figure, the mean score of third graders (20.875) was higher than the mean score of first graders (15.9), which was higher than the mean score of kinder-

Table 16–2

Total Scores as a Function of Group and Grade

Grade		Visually Impaired	Sighted
Kindergartners	M	2.00	12.75
	SD	1.41	3.77
	N	4	4
First Graders	M	13.60	18.20
	SD	3.29	1.09
	N	5	5
Third Graders	M	19.74	22.00
	SD	1.50	.82
	N	4	4
TOTAL	M	11.92	17.69
	SD	3.90	4.09
	N	13	13

Figure 16–3

Total Scores as a Function of Group and Grade

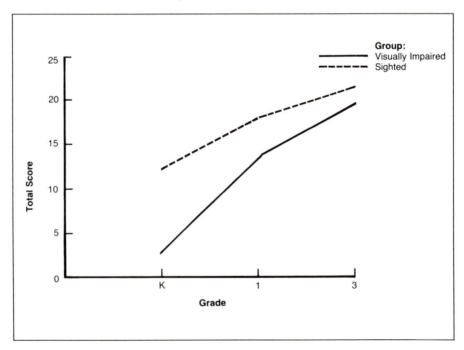

gartners (7.375). Mean scores of sighted children were higher than mean scores of VI children at the kindergarten (12.75; 2.0) and first grade levels (18.2; 13.6). However, mean scores of VI and sighted children were not different at the third grade level.

An additional analysis of variance on the total scores of the first graders was conducted to include the additional group of sighted first graders reading on grade level. The one-way analysis of variance was significant ($F_{2,15} = 8.79$, $p < .01$). The mean score of on-level first grade sighted children (19) was not different from the mean score of below-level first grade sighted children (18.2). However, the mean scores of both groups of sighted children were higher than the mean score of VI children (13.6).

Using a factor analysis procedure, Day and Day (1979) classified the items on Clay's (1972) *Concepts about Print Test* into four dimensions: (1) book orientation concepts, (b) print direction concepts, (c) letter-word concepts, and (d) advanced print concepts. (See Table 16-1 for items included in each of the dimensions.) Scores on items classified in each of these four dimensions and the additional dimension of braille concepts were also calculated. Table 16-3 presents means and standard deviations of scores on each of these five dimensions

Table 16–3

Scores on Five Dimensions as a Function of Group and Grade

Dimension		Visually Impaired			Sighted		
		Kinder-garten	First Grade	Third Grade	Kinder-garten	First Grade	Third Grade
Book	M	1.25	3.00	3.00	3.00	3.00	3.00
Orientation	SD	.96	.00	.00	.00	.00	.00
(3 items)	%*	41.7	100	100	100	100	100
Print	M	.14	5.20	6.00	5.50	7.00	7.00
Direction	SD	.50	1.79	.00	1.92	.00	.00
(7 items)	%	2.0	74.3	85.7	78.6	100	100
Letter-word	M	.50	3.60	5.75	3.75	6.00	6.00
(6 items)	SD	.58	1.14	.50	1.26	.00	.00
	%	8.3	60.0	95.8	62.5	100	100
Advanced	M	.00	1.90	5.50	.50	2.20	6.00
Print	SD	.00	1.79	1.29	1.00	1.09	.82
(7 items)	%	0	27.1	78.6	71.0	31.4	85.7
Braille	M	.00	3.00	4.00	N/A	N/A	N/A
(4 items)	SD	.00	1.73	.00			
	%	0	75.0	100			

*Percentage of items correct within dimension.

in the test. A series of analyses of variance were conducted to examine differences in mean scores in each of the dimensions.

The book orientation dimension included three items. Since all students, except the VI kindergartners, achieved perfect scores on this dimension, an analysis of variance was not conducted. Visually impaired kindergartners received a mean score of 1.25.

The print direction dimension included seven items. The analysis of variance revealed significant main effects for group ($F_{1,20} = 52.823$, $p < .0001$) and grade ($F_{2,20} = 18.11$, $p < .001$). The interaction between group and grade was also significant ($F_{2,20} = 8.459$, $p < .01$). Figure 16-4 displays this interaction. As illustrated in this figure, the mean score of third graders (6.5) was not different than the mean score of first graders (6.1). However, the mean score of kindergartners (2.875) was significantly lower than the mean scores of first and third graders. The mean score of sighted children was higher than the mean score of VI children at the kindergarten level (5.5; .143), but not at the first or third grade levels.

The letter-word dimension contained six items. The analysis of variance re-

Figure 16–4

Print Direction Score as a Function of Group and Grade

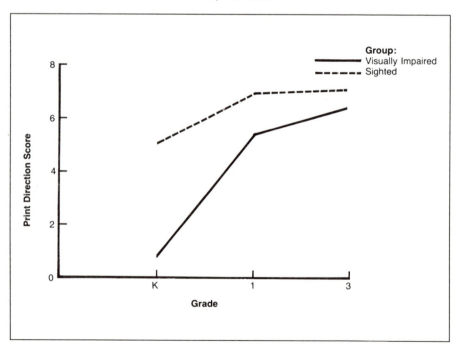

vealed a significant main effect for group ($F_{1,20} = 44.667$, p<.001) and grade ($F_{2,20} = 39.827$, p<.001). The interaction between group and grade was also significant ($F_{2,20} = 5.33$, p<.05). Figure 16-5 displays this interaction. As shown in this figure, the mean score of third graders (5.625) was higher than the mean score of first graders (4.8), which was higher than the mean score of kindergartners (2.125). Mean scores of sighted children were higher than mean scores of VI children at both the kindergarten (3.75; .5) and first grade levels (6.0; 3.6). Again, mean scores of VI and sighted children did not differ at the third grade level.

The advanced print dimension consisted of seven items. The analysis of variance revealed only a significant main effect for grade ($F_{2,20} = 44.459$, p<.0001). Figure 16-6 graphically displays mean scores as a function of grade and group. As shown in this figure, the mean score of third graders (5.75) was higher than the mean score of first graders (2.0), which was higher than the mean score of kindergartners (.50).

Only the VI students were tested on the four items assessing the braille dimension. A one-way analysis of variance revealed a significant effect for grade

Figure 16–5

Letter-Word Score as a Function of Group and Grade

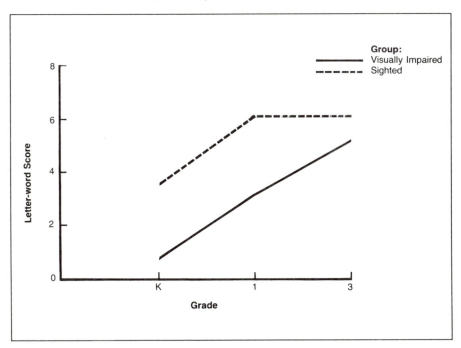

Figure 16–6

Advanced Print Score as a Function of Group and Grade

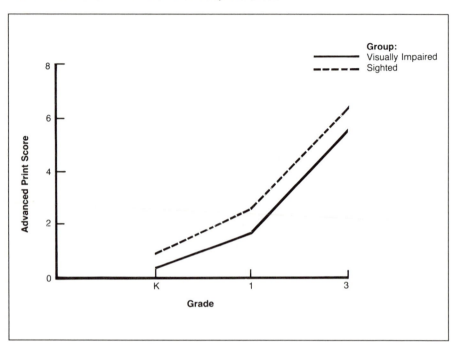

$(F_{2,10} = 14.613, p < .01)$. Mean scores of both first graders (3.0) and third graders (4.0) were higher than the mean score of kindergartners (0). No first graders were able to identify a sign. This would be expected, because signs are not introduced in their reading program until second grade.

Discussion

The purpose of the present study was to examine VI children's emerging concepts about the conventions of written language. Also investigated were differences between VI and sighted children's emerging written language concepts. In order to accomplish these goals, the CAB was designed to provide a measure of VI students' understanding of these concepts. Visually impaired children must learn the same written language concepts that sighted children learn as well as two unique braille concepts, hand movements and signs. Although this instrument shows promise as a research tool, it may be more useful as an informal diagnostic device for teachers of VI students. The print version of the test was developed for this study only.

This study was intended as an initial exploration and suffers from several limitations. These limitations include small sample size, matched rather than random selection of the sample, inability of the CRI to provide precise measures of reading achievement, and lack of validity or reliability data on the CAB. However, in order to provide direction for further research, some tentative inferences have been drawn from the data.

The results indicate that at the end of kindergarten, VI children have acquired only a few written language concepts, correctly answering only a mean of 2.0 items. The two items most frequently answered correctly involved book orientation concepts: (a) identifying the front of the book, and (b) indicating that the text, not pictures (nor tactile objects), is read. The VI children's performance on the CAB improved as a function of grade. Kindergartners, first graders, and third graders achieved mean scores of 2.0, 13.6, and 19.7 respectively, suggesting that their largest gain may be made during first grade. Day and her colleagues (Day & Day, 1979; Day, Day, Spicola & Griffin, 1981) found similarly large gains in (sighted) children's performance on the CAP between the end of the kindergarten and the first grade years. Even though the VI first graders' performance increased in all but one of the five dimensions (advanced print concepts), their mean score (13.6) was only approximately half of the possible score (28). These results suggest that while VI children enter school with little understanding of reading, they quickly acquire many concepts about written language during first grade. However, their growth period may be relatively prolonged, continuing through the primary grades. These conclusions must be approached cautiously as they may be dependent on the students and the program of the particular school from which the sample was selected. Further research is needed to provide additional evidence regarding VI students' acquisition of written language concepts.

Visually impaired and sighted youngsters' performance was compared to provide additional insights into VI children's emerging concepts about written language. As predicted, kindergarten and first grade VI children evidenced knowledge of fewer concepts than did sighted children at those grade levels. Not only did the VI kindergartners score lower than the sighted kindergartners in the present study, but they also scored lower than the lowest scoring *entering* kindergartners in a previous study (Day & Day, 1979). In the present study, the VI kindergartners differed from the sighted kindergartners on three dimensions of written language knowledge: (1) book orientation, (b) print direction, and (c) letter-word concepts. Similarly, the VI first graders scored lower than the sighted first graders and lower than Johns' (1980) similar sample of below average first grade readers. However, the VI first graders differed from the sighted first graders in the present study only in their knowledge of letter-word concepts. Both VI and sighted kindergartners and first graders seemed to know very little about the advanced print concepts. By third grade, both the VI and sighted students had acquired most of the written language concepts measured by the CBT and their performance did not differ.

The findings suggest that the major difference between VI and sighted children's development of written language concepts may be the developmental lag experienced by the VI youngsters. This lag may reflect a difference in the amount of prior experience with written language. While the lag in VI students' development seems to persist through first grade, it becomes less dramatic. Their knowledge of letter-word concepts appear to be the only dimension that is less well developed at the first grade level. The results indicate that while young VI children take longer to develop these concepts, the pattern of overall development seems to be similar for the two groups. This conclusion is not surprising given the similarity between the print and braille written language systems.

The results suggest that knowledge of written language concepts may not be a prerequisite to reading achievement. If it were, sighted first graders who were better readers would be expected to have higher CAB scores than sighted first graders who were poorer readers. However, the sighted first graders who were better readers did not score appreciably higher (19.0) than the poorer readers (18.2). Likewise, the VI and sighted first graders who were reading at comparable levels would be expected to score similarly on the CAB. Yet sighted first graders scored significantly higher (18.2) than the VI first graders (13.6). Day and Day (1979) cautioned that concepts about print may not directly influence reading acquisition. Similarly, Evans, Taylor, and Blum (1979) found that tasks measuring students' ability to focus only on written aspects of language did not predict reading achievement as well as tasks measuring students' ability to focus on both oral and written aspects of language. The results of Evans et al.'s study, as well as of the present study, support Ehri's (1979) suggestion that linguistic awareness may have a reciprocal relationship with reading achievement such that linguistic awareness is both a cause and consequence of learning to read.

Performance of both groups of sighted first graders in the present study was better on the print version of the CAB than the performance of below average readers in Johns' (1980) study on the CAP. In the present study, first graders reading on the preprimer and first grade levels answered 79% and 83% of the items correctly, respectively. In contrast, below average readers (first grade level) in Johns' study answered 63% of the items correctly. Perhaps the tactile component of the CAB enhanced attention to the text. This difference in performance highlights the difficulty in accurately measuring these concepts.

The reactions of the VI children underscore the effect of the tactile component of the text. According to both teachers and students, the tactile book was a unique experience for the VI students. The children were actively involved with the book, eagerly feeling the pages again and again. They were interested in the objects and were anxious to talk about them. One young VI child even rubbed his face back and forth across each page of the test booklet. The sighted students, who had had many more experiences with books, were interested in the tactile book, but they did not equal the enthusiasm and curiosity exhibited by the VI children.

Our substitution of tactile objects for pictures in the CAB highlights a significant difference between VI and sighted children. Visually impaired youngsters lack meaningful experiences with pictures and other graphic symbols, while sighted children use pictures and other symbols to interpret the meaning of environmental print (Hiebert, 1978; Mason, 1980). Also, children use pictures to organize their retellings of favorite stories (Sulzby, 1982). Ferreiro and Teberosky (1982) have investigated (sighted) children's notions of the relationship between pictures and print and how this knowledge influences their growing awareness of the print to speech match. They found that some children move from "viewing written text as a representation of referents" to "viewing it as a representation of the words of an utterance" (p. 150). The value of pictures was not addressed in the present study, but further research is needed to examine the role of pictures and other graphic symbols in children's emerging concepts of written language as well as to investigate how VI children develop an understanding of the print to speech match.

In summary, the *Concepts about Braille Test* represents an attempt to apply the *Concepts about Print Test* to another form of written language, braille. Further research is needed to judge the effectiveness of the test as a research tool; to examine visually impaired students' acquisition of concepts about written language using larger, random samples; and to determine the usefulness of the test as an informal classroom diagnostic tool.

Acknowledgments

The complete text, directions, and scoring procedures of the *Concepts about Braille Test* are available from the authors upon request. The authors appreciate the assistance of faculty and students at the Louisiana School for the Visually Impaired, Baton Rouge, Louisiana, and at Crosstimbers Elementary School, Noble, Oklahoma.

Chapter 17

Childhood Deafness and the Acquisition of Print Concepts

JEAN F. ANDREWS

JANA M. MASON

Children who hear initially use their language for communication purposes, then they gradually begin to analyze written language and attend to language forms in and of themselves (Cazden 1976; Rozin and Gleitman, 1976). Deaf children's use of language, too, progresses from a communicative use to a more analytic or metalinguistic use similar to hearing children but with an alternative symbol system—manual language.

When hearing children begin to read, according to Mason (1980), they first realize print has a function. That is, they realize print can be used to label environmental signs, food labels, and names. After this "contextual" understanding, they use a metalinguistic approach as they pull words apart into sounds or phonemes, letters or graphemes. Given deaf childrens' different communication system, could we identify similar developmental levels? We adapted Mason's theoretical perspective and reasoned that as hearing children map their *oral* communicative language on written forms to learn to read, deaf children match their *manual* language onto print during the early reading stage. Prior to describing these levels, though, several issues regarding the effects of deafness on children's communicative, linguistic, and cognitive abilities need to be discussed, as these issues critically affect emerging reading acquisition.

Issues

About 70,000 preschool children in the United States have a hearing impairment.[1] Such a sensory loss could affect their communicative, linguistic, and cognitive functioning (Meadow, 1968). One dramatic educational effect is underachievement in reading and writing skills. In fact, only 10% of the deaf school age population go beyond the fourth grade in reading achievement (Trybus, Buchanan, & DiFrancesca, 1975). Understanding deaf children's metalinguistic or analytic use of print using manual language could shed light on how they initially learn to read. Such information would be useful to teachers instructing young deaf children in reading.

One speculative reason for reading underachievement is that deaf children learn to communicate in an alternative symbol system—manual language (Jordan, Gustason, & Rosen, 1979)—which differs from oral language in modality, form, and code. As oral language forms the base of alphabetic script, the lack of an auditory-oral language could be problematic for hearing-impaired children learning to read. Instead, deaf children of hearing parents typically use signing systems.[2] These manual systems are derived from American Sign Language (ASL), the language of the adult deaf community in the U.S. (Klima & Bellugi, 1979; Stockoe, 1969). With its own rules of lexical and grammatical formation different from spoken languages, ASL makes use of space and movement to form its lexical items (signs) and grammatical forms rather than the temporal ordering of sounds as in auditory/oral languages. Deaf parents teach their deaf children ASL. Most deaf children, however, have hearing parents and learn a signed system of English rather than ASL (Meadow, 1968). These manual systems of English (see Wilbur, 1979, for linguistic descriptions of these systems) essentially use ASL lexical signs but put them into English word order. Another important part of ASL and signing systems of English is finger spelling. It is used for words in which there are no manual equivalent. Finger spelling has a one-to-one mapping of 26 manual handshapes (and numerals) to the 26 letters of the alphabet. Most deaf children, then, learn the visual-gestural systems of manual signs and finger spelling for communication rather than the auditory-oral system used by hearing children.

While manual language may be effective for communication, it does not map onto alphabetic script as efficiently as oral language does; hence, deaf children cannot learn to decode meaning from a sound-based alphabetic system in the same way hearing children do (Hirsh-Pasek & Treiman, 1982). Contrasting the spoken word with the manual sign illustrates this point. A spoken word is composed of a sequence of sounds or phonemes, whereas a lexical sign is composed of "cheremes" (Stockoe, 1969), the formational parameters of hand configuration, location, movement, and position which are executed at the same time (Klima & Bellugi, 1979; Stockoe, 1973; Battison, 1974). While phonemes have (for the most part) direct mapping onto alphabet letters, the cheremes of lexical signs combine to express concepts which can be tied to the visual discrimination of objects and actions (some signs mime their meaning) as well as express abstract ideas, which in turn can be mapped onto words and phrases. Thus, while hearing children use phonemes to relate their spoken language to print, deaf children relate manual signs to print.

The phonetic mapping inability can be circumvented at the prereading stage, where the identification of words is primary because many lexical signs map into English at the morphemic (word) level rather than at the phonemic level. Since experiments show that deaf individuals remember words better if they know their manual equivalents (Odam, Blanton & McIntyre, 1979), it is likely that deaf children may begin to learn and retain words using manual signs. This, however, may be problematic past the prereading stage, where sentence (Russell, Quigley & Power, 1976) and intersentential relationships (Wilson, 1979) are important.

While deaf children can use manual language to map meaning directly onto print, they are still constricted, as studies show they typically have underdeveloped signing vocabularies (Griswold & Commings, 1974) and syntactic systems (Champie, 1981). Furthermore, they seldom achieve competence in any one system[3] whether it be spoken English, signed English, or ASL. Thus, while hearing children by age 6 hold a well developed internal language (de Villiers & de Villiers, 1978) so they can relate their oral language to print, young deaf children typically lack an auditory-based language (Conrad, 1979; Ling, 1976) and have far fewer sign words (Griswold & Commings, 1974) than normal children have spoken words (Carey, 1977).

Another reason cited for reading difficulties concerns the social effects of deafness on cognitive functioning. While a hearing loss does not cause cognitive deficits (Vernon, 1967), the communication barriers it imposes often isolate the child from interactive experiences with people and the environment necessary for concept development (Furth, 1973). This experiential deficit may create gaps in their world knowledge needed to understand content in stories, for understanding relationships among ideas (Wilson, 1979), as well as for understanding how texts are organized as coherent wholes.

An Instructional Approach for Deaf Prereaders

An instructional model was tested that focused on the communicative and linguistic aspects of reading (Andrews, 1983; Andrews & Mason, 1984). The model was based on two assumptions: (a) Manual signs and finger spelling are prior constructs to learning about print (Greenberg, Vernon, DuBois & McKnight, 1982; Bornstein, 1972), and (b) print knowledge is initially acquired during deaf children's communicative interactions about reading-related activities with their parents and teachers (Henderson, 1976; Schlesinger & Meadow, 1972). To test instructional effects, the *Manual Prereading Test* (MPT), (adapted from Mason, 1980; McCormick & Mason, 1981) was constructed and administered in September to 45 prelingually deaf children in kindergarten and first grade and read-ministered the following May. Parents were also interviewed at the same time. A comparison of two reading instruction treatments provided the evidence for the model-based approach (Andrews, 1983).

This chapter provides a description of deaf children's acquisition of print concepts during the school year, using principally the results of the MPT, disregarding the type of instruction. In the study, 34 children had profound hearing losses (91dB or above in the better ear) and 11 had severe-to-profound losses (71dB or above). All subjects were between the ages of 5 and 8 years old with normal intelligence and no additional handicaps. All had hearing parents and attended state residential schools for the deaf which used speech, signs, and finger spelling for communication.

In this next section, we describe the substantive content of the children's print concept knowledge. The focus is on changes over the school year in the children's letter, word, and story knowledge using manual language. From the analysis of change we identified three developmental levels. These levels show how deaf children progress in print concept knowledge over a full school year.

The Development of Print Concepts

Letter Concepts

Children were shown uppercase magnetic letters and asked to name them manually with finger spelling. Here are some examples which illustrate deaf children's knowledge of letter naming and how it changes into a developing understanding of the alphabet.

Children performing at the lowest level recognized 2 to 4 alphabet letters with finger spelling, usually the first letter of their name would be included. They would typically make random guesses at letters they did not know. For example, JS (age 5, 110dB loss) could identify the letters M, J, V, and made random guesses for other letters, U for T, X/M. She also could print the first letter of her name. Only 4 kindergarten children showed these behaviors in September. Other children's view of letters often meant confusing them with numerals and with punctuation marks. For instance, NB (age 5, 98dB loss) gave the manual numeral 3 for the letter R, 6/X, 1/E. Another child, MS (age 6, 94dB loss), looked at an exclamation point in a book and gave the manual handshape for the letter I. Another letter labeling behavior included giving the name sign of friends when shown a letter. One child signed MIKEY (M on chest)[4] when shown the letter M. Thus, letters were often viewed as labels for friends.

Children who could finger spell about 20 letters typically made errors on graphic similarities. Often they would self-correct themselves, demonstrating active exploration of letter information. For instance, RS (age 7, 100dB loss) could identify 19 letters in September. He confused Q with O, E/B, F/G. When shown M, he finger spelled V, then changed his mind to W, then finally correctly answered M. By May, he could recite as well as print most of the alphabet in sequence and made no errors recognizing letters.

Children with the most knowledge about letter names could finger spell all their letters, recite most in sequence, and print uppercase letters. By the end of first grade, most of our sample were performing at this level. By May, parents reported that their children were more often pointing out letters on road signs and billboards and on food labels and were printing them on drawings. Uppercase letters were recognized more often than lowercase letters.

Comparing our data to hearing children's letter naming abilities (Mason, 1980), we see that by kindergarten deaf children easily acquire knowledge of letter names with finger spelling. Yet an important difference emerges between these two groups. While studies of hearing children show that their letter naming develops into phonological awareness (Gibson & Levin, 1975; Liberman et al., 1977, Mason, 1984), this was not the case with our deaf sample. Instead, letter naming with manual handshapes was used to label letters, finger spell their names, and label friends. Naming letters became a prerequisite for printing letters and spelling other words. In sum, then, our data show that deaf children initially learn to finger spell their names, then they learn other letters of the alphabet, can print them, and use them later to spell short words.

Word Concepts

To measure deaf children's early concepts about printed words, we looked at how they labeled print in the environment and how they recognized isolated printed words.

In the first "word" task, we asked parents to list any environmental words their children were observed signing at home. Even those children who knew the least about print were observed recognizing print on labels and road signs. The word *stop* on the road sign was most frequently mentioned by parents. With other labels children showed a progression from first focusing on a picture or a logo on the label to focusing more on the actual print. For example, CH (age 6, 98dB loss) signed *Krogers* as WHITE HOUSE, *Trix* as RABBIT CEREAL, and *Fruit Loops* as BIRD CIRCLES. Thus, she was attending to a color or a shape or a picture on the label rather than the print. Other children were incorporating finger spelling and numerals in their reading of labels. For instance, McDonalds was frequently signed M with the arch sign and alphabet soup as A-B-C-1-2-3 SOUP. Children also were observed finger spelling the whole label, as in W-E-N-D-Y-S and S-E-A-R-S. In general, children who knew the most about print would finger spell the word in the picture context, while children less aware of print conventions would give the sign for the picture or a color or a shape.[5]

In the second "word" task, we asked the children to read 150 sight words. Isolated words were used because we wanted to see how they were using letter information to identify words. If they did not know the print word, we showed them a picture of the corresponding word to see if they knew the sign.

At the first testing, children who were slower to learn about reading had limited sign vocabularies and would often label several pictures with the same sign. For example, TM (age 6, 83dB loss) overextended the sign DOG by labeling a cow, pig, cat, and dog with this same sign.[6] Other children would pull out a familiar letter in a word. For example, MF (age 6, 92dB loss), when shown the word *car*, finger spelled the letter R. Usually these children would make no attempts at trying to read words.

As children increased their sign vocabularies, their attempts at reading words usually focused on the initial letter or related letter information to other words they knew. For instance, CH (age 6, 98dB loss) was shown the word *eat*, then he signed ALMOST CAT. Thus, children at this stage were beginning to reflect and comment on visual letter patterns in words.

The children who knew the most about reading had acquired 20 or more print words by giving the manual sign equivalent. They had integrated the word meaning into their expressive sign vocabulary. Some of these children gave multiple meanings of words.[7] After they learned the manual sign equivalent for the printed word, they usually were able to segment their language to the level of finger spelling as our next task shows.

Finger Spelling Concepts

Our letter concept data showed that deaf children learned to easily identify printed letters by giving the finger spelled handshape. Many were then able to learn concepts about words as a linear sequence of finger spelled letters. In the manual language we used with the children, single words could be expressed as a single manual sign or a sequence of finger spelled handshapes. How were the children learning to segment their language into finger spelling?

To identify changes in their finger spelling knowledge over the school year, children were asked to finger spell several simple words (as *hat, hot, car, stop, hand* and *trip*) after being given the manual sign.

The first word the children learned to finger spell was their first name. In September, 40 of the 45 children could do this. By May, all but one child could finger spell their first name. Finger spelling other words emerged more slowly. Initially children responded by giving a random string of finger spelled letters with no concept of word length or understanding of consonant-vowel-consonant (CVC) patterns. For instance, SS (age 5, 108dB loss), when asked to finger spell *hot*, responded with the handshapes B-J-S-I-L-R-W-M and would have kept on finger spelling letters had not the experimenter stopped her. Another child, MF (age 5, 92dB loss), limited his letters but had no conception of CVC letter patterns as he spelled *hat* as D-B-L and *car* as Y-J-D.

As children changed in their finger spelling knowledge, they began to focus on the correct initial letter of a word but had difficulty with the other letters. For example, MP (age 7, 103dB loss), when asked to spell hat, finger spelled H-O-E-H. Children at this level became increasingly aware of word length. They also knew how to sequence letters in words. They began conceptualizing a word as a linear string of letters beginning with the leftmost letter and started to monitor their spelling behavior. WB (age 7, 100dB loss), for instance, finger spelled car as C-A, then corrected herself to C-A-A. By May, she was finger spelling it correctly as C-A-R.[8]

Children in our sample with the most skill in reading could finger spell the sign with the correct number of letters in the right sequence. As could be predicted, word length was important, as 3-letter words were learned more accurately than 4-letter words.

In summary, our test responses and parent perceptions reveal that deaf children initially learn about words giving the manual sign equivalent. Usually this occurs with words in picture contexts. Then they learn how to finger spell words and develop notions about word length and letter sequencing. Like hearing children, they begin to analyze words by focusing on the initial letter. However, deaf children's strategies differ from those of hearing children. While hearing children will begin to analyze words by using initial and final letter sounds which they hear in words (Mason, 1980, 1981), the children in our sample considered words as visual strings beginning with the leftmost letter. Confusions were more likely to occur because of visually similar letters instead of phonological similarities, and complexities arise principally from increased word length instead of more complex letter cluster-to-sound patterns. Consistent with our findings, Hirsh-Pasek (1981) found that deaf children use finger spelling strategies to learn sight words. Contrary to our findings, Conrad's experiments (1979) show that at least some orally trained hearing-impaired individuals use articulatory or phonological recoding when reading and remembering words.

Story Concepts

We measured the children's knowledge about story concepts with a book reading and a story reciting task. They were asked to read a simple story with simple words and pictures and to recite a second story after having it signed to them. A book handling and page sequencing task was also included, but we found that all our children could do these tasks. Apparently, deaf children by age 5 have had experiences holding books and sequencing pages.

On the book reading task,[9] several kindergarten level children attended only to the pictures in the book rather than to the printed words. When asked to read the book, they would simply label the pictures with manual signs, not realizing that the pictures were connected with meaning and words to a simple plot.

Children with more knowledge about reading began to attend to several of the nouns and verbs in the story. Pictures were often used to label the words and to predict the text. Other story reading behaviors were also observed. For instance, they were observed to paraphrase the story as they were adding content items. Several children digressed from a content item in the story to "talk" to the experimenter about this item, relating it to their personal experiences. One child began to communicate with the cat in the story, urging it in sign not to cross the street!

Finally, the most skilled children were able to read each word in the text, including articles and conjunctions with the manual sign equivalent. By May, most of the first graders were able to complete this task. Thus, on the book reading task, they progressed from picture reading to reading content words, and to reading content words as well as function words.

To examine the children's story reciting abilities, we presumed that if they had some notions of how stories order ideas, they would be able to retell a simple story that had just been read to them in sign.[10] How did these children recall the story? We found the children to segment the signed story into discrete lexical signs and observed three changes which characterize developmental differences. First, one or two content signs were included in the responses. Second, conjunctions and prepositions were added with the content words. Third, children were able to sequence the content words and function words keeping the story plot in the correct sequence. Most of our sample had no difficulty listing content words from the story but few reached the third level of sequencing story events.

First grade hearing children have been found to be sensitive to the structure of stories (Mandler and Johnson, 1977). In contrast to this, deaf children in our sample had difficulty sequencing story items. One reason for this may be that these children simply lacked experience of having stories read to them, as our parent interviews indicated that many of the children were not read to at home. Rather than understanding this simple text as a cohesive whole, the deaf children seemed to conceive of stories as a listing of discrete lexical signs, not as a series of connected events. That those children who participated in the training aspect of this study made gains in story reciting abilities indicates that training can positively affect their acquisition of story concepts.

Discussion

Our data showed that deaf children learn about letter, word, and story concepts using signs and finger spelling and that changes in their understanding of these concepts can be traced. It was evident, though, that the children were not progressing in their print concept understanding at the same rate. We merged our data across the concept areas of letter, word, and story knowledge so that we could identify developmental patterns in their early print awareness. We placed the 45 children in three levels of development. Each level shows increasing changes in letter, word, finger spelling, and story knowledge.

As shown in Table 17–1, children at the first level were primarily letter oriented, able to identify about 10 print letters, print some letters, and recognize familiar letters in words. In September, 6 children were classified as letter-readers, but by May all of these children had progressed to the next level. These children could hold a book properly, turn the pages in sequence, label pictures with manual signs, but they could not retell a short story in signs. Generally, their finger spelling, signing, and print knowledge were limited.

Level two designated an ability to recognize some words in picture contexts such as *Stop, McDonald's* and *Trix*. In September, 16 of the 45 children were at the picture-context level. But by May, 9 children moved to the next level, leaving only 7 picture-context prereaders. At this level, the children began to finger spell and print their first name and names of family members, recite the manual alphabet, and print most of their letters. Parents observed their children babbling random letters in finger spelling during play, and frequently pointing out letters of the alphabet on road signs, food labels, and in books. Often they would ask an adult to sign a word they could not read. The experimenter observed one child point to each word in a library book, then look up to her teacher to give

Table 17–1

Levels of Increasing Print Awareness

Concepts About Print	I	II	III
Letters	Identify and print 10 letters	Recite most of alphabet Print more letters	Identify and print all 26 letters
Words	Recognize own name in print	Recognize environmental words in picture/logo contexts	Identify 15 or more sight words Print words
Finger spelling	Identify letters in words Finger spell first letter of first name	Finger spell own name and family names Finger spell environmental words	Finger spell short three or four letter words Focus on initial letter to spell other words
Stories	Hold a book properly Sequence pages in book Label pictures with signs Attend to story in sign	Read words in picture context in stories Recite several content items in story Pantomime story ideas	Recall and sequence story ideas

her the manual sign equivalent of the word. While this child could recognize no print words, she had the prereading concept that a word could be expressed as a manual sign. Regarding story knowledge, children at this level could usually recite in a listing fashion several content items, yet they could not accurately sequence story events.

At the third level, the children had integrated the word meaning into their sign language vocabulary. Also, they began to analyze words into letter patterns. In September, 23 children were graphic analyzers, and by May this number had increased to 38, almost 85 percent of the sample. They could identify 15 or more words out of picture contexts, such as the nouns: *ice cream, milk, Dad* and *Mom*. They could identify and print all 26 letters of the alphabet, recite most of the manual alphabet in sequence, and finger spell and print short, three-letter words. Children at this level were aware that word units could be broken down into a specific set of letters. Their word recognition errors and spelling errors further highlight that important developments in breaking down words were taking place. Their word recognition errors (collected in September) indicated that the children were using the initial letter as clues to identify words. For instance, YELLOW was signed for the word *yes*, and FLY for *flower* (see similar results by Ewoldt, 1978, with deaf readers, and Mason, 1980, with hearing readers). The children focused on initial letters when identifying words as well as finger spelling. For example, the word *car* was finger spelled as C-A or C-A-T. Regarding story concept knowledge, these children could recite back most of the content items in a story. The more advanced members in level three could also sequence these items correctly. Three brief case studies which illustrate the three developmental levels of letter, word, finger spelling, and story knowledge follow below.

Case Studies

Level 1: TM

TM was 6 years, 9 months, a black male with an 83 decibel loss. His mother was unmarried and on welfare. TM started preschool at 30 months. He and his mother knew only about 30 signs. He used no speech when communicating or reading.

TM developed from a Level 1 (letter reader) to a Level 2 (picture-context reader) over the school year. In the September interview, he could name about 12 letters and could print only a shaky T for his first name. By December, he still had difficulty labeling pictures with manual signs and reluctantly participated in story-time activities. Instead he preferred to be held by attending adults. By March, he still had difficulty reading from left to right. Often he would pull out finger spelled letters from familiar words. For example, he finger spelled N-O for the word *nose*. By the end of the school year, he could finger spell his name, print his name (with letter reversals), and recognize the word *fish*.

Level 2: CO

CO was 8 years old, a black male with a 71 decibel loss. His father was a factory worker and his mother a housewife. He started preschool at 48 months. He used unintelligible vocalizations when communicating or reading.

CO developed from a Level 2 (picture-context reader) to a Level 3 (word integration reader) from September to May. In the September interview he could use about 110 signs, name 23 letters, finger spell and print his first name. By November, he was reading storybooks depending heavily on picture clues. By the end of the year he was attending to initial letters in words. On the May test, CO recognized 31 words. His finger spelling and word recognition errors showed that he was attending to more letter information.

Level 3: LW

LW was 6 years, 2 months, a while female with a 110 decibel hearing loss. Her father owned a car company and her mother was a housewife. She started preschool at 26 months. LW used unintelligible vocalizations when communicating and reading.

LW increased her skill within Level 3 (word integration reader) over the school year. The September print test indicated that she had a substantial background in letter, word, and story reading knowledge at the beginning of first grade. LW could print and finger spell her first name, finger spell short words, and identify 103 print words. Her parents had read to her in Signed English since infancy, and now she was reading independently from books her parents bought for her through a children's book club. By the end of the school year, LW had increased her sight word vocabulary and was reciting the training storybooks from memory, adding prepositions, conjunctions, articles, and verb tenses.

Facilitating Factors

We wanted to see if we could determine what parent factors and school instructional factors facilitate print knowledge growth in deaf children. More than likely, simple exposure to print in the classroom encourages print knowledge growth. But what home and school instruction factors have had positive effects on children's development of print understanding?

Parent Factors

If deaf children, indeed, were learning about print by matching manual language and meaning in printed forms as our test results indicate, then parental sign competence ought to effect acquisition of print concepts, because the parents could give their child more language experiences using signs. Was there a relationship between the sign language competence of the parents and their deaf child's print knowledge?

In order to address this question, the scores of the sum of all items from the prereading test given in September were divided into three approximately equal groups: high, middle, and low scores. Five items from the parent questionnaire were then examined: number of sign classes mothers had taken, mother's knowledge of the manual alphabet, father's knowledge of the manual alphabet, the number of signs the mother knew and the number of mothers who signed stories to their child. Percentages were computed in each category (see Table 17–2).

Table 17–2

Child Print Knowledge Achievement and Parent Manual Language Competency

Child Print Knowledge Score in September (N = 45)[a]	Parent Manual Language Competency				
	Percentage of Mothers Who Took 2 or More Sign Classes	Mother Knows All Manual Alphabet	Father Knows All Manual Alphabet	Mother Knows 50 or More Signs	Mother Signs Stories Often to Child
High N = 15	73 (N = 11)	100 (N = 15)	60 (N = 9)	80 (N = 12)	80 (N = 12)
Middle N = 14	64 (N = 9)	93 (N = 13)	29 (N = 4)	86 (N = 12)	79 (N = 11)
Low N = 16	31 (N = 5)	81 (N = 13)	44 (N = 7)	44 (N = 7)	12 (N = 2)

Note: From a possible perfect score of 235 points total, the High group scored between 63 and 185 on the September test; the Middle group, 30 to 55 points; and the Low group, 0 to 28 points.

[a]N: number of subjects in each group.

The results indicated that the high print achievers had parents who were more fluent in the use of communicative manual language and frequently signed stories to their children. Those children who knew less about print in September had parents with fewer sign competencies.[11] While they knew about as many manual alphabet letters, they had taken fewer sign classes, knew fewer manual signs, and seldom signed stories to their child. These results must be interpreted with caution, though, as many of our September low print achievers were the youngest in the sample. Thus, age and amount of classroom print experience may be confounding factors. Nonetheless, 12 or the 15 parents of the high print achievers reported that they had been signing books regularly to their child since he/she was young[12] while only 2 of the 16 parents of the low achievers so reported. Parent willingness to learn sign and communicate with their child may have affected their child's print knowledge growth. This needs to be studied further, with other groups of deaf children of the same age.

School Instructional Factors

Another factor which ought to increase print knowledge growth is explicit sign-meaning-print training in the classroom. We asked the question: Would explicit instruction training the child to match manual language and meaning to print result in print knowledge gains? To address this question, a 7-month training program was set up in a state residential school for the deaf in the southeast part of the U.S. Over the school year, 23 children in groups of 5 to 6 each were exposed to a once-a-week 30 minute story-time session. At each session, the experimenter would sign a simple story to the children, using training storybooks (adapted from Mason, 1980). The instructional approach focused on storybook reading modifying reciprocal teaching (Palincsar, 1984) in order to tie children's background experience to word and story concepts. Each session began with the experimenter modeling the story reading, then a discussion took place using the 3 to 5 target words to be taught that session, followed by guided reading and supervised practice. A control group of 22 deaf children from two residential schools in the northeast part of the U.S. received a well-taught cognitive, perceptual, traditional program (see Andrews, 1983, for detailed comparisons and training results). Pre/post testings were performed on both groups in September and again in May.

Our results showed that explicit instruction in training deaf children to match manual language and meaning to printed forms in the context of stories resulted in accelerated learning in early letter, word, finger spelling, and story knowledge.

Discussion

Our descriptive and experimental results indicated that young deaf children become aware of print concepts, using finger spelling and signing strategies. That none of the children in our sample used intelligible vocalizations while reading or any sounding-out strategies to decipher print words, yet all made progress in finger spelling and signing to identify print, suggests that finger spelling and signing are prior constructs. An analysis of word reading errors confirms this interpretation. During word recognition tasks, these deaf children were not processing print in terms of initial, then initial plus final consonant sounds, as hearing children begin analyzing words. Their word development was slower, deviated at the letter-to-sound analytic level, and never achieved the letter-cluster-to-sound analytic level. Instead, they appear to be viewing words as linear strings of visually distinguishable letters. In finger spelling tasks, our sample was observed to spell and learn to recognize words from left to right, rather than spell words according to the sounds as hearing children do.

At this early stage, two interventions were found to facilitate print knowledge growth: parental sign language competence and explicit sign-meaning-print training. Although these interventions encouraged word recognition strategies that do not conform to those initiated by hearing children who utilize the symbol-sound system, the enhanced growth in book reading and recitation as well as word recognition suggests that deaf children begin reading by using a system that they can readily understand.

Considerably more research is needed to find ways to lead these children to analyze and make use of the phonological structure of our language. In the meantime, we believe that early concepts about letters, words, finger spelling, and stories be included in reading curricula for young deaf children, so that a solid foundation will be laid upon which later mature reading skills can be built. By focusing the child's attention on the meaningfulness of print early at home and at school using manual language, analytic strategies for recognizing and spelling words can be acquired.

Notes

[1] This population figure is an estimate with a wide margin of error obtained by applying Shein and Delk's (1974) prevalence figures on deafness to the 1980 census figures of the general population. It takes into account all degrees of hearing impairment from mild to profound. (Office of Demographic Studies, personal communication)

[2] According to Wilbur (1979), manual systems for representing English have been invented by educators who believed that signing English would be more effective in teaching written English syntax than signing ASL. These systems "do not simply take the signs of ASL and put them in English order, they also drastically alter the morphological and phonological processes that users of ASL are accustomed to producing and perceiving" (1979, p. 203). In the study reported here, teachers were observed using speech, Signed English (Bornstein, 1973), and ASL expressions or a Pidgin Signed English (Woodward, 1973) when communicating in the classroom. Most children were observed responding using single ASL lexical signs in one-sign or two-sign combinations or in short phrases. Only a few children were using Signed English morphological markers.

[3] Mothers reported their children to use about 300 to 400 signs in communication. At the upper end of a sign continuum, 7 deaf children were reported to use several thousand signs, while at the lower end, 6 children knew only about 10 signs. In classroom observations, children were using signs in different contexts, in two-sign combinations and

with accompanying pantomimic gestures. Their sign strings were typically of the noun-noun or noun-verb variety. Most children jumbled signs together, as "rope boy girl broke girl fix." Several children used such ASL constructions as the statement, "Sick before better now finish." A few children attempted to sign in English as one child signed, "Girl is fall and be hurt," thus demonstrating a knowledge of emerging syntax.

[4] In this chapter, single uppercase letters designate finger spelled handshapes and words in uppercase designate manual signs.

[5] Often children who knew much about print and were able to finger spell environmental words chose to give a favorite sign expression for the restaurant name or food label. For example, LW would sign BIG COW for a local steak house because of its logo, even though the words steak and cow were in her sight vocabulary.

[6] Hearing children about the age of one- to two-and-a-half years typically overextend their first nouns to objects outside their normal range of application for adults. For example, the word *doggie* is used to refer not only to the family dog but cows, sheep, and cats as well (de Villiers and de Villiers, 1978, p. 126). We observed these overextension behaviors in 5-year-old deaf children learning a sign language vocabulary.

[7] Several children in the May testing were giving multiple meanings of words in their test responses. For example, the word *roll* was recognized with the sign DONUT and the verb sign ROLL (to roll). The word *fall* was signed as FALL (meaning autumn) and the verb sign FALL (meaning to fall).

[8] These kinds of finger spelling strategies occurred more frequently as the children learned more words.

[9] This story, *Stop Sign*, read: Stop, car (picture of stop sign and car). Stop, bus (picture of stop sign and bus). Stop, truck (picture of stop sign and truck). Stop, stop, stop (picture of car, bus, truck stopping at a stop sign). Stop for the cat (cat walking across street in front of car and truck). (Mason, 1980)

[10] This story, *Pick Up Toys*, read: Pick up toys (picture of bus, ball, rabbit, bear, blocks). Pick up ball (picture of boy picking up ball and box of toys). Pick up boat (picture of boy picking up boat). Bear and bunny (picture of boy with bear and bunny in arms, toy box nearby). Pick up bus (picture of boy picking up bus). Books and bus (picture of boy with books and blocks in his arms, toy box nearby). Put in box (picture of box of toys). Oh, Oh, Boom! (picture of boy dropping box of toys). (Mason, 1980)

[11] At the September testing, TM had sign language vocabulary of about 10 signs. He came from a home where his mother knew few signs and had taken no sign language classes. However, that year he moved into the school dormitory, during which he had more hours interacting with the dorm parents and other children. By the May testing, his teacher reported that he knew and used several hundred signs.

[12] Parents reported a variety of book-sharing behaviors with their children. Some parents signed the pictures in storybooks. Other parents would condense the story plots, using what signs they knew. One exceptional mother, a former teacher of French and a skilled user of ASL, approached reading to her deaf son as if she were reading in a second language. She translated English words, idioms, and sentences into a Pidgin Sign English (Woodward, 1973), making sure he understood the meanings of the English structures. She often would bracket groups of words in pencil, then explain the meaning in context and conceptually in signs. (B. Thomas, personal communication)

Section 8

Summary and Synthesis

Chapter 18

Metalinguistic Awareness: A Synthesis and Beyond

SHANE TEMPLETON

Retrospective metalinguistic reflections of accomplished writers may understandably be a trifle suspect. One cannot escape, however, an impression of keen precision between the fact and the recollection in the memories of Eudora Welty, one of the most accomplished, powerful, and gracious Southern writers. Her accounts of the many "literacy events" in which she was engaged, beginning in her earliest preschool years, are captivating and ofttimes poignant. They elaborate what for so many literate individuals are merely dim, inexpressible though vaguely pleasureable impressions. Welty recalls, for example, the rhythmic tick of the rocker in which she sat upon her mother's lap as she was read to, "as though we had a cricket accompanying the story." She confesses that she "cannot remember a time when I was not in love . . . with the books themselves, cover and binding and the paper they were printed on, with their smell and their weight and with their possession in my arms, captured and carried off to myself." About the letters of the alphabet she recalls, "In my own storybooks, before I could read them for myself, I fell in love with various winding, enchanted-looking initials . . . at the heads of fairy tales." Welty also remembers the disappointment in discovering "that storybooks had been written by *people*, that books were not natural wonders coming up of themselves like grass."

One of Welty's most engrossing recollections involves her first awareness of "the *word*." A specific event precipitated the coalescence of innumerable experiences and tacit knowledges into a conscious understanding of the connection between the "word" and what it stands for:

At around age six, perhaps, I was standing by myself in our front yard waiting for supper, just at that hour in a late summer day when the sun is already below the horizon and the risen full moon in the visible sky stops being chalky and begins to take on light. There comes the moment, and I saw it then, when the moon goes from flat to round. For the first time it met my eyes as a globe. The word "moon" came into my mouth as though fed to me out of a silver spoon. Held in my mouth the moon became a word. It had the roundness of a Concord grape Grandpa took off his vine and gave me to suck out of its skin and swallow whole . . .

The concept of "word," as several of this volume's contributors have noted, is a seminal event in the development of metalinguistic thought and for most children its onset follows upon an immersion in the multifaceted reality of print or visual language (Templeton, 1980). It is an intriguing and perhaps instructive observation that, even for a childhood as rich in literacy experiences as Eudora Welty's, a metalinguistic concept as basic as the relationship between word and referent is relatively late in appearance. Such observations, however, require explanation; thus the focus of the research, implications, and conclusions presented in this volume.

The contributors to this collection have in various ways attempted to divine what children actually experience as they live in, through, and to a degree because of language. They are seeking answers to questions regarding what the processes accompanying metalinguistic awareness afford in a specific culture, and what these processes afford in a "universal" sense. It is in part through the various phenomena of metalinguistic awareness that it becomes possible to observe children's emancipation from near total governance by the tacit dimension to join the company of those who assume the reflective stance and see, in Luria's famous metaphor, not only what is beyond the glass but the glass itself. It is through investigating the processes in which reflection evolves out of action, too, that more informed speculation about the nature and workings of this tacit dimension may occur. For each of the investigators represented in this volume, the overriding desire to discern processes underlying the construction or transmission of metalinguistic knowledge has infused the research endeavor.

Despite the range of methodologies, data, and interpretations evidenced in this collection, the efforts seem to weave into a fugue of more harmonic than dissonant themes. In its most robust expression, metalinguistic awareness requires an examination of broader psychological and cultural consequences. In a coda for this volume, therefore, the themes developed throughout will be elaborated from a more encompassing perspective of the domain and the importance of metalinguistic awareness.

The following issues will be briefly considered in this concluding chapter: the nature of methodology in the metalinguistic research domain; the "tool" metaphor for literacy to which Downing and Dyson refer and the cognitive "hand" that creates and uses the tool; the context in which the hand and the tool interact; the parallels between cultural/historical and psychogenetic development in the construction and use of the tool and the accompanying development in metalinguistic awareness; and the effects of beginning instruction in literacy and the more general meaning and effects of metalinguistic awareness and literacy.

First, however, a final reflection upon some conceptual distinctions.

A Terminological Postlude

Most of the contributors to this volume concur that metalinguistic awareness is a part of metacognition. It is one piece in a constellation of competencies and resultant "awarenesses" that children must construct. Given the literacy imperative of our culture, however, metalinguistic awareness has assumed preeminent proportions. As the term has been used by most contributors to this volume, metalinguistic awareness is understood to refer to the ability to reflect upon and analyze the structures of both spoken and written language—regardless of whether this reflection and analysis evidences "conventional" understandings. In the case of visually or auditorially impaired individuals, the reflection is directed toward the mode or medium into which the external text is encoded—touch for visually impaired and sight for auditorially impaired.

As noted in the introductory chapter, a distinction is often drawn between metalanguage and metalinguistic awareness. The former refers to language about language; the latter is recognition of and reflection upon *instantiations* of particular linguistic concepts represented by this metalanguage—word, letter, sound, sentence, and so forth. Young children, for example, will *use* terms such as *letter, word, sound*, and *writing*, but cannot reliably identify instantiations of them or make very sophisticated judgments about them. In most instances, contributors to this collection have used the term according to its more general domain, that is, referring to both recognition of instantiations and reflections on or analysis of those instantiations.

Literacy has similarly resisted efforts to affix a fairly specific definition. Collapsing across several more subtle subcultural boundaries, in contemporary Western society literacy is taken to refer to the ability to obtain the message encoded in a particular nonspoken mode, usually though not exclusively visual, and to encode a message into one of these modes. Criterion levels of competence, of course (and in some cases unfortunately), remain elusive. Some researchers have defined literacy such that it includes any pattern of discourse (for example, Scollon & Scollon, 1982). This conceptualization in one sense may be helpful in moving beyond the parochialism of culture-bound and culturally biased definitions, but when considered for its educational significance, may leave behind a disquieting wake of pedagogical impotence.

The Context of Inquiry: Methodological Considerations

Broadly conceived, research in the field of metalinguistic awareness may be characterized by (a) the levels or *degrees of explicitness* of metalinguistic reflection required of children, and (b) the context in which the levels are investigated—the degree to which they are structured.

E. Clark (1978) was one of the first theorists to point out that there are degrees of metalinguistic awareness. Notably, however, Clark's levels do not include explicit reference to the role of *writing* in the development of this knowledge. Much of the work in metalinguistic awareness has reflected the implicit assumption that writing, being a second-order symbol system, "piggybacks" on speech, therefore emphasizing a primary role for spoken language in the development of these concepts (see Tunmer et al., 1984). Many researchers, however, now appreciate the function of print in literate cultures not only in facilitating the development of metalinguistic concepts—"freezing" aspects of speech in a visual medium—but in the development of the native tongue as well (see for example Olson, 1984).

Research in metalinguistic awareness has evidenced the paradigm shift in methodology and design characteristic of much of contemporary psychological, sociological, and educational research: The highly-controlled traditional or "experimental" paradigm is being replaced by the more "naturalistic" or ethnographic paradigm. In contrast to the traditional designs and methodologies of experimental psychology, the traditional approaches of anthropology/ethnography admit all aspects of a context in the interpretation of the observable phenomena (e.g., Harste, Woodward, & Burke, 1984). This methodological orientation is important because it unmasks the significant nuisance variable adults may introduce when they sit down with young children intending to divine through conversation what the children may know, for example, about syntactic, lexical or phonological features of language. Such tasks may elicit task-specific behaviors and judgments, the generalizability of which may be questionable.

It has been argued that this newer naturalistic, ethnographic, or "transactional" paradigm often provides a realistic counterpoint to the ecological invalidity of the laboratory approach. Without appropriate caveats, however, this paradigm may carry the threat of experimental nihilism: If all responses depend on the immediate and usually quite unique context, what generalizations of any worth is it possible to draw from observation? In her chapter Sulzby comments that "we need both naturalistic and experimental designs and much longitudinal evidence from children's activities in reading and writing." Her sense of experimental balance is well taken; setting up an experiment to learn something about children's minds does not necessarily entail the "decontextualization" often feared by some ethnographers. This perspective is implicit in Dyson's work when she comments, "Although, as researcher, I did not structure the writing situation by giving children explicit directions, I legitimized writing (by asking the children to 'Come write'), and I *caused* reflection by asking, 'Tell me about that' " (emphasis added). The studies reported by Vellutino and Scanlon exemplify the care and precision of well-designed experimental research; despite the use of pseudowords in the learning tasks, subjects were less likely to be confused by context or experimenter expectation. In addition, as other researchers have cleverly demonstrated, it is possible to create a context that does not challenge the child's perspective; Read's puppets that elicited phonetic judgments from young children (1975) and McGarrigle's "Naughty Teddy" that provided a delightful—and interpretable—context to classic Piagetian tasks (cited in Donaldson, 1978) are but two compelling examples.

As the paradigms shift, then, a methodological warning may be in order: The disdain in some quarters for the experimental psychological paradigm and the current praise for the new naturalistic paradigm may inadvertently lead to the same type of tunnel vision attributed to the traditional experimentalists. *Both* paradigms offer considerable strengths (Templeton & Scarborough-Franks, 1985); researchers need to continue to assess the relative merits of each in the investigation of particular metalinguistic phenomena.

The Hand, the Tool, the Context

In discussing the implications of cross-cultural research in cognition, Olson (1981) commented that "the cognitive resources of an individual remain relatively invariant across differences in culture, while the goals to which these resources are applied and the levels of performance which may be achieved differ considerably" (p. 4). One of the challenges to investigators in metalinguistic awareness is the characterization of young children's invariant cognitive resources, and consequently their predispositions to construct knowledge about the correspondence medium and what it symbolizes. Children are "set up" to attribute symbolic properties to aspects of their world; the contemporary debate in some theoretical circles hinges upon whether there is a single "semiotic function" or several (Piatelli-Palmarini, 1980).

Awareness of symbolic processes can be examined in part through the graphic behaviors described by several contributors. Not only are young children observed to create an object and comment on it in the doing of it, but their gradual differentiation of "writing" from "drawing" affords insight into the development of symbolic functions; second order symbolism becomes gradually separated from first order symbolism and eventually may be characterized, as Vygotsky so engagingly suggested, as "drawing speech" (1978). This process is not apparent in conscious reflection in structured interviews until much later, though as Rowe and Harste indicate, *spontaneous* comments by young children as they are in the act of creating suggest some degree of metalinguistic competence. Children learn much about aspects of printed language that have simply to do with the representational and structural features of print exclusive of spoken language considerations. "Conscious reflection" may at first be directed primarily towards print, with the beginning awareness of print/speech correspondence developing sometime later.

Keen insight into the development and application of children's cognitive resources may be afforded by considering the populations Tompkins and McGee and Andrews and Mason have investigated: the visually- and hearing-impaired. When considering their learning of literacy and the nature of their metalinguistic awareness, what is so singular about these populations is not so much the surface dissimilarity in the coding medium and the accompanying rules of correspondence to be learned; rather, it is the apparent commonalities in developmental sequence with nonimpaired children. The writing and reading behaviors of the hearing-impaired children, for example, move from the facilitative effects of situational and historical contexts to the finger spelling and printing of their names and those of family members; accompanying this latter performance the children were observed "babbling random letters in finger spelling during play." The parallel with nonimpaired children's experimenting with letter-like forms in their writing/drawing experiences is striking. The next developmental level evidences the analysis of words into constituent patterns: Word recognition errors reflect attention to initial letters. Not surprisingly in light of this parallel, invented spellings reflect letter errors on the basis of similar *visual* features as opposed to similar *phonetic* features as would be the case for nonimpaired children.

Tompkins and McGee note a similar developmental sequence with a visually impaired population. Acknowledging parallel concepts about print between these children and the nonimpaired subjects in their study, they point out the two concepts unique to visually impaired children: directional hand movements and identification of signs. Although the correspondence system is indeed unique, these children may share with nonimpaired children the similar underlying competence in learning directionality and signs. In the former instance, hands rather than eyes are the directional trackers; in the latter instance, Grade 2 braille or contracted forms are learned in place of more "predictable" Grade 1 forms—this is similar to nonimpaired children learning high frequency/low decodability words during the period of formal beginning reading instruction. In each case—Grade 2 forms and high frequency/low decodability—the correspondence governing the word-referent relationship is potentially more arbitrary, but with appropriate instruction children should have fewer problems in learning such correspondence (Curry, 1975).

And what of the tool? As Holdaway observes, print is a "highly suggestive husk"; this husk embraces many *potential* meanings. The child must learn to penetrate this husk in order to grasp one or perhaps several semiotic cores.

Reflecting its structure, the hand shapes the tool, and thence the tool shapes the "hand." The strong form of the latter argument is expressed by Ong (1977): "The mind does not enter into the alphabet or the printed book or the computer so much as the alphabet or print or the computer enters the mind, producing new states of awareness there" (p. 47). Downing and Henderson emphasize how different orthographies make different demands depending on the basic constituent unit of the orthographic system. Although in theory an infinite number of orthographic systems could be developed, those actually developed and which have been in existence for some time represent ever more fine-grained analyses directed toward economy in representation while retaining richness in semantic expression of the message. This representation is usually at the expense of unambiguous sound/symbol, gesture/symbol, or tactile/symbolic representation. The consequent metalinguistic demands may be greater, but the richness of the literate experience—functionally and aesthetically—may justify these demands.

The interaction of hand and tool coalesces about the issue of the degree to which metalinguistic awareness causes, is a consequence of, or is coterminous with beginning literacy. Often obscured in the issue is the specificity regarding what type or level of metalinguistic awareness is being investigated. Part of the Western literacy imperative holds that because formal schooling begins roughly at the age of six or seven, it is important that children begin "conventional" reading instruction at this time. The most significant aspect of conventional instruction is of course considered to be mastery of the "code"—the phoneme/grapheme relationships in English. Therefore the "criterion" of success, phonemic segmentation, is the type of metalinguistic awareness most often interpreted as being what children "need" to be successful in their beginning literacy attempts. Regardless of the sociocultural context from which a child comes, his or her success in beginning reading most often will rest upon performance on this one particular criterion measure. Dyson succinctly states the conventional metalinguistic challenge in our culture: "Teachers tend to value knowledge of the discrete parts of written language (the names, sounds, and formations of the alphabet) more than knowledge of the uses of print."

Ehri acknowledges that some studies demonstrate the possibility of teaching phoneme segmentation before formal reading instruction is begun. One study in particular has generated no small degree of excitement in suggesting a causal connection between phonemic segmentation training and success in reading (Bradley & Bryant, 1983). Rather than resolving the causal controversy, however, upon closer examination this study is qualified by the following observations: (a) There was no actual segmentation training at the phonemic level prior to formal schooling; (b) some rather constrained criterion measures of reading performance were used; (c) confounding variables exist, such as the most successful group using visual markers, that is, manipulating plastic letters; and (d) only a small percentage of variance is accounted for by phonemic awareness (Yaden, this volume). Reality, then, offers a more intricate picture of the relationship between beginning reading and phonemic segmentation. There remain difficulties in attempting to tease out discrete and highly specific causal factors underlying individuals' ability to assume an objective, reflective, or "decontextualized" stance vis-a-vis language and to master phonemic segmentation.

Some researchers are beginning to question the role of a writing system in facilitating the decontextualized stance necessary for metalinguistic reflection, and more broadly in effecting the generalized cognitive consequences for abstract thinking. Based on their data from adult subjects in Liberia, for example, Scribner and Cole (1981) have suggested it is not literacy that produces such decontextualized thinking, but schooling. Interestingly, if extended logically, the following argument may be made: If it is not literacy for which a society prepares its children in the preschool and primary years, then it is the "decontextualization" of schooling. If decontextualized thought is the real if not apparent objective, then in a curious turnaround literacy retains importance, for as Olson (1984) has suggested, it may be primarily through preschool literacy events that we are teaching the readiness for decontextualization or different patterns of cohesion (Tannen 1982; Scollon & Scollon, 1983). Metalanguage is used to help develop this decontextualized stance, and metalinguistic terms are an integral part of this development.

Children, History, and Literacy: Some Parallels

Historically, the juxtaposition among literacy, schooling, and decontextualized thinking appears to be reciprocal or "relational" (Ong, 1977). There is considerable evidence that this state of affairs characterizes psychogenetic development as well. Such comparisons invite further investigation: Within the perspective of metalinguistic awareness, what is the nature of the parallels between the historical development of writing and literate behavior and psychogenetic development in children?

Often considered as little more than a parlor game for diachronic linguists, the ontogenetic or psychogenetic recapitulation of phylogenetic development becomes of significant use when it is inquired whether alphabetic systems that require a high degree of metalinguistic reflection "pay off," as it were, in qualitatively richer semiotic potential and generalized cognitive consequences. Is it indeed possible to observe in children a recapitulative foreshortening of the consequences of the interaction between culture and literacy?

Ferreiro and Teberosky (1982) and Papandropoulou and Sinclair (1974) have sketched some engaging parallels between children's development in literacy and their metalinguistic reflections and the historical development of alphabetic orthographies. Several of the contributors to this collection report findings that support and extend such arguments. If the investigation of these parallels has in the past been viewed somewhat disparagingly, it is probably because the parallels often were overdrawn and oversimplified. Simply living in cultures in which alphabetic orthographies exist will not inevitably lead to the full realization of literacy, an observation painfully obvious to educators but occasionally forgotten by historical linguists. Indeed, it is when the beneficial consequences of literacy to certain cultures are assumed to accrue inevitably to the child who "cracks the alphabetic code" that an unfortunate pedagogical error is committed. As Cole and Griffin (1981) noted, *"The tool must be in the hand of the user"* and it must be *applied.* Most children, then, appear to approximate the phylogenetic sequence if given an exposure to and feedback about the visible language—information that is reasonable in both quality and format.

With the foregoing qualifications in mind, it is interesting to juxtapose certain pre-, semi-, and conventionally literate cultural phenomena with pre-"conventional" literate children's behavior. The memorized oral narratives and ritualistic scripts that characterized pre- and semi-literate societies followed predictable formulas (Havelock, 1982; Lord, 1960). Built into these narratives and scripts were rhymes and rhythms that facilitated recall and performance. In those instances where these narratives and scripts were written down in prealphabetic orthographies, the text served merely to "remind" or prompt the reader of what he or she already knew. The significant aspect here is the structure supported by rhythm and rhyme—characteristics of young children's oral play, either for its own sake or as an accompaniment to physical play. Young children use their memory well when perusing a favorite book; having heard it read many times by an obliging adult or sibling they "tell" the story to the page. What is on the page is merely a prompt to something that is already known; the structure of speech facilitates and supports this recall. Children, like societies, may pass through a "lyrical" or formulaic phase. Because they are presented with an alphabetic script that can do more than merely prompt recall, however, the children do not remain, as did so many semiliterate cultures, at the "prompting what is already known" stage.

In his chapter, Holdaway observes that "There has been much speculation as to why alphabetic learning normally precedes, and somehow facilitates, phonetic learning developmentally." One of the most intriguing speculations regarding children's recapitulative understanding of an alphabetic orthography has to do with an issue Holden mentions in the preface to this volume: the conflict between syllabic and phonemic segmentation of speech. Historically, of course, the Greeks resolved this conflict. They were confronted with the following circumstances. They had the Phoenician alphabet, which represented not phonemes but syllables in a Semitic tongue; this alphabet did not, however, resonate well with the Greek tongue. The conflict, then, was between the symbol system and the demands of the spoken language. The singular achievement of the Greeks was to resolve this conflict by splitting the syllable into its consonant and vowel constituents. This split involved an analysis that went beyond that which was perceptually apparent; most consonants do not have an isolable physical reality, but rather overlap with vocalic segments. The Greeks represented those fleeting and less-than-obvious actions of the supralaryngeal systems—lips, tongue, palate, and so on—upon the column of air. As Havelock concluded, "The consonant represented an object of *thought,* not of *sense . . .*" (p. 82, emphasis added).

It is instructive to note that the alphabet the Greeks used *preceded* rather than followed phonemic segmentation at the consonant/vowel level. It was, after all, the attempt to apply the alphabet to their language that created the necessary "conflict" out of which arose the need to effect the conceptual split between consonant and vowel. Children are presented with a similar conflict; phonemic segmentation of the type expected in beginning reading programs appears to follow rather than precede conventional understanding of the alphabetic principle.

When children split the consonant from the vowel in their invented spellings, does their metalinguistic behavior suggest a qualitative leap in their conceptualization of the correspondence between written and spoken language? The evidence suggests that this may be the case. The children exhibit a conventional understanding of what a "word" is, although they may not include *spaces* in their writing, a critical defining attribute of words. They can, however, point to words in print. They are able to assume a metalinguistic stance vis-a-vis words and comment on both structural and significatory features. In the historical development of writing, such metalinguistic reflection also followed upon the entrenchment of the alphabetic principle.

In an engaging speculation, Papandropoulou and Sinclair (1974) noted that children's comments on words prior to their attainment of the concept of word and of the alphabetic principle evidence the characteristics of classical thought. In Plato's *Cratylus* the confusion of the word with the referent is at issue; young children evidence similar confusion (Templeton & Spivey, 1980; Templeton & Thomas, 1984). Even when metalinguistic awareness becomes more sophisticated, some words—such as conjunctions and articles—are rejected by children as not being words. Historically, this same conceptual distinction between grammatical morphemes and contentives was also problematic. Ironically, it may not be until the concept of word coalesces and the vowel/consonant split occurs that children are able to understand the tasks entailed in the more systematic presentation of many readiness skills in basal reading programs. It is difficult to avoid noting another bit of irony: Children's ability to reflect upon syntactic categories and parts of speech in a conventional sense occurs quite some time after they have mastered the basic conventions of the alphabetic orthography; interestingly, Havelock notes that for the Greeks these concepts did not become objects of reflection until nearly three hundred years had elapsed after the alphabetic principle was established.

According to Havelock, the most significant consequence of the precision of expression afforded by the alphabetic legacy is that it allows the study of propositions as well as the description of events. This movement from "action" to "reflection" may create, in a more formal sense, the argumentative out of the narrative form.

Examining particulars in psychogenetic development entails addressing the issue of "stages." Not all societies, of course, have pursued the alphabetic path— just as not all children appear to follow the phylogenetic sequence as it unfolded in its alphabetic phase. That so many children *do* follow this sequence, however, suggests parameters within which educators might respond.

Children do need to learn to perceive commonalities across different contexts; they need to learn the different "patterns of cohesion" that characterize different social (learning) contexts and texts to be read. Learning how to function within and between these various contexts is developmental, and if tasks are requested of the children, the commonalities among the strategies expressed tell us much about the organization, function, and development of symbolic understanding. When speaking of stage theories, H. Gardner's (1983) observation in this regard is relevant: "It is difficult . . . to adhere to a rigid view of the stage theory. Nonetheless, in my own view, there is still utility in recognizing *different mental organizations associated with different levels of understanding* (for example, in the picture of symbolic development I have rendered)" (p. 315, emphasis added). Traditionally, the objection to stage theories has hinged on the acceptance of *specific* "context free" behaviors as evidence of developmental level. If the focus is on a fairly wide range of behaviors and strategies, then the parameters—characterizing different levels of understanding—are more instructive to the researcher and potentially of greater benefit to children in the instructional setting.

Educational Implications

One of the most direct consequences of research in metalinguistic awareness and beginning literacy has been the redefinition if not rejection of the term "readiness." Pedagogical reality, of course, ensures that the term will not pass into obscurity. Assessments that fall within the classification of "readiness" nevertheless may serve a significant purpose. As Yaden and Day and Day have demonstrated, tasks such as those presented in Clay's early diagnostic survey (1979a) and the *Linguistic Awareness and Reading Readiness* test (Downing, Ayers, and Schaefer, 1983) provide more appropriate assessments than those obtained through traditional readiness tests. This may in time vitiate the longstanding concern with relationships between prediction and criterion measures that often obscure the value of ongoing assessment; the success of Clay's ongoing program in New Zealand schools demonstrates not only that teachers benefit in terms of the instruction they are able to provide their young pupils, but that administrators, too, are pleased with the ongoing as opposed to beginning-of-year/end-of-year assessment. One would hope that assessment in other countries would emulate the program in New Zealand and, in following Clay's lead and the lead of several researchers who have shared their efforts in this volume, evaluate the information expressed in children's *writing* as well.

The power of the pedagogical implications offered in this volume grows out of the nature of much of the research: The character and course of children's metalinguistic understanding develops in a context that *is* a pedagogical environment. What pedagogical factors support beginning literacy and those metalinguistic behaviors arguably associated with this development?

As several contributors have implied, more "structured" and elaborated dialogue with children will unavoidably reflect the characteristics of printed language—the perspective of decontextualization or different patterns of cohesion that are necessary for metalinguistic awareness and for understanding the primary character of formal literacy instruction in Western culture. Torrey's (1979) famous case study notwithstanding, for most children it is not enough simply to be around print. What the children's attention is directed toward is of importance as well as the *language* used in directing that attention. Much of this volume has been given over to an examination of the forum and the context for this focusing. A few thoughts will be directed here toward those forums and contexts: the home, the preschool, and the primary grades.

Hiebert, Taylor, and Mason et al. have outlined some excellent procedures for meaningful print-related experience in the preschool years and have illustrated the relative efficacy of different styles of interaction with children. In such contexts a *functional* albeit implicit knowledge about print develops; the metalanguage exists as a pointer or highlighter for categories that will in time assume a more conventional elaboration. As Sulzby has indicated, children create a *textual entity* separate from the rest of their speech, which they can comment on and treat as an object. The role of an adult or literate sibling in assisting at this creation becomes seminal. As Hiebert and Sulzby have demonstrated, such knowledgeable literates are engaged in a cooperative effort with the young child. When considered in light of Hiebert's suggestion that school ought to continue in the same vein as good home and preschool programs, these research implications underscore the importance of trying to respond to what the child is attempting to do; this imperative, now unfortunately a cliché, nevertheless continues to be violated every day in the context of "formal" education.

It was noted earlier that more commonalities underlie developing literacy and metalinguistic strategies of normal and impaired children than would at first appear to be the case. Strategies for responding to special populations are strikingly similar as well. Consider Andrews and Mason's conclusion: "By focusing the child's attention on the meaningfulness of print early at home and at school using manual language, analytic strategies for recognizing and spelling words can be acquired." Both the possibilities for and the necessity of establishing meaningful connections between the correspondence medium and the natural language mode among impaired children are poignantly illustrated by the child in Tompkins and McGee's research who rubbed his face across the page in the tactile book.

Related to the issue of the home/school transition, some recent research has contradicted a predominant traditional belief: Literacy events and the potential for metalinguistic "events" occur across all socioeconomic/cultural groups (Heath 1982; Anderson, Teale & Estrada, 1980). The issue, made so apparent by research in metacognition and metalinguistic awareness, is not whether or not children are capable of certain behaviors, but whether they will marshal the appropriate cognitive resources to the demands of specific literacy tasks. Herein lies the challenge, as the demands of traditional school literacy tasks are usually at variance with the experiences of children from non-middle class backgrounds. Children do not approach literacy in a natural state of cognitive confusion, as Downing in his modified postulates has noted. If they are confronted with inappropriate instruction, however, a most unnatural state may indeed develop.

And what of the implications of the earliest research in what has come to be known as metalinguistic or metacognitive awareness? Johns reviews those studies that, while laudably noting the discrepancy between what children thought about reading and what teachers thought they were teaching, enjoined teachers to teach children that "reading has a purpose" and that teachers should "help them want to learn to read" (Denny & Weintraub, 1963). Teachers should teach the "direct perception of the reading process . . . directly and thoroughly." What has become apparent since those early studies, however, is that knowledge of process and purpose cannot be *directly* taught. Moreover, as Olson (1984) pointed out in contrasting what he termed the "developmentalist" and "cultural/historical" learning perspectives, what is learned is not necessarily what is taught. If on the other hand instruction is effectively meaning-based, instruction should carry the idea of "purpose" along with it. Again, as Downing observes, the tacit understanding of *function* precedes *features*.

How is the challenge of meaning-based instruction addressed? Some recent research belies the most obvious solutions; Heath (1982) has concluded for example that in a lowerclass minority community "no amount of books suddenly poured into the community, or public service programs teaching parents how to help their children learn to read, would have made an appreciable difference" (p. 111). It is possible, however, that the outlook may not be so bleak as Heath suggests. Rather than setting community dynamics against school dynamics, a closer approximation between both should be sought; broader societal transformations demand that this be done. Heath is addressing issues more fundamental than methodological; it should be noted on the other hand that, although real, the gap between the expectations and experiences of members of different socioeconomic and ethnic groups vis-a-vis schooling can be spanned. Indeed, the very type of community Heath describes, for which the usual solutions are held to be inappropriate, offers a particularly favorable context in which the meaning of written texts can be constructed, elaborated, and refined through interaction within a group. Heath observed that in the community she referred to as Trackton, written texts "had to be renegotiated into an informal style, one which led to discussion and debate among several people," and later, "they might or might not follow up on the message of the written information, but what they had come to know had come to them from the text through the *joint negotiation of meaning*" (p. 111, emphasis added). This type of interaction among individuals after a reading is precisely the sort that has been advocated in decades past by several reading educators. The only difference between this "joint negotiation of meaning" and an interactive, critical reading activity in school is that in the latter context all participants read the text; beyond this, the dynamics of the interchange should reflect in large measure precisely the dynamics that characterize the interchange in communities such as Heath's Trackton. For young children with minimal "conventional" literacy knowledge, the only adjustment is that the teacher reads the story, after which—or in some cases during which—the joint negotiation of meaning will ensue. In such contexts the relevant metalinguistic terms will also be used and reinforced.

Teachers thus facilitate not only the social negotiation of meaning for written texts but, in the beginning, the social mediation of print as well. Teachers carry out actions upon the written language. It is precisely for this reason that "language experience" activities work so well (Stauffer, 1980; Hall, 1981; Henderson, 1981). In such activities, *every* convention of written language is modeled for the children, including the formation of basic letter units—a very subtle series of actions which as Henderson suggests becomes, when undertaken by the child, an intrinsic component of the organic relationship between spoken and written language. The fact remains that alphabetic orthographies place greater demands on young learners than syllabic orthographies. This should be appreciated and the necessary "actions" should be allowed to arise before expecting awareness. The social setting for reading and writing is not decontextualized; it is the content of what is to be read and written that *may* be. The "important" functions of literacy are conveyed through the features that teachers appear to value and the tasks that teachers require.

Noted earlier were the engaging parallels between the historical development of the writing system and its psychogenetic recapitulation. Not noted were the somewhat less captivating parallels between the predominant contemporary and historical methods of teaching beginning reading. In each generation there are proponents, usually quite vocal, of the direct approach: Select the smallest constituent in the orthography and teach it early and directly. While often decrying the egocentricity of the child, these adults rather peculiarly cannot or will not overcome the entrenched egocentrism of the adult orthographic perspective. On the other hand, research conducted in metalinguistic and metacognitive awareness and on the phylogenetic/psychogenetic parallels in literacy development strongly suggests the following: The problems young children experience with reading and with writing probably lie not so much with the alphabet, but with the adults who may have lost touch with the literate soul of a phylogenetic heritage.

Conclusions: Policy Implications and Beyond

What Needs to Be Done?

The high degree of metalinguistic awareness required in our culture is a function of two factors: (1) our alphabetic system and (2) our manner of instruction. Nothing can be done about the first; the second, however, can and ought to be addressed. How can the insights gained from research in metalinguistic awareness and related areas be applied at a level of any consequence?

Those who will genuinely and favorably affect policy have greater potential at the very age levels with which this volume has been concerned: preschool- and primary-age children. Arguments must be advanced for the necessity of structuring a facilitative environment and against the regimen that those who are mis- or un-informed would place upon the schools in the hopes of advancing literacy. Much of the research in this collection reveals that this latter orientation, in the name of consistency and the standardization of instruction in the "basics," involves more decontextualization and an implicit insensitivity to sociocultural differences. The following trend effectively represents the challenge to be addressed: By administrative fiat in some large school systems, "reading" should be taught not only in kindergarten but in the pre-kindergarten year—and in one large metropolitan system, a superintendent has said that he desires the so-called "nursery school" year (which precedes the *pre*-kindergarten year) to offer instruction in reading as well. What type of reading? The children will *begin* with phonics . . .

Unlike the participants at a recent conference on beginning literacy, researchers cannot avoid for whatever reason defining their domains of inquiry and offering some solid supportive action for teachers (Goelman et al., 1984). Indeed, "above the fray" conclusions are precisely what the classroom teacher has come to expect from the research community, and often mitigate against teachers themselves becoming involved in the research endeavor. The "true" social context and the "true" interactive dialogue between literate adult and young child have not yet and of course can never be identified; the weak qualifier that "further research is needed" may discredit our undertaking. We have learned a great deal, and we ought to be ready to offer and to press for some specific actions. This is not the forum for an exhaustive listing of the fronts on which these efforts will be mounted, but a few broad domains should be briefly noted.

On two established fronts, preservice and inservice teacher education, there is already much underway, yet much remains to be accomplished. Well-known criticisms notwithstanding, one senses that preservice elementary teachers intending to teach at the primary level are getting a far better education in the area of beginning literacy than was the case in years past. Practica experiences prior to student teaching are increasing and, it is hoped for better than for worse, more researchers in this area will find themselves not only teaching these undergraduate practica but as a consequence sharing the excitement of the research and implications with their students. For a multitude of reasons education for inservice teachers is a more complex matter. There are admittedly more teachers at the kindergarten and primary levels than would be preferred who reflect attitudes and approaches that run directly counter to the orientation reflected in this volume. Experience suggests, however, that a significant number of these teachers teach as they do not because they are unable to teach otherwise but simply because they are not *aware*. As concern with teacher competency and evaluation leads to more supportive inservice and certification renewal programs, the issue of awareness and subsequent action may be addressed. Where inservice education is concerned, incidentally, administrators—and if at all possible, school board members—should definitely be included.

As many states move toward establishing more rigorous programs of certification for preschool educators, efforts must be made at the state and local levels to ensure that learning and instruction in language and literacy rest on an informed and enlightened foundation rather than on the simplistic solution of moving the kindergarten curriculum up to the nursery school year and the nursery school year to the preschool. Neither preschool nor primary curricular changes will enjoy much success, however, if decision-making entities are not approached, worked with, and in many cases, educated. One is often delightfully impressed with how effective a half-hour presentation can be in which examples of young children's reading and writing are shared and explained, whether the forum is a PTA meeting, a group of principals, a session of the board of education, or an education subcommittee of the state legislature. There must be systematic follow-up, of course, but in most cases the attractiveness of bedrock back-to-basics approaches will at least have begun to be questioned.

Educational publishers, particularly those of basal reading series, have been attempting to respond to research. Those publishers who pursue their mission honorably are engaged in a perpetual balancing act between incorporating the implications of research and responding to the exigencies of the marketplace—

exigencies that often follow rather unpredictable trends. The research foundation is probably weakest, however, at the beginning or readiness levels of most basal series (Templeton, in press); specifically, with the introduction and development of both print conventions and metalinguistic terms. As researchers in metalinguistic awareness and beginning literacy work closely with the publishers, this void may in the future be filled.

Conceptualizing What It Means

This volume has addressed the role of metalinguistic awareness in the onset of literacy—"conventional" or otherwise. Some of the research in this domain has ironically called into question the cognitive consequences so often claimed for literacy (for example, Scribner and Cole, 1981). This challenge entails an unsettling question about justifying the time if not the current methodologies of teaching reading and writing—the ways in which the literate members of society attempt to mediate the influences of this cultural artifact. The role literacy plays in a culture is questioned; the stance a conventionally literate society assumes vis-a-vis cultures with little or no tradition of literacy is examined; what, after all, can metalinguistic insights afford?

Unlike most other visual stimuli that announce themselves more dramatically to the perceiver, print belies this most dynamic and unique nature by the simple fact of its apparent static character. It is, on its surface, the most modest of the visual arts. In this superficially humble appearance, print can affect our consciousness and our sense of ourselves without effecting a sea change in the cognitive *operations* of individuals or of cultures. Literacy affords access to and reflection upon "decontextualized" information to a greater degree than in nonliterate societies. Thus, although some social historians have suggested that the effects of literacy on more formal, abstract types of thinking are minimal (e.g., Cressy, 1980), it may be argued that literacy affords the modeling and the fine-tuning of these types of thinking processes. If not in affording more generalized cognitive consequences, its role may be in supplying the ideas and data on which our cognitive processes operate. Although literacy demands may be protean, in a more fundamental sense the aesthetic or affective traces often left by the content of the processes of literacy may not be so mutable.

In many nonliterate cultures the knowledge and wisdom out of which fundamental truths are perceived and understood arise through interaction between storyteller and audience. Significantly, for those cultures in whom the stewardship of humankind for the moment resides, the historical analogues of contemporary conflicts and problems are perceived and understood primarily through written texts. Such a society, therefore, would be well-advised to be sensitive not only to the functions that literacy can serve in daily on-the-job or obtaining-a-job life, but also to the functions it can serve in the fundamental sense its members make of their lives. More "pragmatic" orientations towards literacy and its consequences (e.g., Heath, 1982; Venezky, 1982) may argue to a point for an increased emphasis on the "functional" vs. "aesthetic" uses of literacy in the culture. One grows a bit uneasy, however, lest the balance be irretrievably tipped simply because its complement is not currently valued by a particular group or does not lead inevitably to a higher level on the wage or salary scale.

If we as educators do our job well, then children who explore literacy during their beginning school years may attend to and heed a quite special phenomenon described by the writer with whom this coda was begun:

. . . the feeling that resides in the printed word, reaches me through the inner voice. I have supposed, but never found out, that this is the case with all readers—to read as listeners—and with all writers, to write as listeners. . . . My own words, when I am at work on a story, I hear too as they go, in the same voice that I hear when I read in books. When I write and the sound of it comes back to my ears, then I act to make my changes. I have always trusted this voice.

This voice may be as real to most children as it is to Eudora Welty; for the others it may remain simply a metaphor. Regardless, those who explore metalinguistic awareness and beginning literacy have accepted the challenge of reaching the genesis of this voice. Beyond that, the challenge is to ensure that literacy experiences in the contexts of home and school reassure children that they, too, may trust their inner voice.

And what of the role of literacy once the voice is trusted? Though it may not be the penultimate cognitive achievement, literacy nevertheless can be a powerful tool when in the hands of the user. The hand is shaped to accept it because the hand once created it. Regardless of however magnificent or prosaic may be the uses to which it is put, no child should be prevented from grasping that tool. When the child trusts the inner voice, then the grasp is secure.

References

Adams, C. S., & Hiebert, E. H. (1983, April). *Fathers' and mothers' perceptions of their preschool children's print awareness.* Paper presented at the annual meeting of the American Educational Research Association, Montreal.

Albrow, K. H. (1972). *The English writing system: Notes towards a description.* London: Longmans.

Allan, K. K. (1982). The development of young children's metalinguistic understanding of the word. *Journal of Educational Research, 76,* 89–93.

Almy, M. C. (1949). *Children's experiences prior to first grade and success in beginning reading.* New York: Teachers College, Columbia University.

Anderson, A. B., Teale, W. B., & Estrada, E. (1980). Low-income children's preschool literacy experiences: Some naturalistic observations. *The Quarterly Newsletter of the Laboratory of Comparative Human Cognition, 2,* 59–65.

Anderson, L., Evertson, C., & Brophy, J. (1979). An experimental study of teaching effectiveness in first grade reading groups. *Elementary School Journal, 79,* 193–223.

Andrews, J. (1983). *A study of the letter, word, and story reading abilities of forty-five young deaf residential children: A longitudinal perspective.* Unpublished doctoral dissertation, University of Illinois at Urbana-Champaign.

Andrews, J. F., & Mason, J. M. (in press). How do deaf children learn to read: An instructional model of deaf children's emerging reading behaviors. *American Annals of the Deaf.*

Ashcroft, S. C. & Henderson, F. (1963). *Programmed instruction in braille.* Pittsburgh: Stanwix House.

Ashton-Warner, S. (1971). *Teacher.* New York: Bantam Books.

Au, K., & Mason, J. (1981). Social organizational factors in learning to read: The balance of rights hypothesis. *Reading Research Quarterly, 17,* 115–152.

Aulls, M. (1982). *Developing readers in today's elementary school.* Boston: Allyn and Bacon.

Austin, R. G. (1974). *Cognitive clarity and success at the reading task.* Unpublished B.Ed. Honors Paper, Flinders University of South Australia.

Ayers, D., & Downing, J. (1982). Testing children's concepts of reading. *Educational Research, 24,* 277–283.

Ball, S., & Bogatz, G. A. (1970). *The first year of "Sesame Street": An evaluation.* Princeton, NJ: Educational Testing Service.

Barton, D., Miller, R., & Macken, M. A. (1980). Do children treat clusters as one unit or two? *Papers and reports on child language development, 18,* 105–137, Stanford University Department of Linguistics.

Battison, R. (1974). Phonological deletion in American Sign Language. *Sign Language Studies, 5,* 1–19.

Becker, H. J., & Epstein, J. L. (1982). Parent involvement: A survey of teacher practices. *Elementary School Journal, 83,* 85–102.

Beers, J. W., & Henderson, E. H. (1977). A study of developing orthographic concepts among first graders. *Research in the Teaching of English, 11,* 133–148.

Beliakova, G. P. (1971). *Teaching the oldest preschoolers how to segment spoken sentences into words.* Paper presented at the All-Union Scientific Conference on the Education and Instruction of the Oldest Preschoolers in Kindergarten, Minsk, USSR.

Beliakova, G. P. (1973, June). *The segmentation of speech into words by the oldest preschool children.* Paper presented at the Conference of Fostering Independence and Activity in Children of Preschool Age, Moscow, USSR.

Bell, A. A. L. (1982). *Phoneme segmentation in the acquisition of reading.* Unpublished master's thesis, University of Victoria, Victoria, BC, Canada.

Bell, R. Q., & Harper, L. V. (1977). *Child effects on adults.* Hillsdale, NJ: Lawrence Erlbaum Associates.

Berthoud-Papandropoulou, I. (1978). An experimental study of children's ideas about language. In A. Sinclair, R. J. Jarvella, & W. J. M. Levelt (Eds.), *The child's conception of language.* New York: Springer-Verlag.

Berthoud-Papandropoulou, I. (1980). *La reflexion metalinguistique chez l'enfant.* Unpublished doctoral dissertation, University of Geneva, Switzerland.

Betts, E. A. (1946). *Foundations of reading instruction.* New York: American Book Company.

Bezrukova, I. A. (1971). *Using educational speech games in the family to prepare children for school.* Paper presented at the All-Union Scientific Conference on Education and Instruction of the Oldest Preschoolers in Kindergarten, Minsk, USSR.

Bialystok, E., & Ryan, E. B. (1983). Two dimensions in the development of metalinguistic ability. In *Metacognition: Development of metalinguistic and cognitive skills.* Symposium conducted at the Biennial Meeting of the Society for Research in Child Development, Detroit.

Bissex, G. (1982). *GYNS AT WRK: A child learns to write and read.* Cambridge, MA: Harvard University Press.

Bissex, G. (1984). The child as teacher. In H. Goelman, A. A. Oberg, & F. Smith (Eds.), *Awakening to literacy.* Portsmouth, NH: Heinemann Educational Books.

Blank, M. (1973). *Teaching learning in the preschool: A dialogue approach.* Columbus, OH: Merrill.

Blank, M. (1982, December). *Grammatical morphemes: A critical neglected ingredient in reading.* Paper presented at the annual meeting of the National Reading Conference, Clearwater Beach, FL.

Blum, I. H., Taylor, N. E., & Blum R. A. (1979). Methodological considerations and developmental trends in children's awareness of word boundaries. In M. L. Kamil & A. J. Moe (Eds.), *Twenty-eighth Yearbook of the National Reading Conference* (pp. 33–38). Clemson, SC: National Reading Conference.

Bogatz, G. A., & Ball, S. (1971). *The second year of "Sesame Street": A continuing evaluation.* Princeton, NJ: Educational Testing Service.

Bogush, A. M. (1971). *Children's speech preparation for schools in bilingual situations.* Paper presented at the All-Union Scientific Conference of the Education and Instruction of the Oldest Preschoolers in Kindergarten, Minsk, USSR.

Bolinger, D. (Ed.) (1972). *Intonation.* Harmondsworth, England: Penguin Books.

Bormuth, J. R. (1978). Literacy policy and reading and writing instruction. In R. Beach & P. D. Pearson (Eds.), *Perspectives on literacy,* (pp. 13–41). Minneapolis: College of Education, University of Minnesota.

Bornstein, H. (1973). A description of some current sign systems designed to represent English. *American Annals of the Deaf, 118,* 454–463.

Bougere, M. (1969). Selected factors in oral language related to first grade reading achievement. *Reading Research Quarterly, 5,* 31–58.

Bradley, H. (1919). *On the relations between spoken and written language with special reference to English.* London: Oxford University Press.

Bradley, L., & Bryant, P. E. (1983). Categorizing sounds and learning to read—a causal connection. *Nature, 301,* 419–421.

Bright, W. (1960). Linguistic change in some Indian caste dialects. In C. A. Ferguson & J. J. Gumperz (Eds.), *Linguistic diversity in South Asia, 26,* 19–26, *International Journal of American Linguistics.*

Bright, W., & Ramanujan, A. J. (1962). Sociolinguistic variation and language change. In H. G. Lunt (Ed.), *Proceedings of the Ninth International Congress of Linguists.* Cambridge, MA: Mouton & Co.

Brittain, M. M. (1970). Inflectional performance and early reading achievement. *Reading Research Quarterly, 6,* 34–48.

Brittain, W. L. (1979). *Creativity, art, and the young child.* New York: Macmillan.

Brown, A. L. (1977, June). *Knowing when,*

where, and how to remember: A problem of metacognition. (Technical Report No. 47.) Champaign, IL: University of Illinois, Center for the Study of Reading.

Brown, A. L. (1980). Metacognitive development and reading. In R. J. Spiro, B. C. Bruce, & W. F. Brewer (Eds.), *Theoretical issues in reading comprehension* (pp. 453–479). Hillsdale, NJ: Lawrence Erlbaum Associates.

Brown, A. L. (1980, March). *Learning and development: The problems of compatibility, access, and induction.* (Technical Report No. 165.) Champaign, IL: University of Illinois, Center for the Study of Reading.

Brown, A. L., Bransford, J., Ferrara, R., & Campione, J. (1982, June). *Learning, remembering, and understanding.* (Technical Report No. 244). Urbana, IL: University of Illinois, Center for the Study of Reading.

Brown, A. L., & Palincsar, A. S. (1982). Inducing strategic learning from texts by means of informed, self-control training. *Topics in Learning and Learning Disabilities, 2*(1), 1–17.

Brown, R. W. (1973). *A first language: The early stages.* Cambridge, MA: Harvard University Press.

Bruce, D. J. (1964). The analysis of word sounds by young children. *British Journal of Educational Psychology, 34*, 158–170.

Bruner, J. S. (1962). On learning mathematics. In J. S. Bruner (Ed.), *On knowing: Essays for the left hand.* Cambridge, MA: Harvard University Press.

Bruner, J. S. (1971). *The relevance of education.* London: Allen & Unwin.

Brzeinski, J. E. (1964). Beginning reading in Denver. *Reading Teacher, 18*, 16–21.

Buck-Smith, R. (1983). The effectiveness of teaching understandings about reading to first graders. *Reading–Canada–Lecture, 2*, 7–11.

Burchfield, R. W. (1976). *A supplement to the Oxford English Dictionary: Vol. 2 (H-N).* Oxford: Clarendon Press.

Butler, D. (1980a). *Babies need books.* New York: Atheneum.

Butler, D. (1980b). *Cushla and her books.* Boston: The Horn Book.

Byrne, B., & Shea, P. (1979). Semantic and phonetic memory codes in beginning readers. *Memory and Cognition, 7*, 333–338.

Calfee, R. C., Lindamood, P., & Lindamood, C. (1973). Acoustic-phonetic skills and reading—kindergarten through twelfth grade. *Journal of Educational Psychology, 64*, 293–298.

Callaway, B. (1968). Relationship of specific factors to reading. In *Proceedings of the Thirteenth An-*

nual Convention of the International Reading Association, Part 1, Vol. 13. Newark, DE: International Reading Association.

Canney, G., & Winograd, P. (1979). *Schemata for reading and reading comprehension performance* (Technical Report No. 120). Urbana, IL: University of Illinois Center for the Study of Reading. (ERIC Document Reproduction Service No. ED 109 520)

Carey, S. (1977). The child as word learner. In M. Halle, J. Bresnan, & G. Miller (Eds.), *Linguistic theory and psychological reality.* Cambridge, MA: The MIT Press.

Carrier, A. (1984). University of Papua New Guinea. Port Moresby, Papua New Guinea. (Private communication).

Carrillo, L. W. (1973). Developing flexibility of reading rate. In M. Clark & A. Milne (Eds.), *Reading and related skills.* London: Ward Lock.

Carswell, M. D. (1979). *Attainment of selected concepts related to reading by kindergarten and first grade children.* Athens GA: University of Georgia. (ERIC Document Reproduction Service No. ED 177 481)

Cazden, C. B. (1974a). Play and metalinguistic awareness: One dimension of language experience. *Urban Review, 7*, 28–39.

Cazden, C. B. (1974b). Two paradoxes in the acquisition of language structure and function. In K. Connally and J. Bruner (Eds.), *The growth of competence.* New York: Academic Press.

Cazden, C. B. (1975). Play with language and metalinguistic awareness: One dimension of language experience. In C. B. Winsor (Ed.), *Dimensions of language experience.* New York: Agathon.

Cazden, C. B. (1976). *Play with language and metalinguistic awareness.* In J. Bruner, A. Jolly, & K. Sylva (Eds.), *Play—Its role in development and evolution.* New York: Basic Books.

Chall, J. S. (1967). *Learning to read: The great debate.* New York: McGraw-Hill.

Champie, J. (1981). Language development in one preschool child. *American Annals of the Deaf, 126*, 43–48.

Cherry, C. (1980). *On human communication: A review, a survey, and a criticism* (3rd ed.). Cambridge, MA: The MIT Press.

Chomsky, C. (1970). Reading, writing, and phonology. *Harvard Educational Review, 40*, 287–309.

Chomsky, C. (1979). Approaching reading through invented spelling. In L. B. Resnick & P. A. Weaver (Eds.), *Theory and practice of early reading, Vol. 2.* Hillsdale, NJ: Lawrence Erlbaum Associations.

Chomsky, N. (1968). *Language and mind.* New York: Harcourt, Brace, and World.

Chomsky, N. (1970). Phonology and reading. In H. Levin & J. Williams (Eds.), *Basic studies in reading.* New York: Basic Books.

Chomsky, N., & Halle, M. (1968). *The sound pattern of English.* New York: Harper & Row.

Clark, E. V. (1977, May). *Awareness of language: Some evidence from what children say and do.* Paper presented at the discussion meeting of the Child's Conception of Language, Nijmegen, Netherlands.

Clark, E. V. (1978). Awareness of language: Some evidence from what children say and do. In A. Sinclair, R. J. Jarvella, & W. J. M. Levelt (Eds.), *The child's conception of language* (pp. 17–43). Berlin: Springer-Verlag.

Clark, M. M. (1976). *Young fluent readers.* London: Heinemann Educational Books.

Clay, M. M. (1967). The reading behavior of five year old children: A research report. *New Zealand Journal of Educational Studies, 2,* 11–31.

Clay, M. M. (1969). Reading errors and self-correction behavior. *British Journal of Educational Psychology, 39,* 47–56.

Clay, M. M. (1972a). *The early detection of reading difficulties: A diagnostic survey.* Auckland, NZ: Heinemann Educational Books.

Clay, M. M. (1972b). *Sand—Concepts about Print Test.* Auckland, NZ: Heinemann Educational Books.

Clay, M. M. (1975). *What did I write?* Auckland, NZ: Heinemann Educational Books.

Clay, M. M. (1979a). *The early detection of reading difficulties: A diagnostic survey with recovery procedures.* Auckland, NZ: Heinemann Educational Books.

Clay, M. M. (1979b). *Reading: The patterning of complex behavior* (2nd ed.). Auckland, NZ: Heinemann Educational Books.

Clay, M. M. (1979c). *Stones—Concepts About Print Test.* Auckland, NZ: Heinemann Educational Books.

Clay, M. M. (1981). *What did I write? Beginning writing behavior.* Auckland, NZ: Heinemann Educational Books.

Clay, M. M. (1982). *Observing young children: Selected papers.* Portsmouth, NH: Heinemann Educational Books.

Cochran-Smith, M. (1984). *The making of a reader.* Norwood, NJ: Ablex.

Cohen, J. (1977). *Statistical power analysis for the behavioral sciences* (rev. ed.). New York: Academic Press.

Conrad, R. (1979). *The deaf school child: Language and function.* London: Harper & Row.

Cook-Gumperz, J., & Gumperz, J. J. (1981). From oral to written culture: The transition to literacy. In M. F. Whiteman (Ed.), *Variation in writing: Functional and linguistic-cultural differences.* Hillsdale, NJ: Lawrence Erlbaum Associates.

Corcoran, J. (1983). [Editor's introduction to the revised edition.] In A. Tarski, *Logic, Semantics, Metamathematics* (2nd. ed.) (pp. xv–xxvii). Indianapolis: Hackett Publishing Company.

Cressy, D. (1980). *Literacy and the social order: Reading and writing in Tudor and Stuart England.* Cambridge: Cambridge University Press.

Cronbach, L. J. (1977). *Educational psychology* (3rd ed.). New York: Harcourt Brace Jovanovich.

Cunningham, P., Moore, S., Cunningham, J. & Moore, D. (1983). *Reading in elementary classrooms.* New York: Longman.

Curry, R. (1975). Using LEA to teach blind children to read. *Reading Teacher, 29,* 3, 272–279.

Davis, D. C. (1972). Code systems found in initial reading materials: A taxonomy. *Elementary English, 49,* 27–32.

Day, H. D., & Day, K. C. (1979a). *Item and factor analysis of the Concepts About Print Test: Patterns in the Sand.* Unpublished manuscript, Texas Woman's University, Denton, TX.

Day, H. D., & Day, K. C. (1979b, June). *Some relations among the Record of Oral Language, the Concepts About Print, and the Metropolitan Readiness Tests.* Paper presented at the meeting of the IRA/University of Victoria International Reading Research Seminar on Linguistic Awareness and Learning to Read, Victoria, BC, Canada.

Day, H. D., & Day, K. C. (1980a). *The reliability and validity of the Concepts About Print and Record of Oral Language.* Denton, TX: Texas Woman's University. (ERIC Document Reproduction Service No. ED 179 932)

Day, H. D., Day, K. C., & Hollingsworth, S. (1981, October). *Gender differences in the relationship between preschool knowledge of print conventions and other cognitive abilities.* Paper presented at the 12th Annual Meeting of the Rocky Mountain Educational Research Association, Dallas, TX.

Day, H. D., Day, K. C., Hollingsworth, S., McClelland, D. K. (1980b). Sex differences in orthographic linguistic awareness. *Journal of the Illinois Reading Association, 8,* 21–28.

Day, H. D., & Hollingsworth, S. (1983). Gender differences in the relationship of nascent conservation and reading abilities. *Journal of Educational Research, 76,* 347–350.

Day, K. C., & Day, H. D. (1978). *Observations of kindergarten and first grade children's development of oral language concepts about print and reading readiness*. Denton, TX: Texas Woman's University. (ERIC Document Reproduction Service No. ED 176 212)

Day, K. C., & Day, H. D. (1979). Development of kindergarten children's understanding of concepts about print and oral language. In M. L. Kamil & A. H. Moe (Eds.), *Twenty-eighth Yearbook of the National Reading Conference* (pp. 19–22). Clemson, SC: National Reading Conference.

Day, K. C., & Day, H. D. (1984). Kindergarten knowledge of print conventions and later school achievement: A five-year follow-up. *Psychology in the Schools, 21,* 393–396.

Day, K. C., Day, H. D., Spicola, R., & Griffin, M. (1981). The development of orthographic linguistic awareness in kindergarten children and the relationship of this awareness to later reading achievement. *Reading Psychology, 2,* 76–87.

Dean, E. K. (1965). *Significant factors associated with reading achievement in the primary grades: A longitudinal study*. New York: The American Press.

Denny, T. P., & Weintraub, S. (1963). Exploring first graders' concepts of reading. *The Reading Teacher, 16,* 363–365.

Denny, T. P., & Weintraub, S. (1966). First graders' responses to three questions about reading. *Elementary School Journal, 66,* 441–448.

Desberg, P., Elliott, D., & Marsh, G. (1980). American Black English and spelling. In U. Frith (Ed.), *Cognitive processes in spelling*. London: Academic Press.

DeStefano, J. S. (1972). *Some parameters of register in adult and child speech*. Louvain, Belgium: Institute of Applied Linguistics.

de Villiers, J. G., & de Villiers, P. A. (1974). Competence in child judgment: Are children really competent to judge? *Journal of Child Language, 1,* 11–22.

de Villiers, J. G., & de Villiers, P. A. (1978). *Language acquisition*. Cambridge, MA: Harvard University Press.

Dewitz, P., Stammer, J., & Jenson, J. (1980). *The development of linguistic awareness in young children from label reading to word recognition*. Paper presented at the annual meeting of the National Reading Conference, San Diego, CA.

Dillon, D., & Searle, D. (1982). *The role of language in one grade one classroom*. Edmonton, Alberta: University of Alberta.

Doake, D. (1981). *Book experience and emergent reading behavior*. Unpublished doctoral dissertation, University of Alberta, Edmonton, Alberta.

Downing, J. (1969). How children think about reading. *Reading Improvement, 23,* 217–230.

Downing, J. (1970a). Children's conceptions of language in learning to read. *Education Research, 12,* 106–112.

Downing, J. (1970b). The development of linguistic concepts in children's thinking. *Research in the Teaching of English, 4,* 5–19.

Downing, J. (1971–72). Children's developing concepts of spoken and written language. *Journal of Reading Behavior, 4,* 1–19.

Downing, J. (1973a). *Comparative reading*. New York: Macmillan.

Downing, J. (1973b). A summary of evidence related to the cognitive clarity theory of reading. In P. O. Nack (Ed.), *Twenty-second Yearbook of the National Reading Conference: Vol. 1* (pp. 178–184). Boone, NC: National Reading Conference.

Downing, J. (1976). The reading instruction register. *Language Arts, 53,* 762–766.

Downing, J. (1979). *Reading and reasoning*. New York: Springer-Verlag, and Edinburgh: Chambers.

Downing, J. (1983). *Evaluation of the consultancy inservice education project on Reading to Learn at Bundaberg High School and cooperating high schools*. Unpublished report, QINSEC Inservice Education Committee, Brisbane, Queensland, Australia.

Downing, J. (1984a). A source of cognitive confusion for beginning readers: Learning in a second language. *Reading Teacher, 37,* 366–370.

Downing, J. (1984b). Task awareness in the development of reading skill. In J. Downing & R. Valtin (Eds.), *Language awareness and learning to read* (pp. 27–55). New York: Springer-Verlag.

Downing, J. (in preparation). *Foundations of reading instruction in Russia*.

Downing, J., Ayers, D., & Schaefer, B. (1978). Conceptual and perceptual factors in learning to read. *Educational Research, 21,* 11–17.

Downing, J., Ayers, D., & Schaefer, B. (1982). *Linguistic Awareness in Reading Readiness (LARR) Test*. Slough, England: The NFER-Nelson Publishing Company.

Downing, J., & Downing, M. (1983). Metacognitive readiness for literacy learning. *Papua New Guinea Journal of Education, 19,* 17–40.

Downing, J., & Leong, C. K. (1982). *Psychology of reading*. New York: Macmillan.

Downing, J., & Oliver, P. (1973–74). The child's concept of a word. *Reading Research Quarterly, 9,* 568–582.

Downing, J., Ollila, L., & Oliver, P. (1975). Cultural differences in children's concepts of reading and writing. *British Journal of Educational Psychology, 45,* 312–316.

Downing, J., Ollila, L., & Oliver, P. (1977). Concepts of language in children from differing socioeconomic backgrounds. *Journal of Educational Research, 70,* 277–281.

Downing, J., & Valtin, R. (Eds.). (1984). *Language awareness and learning to read.* New York: Springer-Verlag.

Dunn, L. M., & Markwardt, Jr., F. C. (1970). *Peabody Individual Achievement Test.* Circle Pines, MN: American Guidance Service.

Dunn, N. E. (1981). Children's achievement at school entry age as a function of mothers' and fathers' teaching sets. *Elementary School Journal, 81,* 245–253.

Durkin, D. (1966). *Children who read early.* New York: Teachers College Press.

Durkin, D. (1974–75). A six-year study of children who learned to read in school at the age of four. *Reading Research Quarterly, 10,* 9–61.

Dyson, A. H. (1982). The emergence of visible language: Interrelationships between drawing and early writing. *Visible Language, 16*(4), 360–381.

Dyson, A. H. (1983). The role of oral language in early writing processes. *Research in the Teaching of English, 17*(1), 1–30.

Dyson, A. H. (1984). Learning to write/Learning to do school: Emergent writers' interpretations of school literacy tasks. *Research in the Teaching of English, 18,* 233–264.

Dyson, A. H. (in press). Individual differences in emerging writing. In M. Farr (Ed.), *Advances in writing research, Vol. 1.* Norwood, NJ: Ablex.

Edwards, D. L. (1958). Reading from the child's point of view. *Elementary English, 35,* 239–241.

Edwards, D. L. (1962). The relation of concept of reading to intelligence and reading achievement of fifth grade children. *Dissertation Abstracts International, 23,* 1603–1604. (University Microfilms No. 62-04637).

Edwards, P. (Ed). (1972). *The encyclopedia of philosophy: Vol. 5.* New York: Macmillan Publishing Company & The Free Press.

Ehri, L. C. (1975). Word consciousness in readers and prereaders. *Journal of Educational Psychology, 67,* 204–212.

Ehri, L. C. (1976). Word learning in beginning readers and prereaders: Effects of form class and defining contexts. *Journal of Educational Psychology, 68,* 832–842.

Ehri, L. C. (1979). Linguistic insight: Threshold of reading acquisition. In T. G. Waller & G. E. MacKinnon (Eds.), *Reading research: Advances in theory and practice, Vol. 1* (pp. 63–114). New York: Academic Press.

Ehri, L. C. (1980a). The development of orthographic images. In U. Frith (Ed.), *Cognitive processes in spelling.* London: Academic Press.

Ehri, L. C. (1980b). The role of orthographic images in learning printed words. In J. F. Kavanagh & R. L. Venezky (Eds.), *Orthography, reading, and dyslexia.* Baltimore: University Park Press.

Ehri, L. C. (1984). How orthography alters spoken language competencies in children. In J. Downing & R. Valtin (Eds.), *Language awareness and learning to read* (pp. 118–147). New York: Springer-Verlag.

Ehri, L. C. (1985). Effects of printed language acquisition on speech. In D. O. Olson, A. Hildyard, & N. Torrance (Eds.), *The nature and consequences of literacy* (pp. 333–367). Cambridge University Press.

Ehri, L. C., & Wilce, L. S. (1979). The mnemonic value of orthography among beginning readers. *Journal of Educational Psychology, 71,* 26–40.

Ehri, L. C. & Wilce, L. S. (1980). The influence of orthography on readers' conceptualization of the phonemic structure of words. *Applied Psycholinguistics, 1,* 371–385.

Ehri, L. C., & Wilce, L. S. (1982). The salience of silent letters in children's memory for word spellings. *Memory and Cognition, 10,* 155–166.

Elkonin, D. B. (1963). The psychology of mastering the elements of reading. In B. Simon & J. Simon (Eds.), *Educational Psychology in the USSR.* London: Routledge & Kegan Paul.

Elkonin, D. B. (1973). Methods of teaching reading: USSR. In J. Downing (Ed.), *Comparative reading: Cross-national studies of behavior and processes in reading and writing* (pp. 551–578). New York: Macmillan.

Elkonin, D. B. (1982, June). Personal communication to J. Downing.

Evanechko, P., Ollila, L., Downing, J., & Braun, C. (1973). Investigation of the reading readiness domain. *Research in the Teaching of English, 7,* 61–78.

Evans, M. (1975). Children's ability to segment sentences into individual words. In G. McNinch & W. D. Miller (Eds.), *Twenty-fourth Yearbook of the National Reading Conference* (pp. 177–180). Clemson, SC: National Reading Conference.

Evans, M., Taylor, N., & Blum, I. (1979). Children's written language awareness and its relation to reading acquisition. *Journal of Reading Behavior, 11*, 331–341.

Ewoldt, C. (1978). *A psycholinguistic description of selected deaf children reading in sign language.* Unpublished doctoral dissertation, University of Arizona.

Ferreiro, E. (1978). What is written in a written sentence? A developmental answer. *Journal of Education, 160*(4), 24–39.

Ferreiro, E. (1980, May). *The relationship between oral and written language: The children's viewpoints.* Paper presented at the International Reading Association, St. Louis, MO.

Ferreiro, E. (1984). The underlying logic of literacy development. In H. Goelman, A. A. Oberg, & F. Smith (Eds.), *Awakening to literacy.* Portsmouth, NH: Heinemann Educational Books.

Ferreiro, E. (in press). The interplay between information and assimilation in beginning literacy. In W. H. Teale & E. Sulzby (Eds.), *Emergent literacy: Writing and reading.* Norwood, NJ: Ablex Publishing Corporation.

Ferreiro, E., & Gómez, P. M. (1982). Reconsideración del fracaso escolar inicial: Conclusiones generales. *Análisis de las perturbaciones en el proceso de aprendizaje de la lecto-escritura* (Vol. 5). Mexico: SEP-OEA.

Ferreiro, E., & Teberosky, A. (1979). *Los sistemas de escritura en el desarrollo del niño.* Mexico: Siglo Veintiuno Editores, S.A.

Ferreiro, E., & Teberosky, A. (1982). *Literacy before schooling.* Portsmouth, NH: Heinemann Educational Books.

Fitts, P. (1962). Factors in complex skill training. In R. Glaser (Ed.), *Training research and education.* Pittsburgh, PA: University of Pittsburgh Press.

Flavell, J. H. (1976). Metacognitive aspects of problem solving. In L. B. Resnick (Ed.), *The nature of intelligence* (pp. 231–236). Hillsdale, NJ: Lawrence Erlbaum Associates.

Flavell, J. H. (1979). Metacognition and cognitive monitoring: A new area of cognitive-developmental inquiry. *American Psychologist, 34*, 906–911.

Fleming, C. M. (1975). Socioeconomic level and test performance. *British Journal of Educational Psychology, 12*, 74–83.

Flood, J. E. (1975). Predictors of reading achievement: An investigation of selected antecedents to reading. *Dissertation Abstracts International, 36*, 2711A–2712A. (University Microfilms No. 75-25,524)

Flood, J. E. (1977). Parental styles in reading episodes with young children. *Reading Teacher, 30*, 864–867.

Flood, J. E., & Menyuk, P. (1979, November). *Detection of ambiguity and production of paraphrase in written language.* Final report to the National Institute of Education.

Fox, B., & Routh, D. K. (1980). Phonemic analysis and severe reading disability in children. *Journal of Psycholinguistic Research, 9*, 115–119.

Francis, H. (1973). Children's experience of reading and notions of units in language. *British Journal of Educational Psychology, 43*, 17–23.

Francis, H. (1975). *Language in childhood.* London: Paul Elek.

Francis, H. (1977). Reading abilities and disabilities: Children's strategies in learning to read. *British Journal of Educational Psychology, 47*, 117–125.

Franklin, M. B. (1979). Metalinguistic functioning in development. In N. R. Smith & M. B. Franklin (Eds.), *Symbolic functioning in childhood.* Hillsdale, NJ: Lawrence Erlbaum Associates.

French, M. A. (1976). Observations on the Chinese script and the classification of writing systems. In Hass, W. (Ed.) *Writing without letters.* Manchester, England: Manchester University Press.

Fry, M. A., Johnson, C. S. & Muehl, S. (1970). Oral language production in relation to reading achievement among select second graders. In D. J. Bakker & P. Satz (Eds.), *Specific reading disability: Advances in theory and method.* Rotterdam: Rotterdam University Press.

Furth, H. G. (1973). *Thinking without language: Psychosocial approach.* Belmont, CA: Wadsworth Publishing Company.

Garcia de Lorenzo, M. E. (1975). Frontier dialect: A challenge to education. *Reading Teacher, 28*, 653–658.

Gardner, H. (1983). *Frames of mind: The theory of multiple intelligences.* New York: Basic Books.

Gates, A. I., & MacGinitie, W. (1965). *Gates-MacGinitie Reading Tests: Primary I.* New York: Teachers College Press.

Gelb, I. J. (1963). *A study of writing.* Chicago: University of Chicago Press.

Geschwind, N. (1974). Selected papers in language and the brain. In R. S. Cohen and M. W. Wartofsky, *Boston studies in the philosophy of science, 16.* Boston: D. Reidel Publishing Company.

Gibson, E. J., & Levin, H. (1975). *The psychology of reading.* Cambridge, MA: The MIT Press.

Ginsberg, H., & Opper, S. (1969). *Piaget's theory of intellectual development: An introduction.* Englewood Cliffs, NJ: Prentice Hall Inc.

Glass, G. G. (1968). Students' misconceptions concerning their reading. *The Reading Teacher, 21*, 765–768.

Gleitman, H., & Gleitman, L. (1979). Language use and language judgment. In C. J. Fillmore, D. Kempler, & W. S.-Y. Wang (Eds.), *Individual differences in language ability and language behavior* (pp. 103–126). New York: Academic Press.

Gleitman, L. R., Gleitman, H., & Shipley, E. F. (1972). The emergence of the child as grammarian. *Cognition, 1*, 137–163.

Gleitman, L. R., & Rozin, P. (1973). Teaching reading by use of a syllabary. *Reading Research Quarterly, 8*, 447–483.

Goelman, H., Oberg, A., & Smith, F. (Eds.) (1984). *Awakening to literacy*. Portsmouth, NH: Heinemann Educational Books.

Goldman, S. R. (1976). Reading skill and the minimum distance principle: A comparison of listening and reading comprehension. *Journal of Experimental Child Psychology, 22*, 123–142.

Goldsmith, S. (1977, September/October). *Reading disability: Some support for a psycholinguistic base*. Paper presented at the Boston University Conference on Language Development, Boston, MA.

Golomb, C. (1974). *Young children's sculpture and drawing*. Cambridge, MA: Harvard University Press.

Goodacre, E. J. (1971). *Children and learning to read*. London: Routledge & Kegan Paul.

Goodman, K. (1976). Reading: A psycholinguistic guessing game. In H. Singer & R. Ruddell (Eds.), *Theoretical models and processes of reading* (pp. 497–508). Newark, DE: International Reading Association.

Goodman, K., & Goodman, Y. M. (1978). Learning to read is natural. In L. B. Resnik & P. Weaver, *Theory and practice of early reading: Vol. 1* (pp. 137–154). Hillsdale, NJ: Lawrence Erlbaum Associates.

Goodman, Y. M. (1981). Test review: Concepts About Print Test. *The Reading Teacher, 34*, 445–448.

Goodman, Y. M. (1983). Beginning reading development: Strategies and principles. In R. P. Parker & F. A. Davis (Eds.), *Developing literacy: Young children's use of language*. Newark, DE: International Reading Association.

Goodman, Y. M. (1984). The development of initial literacy. In H. Goelman, A. A. Oberg, & F. Smith (Eds.), *Awakening to literacy* (pp. 102–109). Portsmouth, NH: Heinemann.

Goodman, Y. M. & Burke, C. (1980). *Reading strategies: Focus on comprehension*. New York: Holt, Rinehart, and Winston.

Gough, P. B. (1976). One second of reading. In H. Singer & R. B. Ruddell (Eds.), *Theoretical models and processes of reading* (pp. 509–535). Newark, DE: International Reading Association.

Graves, D. H. (1979). Let children show us how to help them write. *Visible Language, 13*, 16–28.

Graves, D. H. (1983). *Writing: Teachers and children at work*. Portsmouth, NH: Heinemann Educational Books.

Green, E. (1970). On the contribution of studies in aphasia to psycholinguistics. *Cortex, 6*, 216–235.

Greenberg, J., Vernon, M., Dubois, J., & McKnight, J. (1982). *The language arts handbook*. Baltimore, MD: University Park Press.

Griswold, E., & Commings, J. (1974). The expressive vocabulary of preschool deaf children. *American Annals of the Deaf, 119*, 16–28.

Grove, M. K. (1983). Clarifying teachers' beliefs about reading. *The Reading Teacher, 37*, 261–268.

Gumperz, J. C., & Gumperz, J. J. (1981). From oral to written culture: The transition to literacy. In M. F. Whiteman (Ed.), *Writing: The nature, development, and teaching of written communication: Vol. 1. Variations in writing: Functional and linguistic-cultural differences*. Hillsdale, NJ: Lawrence Erlbaum Associates.

Gumperz, J. J. (1982). *Discourse strategies: Studies in interactional sociolinguistics: 1*. Cambridge, MA: Cambridge University Press.

Guszak, F. (1967). Teacher questioning and reading. *Reading Teacher, 21*, 228–234.

Haber, L. (1980). Language acquisition and language delay. In R. Shuy & A. Shnuxal (Eds.), *Language use and the uses of language*. Washington, DC: Georgetown University Press.

Hakes, D. T. (1980). *The development of metalinguistic abilities in children*. New York: Springer-Verlag.

Hall, M. (1981). *Teaching reading as a language experience* (3rd Ed.). Columbus: Charles E. Merrill.

Halliday, M. A. K. (1980). *The sociolinguistic constraints of literacy*. Speech given at the Annual Meeting of the National Conference on Research in English, Boston.

Harste, J. C., & Burke, C. L. (1978). Toward a socio-psycholinguistic model of reading. *Viewpoints on Teaching and Learning, 58*(3), 9–34.

Harste, J. C., Burke, C., & Woodward, V. A. (1981). *Children, their language and world: Initial encounters with print*. Final Report. Bloomington, IN: Indiana University, Language Education Department.

Harste, J. C., Burke, C. L., & Woodward, V.

A. (1982). Children's language and world: Initial encounters with print. In J. Langer & M. Smith-Burke (Eds.), *Bridging the gap: Reader meets author.* Newark, DE: International Reading Association.

Harste, J. C., Burke, C. L., & Woodward, V. A. (1983). *The young child as writer-reader, and informant. Final report.* Bloomington, IN: Indiana University, Language Education Department.

Harste, J. C., Woodward, V. A., & Burke, C. L. (1984). *Language stories and literacy lessons.* Portsmouth, NH: Heinemann Educational Books.

Haugen, E. (1951). Directions in modern linguistics. *Language, 27,* 211–222.

Havelock, E. (1982). *The literate revolution in Greece and its cultural consequences.* Princeton, NJ: Princeton University Press.

Heath, S. B. (1982). Protean shapes in literacy events: Ever-shifting oral and literate traditions. In D. Tannen (Ed.), *Spoken and written language: Exploring orality and literacy.* Norwood, NJ: Ablex.

Heath, S. B. (1983). *Ways with words: Language, life, and work in communities and classrooms.* New York: Cambridge University Press.

Helfgott, J. (1976). Phonemic segmentation and blending skills of kindergarten children: Implications for beginning reading acquisition. *Contemporary Educational Psychology, 1*(2), 157–169.

Henderson, E. H. (1976). *The cloth book.* Unpublished manuscript, University of Virginia.

Henderson, E. H. (1981). *Learning to read and spell: The child's knowledge of words.* DeKalb, IL: Northern Illinois University Press.

Henderson, E. H. (1984). *Teaching spelling.* Boston, MA: Houghton Mifflin Company.

Henderson, E. H. & Beers, J. W. (Eds.). (1980). *Developmental and cognitive aspects of learning to spell.* Newark, DE: International Reading Association.

Henderson, J. M. (1976). Learning to read: A case study of a deaf child. *American Annals of the Deaf, 121,* 502–506.

Hess, R. D., Holloway, S., Price, G. G., & Dickson, W. (1979, November). *Family environments and acquisition of reading skills: Toward a more precise analysis.* Paper presented at the Conference on the Family as a Learning Environment, Educational Testing Service, Princeton, NJ.

Hess, R. D., Holloway, S., Price, G., & Dickson, W. P. (1982). Family environments and the acquisition of reading skills. In L. Laosa & I. Siegel (Eds.), *Families as learning environments for children.* New York: Plenum Press.

Hiebert, E. (1978). Preschool children's understanding of written language. *Child Development, 49,* 1231–1234.

Hiebert, E. (1980). The relationship of logical reasoning ability, oral language comprehension, and home experiences to preschool children's print awareness. *Journal of Reading Behavior, 12,* 313–324.

Hiebert, E. (1981). Developmental patterns and interrelationships of preschool children's print awareness. *Reading Research Quarterly, 16,* 236–260.

Hiebert, E. (in press). Knowing about reading before reading: Preschool children's conceptions of reading. *Reading Psychology.*

Hiebert, E. H., & Coffey, M. W. (1981, October). *Learning to read is natural: Do parents agree?* Paper presented at the annual meeting of the College Reading Association, Louisville, KY.

Hiebert, E. H., & Ham, D. (1981, December). *Young children and environmental print.* Paper presented at the annual meeting of the National Reading Conference, Dallas, TX.

Hildreth, G. (1936). Developmental sequences in name writing. *Child Development, 7,* 291–302.

Hirsh-Pasek, K. (1981). *Phonics without sound: Reading acquisition in the congenitally deaf.* Unpublished doctoral dissertation, University of Pennsylvania.

Hohn, W. E., & Ehri, L. C. (1983). Do alphabet letters help prereaders acquire phonemic segmentation skill? *Journal of Educational Psychology, 75,* 752–762.

Holdaway, D. (1979). *The foundations of literacy.* Sydney: Ashton Scholastic.

Holdaway, D. (1983). *Stability and change in literacy learning.* London, Ontario: University of Western Ontario in association with Heinemann Educational Books.

Holden, M. H. (1972). Metalinguistic performance and cognitive development in children five to seven. *Dissertation Abstracts International, 33,* 2791B–2792B. (University Microfilms No. 72-31, 214)

Holden, M. H. (1977). Word awareness, reading, and development. *Perceptual and Motor Skills, 44,* 203–206.

Holden, M. H., & MacGinitie, W. H. (1972). Children's conceptions of word boundaries in speech and print. *Journal of Educational Psychology, 63,* 551–557.

Holden, M. H., & MacGinitie, W. H. (1973). *Metalinguistic ability and cognitive performance in children from five to seven.* Paper presented at the meeting of the American Educational Research Association, New Orleans. (ERIC Document Reproduction Service No. ED 078 436)

Hollingsworth, S. (1977). An investigation of

the cognitive, environmental, and personal differences in the reading performance of preschool children. (Doctoral dissertation, The Ohio State University, 1977). *Dissertation Abstracts International, 38,* 4667A.

Holmes, J. A. (1970). The substrata-factor theory of reading: Some experimental evidence. In H. Singer & R. B. Ruddell (Eds.), *Theoretical models and processes of reading.* Newark, DE: International Reading Association.

Hoole, C. (1966). *A new discovery of the old art of teaching school.* Menston, Yorkshire, England: Scolar Press Ltd.

Horne, M. D., Powers, J. E., & Mahabub, P. (1983). Reader and nonreader's conception of the spoken word. *Contemporary Educational Psychology, 8,* 403–418.

Huey, E. B. (1908). *Psychology and pedagogy of teaching reading.* New York: The Macmillan Publishing Company.

Hutson, B. A. (1979). *Macro-theory and microtheory in the study of concepts about language and reading.* Paper presented at the University of Victoria/IRA Research Seminar on Linguistic Awareness and Learning to Read, Victoria, BC, Canada.

Huttenlocher, J. (1964). Children's language: Word-phrase relationship. *Science, 143,* 264–265.

Hymes, D. H. (1972). Models of the interactions of language and social life. In J. J. Gumperz & D. Hymes (Eds.), *Directions in sociolinguistics.* New York: Holt, Rinehart, & Winston.

Invernizzi, M. (1984). *A cross-sectional analysis of children's recognition and recall of word elements.* Unpublished doctoral dissertation, University of Virginia, Charlottesville, VA.

Istomina, Z. M. (1975). The development of voluntary memory in preschool-age children. *Soviet Psychology, 13,* 5–64.

Jakimik, J., Cole, R. A., & Rudnicky, A. I. (1980, November). *The influence of spelling on speech perception.* Paper presented at the annual meeting of the Psychonomic Society, St. Louis, MO.

Jakobson, R. (1980). Metalanguage as a linguistic problem. In R. Jakobson, *The framework of language* (pp. 81–92). Ann Arbor, Michigan: Michigan Studies in the Humanities, Horace H. Rackum School of Graduate Studies.

Jensen, H. (1970). *Sign, symbol, and script: An account of man's efforts to write.* London: Allen & Unwin.

Johns, J. (1970). Reading: A view from the child. *The Reading Teacher, 23,* 647–648.

Johns, J. (1972). Children's concepts of reading and their reading achievements. *Journal of Reading Behavior, 4,* 56–57.

Johns, J. (1974). Concepts of reading among good and poor readers. *Education, 95,* 58–60.

Johns, J. (1977). Children's conceptions of a spoken word: A developmental study. *Reading World, 16,* 248–257.

Johns, J. (1980a). First graders' concepts about print. *Reading Research Quarterly, 15,* 529–549.

Johns, J. (1980b). The growth of children's knowledge about spoken words. *Reading Psychology, 1,* 103–110.

Johns, J. (1982). Does our language of instruction confuse beginning readers? *Reading Psychology, 3,* 37–41.

Johns, J. (1984). Students' perceptions of reading: Insights from research and pedagogical implications. In J. Downing & R. Valtin (Eds.), *Language awareness and learning to read* (pp. 57–77). New York: Springer-Verlag.

Johns, J. L., & Ellis, D. W. (1976). Reading: Children tell it like it is. *Reading World, 16,* 115–128.

Johns, J. L., & Johns, A. L. (1971). How do children in the elementary school view the reading process? *The Michigan Reading Journal, 5,* 44–53.

Jordan, I., Gustason, G., & Rosen, R. (1979). An update on communication trends at programs for the deaf. *American Annals of the Deaf, 124,* 350–357.

Karpova, S. N. (1966). The preschooler's realization of the lexical structure of speech. In F. Smith & G. Miller (Eds.), *The genesis of language: A psycholinguistic approach.* Cambridge, MA: The MIT Press.

Karpova, S. N. (1977). *The realization of the verbal composition of speech by preschool children.* The Hague: Mouton.

Kawai, Y. (1966). Physical complexity of the Chinese letter and learning to read it. *Japanese Journal of Educational Psychology, 14,* 129–138, 188.

Kederis, C. J., Siems, J. R., & Haynes, R. L. (1965). A frequency count of the symbology of English braille grade 2, American usage. *International Journal for the Education of the Blind, 15,* 38–46.

Kellogg, R. (1970). *Analyzing children's art.* Palo Alto, CA: National Press Books.

Kerek, A. (1976). The phonological relevance of spelling pronunciation. *Visible Language, 10,* 323–338.

Kingston, A. J., Weaver, W. W., & Figa, L. E. (1972). Experiments in children's perceptions of word and word boundaries. In F. P. Green (Ed.), *Twenty-first Yearbook of the National Reading Conference: Vol. 2* (pp. 91–99). Milwaukee, WI: National Reading Conference.

Kinsbourne, M. (1976). Looking and listening

strategies and beginning reading. In J. Guthrie (Ed.), *Aspects of reading acquisition*. Baltimore: Johns Hopkins Press.

Klima, E., & Bellugi, U. (1979). *The signs of language*. Cambridge, MA: Harvard University Press.

Konstandian, N. A. (1971). *Occurrences of lexical interference in a bilingual environment*. Paper presented at the All-Union Scientific Conference on Education and Instruction of the Oldest Preschoolers in Kindergarten, Minsk, USSR.

Kontos, S., & Huba, M. (1983, April). *The development and function of print awareness*. Paper presented at the biennial meeting of the Society for Research in Child Development, Detroit, MI.

Kugelmass, J. A. (1951). *Louis Braille: Windows for the blind*. New York: Julain Messner, Inc.

Lado, R. (1957). *Linguistics across cultures*. Ann Arbor, MI: University of Michigan Press.

Lansdown, R. (1974). *Reading: Teaching and learning*. London: Pitman.

Laosa, L., & Siegal, I. (Eds.). (1982). *Families as learning environments for children*. New York: Plenum Press.

Larson, M. L., & Davis, P. M. (1981). *Bilingual education: An experience in Peruvial Amazonia*. Washington, DC: Center for Applied Linguistics, & Dallas, TX: Summer Institute of Linguistics.

Lavine, L. O. (1977). Differentiation of letter-like forms in prereading children. *Developmental Psychology, 13*, 89–94.

Lenneberg, E. (1967). *Biological foundations of language*. New York: John Wiley & Sons.

Leong, C. K. (1970). *An experimental study of the vocabulary of written Chinese among primary III children in Hong Kong*. Paper presented at the annual convention of the International Reading Association, Anaheim, CA.

Leong, C. K., & Haines, C. F. (1978). Beginning readers' analysis of words and sentences. *Journal of Reading Behavior, 10*, 393–407.

Lerner, R. M., & Spanier, G. B. (1978). A dynamic interactional view of the child and family development. In R. M. Lerner & G. B. Spanier (Eds.), *Child influences on marital and family interaction*. New York: Academic Press.

Lerner de Zunino, D. (1982, November). *Una propuesta didáctica centrada en el proceso espontáneo de construcción de la lengua escrita*. Paper presented by members of the Venezuelan Institute of Audio-Linguistics at the First National Meeting on Reading, Caracas, Venezuela.

Leroy-Boussion, A. (1975). Une habilité auditivo-phonetique necessaire pour apprendre a lire: La fusion syllabique. Nouvelle étude genetique entre 5 et 8 ans. *Enfance, 2*, 164–190.

Leroy-Boussion, A., & Martinez, F. (1974). Un pre-requis auditivo-phonetique pour l'apprentissage du langage ecrit: L'analyse syllabique. Etude genetique longitudinale entre 5 et 8 ans. *Enfance, 1–2*, 111–130.

Lewis, M., & Rosenblum, L. A. (Eds.). (1974). *The effect of the infant on its caregiver*. New York: Wiley.

Liberman, A. M., Cooper, F. S., Shankweiler, D., & Studdert-Kennedy, M. (1967). Perception of the speech code. *Psychological Review, 74*, 431–461.

Liberman, I. Y. (1973). Segmentation of the spoken word. *Bulletin of the Orton Society, 23*, 65–77.

Liberman, I. Y., & Shankweiler, D. (1979). Speech, the alphabet and teaching to read. In L. Resnick & P. Weaver (Eds.), *Theory and practice of early reading, Vol. 2*. Hillsdale, NJ: Lawrence Erlbaum Associates.

Liberman, I. Y., Shankweiler, D., Fischer, F. W., & Carter, B. (1974). Explicit syllable and phoneme segmentation in the young child. *Journal of Experimental Child Psychology, 18*, 201–212.

Liberman, I., Shankweiler, D., Liberman, A., Fowler, C., & Fischer, F. (1977). Phonetic segmentation and recoding in the beginning reader. In A. Reber & D. Scarborough (Eds.), *Toward a psychology of reading: The proceedings of the CUNY conferences*. Hillsdale, NJ: Lawrence Erlbaum Associates.

Lieberman, P. (1975). *On the origins of language: An introduction to the evolution of human speech*. New York: Macmillan Publishing Company.

Lindamood, C. H., & Lindamood, P. C. (1971). *Lindamood Auditory Conceptualization Test*. Boston, MA: Teaching Resources Corporation.

Lindamood, C. H., & Lindamood, P. C. (1975). *The A.D.D. Program: Auditory Discrimination in Depth*. Boston, MA: Teaching Resources Corporation.

Ling, D. (1976). *Speech and the hearing-impaired child: Theory and practice*. Washington, DC: Alexander Graham Bell Association for the Deaf.

Lowenfeld, B., Abel, G. L., & Hatlen, P. H. (1969). *Blind children learn to read*. Springfield, IL: Charles C. Thomas Books.

Lundberg, I., & Torneus, M. (1978). Nonreaders' awareness of the basic relationship between spoken and written words. *Journal of Experimental Child Psychology, 25*, 404–412.

Lundberg, I., Wall, S., & Olofsson, A. (1980). Reading and spelling skills in the first school years predicted from phonemic awareness skills in kindergarten. *Scandinavian Journal of Psychology, 21*, 159–173.

Luria, A. R. (1946). On the pathology of grammatical operations. *Izvestija APN RSFSR*, No. 17.

Luria, A. R. (1976). *Cognitive development: Its cultural and social foundations*. Cambridge, MA: Harvard University Press.

Luukkonen, J. (1979). *Linguistic awareness in reading readiness among Finnish preschool children*. Paper presented at the IRA Seminar on Linguistic Awareness and Learning to Read, University of Victoria, BC, Canada.

Luukkonen, J. (1984, May). *Longitudinal study of the predictive validity of linguistic awareness testing in Finnish kindergartens*. Paper presented at the IRA Annual Convention, Atlanta, GA.

Macnamara, J. (1966). *Bilingualism and primary education*. Edinburgh: Edinburgh University Press.

Madden, R., Gardner, E. F., Rudman, H. C., Karlsen, B., & Merwin, J. C. (1972). *Stanford Achievement Test: Primary Level I*. New York: Harcourt Brace Jovanovich.

Makita, K. (1968). The rarity of reading disability in Japanese children. *American Journal of Orthopsychiatry, 38*, 599–614.

Maksakov, A. I. (1971). *The sound analysis of a word in children with articulation defects*. Paper presented at the All-Union Scientific Conference on the Education and Instruction of the Oldest Preschoolers in Kindergarten, Minsk, USSR.

Malinowski, B. (1965). *Coral gardens and their magic.* (Vol. 2). Bloomington: Indiana University Press.

Mandler, J. M., & DeForest, M. (1979). Is there more than one way to read a story? *Child Development, 50*, 886–889.

Mandler, J. M., & Johnson, M. S. (1977). Remembrance of things parsed: Story structure and recall. *Cognitive Psychology, 9*, 111–151.

Mangold, S. S. (1978). Tactile perception and braille letter recognition: Effects of developmental teaching. *Journal of Visual Impairment and Blindness, 72*, 259–266.

Mann, V. A., Liberman, I. Y., & Shankweiler, D. (1980). Children's memory for sentences and word strings in relation to reading ability. *Memory and Cognition, 8*, 329–335.

Mark, L. S., Shankweiler, D., Liberman, I. Y., & Fowler, C. A. (1977). Phonetic recoding and reading difficulty in beginning readers. *Memory and Cognition, 5*(6), 623–629.

Markman, E. M. (1976). Children's difficulty with word referent differentiation. *Child Development, 47*, 742–749.

Marshack, A. (1972). *The roots of civilization: The cognitive beginning of man's first art, symbol, and notation.* New York: McGraw-Hill.

Marshall, J. C., & Morton, J. (1978). On the mechanics of Emma. In A. Sinclair, R. J. Jarvella, & W. J. M. Levelt (Eds.), *The child's conception of language* (pp. 225–239). Berlin: Springer-Verlag.

Martin, B., & Brogan, P. (1972). *Sounds of language*. New York: Holt, Rinehart, & Winston.

Mason, G. E. (1967). Preschoolers' concepts of reading. *The Reading Teacher, 21*, 130–132.

Mason, J. M. (1980). When do children begin to read: An exploration of four-year-old children's letter and word reading competencies. *Reading Research Quarterly, 15*, 203–227.

Mason, J. (1981). *Prereading: A developmental perspective* (Technical Report No. 198). Urbana, IL: University of Illinois, Center for the Study of Reading.

Mason, J. (1982, December). *Acquisition of knowledge about reading: The preschool period* (Technical Report No. 267). Champaign, IL: University of Illinois, Center for the Study of Reading.

Mason, J., & Au, K. (1984). Learning social context characteristics in prereading lessons. In J. Flood (Ed.), *Promoting reading comprehension.* Newark, DE: International Reading Association.

Mason, J., & McCormick, C. (1981). *An investigation of prereading instruction: A developmental perspective* (Technical Report No. 224). Urbana, IL: University of Illinois, Center for the Study of Reading.

Mason, J. M., & McCormick, C. (1983, April). *Intervention procedures for increasing preschool children's interest in and knowledge about reading.* Paper presented at the annual meeting of the American Educational Research Association, Montreal.

Mason, J. M. & McCormick, C. (1985). *Little Books*. Charleston IL: Pintsized Prints.

Masonheimer, P. (1983, April). *Information used by preschool readers and nonreaders.* Paper presented at the biennial meeting of the Society for Research in Child Development, Detroit, MI.

Matluck, J. H., & Mace-Matluck, B. J. (1983, May). Metalinguistic skills and reading achievement. In *The development of school-related language and reading skills by Spanish-English bilingual children.* Symposium conducted at the 28th Annual Convention of the International Reading Association, Anaheim, CA.

Mattingly, I. G. (1972). Reading, the linguistic process, and linguistic awareness. In J. F. Kavanaugh & I. G. Mattingly (Eds.), *Language by ear and by eye: The relationships between speech and reading* (pp. 133–148). Cambridge, MA: The MIT Press.

Mattingly, I. G. (1979). The psycholinguistic basis for linguistic awareness. In M. L. Kamil & A. J. Moe (Eds.), *Twenty-eighth Yearbook of the National Reading Conference* (pp. 274–278). Clemson, SC: National Reading Conference.

Mattingly, I. G. (1984). Reading, linguistic awareness, and language acquisition. In J. Downing & R. Valtin (Eds.), *Language awareness and learning to read* (pp. 9–25). New York: Springer-Verlag.

Mayfield, M. I. (1983). Code systems instruction and kindergarten children's perceptions of the nature and purpose of reading. *Journal of Educational Research, 76*, 161–168.

McConkie, G. W. (1959). *The perceptions of a selected group of kindergarten children concerning reading.* Unpublished doctoral dissertation, Teacher's College, Columbia University.

McCormick, C., & Mason, J. (1981). What happens to kindergarten children's knowledge about reading after a summer vacation? *The Reading Teacher, 35*, 164–172.

McCormick, C., & Mason, J. (in press). Intervention procedures for increasing preschool children's interest in and knowledge about reading. In W. Teale & E. Sulzby (Eds.), *Emergent literacy: Writing and reading.* New York: Ablex.

McDonell, G. M., & Osburn, E. B. (1978). New thoughts about reading readiness. *Language Arts, 55*, 26–29.

McGee, L. M., Charlesworth, R., Cheek, M., & Cheek, E. (1982). Metalinguistic knowledge: Another look at beginning reading. *Childhood Education, 59*, 123–127.

McNinch, G. (1974). Awareness of aural and visual word boundary within a sample of first graders. *Perceptual and Motor Skills, 38*, 1127–1134.

Meadow, K. (1968). Early manual communication in relation to the deaf child's intellectual, social, and communicative functioning. *American Annals of the Deaf, 113*, 29–41.

Meares, O. (1980). Figure/ground, brightness contrast, and reading disabilities. *Visible Language, 14*, 13–29.

Mehan, H. (1979). *Learning lessons.* Cambridge, MA: Harvard University Press.

Meltzer, N. S., & Herse, R. (1969). The boundaries of written words as seen by first graders. *Journal of Reading Behavior, 1*, 3–13.

Mickish, V. (1974). Children's perceptions of written word boundaries. *Journal of Reading Behavior, 6*, 19–22.

Miller, W. H. (1969). Home prereading experiences and first grade reading achievement. *Reading Teacher, 22*, 641–645.

Miller, W. H. (1970). An examination of children's daily schedules in three social classes and their relation to first grade reading achievement. *California Journal of Education Research, 21*, 100–110.

Modiano, N. (1973). *Indian education in the Chiapas Highlands.* New York: Holt, Rinehart & Winston.

Mohanty, A. K., & Babu, N. (1983). Bilingualism and metalinguistic ability among Kond tribals in Orissa, India. *The Journal of Social Psychology, 212*, 15–22.

Mommers, M. I. C. *Linguistisch bewustzijn en leren lezen.* Unpublished manuscript, Instituut voor Oonderswijskunde, Nijmegen, Holland.

Montgomery County Public Schools. (1982). *Program of Studies, English Language Arts K-8 Part I, Reading and Listening.* Rockford, MD: Author.

Moore, A. E., Betzner, J., & Lewis, M. (1927-28). *The classroom teacher: Vol. 3, Primary language and literature for children.* Chicago: The Classroom Teacher.

Moore, D. W. (1984, May). *Acquiring the initial concepts about print in Papua, New Guinea community schools.* Paper presented in the University of Papua, New Guinea Education Faculty Research Seminar Series, Papua, New Guinea.

Morais, J., Cary, L., Alegria, J., & Bertelson, P. (1979). Does awareness of speech as a sequence of phones arise spontaneously? *Cognition, 7*, 323–331.

Morris, D. (1980). Beginning readers' concept of word and its relationship to phoneme segmentation ability. *Dissertation Abstracts International, 41*, 3760A–4197A. (University Microfilms No. 8026632)

Morris, D. (1983). Concept of word and phoneme awareness in the beginning reader. *Research in the Teaching of English, 17* (4), 359–373.

Morris, D., & Henderson, E. (1981). Assessing the beginning reader's "concept of a word." *Reading World, 20*, 279–285.

Morrow, L. (1984). *The effects of story structure and traditional questioning strategies on comprehension.* Paper presented at the American Educational Research Association Convention, New Orleans, LA.

Myers, M., II, & Paris, S. G. (1978). Children's metacognitive knowledge about reading. *Journal of Educational Psychology, 70*, 680–690.

Ninio, A. (1980). Picture-book reading in mother-infant dyads belonging to two subgroups in Israel. *Child Development, 51*, 587–590.

Ninio, A., & Bruner, J. (1978). The achievement and antecedents of labeling. *Journal of Child Language, 5*, 5–15.

Odam, O., Blanton, R., & McIntyre, C. (1970). Coding medium and word recall by deaf and hearing subjects. *Journal of Speech and Hearing Research, 13,* 54–58.

Oliver, M. E. (1975). The development of language concepts of preprimary Indian children. *Language Arts, 52,* 865–869.

Ollila, L., Johnson, T., & Downing, J. (1974). Adapting Russian methods of auditory discrimination training for English. *Elementary English, 51,* 1134–1141, 1145.

Olson, D. R. (1977). From utterance to text: The bias of language in speech and writing. *Harvard Educational Review, 17*(3), 257–281.

Olson, D. R. (Ed.). (1981). *The social foundations of language and thought: Essays in honor of Jerome S. Bruner.* New York: W. W. Norton & Company.

Olson, D. R. (1982). What is said and what is meant in speech and writing. *Visible Language, 16,* 151–161.

Olson, D. R. (1984). See! Jumping! Some social antecedents to literacy. In H. Goelman, A. Oberg, & F. Smith (Eds.), *Awakening to literacy* (pp. 185–192). Portsmouth, NH: Heinemann Educational Books.

Olson, D. R., & Hildyard, A. (1981). Assent and compliance in children's language. In W. P. Dickson (Ed.), *Children's oral communication styles.* New York: Academic Press.

Olson, R. K., Kliegel, R., Davidson, B. J., & Foltz, G. (1984). Individual and developmental differences in reading disability. In T. G. Waller (Ed.), *Reading research: Advances in theory and practice.* New York: Academic Press.

Ong, W. J. (1977). *Interfaces of the word.* Ithaca, NY: Cornell University Press.

Orlova, A. M. (1965). Developing syntactical concepts in primary school students. In N. S. Rozhdestvensky (Ed.), *The foundation of the methodology of the initial teaching of the Russian language.* Moscow: Prosveshchenie.

Osterberg, T. (1961). *Bilingualism and the first school language.* Umea, Sweden: Vasterbottens Tryckeri, AB.

Otis, A. S., & Lennon, R. T. (1979). *Otis-Lennon School Ability Test: Primary I.* New York: Harcourt Brace Jovanovich.

Otto, B. (1982). Tracking emergent reading behaviors through storybook reenactments. (ERIC Document Reproduction Service No. ED 229 722)

Otto, B., & Sulzby, E. (1981). *Judging the emergent reading abilities of kindergarten children.* Washington, DC: National Institute of Education.

(ERIC Document Reproduction Service No. ED 216 332)

Paivio, A. (1971). *Imagery and verbal processes.* New York: Holt, Rinehart, and Winston.

Paivio, A., & Begg, I. (1971a). Imagery and comprehension latencies as a function of sentence concreteness and structure. *Perception and Psychophysics, 10,* 408–412.

Paivio, A., & Begg, I. (1971b). Imagery and associative overlap in short-term memory. *Journal of Experimental Psychology, 89,* 40–45.

Palincsar, A. S. (1984). The quest for meaning from expository text: A teacher-guided journey. In G. Duffy, L. Roehler, & J. Mason (Eds.), *Comprehension instruction: Perspectives and suggestions.* New York: Longman, Inc.

Papandropoulou, I., & Sinclair, H. (1974). What is a word? Experimental study of children's ideas on grammar. *Human Development, 17,* 241–258.

Papert, S. (1980). *Mindstorms: Children, computers, and powerful ideas.* New York: Basic Books.

Paris, S. G. (1983). Becoming a strategic reader. *Contemporary Educational Psychology, 8,* 293–316.

Paris, S. G., & Jacobs, J. E. (1984). The benefits of informed instruction for children's reading awareness and comprehension skills. *Child Development, 55,* 2083–2093.

Park, B. (1982). The big book trend: A discussion with Don Holdaway. *Language Arts, 59,* 815–821.

Pei, M. A., & Gaynor, F. (1954). *A dictionary of linguistics.* New York: Philosophical Library.

Perfetti, C. A., & Lesgold, A. M. (1979). Coding and comprehension in skilled reading and implications for reading instruction. In L. B. Resnick & P. A. Weaver (Eds.), *Theory and practice of early reading: Vol. 1.* Hillsdale, NJ: Lawrence Erlbaum Associates.

Piaget, J. (1974). *The language and thought of the child.* New York: New American Library. (Originally published 1924).

Piatelli-Palmarini, M. (Ed.) (1980). *Language and learning: The debate between Jean Piaget and Noam Chomsky.* Cambridge, MA: Harvard University Press.

Pike, R. (1977, April). *Linguistic structure, memory, and reading.* Paper presented at the annual meeting of the American Educational Research Association, New York.

Plessas, G., & Oakes, C. (1964). Prereading experiences of selected early readers. *The Reading Teacher, 17,* 241–243.

Poizner, H., Newkirk, D., Bellugi, V., & Klima, E. S. (1981). Representation of inflected signs from American sign language in short-term memory. *Memory and Cognition, 9,* 121–131.

Postman, N., & Weingartner, C. (1966). Beyond linguistics. In N. Postman & C. Weingartner, *Linguistics: A revolution in teaching.* New York: Delacorte Press, 1966.

Prescott, G. A., Balow, I. H., Hogan, T. P., & Farr, R. C. (1971). *Metropolitan Achievement Tests.* New York: Harcourt Brace Jovanovich.

Rapin, I., & Allen, D. (1982). Progress toward a nosology of developmental dysphasia. In M. Yfuku-yama (Ed.), *Child Neurology.* Princeton, NJ: Excerpta Medica.

Read, C. (1971). Preschool children's knowledge of English phonology. *Harvard Educational Review, 41,* 1–34.

Read, C. (1973). Children's judgments of phonetic similarities in relation to English spelling. *Language Learning, 23,* 17–38.

Read, C. (1975a). *Children's categorization of speech sounds in English.* Urbana, IL: National Council of Teachers of English.

Read, C. (1975b). Lessons to be learned from preschool orthographers. In E. Lenneberg & E. Lenneberg (Eds.), *Foundations of language development: A multidisciplinary approach: Vol. 2.* New York: Academic Press.

Read, C. (1978). Children's awareness of language, with emphasis on sound systems. In A. Sinclair, R. J. Jarvella, & W. J. M. Levelt (Eds.), *The child's conception of language* (pp. 65–82). New York: Springer-Verlag.

Reder, S. (1981). The written and the spoken word: Influence of Vai literacy on Vai Speech. In S. Scribner & M. Cole, *The psychology of literacy* (pp. 187–199). Cambridge, MA: Harvard University Press.

Reid, D. K., Hresko, W. P., & Hammill, D. D. (1981). *TERA: The Test of Early Reading Ability.* Pro-ed (Services for Professional Educators), 333 Perry Brooks Building, Austin, TX.

Reid, J. F. (1966). Learning to think about reading. *Educational Research, 9,* 56–62.

Robinson, H. A., Lazarus, A., & Costello, G. (1983). Beginning readers' concept of reading: An international survey. *Reading-Canada-Lecture, 2,* 12–17.

Rosner, J. (1972). *Phonetic analysis training and beginning reading skills.* Pittsburgh, PA: University of Pittsburgh Learning Research and Development Center.

Rowe, D. W. (1982). *The effect of two instruc-tional strategies using predictable texts on kindergartners' concept of word.* Unpublished master's thesis, Wake Forest University.

Rowe, D. W., & Cunningham, P. M. (1983). The effect of two instructional strategies on kindergarteners' concept of word. In J. A. Niles & L. A. Harris (Eds.), *Thirty-second yearbook of the National Reading Conference* (pp. 226–230). Rochester, NY: The National Reading Conference.

Rozin, P., Bressman, B., & Taft, M. (1974). Do children understand the basic relationship between speech and writing? The mow-motorcycle test. *Journal of Reading Behavior, 6,* 327–334.

Rozin, P., & Gleitman, L. R. (1977). The structure and acquisition of reading II: The reading process and the acquisition of the alphabetic principle. In A. S. Reber & D. Scarborough (Eds.), *Toward a psychology of reading* (pp. 55–141). Hillsdale, NJ: Lawrence Erlbaum Associates.

Rozin, P., Poritsky, S., & Sotsky, R. (1971). American children with reading problems can easily learn to read English represented by Chinese characters. *Science, 171,* 1264–1267.

Rubin, A. (1980). A theoretical taxonomy of the differences between oral and written language. In R. J. Spiro, B. C. Bruce, & W. F. Brewer (Eds.), *Theoretical issues in reading comprehension.* Hillsdale, NJ: Lawrence Erlbaum Associates.

Russell, W., Quigley, S., & Power, D. (1976). *Linguistics and deaf children.* Washington, DC: Alexander Graham Bell Association.

Ryan, E. B. (1980). Metalinguistic development and reading. In F. B. Murray (Ed.), *Language awareness and reading* (pp. 38–59). Newark, DE: International Reading Association.

Ryan, E. B., & Ledger, G. W. (1984). Learning to attend to sentence structure: Links between metalinguistic development and reading. In J. Downing and R. Valtin (Eds.), *Language awareness and learning to read* (pp. 149–171). NY: Springer-Verlag.

Ryan, E. B., McNamara, S. R., & Kenney, M. (1977). Linguistic awareness and reading performance among beginning readers. *Journal of Reading Behavior, 9,* 399–400.

Sales, B. D., Haber, R. N., & Cole, R. A. (1969). Mechanisms of aural encoding. IV: Hearsee, say-write interactions for vowels. *Perception and Psychophysics, 6,* 385–390.

Samuels, S. J. (1971). Letter name versus letter sound knowledge in learning to read. *Reading Teacher, 24,* 604–608.

Sanders, T. S. (1981). Three first graders' concept of word and concepts about the language of literacy instruction. In M. L. Kamil & A. J. Moe (Eds.), *Thirtieth Yearbook of the National Reading Conference* (pp. 266–272). Clemson, SC: National Reading Conference.

Schein, J., & Delk, M. (1974). *Deaf population in the U.S.* Silver Spring, MD: National Association of the Deaf.

Schieffelin, B. B. & Cochran-Smith, M. (1984). Learning to read culturally: Literacy before schooling. In H. Goelman, A. A. Oberg, & F. Smith (Eds.), *Awakening to literacy* (pp. 3–23). Portsmouth, NH: Heinemann Educational Books.

Schlesinger, H., & Meadow, K. (1972). *Sound and sign: Childhood deafness and mental health.* Berkeley: University of California Press.

Scollon, R., & Scollon, S. B. K. (1981). *Narrative, literacy, and face in interethnic communication.* Norwood, NJ: Ablex Publishing Corporation.

Scott, E.P. (1982). *Your visually impaired student: A guide for teachers.* Baltimore: University Park Press.

Scribner, S., & Cole, M. (1973). Cognitive consequences of formal and informal education. *Science, 18,* 553–559.

Scribner, S., & Cole, M. (1981). *The psychology of literacy.* Cambridge, MA: Harvard University Press.

Seidenberg, M.S., & Tanenhaus, M.K. (1979). Orthographic effects on rhyme monitoring. *Journal of Experimental Psychology: Human Learning and Memory, 5,* 546–554.

Shatz, M. (1984, March). *Songs without music: The consequences of processing constraints on the oral and written narratives of young children.* Paper presented at the Twenty-fifth Annual Georgetown University Round Table on Languages and Linguistics.

Sheldon, W. D., & Carrillo, L. (1952). Relation of parents, home, and certain developmental characteristics to children's reading ability: II. *Elementary School Journal, 53,* 517–521.

Shinn, M. (1978). Father absence and children's cognitive development. *Psychological Bulletin, 8,* 295–324.

Siegel, I. (1982). The relationship between parental distancing strategies and the child's cognitive behavior. In L. Laosa & I. Siegel (Eds.), *Families as learning environments for children.* New York: Plenum Press.

Siegel, L., & Ryan, E. B. (1984). Reading disability as a language disorder. *Remedial and Special Education, 5,* 28–33.

Silvaroli, N. J. (1976). *Classroom Reading Inventory.* New York: William C. Brown Company.

Simons, H. D. (1975). Transformational phon-

ology and reading acquisition. *Journal of Reading Behavior, 7,* 49–59.

Sinclair, A. (1980). Thinking about language: An interview study of children aged three to eight. *International Journal of Psycholinguistics, 4–7,* 19–40.

Sinclair, A., & Berthoud-Papandropoulou, I. (1984). Children's thinking about language and their acquisition of literacy. In J. Downing & R. Valtin (Eds.), *Language awareness and learning to read* (pp. 79–92). New York: Springer-Verlag.

Sinclair, A., & Coulthardt, R. (1975). *Toward an analysis of discourse.* London: Oxford University Press.

Sinclair, A., Jarvella, R. J., Levelt, W. J. M. (Eds.). (1978). *The child's conception of language.* Berlin: Springer-Verlag.

Singer, H. (1966). Conceptualization in learning to read. In G. B. Schick & M. M. May (Eds.), *New frontiers in college-adult reading* (pp. 116–132). Milwaukee, WI: National Reading Conference.

Skousen, R. (1982). English spelling and phonemic representation. *Visible Language, 16,* 28–38.

Slosson, R. L. (1963). *Slosson Oral Reading Test.* East Aurora, NY: Slosson Educational Publications.

Smith, F. (1973a). *Psycholinguistics and reading.* New York: Holt, Rinehart, and Winston.

Smith, F. (1973b). Twelve easy ways to make reading difficult. In F. Smith (Ed.), *Psycholinguistics and reading* (pp. 183–196). New York: Holt, Rinehart, and Winston.

Smith, F. (1976). Learning to read by reading. *Language Arts, 53,* 297–299.

Smith, F. (1977). The uses of language. *Language Arts, 54,* 638–644.

Smith, F. (1978). *Understanding reading.* New York: Holt, Rinehart, and Winston.

Smith, F. (1982a). *Understanding reading* (3rd ed.). New York: Holt, Rinehart, and Winston.

Smith, F. (1982b). *Writing and the writer.* New York: Holt, Rinehart, and Winston.

Smith, F. (1983). *Essays into literacy.* Portsmouth, NH: Heinemann Educational Books.

Smith, H. K. (1967). The responses of good and poor readers when asked to read for different purposes. *Reading Research Quarterly, 3,* 53–83.

Smith, H. K. (1972). Reading for different purposes. In V. Southgate (Ed.), *Literacy at all levels.* London: Ward Lock.

Smith, H. L., & Trager, G. L. (1952). [Forward to the metalinguistics issue]. *ETC, 9,* 163–164.

Snow, C. (1983). Literacy and language: Relationships during the preschool years. *Harvard Educational Review, 53,* 165–189.

Snow, C., Dubber, C., & DeBlauw, A. (1982). Routines in mother-child interaction. In L. Feagans & D. Farran (Eds.), *The language of children reared in poverty: Implications for evaluation and intervention.* New York: Academic Press.

Soderberg, R. (1971). *Reading in early childhood: A linguistic study of a Swedish preschool child's gradual acquisition of reading ability.* Stockholm: Kungl, Boktryckerict P. A. Harstedt & Sons.

Sokhin, F. A. (1974). Preschoolers' awareness of speech and preparation for learning literacy. *Voprosy Psikhologii, 20,* 138–142.

Stauffer, R. G. (1969). *Directing reading maturity as a cognitive process.* New York: Harper & Row.

Stauffer, R. G. (1970). *The language experience approach to the teaching of reading.* New York: Harper & Row.

Stauffer, R. G. (1980). *The language experience approach to the teaching of reading* (2nd ed.). New York: Harper & Row.

Stein, N. L., & Glenn, C. G. (1977). An analysis of story comprehension in elementary school children. In R. O. Freedle (Ed.), *Multidisciplinary perspectives in discourse comprehension.* Hillsdale, NJ: Ablex, Inc.

Stockoe, W. (1969). *Sign language structure: An outline of the visual communication systems of the American deaf* (Studies in Linguistics, Occasional Paper No. 8). Washington, DC: Gallaudet College.

Stockoe, W. (1973). *Sign language structure.* Silver Spring, MD: Linstock Press.

Sulzby, E. (1978). Children's explanations of word similarities in relation to word knownness. In P. D. Pearson & J. Hansen (Eds.), *Twenty-seventh Yearbook of the National Reading Conference* (pp. 51–55). Clemson, SC: National Reading Conference.

Sulzby, E. (1979). Semantic salience in relation to word knownness. In M. L. Kamil & A. J. Moe (Eds.), *Twenty-eighth Yearbook of the National Reading Conference* (pp. 49–54). Clemson, SC: National Reading Conference.

Sulzby, E. (1980). Word concept development activities. In E. H. Henderson & J. W. Beers (Eds.), *Developmental and cognitive aspects of learning to spell: A reflection of word knowledge.* Newark, DE: International Reading Association.

Sulzby, E. (1981, August). *Kindergarteners begin to read their own compositions: Beginning readers' developing knowledge about written language projects* (Final report to the Research Foundation of the National Council of Teachers of English). Evanston, IL: Northwestern University. (ERIC Document Reproduction Service No. 204 738)

Sulzby, E. (1981, December). *Kindergarteners*

deal with word boundaries. Paper presented at the annual meeting of the National Reading Conference, Dallas, TX.

Sulzby, E. (1982a). *Children's emergent reading of favorite storybooks.* Paper presented at the National Reading Conference, Clearwater Beach, FL.

Sulzby, E. (1982b). Oral and written mode adaptations in stories by kindergarten children. *Journal of Reading Behavior, 14,* 51–59.

Sulzby, E. (1983, September). *Beginning readers' developing knowledges about written language.* Final report to the National Institute of Education (NIE-G-80-0176). Evanston, IL: Northwestern University.

Sulzby, E. (1983, November). *Children's emergent abilities to read favorite storybooks.* Final report to the Spencer Foundation. Evanston, IL: Northwestern University.

Sulzby, E. (in press, a). Children's development of prosodic distinctions in telling and dictating modes. In A Matsuhashi (Ed.), *Writing in real time: Modeling production processes.* New York: Longman.

Sulzby, E. (in press, b). Children's emergent reading of favorite storybooks: A developmental study. *Reading Research Quarterly.*

Sulzby, E. (in press, c). *Emergent writing and reading in 5–6 year olds: A longitudinal study.* Norwood, NJ: Ablex Publishing Corporation.

Sulzby, E. (in press, d). Kindergarteners as writers and readers. In M. Farr (Ed.), *Advances in writing research, Vol. I: Children's early writing development.* Norwood, NJ: Ablex Publishing Corporation.

Sulzby, E. (in press, e). Writing and reading: Signs of oral and written language organization in the young child. In W. H. Teale & E. Sulzby (Eds.), *Emergent literacy: Writing and reading.* Norwood, NJ: Ablex Publishing Corporation.

Sulzby, E., & Otto, B. (1982). "Text" as an object of metalinguistic knowledge: A study in literacy development. *First Language, 3,* 181–199.

Sulzby, E., & Templeton, S. (1980, December) *The development and validation of metalinguistic tasks assessing the child's concept of word.* Paper presented at the 30th annual meeting of the National Reading Conference, San Diego, CA.

Tannen, D. (Ed.) (1982). *Spoken and written language: Exploring orality and literacy.* Norwood, NJ: Ablex Publishing Corporation.

Tarski, A. (1983). *Logic, semantics, metamathematics* (2nd ed.). Indianapolis, IN: Hackett Publishing Company.

Taylor, D. (1981). *Family literacy: The social context of learning to read and write.* Unpublished doctoral dissertation, Teachers College, Columbia University.

Taylor, D. (1983). *Family literacy: Young children learning to read and write.* Portsmouth, NH: Heinemann Educational Books.

Taylor, N. E., & Blum, I. H. (1980). *Written Language Awareness Test* (Experimental edition). Washington, DC: The Catholic University.

Taylor, N. E., & Blum, I. H. (1981). *The effects of written language awareness on first grade reading achievement.* Paper presented at the Annual Meeting of the American Educational Research Association, Los Angeles, CA.

Taylor, N. E., Blum, I. H., Logsdon, D. M., & Moeller, G. D. (1982). *The development of written language awareness: Environmental aspects and program characteristics.* Paper presented at the annual meeting of the American Educational Research Association, New York.

Taylor, N. E., Moeller, G., & Blum, I. H. (1982). Learning to read: The meaningful and functional use of written language. *Reading-Canada-Lecture, 1*(4), 48–56.

Taylor, N. E., & Vauter, J. (1978). Helping children discover the functions of written language. *Language Arts, 55*(8), 941–945.

Teale, W. H. (1978). Positive environments for learning to read: What studies of early readers tell us. *Language Arts, 55,* 922–932.

Teale, W. H., Estrada, E., & Anderson, A. (1981). How preschoolers interact with written communication. In M. L. Kamil (Ed.), *Thirtieth Yearbook of the National Reading Conference.* Washington, DC: The National Reading Conference.

Teale, W. H., & Sulzby, E. (in press). Emergent literacy as a perspective: How young children become writers and readers. In W. H. Teale & E. Sulzby (Eds.), *Emergent literacy: Writing and reading.* Norwood, NJ: Ablex Publishing Corporation.

Temple, C. A. (1978). *An analysis of spelling errors from Gates, 1936.* Unpublished master's thesis, University of Virginia.

Temple, C. A., Nathan, R. G., & Burris, N. A. (1982). *The beginnings of writing.* Boston: Allyn and Bacon.

Templeton, S. (1980). What is a word? In E. H. Henderson & J. W. Beers (Eds.), *Developmental and cognitive aspects of learning to spell: A reflection of word knowledge.* Newark, DE: International Reading Association.

Templeton, S. (in press). Literacy, readiness, and basals. *The Reading Teacher.*

Templeton, S., & Scarborough-Franks, L. (1985). The spelling's the thing: Knowledge of derivational morphology in phonology and orthography

among older students. *Applied Psycholinguistics, 6,* 371–389.

Templeton, S., & Spivey, E. (1980). The concept of word in young children as a function of level of cognitive development. *Research in the Teaching of English, 14,* 265–278.

Templeton, S., & Thomas, P. (1984, January/February). Performance and reflection: Young children's concept of word. *Journal of Educational Research, 77,* 3, 139–146.

Tobin, A. W. (1981). *A multiple discriminant cross-validation of the factors associated with the development of precocious reading achievement.* Unpublished doctoral dissertation, University of Delaware.

Tobin, A. W., & Pikulski, J. J. (1983, April). *Parent and teacher attitudes toward early reading instruction.* Paper presented at the annual meeting of the American Educational Research Association, Montreal.

Torrey, J. W. (1969). Learning to read without a teacher: A case study. *Elementary English, 46,* 550–556, 658.

Torrey, J. W. (1979). Reading that comes naturally: The early reader. In T. G. Waller & G. E. MacKinnon (Eds.), *Reading research: Advances in theory and practice: Vol. 1.* New York: Academic Press.

Tovey, D. R. (1976). Children's perceptions of reading. *The Reading Teacher, 29,* 536–540.

Tovey, D. R. (1983). Teachers' understanding of the reading process. *Reading-Canada-Lecture, 2,* 5–12.

Trager, G. L. (1966). *The field of linguistics.* New York: Johnson Reprint Corporation.

Treiman, R. A. (1976). *Children's ability to segmet speech into syllables and phonemes as related to their reading ability.* Unpublished manuscript, Yale University.

Treiman, R., & Baron, J. (1981). Segmental analysis ability: Development and relation to reading ability. In G. E. MacKinnon & T. G. Waller (Eds.), *Reading research: Advances in theory and practice: Vol. 3* (pp. 159–198). New York: Academic Press.

Treiman, R., & Baron, J. (1983). Phonemic analysis training helps children benefit from spelling-sound rules. *Memory and Cognition, 11,* 382–389.

Trybus, R., Buchanan, C., & DiFrancesca, S. (1975). *Studies in achievement testing, hearing-impaired students.* Washington, DC: Gallaudet College, Office of Demographic Studies.

Tunmer, W. E., Bowey, J. A., & Grieve, R. (1983). The development of young children's awareness of the word as a unit of spoken language. *Journal of Psycholinguistic Research, 12,* 567–594.

Tunmer, W. E., & Fletcher, C. M. (1981). The relationship between conceptual tempo, phonological awareness and word recognition in beginning readers. *Journal of Reading Behavior, 13,* 173–185.

Tunmer, W. E., & Herriman, M. L. (1984a). The development of metalinguistic awareness: A conceptual overview. In W. E. Tunmer, C. Pratt, & M. L. Herriman (Eds.), *Metalinguistic awareness in children* (pp. 12–35). New York: Springer-Verlag.

Tunmer, W. E., Pratt, C., & Herriman, M. L. (1984b). *Metalinguistic awareness in children.* New York: Springer-Verlag.

Turnbull, K. (1970). Children's thinking: When is a letter a number? *Curriculum and Research Bulletin* (pp. 126–131). Victoria, Australia.

Valtin, R. (1984a). The development of metalinguistic abilities in children learning to read and write. In J. Downing & R. Valtin (Eds.), *Language awareness and learning to read* (pp. 207–226). New York: Springer-Verlag.

Valtin, R. (1984b). Featural and functional concepts of language. In J. Downing & R. Valtin (Eds.), *Language awareness and learning to read* (pp. 227–260). New York: Springer-Verlag.

Van der Vlught, H. (1979). Aspects of normal and abnormal neuropsychological development. In M. S. Gazzaniga (Ed.), *Neuropsychology.* New York: Plenum Press.

Van Dongen, D. (1979). *Preventie van leesmoeilijkheden Deelrapport 3, Opzet van het longitudinale onderzoek.* Nijmegen, Holland: Instituut voor Oonderwijskunde.

Van Dongen, D., Bosch, R., & Mommers, M. (1981). *Preventie van leesmoeilijkheden, Deelrapport 5. Eerste analyses op de data van het longitudinale onderzoek. Analyses op het niveau van de afzonderlijke meetinstrumenten voor het eerste leerjaar op voor de periode daaraan voorafgaand.* Nijmegen, Holland: Instituut voor Oonderwijskunde.

Van Dongen, D., & van Leent, H. (1981). *Preventie van leesmoeilijkheden, Deelrapport 4. Opzet van het eerste deel van het exploratieve onderzoek.* Nijmegen, Holland: Instituut voor Oonderwijskunde.

Van Dongen, D., & Wolfshage, I. (1981). *Predictability of reading ability.* Unpublished manuscript, Instituut voor Oonderwijskunde, Nijmegen, Holland.

Van Leent, H. (1982, May). *Het exploratieve onderzoek naar de ontwikkeling van de leesvaardigheid in het eerste leefjaar van de lagere school.* Paper presented at the Onderwijs Research Dagen, Tilburg, Holland.

Van Leent, H. (in press). Auditieve analyse en leren lesen. *Pedagogiche Studien.*

Vargus, N. R. (1982). *Letter writing over time:*
Sociocognitive constraints in transition. Unpublished doctoral dissertation, Indiana University, School of Education.

Vellutino, F. R. (1979). *Dyslexia: Theory and research.* Cambridge, MA: The MIT Press.

Vellutino, F. R., Harding, C. J., Phillips, R., & Steger, J. (1975). Differential transfer in poor and normal readers. *Journal of Genetic Psychology, 126,* 3–18.

Vellutino, F. R., & Scanlon, D. M. (1979, April). *The effect of phonemic segmentation training and response acquisition on coding ability in poor and normal readers.* Paper presented at the American Educational Research Association Annual Meeting, San Francisco, CA.

Vellutino, F. R., & Scanlon, D. M. (1982). Verbal processing in poor and normal readers. In C. J. Brainerd & M. Pressley (Eds.), *Verbal processes in children.* New York: Springer-Verlag.

Vellutino, F. R., & Scanlon, D. M. (1984). *Developmental differences in encoding the featural attributes of printed words in poor and normal readers.* Manuscript in preparation.

Vellutino, F. R., & Scanlon, D. M. (1985). Free recall of concrete and abstract words in poor and normal readers. *Journal of Experimental Child Psychology, 39,* 363–380.

Vellutino, F. R., Scanlon, D. M., DeSetto, L., & Pruzek, R. M. (1981). Developmental trends in the salience of meaning versus structural attributes of written words. *Psychological Research, 3,* 131–153.

Vellutino, F. R., Steger, J. A., Harding, C. J., & Phillips, F. (1975). Verbal vs. nonverbal paired associates learning in poor and normal readers. *Neuropsychologia, 13,* 75–82.

Venezky, R. L. (1970). *The structure of English orthography.* The Hague: Mouton.

Venezky, R. L. (1982). The origins of the present-day chasm between adult literacy needs and school literacy instruction. *Visible Language, 16,* 2, 113–125.

Vernon, M. D. (1957). *Backwardness in reading.* Cambridge, England: Cambridge University Press.

Vernon, M. D. (1967). Relationship of language to the thinking process. *Archives of General Psychiatry, 16,* 325–333.

Vernon, M. D. (1971). *Reading and its difficulties.* Cambridge, England: Cambridge University Press.

Vogel, S. A. (1974). Syntactic abilities in normal and dyslexic children. *Journal of Learning Disabilities, 7*(2), 103–109.

Vygotsky, L. S. (1962). *Thought and language.* Cambridge, MA: The MIT Press.

Vygotsky, L. S. (1978). *Mind in society* (M. Cole, V. John-Steiner, S. Scribner, & E. Souberman, Eds.). Cambridge, MA: Harvard University Press.

Wagoner, S. A. (1983). Comprehension monitoring: What it is and what we know about it. *Reading Research Quarterly, 18,* 328–346.

Wallach, M. A., & Wallach, L. (1975). *Teaching all children to read.* Chicago: University of Chicago Press.

Waller, T. G. (1976). Children's recognition memory for written sentences: A comparison of good and poor readers. *Child Development, 47,* 90–95.

Watkins, C. (1970). Language of gods and language of men: Remarks on some Indo-European metalinguistic traditions. In J. Puhvel (Ed.), *Myth and law among the Indo-Europeans: Studies in Indo-European comparative mythology* (pp. 1–17). Berkeley: University of California Press.

Watson, A. J. (1979, June). *Cognition and units of print in early reading.* Paper presented at the meeting of the IRA University of Victoria International Reading Research Seminar on Linguistic Awareness and Learning to Read, Victoria, BC, Canada.

Watson, A. J. (1984). Cognitive development and units of print in early reading. In J. Downing & R. Valtin (Eds.). *Language awareness and learning to read* (pp. 93–118). New York: Springer-Verlag.

Watson, D. J. (in preparation). *A description of teacher-student language productions and attitudes in two first grade classrooms.* Columbia, MO: University of Missouri-Columbia, Department of Elementary Education.

Weimer, W., & Weimer, A. (1977). *Reading Readiness Inventory.* Columbus, OH: Charles E. Merrill Publishing Company.

Weintraub, S., & Denny, T. P. (1965). What do beginning first graders say about reading? *Childhood Education, 41,* 326–327.

Welty, E. (1983). *One writer's beginnings.* Cambridge, MA: Harvard University Press.

Wepman, J. P. (1958). *Wepman Auditory Discrimination Test.* Chicago: Language Research Associates.

Werner, H., & Kaplan, B. (1963). *Symbol formation: An organismic-developmental approach to language and the expression of thought.* New York: John Wiley & Sons.

Whiting, H. T. A., & den Brinker, E. (1982). Image of the act. In J. P. Das, R. F. Mulcahy, & A. E. Wall (Eds.), *Theory and research in learning disabilities.* New York: Plenum Press.

Wilbur, R. B. (1979). *American Sign Language and sign systems.* Baltimore, MD: University Park Press.

Williams, J. P. (1979). The ABD's of reading: A program for the learning-disabled. In L. B. Resnick & P. A. Weaver (Eds.), *Theory and practice of early reading: Vol. 3.* Hillsdale, NJ: Lawrence Erlbaum Associates.

Williams, J. P. (1980). Teaching decoding with an emphasis on phoneme analysis and phoneme blending. *Journal of Educational Psychology, 72,* 1–15.

Winetsky, C. S. (1978). Comparisons of the expectations of parents and teachers for the behavior of preschool children. *Child Development, 49,* 1146–1154.

Wolf, D., & Gardner, H. (1981). On the structure of early symbolization. In R. L. Schiefelbusch & D. D. Bricker (Eds.), *Early language: Acquisition and intervention.* Baltimore: University Park Press.

Wood, M. (1982). Invented spelling. *Language Arts, 59,* 707–717.

Woodward, J. (1973). Some characteristics of pidgin sign English. *Sign Language Studies, 2,* 37–46.

Yaden, Jr., D. B. (1982). A multivariate analysis of first graders' print awareness as related to reading achievement, intelligence, and gender. *Dissertation Abstracts International, 43,* 1912A. (University Microfilms No. 8225520)

Yaden, Jr., D. B. (1983). *A categorization of two children's questions about print as they learn to read: A case study.* Paper presented at the annual meeting of the Oklahoma Reading Council, Lawton, OK. (ERIC Document Reproduction Service No. ED 227–472)

Yaden, Jr., D. B. (1984). Research in metalinguistic awareness: Findings, problems, and classroom applications. *Visible Language, 18* (Winter), 5–47.

Yaden, Jr., D. B., & McGee, L. M. (1984). Reading as a meaning-seeking activity: What children's questions reveal. In J. A. Niles & L. A. Harris (Eds.), *Thirty-third Yearbook of the National Reading Conference* (pp. 101–109). Rochester, NY: National Reading Conference.

Yanez, J. L. (1984). *Cross-cultural examination of reading readiness.* Unpublished master's thesis, University of Victoria, BC, Canada.

Zhiukov, S. F. (1965). The formation of morphological concepts in the youngest school children. In N. S. Rozhdestvensky (Ed.), *The foundation of the methodology of the initial teaching of the Russian language.* Moscow: Prosveshchenie.

Zifcak, M. (1976). *Phonological awareness and reading acquisition in first grade children.* Unpublished doctoral dissertation, University of Connecticut.

Author Index

Subject Index